SOTHIS PRESS

Sothis Press aims to completely reimagine the public domain book with an emphasis on universal access to captivatingly designed print editions. We believe that technology will enable every single book ever published to be perpetually accessible in beautiful print form. Sothis is beauty in ubiquity.

www.sothis.press
1 Waterhouse Square, London, ECIN 2ST

A Treatise on Private International Law, or the Conflict of Laws

With Principal Reference to Its Practice
in the English and Other Cognate Systems
of Jurisprudence, and Numerous
References to American Authorities

John Westlake

SOTHIS PRESS

ISBN 978-1-0365-0786-2

A Treatise on Private International Law, or the Conflict of Laws
is in the public domain.

This edition is published by
Sothis Press © 2023. The company
is registered in England and Wales.
The Company Number is 14900389.

A TREATISE

ON

rivate International Law,

OR

THE CONFLICT OF LAWS,

ITH PRINCIPAL REFERENCE TO ITS PRACTICE IN THE ENGLISH AND OTHER COGNATE SYSTEMS OF JURISPRUDENCE.

BY

JOHN WESTLAKE,

OF LINCOLN'S INN, ESQ., BARRISTER-AT-LAW,

AND FELLOW OF TRINITY COLLEGE, CAMBRIDGE.

LONDON:

W. MAXWELL, 32, BELL YARD, LINCOLN'S INN;

HODGES, SMITH AND CO. DUBLIN.

1858.

LONDON:
PRINTED BY C. ROWORTH AND SONS,
BELL YARD, TEMPLE BAR.

PREFACE.

The following work treats of private international jurisprudence, but regarded as a department of English law; and on the subject so defined it undertakes to furnish the profession with a volume at once compendious and useful. Such an undertaking imposed both positive and negative duties.

First in the former class I reckon the duty of taking as groundwork the English decisions, and not the writings of foreign jurists, though using the latter freely for collateral and subordinate purposes. Such a course implies no disrespect to the great foreign lawyers who have created this portion of juristic science, but is made necessary by the binding authority of precedents among us, from the moment at least that enough of those precedents has accumulated to cover the field: and that this time has arrived is shown by the number of English cases here collected, whatever be the merit of any particular deduction I have made from them. I hope indeed that our cases, though I have sometimes been obliged to dissent from them, will appear from the present work to contain on the whole a connected and reasonable system of private international jurisprudence.

Next, if it be not a part of the same duty, was that of suiting the order of treatment to the common classifications of English law. Personal relations occupy in our jurisprudence so small a space as compared with pecuniary, and our subdivision of the latter into those of real and personal property is so unlike the common subdivision into the relations of property and obligation, that to have set out from the law and jurisdiction affecting the person as such, or to have developed the international law of property in one chapter, would have vastly increased the difficulty of founding a connected system on the English decisions, besides perhaps bewildering the English student. Indeed, in the arrangement, I have mainly considered the order in which a student reading the work as a whole had best be introduced to its topics; and have therefore not shrunk from letting principles be first seen in particular applications, or from any other course which seemed to carry him on most naturally from the knowledge with which he may be presumed to start. The practising lawyer is more likely to refer to the book than to peruse it, and I trust the index may be found copious enough to guide him readily to what he may require.

The negative duties of my undertaking—were not to treat *ex professo* of topics which neither illustrate principles nor enter into English practice, although their importance in foreign legal systems may have caused them to occupy a more or less prominent place in other treatises; and to observe strictly the limits of my subject. Thus, for example, the rights of aliens in England, and the questions which have been raised on our statutes of copyright as to works composed and published abroad, belong to English law as speaking for itself, and not as adopting international maxims: while the occasional acts of sovereign states, as distinguished from their regular laws, and the laws of war, with the modifications introduced into them by treaties, though often in question in private causes, must be discussed on public international principles. Criminal jurisprudence also does not fall within the scope of private law: and my subject, within its own limits, is vast enough.

LINCOLN'S INN,
November 11*th*, 1858.

CONTENTS.

LIST OF CASES CITED.

(*The* NUMBERS *are those of the* PAGES.)

ERRATA ET ADDENDA.

Page 101, line 21: the citation is from *Bayley* v. *Edwards*, 3 Swan. 711.
,, 104, ,, 2 from bottom: *for* "know" *read* "knew."
,, 123, ,, 10: *for* "five" *read* "seven."
,, 180, ,, 18: the citation is from *Forbes* v. *Cochrane*, 2 B. & Cr. 471.
,, 207, ,, 29: }
,, 208, ,, 6: } *for "solido" read "solidum."*
,, 215, ,, 12: }
,, 217, ,, 14: *for* "are" *read* "were."
,, 232, note (*i*): *add* "2 Cl. & F. 544."
,, 368, line 3 of note (*y*): *add* "3 C. B. N. S. 597."

PRIVATE INTERNATIONAL LAW.

CHAPTER I.

Definition of the Subject.

1. Private International Law is that department of private jurisprudence which determines before the courts of what nation each suit should be brought, and by the law of what nation it should be decided. It may be farther defined by its differences from the departments which respectively border on it—private municipal and public international law.

2. Public international law respects disputes between states, which acknowledge no human superior, and it is consequently not judicially administered: indeed it is therefore a great question whether it deserves the name of law in any other than a figurative sense. Private international law respects the disputes between private persons, or at least, if a government be a party, it is then only when such government is considered as a private body in respect of its pecuniary rights; and the cases to which it applies come before ordinary tribunals. The name of the subject is derived from those instances in which the parties, as members of different states, acknowledge no common human superior; and we shall have to consider whether any, and what, principles of law, strictly so called, are applicable to such parties. But the subject includes also many questions arising between members of

the same state, and which are classed with the properly international ones from the similarity of the reasoning employed on them.

3. Municipal law contemplates no exception to the jurisdiction but such as would carry the cause to another court of the same state; but cases arise where the jurisdiction of the court is questioned, because that of the state is questioned, either over the person of a party generally, or in reference to the matter in dispute. Again, if the jurisdiction be granted, still a municipal law is sometimes invoked foreign to that commonly administered by the court. For example, I become at my home a surety, and, relying on the law there existing, which, we will suppose, allows me to require that the principal debtor be first proceeded against, I omit to stipulate expressly for that privilege; then, through change of domicile or some other cause, being sued in a country where the general law does not provide that privilege for sureties, I say it would be unjust that I should lose my advantage. Or again, if I marry where marriage is only a civil contract, it may interest public morals no less than myself that my marriage should still be held valid, notwithstanding my removal to a country where a religious ceremony would have been necessary to it. In both these instances, the foreign law is invoked on account of facts which occurred beyond the jurisdiction, and such foreign facts may occur as well in the mutual dealings of members of the same state as in those of members of different states; whence flows the result already mentioned, that many disputes between fellow-citizens are, from the similarity of the reasoning, included in private international jurisprudence.

4. Private international law, then, regulates private rights as dependent on a diversity of municipal laws and jurisdictions, applicable, or conceivably applicable, to the persons, facts or things in dispute: wherefore it is also

called *The Conflict of Laws.* Public international law often, and only, refers to municipal laws as furnishing analogies or principles: the conflict of laws treats them as of force in their own character, and its problem is to ascertain the principles on which any municipal law can, as such, be of force between members of different nations, or where extra-territorial facts or things are in dispute; and to point out which municipal law must, on those principles, be applied in every particular case. These principles, too, must nesessarily be arrived at by considerations external to all the several municipal laws which in any case may compete; but, since this department of jurisprudence is administered by judges commissioned by human superiors, it follows that if the law of any state has expressly defined the limits of its own applicability, the judges of that state will be bound by such definition, however incorrect in principle it may appear to them to be. It is only where the municipal law is silent as to its own limits, that the jurisprudence which is the subject of this Treatise admits of judicial enforcement.

5. The preliminary questions of this subject are two. First, how must it be determined of what nation each person is a member? what are the rules concerning national character? But then many nations include separate jurisdictions administering different laws, as the British, in which the several colonies and portions of the United Kingdom have each its own law; and these diversities, no less than national ones, must occasion the conflict of laws: therefore, secondly, how are the members of such a nation permanently related to its several subdivisions? by what rules is each citizen's domicile to be ascertained? With these questions I shall therefore begin. They will determine the facts as to the several persons, with whose rights, when they have been classed by nationality and domicile, we shall afterwards have to deal. There may of course be

different domiciles within the empire of the same law, as within England or within Scotland; but these will not give rise to international questions. Also the member of one nation may be domiciled in the territory of another, and it will be a point for us, whether and how that affects private international rights; so that for this application also our investigation of the rules concerning domicile will have been indispensable.

6. These preliminary questions disposed of, we shall have to consider the principles on which persons are amenable to municipal laws and jurisdictions, and to apply those principles to the determination of particular cases.

CHAPTER II.

NATIONAL CHARACTER.

7. THERE are no rules of quite universal acceptance by which states are guided in claiming or rejecting persons as their members. The leading feature in the disagreement which exists on this subject has been the contest between the feudal and Roman principles, of which the former, subordinating all other relations to those of the soil, made allegiance to depend on the place of birth, while the latter applied to citizenship the general rule that children follow the condition of their parents. The feudal principle has progressively given away, but retains so much influence in England and some other countries, while in all it has so much the character of a groundwork into which the modifications arising from the other principle have been introduced, that the historical method is best suited for describing the doctrines now current in different states.

1. *History of the Doctrine of Allegiance in England and France.*

8. The mediæval doctrine of allegiance had two sources, corresponding to the two sections of the population over which the Frankish and other barbarian kings reigned.

The first of these was the military oath of fidelity to the Roman emperor, which was ultimately imposed on the provincials as well as the citizens, and which the Frankish kings, conceiving themselves to inherit the rights of the empire over its subjects, occasionally exacted from the cities, since it was in them that the bulk of their Roman subjects dwelt. The second, and far more important source, as it concerned the king's relation to his own Teutonic people, existed in the habit common to all the German tribes, by which a chief was surrounded by warriors who had voluntarily attached themselves to him, who were his *men*, and who were understood to owe him *fidelity* and *allegiance* in return for the *benefits* which he conferred upon them. These benefits at first might be limited to a bench at his table, and the gift of horses and arms, but, when the patrons acquired territorial wealth through the conquest of the empire, the name came to be appropriated to the gifts of land, which were known as *benefices*, and afterwards as fiefs. Then, as it became continually more difficult for an independent allodial proprietor to maintain himself in the midst of the general violence and confusion, the habit of thus *commending* one's-self to a *lord* extended until all society had been brought under the feudal form. In this simple form, however, the chain of commendation was extended from the highest to the lowest through the intermediate links of the mesne lords, and a direct personal relation was far from existing between the kings and the whole proprietary, still less between them and the whole population. But the kings naturally sought to avail themselves of the tie which appeared to be most efficacious in the society around them, and sometimes encouraged, sometimes commanded, their subjects generally to incur towards them immediately the personal obligations of allegiance. At whatever period, and with whatever variation of details this took place in any one Teutonic state, the character of the innovation was identical in them all, and I shall therefore cite the clearest description of it, that given by Guizot for the case of Charlemagne; premising that whether from the personal weakness of his successors, or from the difficulties which surrounded them, his scheme had in France no permanent effect.

9. " Ainsi se formait peu à peu cette hiérarchie des propriétés et des personnes qui devait devenir la feódalité; ainsi, par la division progressive des bénéfices s'étendait de jour en jour cette série de vassaux et d'arrière-vassaux, liés les uns aux autres par des obligations semblables, et toujours comprises dans cette condition de la fidélité qui était le titre même de leur possession. Bien que, dans leur enchaînement graduel et d'intermédiaire en intermédiaire, ces obligations rattachassent au trône la plupart des bénéfices, et qu'ainsi le monarque eût des droits, directs au indirects, à la fidélité du plus grand nombre des bénéficiers, cependant, dans une société violente et grossière, une relation si lointaine était nécessairement bien peu puissante, et l'unité sociale ou monarchique qui en devait résulter ne pouvait être réelle. Les liens fondés sur des rapports prochains et personnels étaient seuls efficaces; seuls ils correspondaient aux anciennes habitudes des Barbares; et de même que le compagnon ne connaissait guère autrefois que le chef de sa bande, de même le vassal ne tenait vraiment qu'à son propre seigneur. Charlemagne s'efforça de rattacher plus immédiatement tous ses sujets à sa personne et à son pouvoir . . . . . . Il entreprit de traverser la hiérarchie féodale qui se constituait, d'entrer en communication directe avec tous les hommes libres, et de faire prédominer la relation du roi au citoyen sur celle du seigneur au vassal. La fidélité, qui jusque-là n'avait été qu'une obligation personnelle contractée envers le chef auquel chaque homme libre

s'était attaché et dont il avait reçu quelque avantage, devint, par les ordres de Charlemagne, une obligation publique imposée à tout homme libre envers le roi, qu'il en tint, ou non, quelque bénéfice médiat ou immédiat, et réclamée au nom de la seule royauté . . . . . . Un tel système affranchissait évidemment la royauté de toutes les relations féodales, fondait son empire hors de la hiérarchie des personnes ou des terres, et la rendait partout présente, partout puissante, à titre de pouvoir public et par son propre droit" (*a*).

10. Such was the system of allegiance in general: I must now ask attention to its history in England in particular. It is stated by Bromton (*b*), that King Edmund the elder ordered all men to swear fidelity to him, and though nothing of the sort appears in the extant collection of his laws, it is not in itself improbable, since the Anglo-Saxons monarchs from Egbert imitated the Carlovingian system in many particulars. But it is certain that no such oath was in fact generally enforced by the Anglo-Saxon kings, and the first real establishment in England of the doctrine of a personal fidelity due to the king as such must be referred to the Conqueror. 1. In the beginning of his reign he compelled the principal inhabitants of Exeter to take an oath to himself, which they, though not refusing him as king, had declined as not due from them (*c*). 2. In the document known as the *carta de quibusdam statutis*, referred by Guizot to the year 1071, he imposed on all freeholders the oath of fidelity to himself (*d*). This oath was actually sworn in 1086 by "all

(*a*) Guizot, Ess. sur l'Hist. de France, 8ème édit. p. 105—107.

(*b*) Cap. 859, quoted in Allen's Inquiry into the Rise and Growth of the Royal Prerogative in England, p. 65, edit. of 1849.

(*c*) Ordericus Vitalis, l. 4, apud Allen, p. 70.

(*d*) Leg. Will. Conq. iii. 2, in Anc. Laws and Inst. of England, vol. i. p. 490; Guizot, Essais sur l'Hist. de France, p. 275, note. Freeholders is, for the Conqueror's reign, the most correct translation of *liberi homines*:

landholders of any account throughout England" (*e*). 3. Charlemagne had left open the comparative force of the obligations which were to be incurred to him and to the vassal's lord; Edmund is said by Bromton to have placed them on a par, but the oath imposed by William was one of fidelity to him "against all other men" (*f*). The example was followed by Frederic Barbarossa, who at the diet of Roncaglia in 1158 enacted that in every oath of fidelity from a vassal to his lord the emperor should be excepted by name, and a similar reservation in favour of the king appears from Glanville to have already at the same period become the common law of England (*g*).

11. By the total result of these innovations, for every piece of ground in the kingdom, whether within or without a borough, there was some one compellable to incur the personal obligations of fealty towards the king, nor does there appear any trace of fealty due to the king on other grounds than those connected with the soil. There was, therefore, a natural tendency to regard allegiance as something geographical, and the term itself came to be used in a geographical sense, persons being expressed as born within or without the king's allegiance when little more was meant than that they were born within or without the realm (*h*): and men were thus predisposed to resolve

---

villani, bordarii, &c. are excluded as well as *servi*. See Ellis's Int. to Domesday Book, vol. i. p. 63 *et seq.*

(*e*) Saxon Chronicle, sub ann.

(*f*) Saxon Chron. *ubi supra.*

(*g*) L. 9, c. 1.

(*h*) It is no real exception to such a geographical sense, that the children of ambassadors born abroad are said to have been by the old common law born within the allegiance; for an ambassador's house is reputed part of his sovereign's realm, and the 25 Edw. 3, st. 2, presently to be quoted, shows that the same exception was not made in favour of children whose parents served the king abroad in any other capacity. The children, however, of the king's enemies, born within any portion of the realm of which their parents might be in hostile occupation, were not reputed born within the allegiance. See *Calvin's case*, 7 Coke, 18 *a*.

by the same test those questions which still had to be asked, concerning the persons who under the system, so far as we have now traced its development, had not yet been called upon to place themselves in a direct relation with the king. And these questions were chiefly two: who, if taken in arms against the king, must be treated as an enemy and not as a traitor? and in whom is there such an incapacity for the personal obligation of allegiance towards the King of England, that he cannot acquire here land which would entail that obligation? Under the presumption that every one must be personally bound to some one sovereign, it was necessary that these questions should receive coincident answers, which again, in accordance with the tendency noticed, were made to depend on the accident of birth within or without the so-called "allegiance."

12. With regard to the former branch of this simple rule, that which would impose the duty of allegiance on all those born *inter quatuor maria*, we cannot believe that it was ever so strictly carried out, as that if a son was born in England to a foreign merchant, such son, on being afterwards taken in arms—a case, one would imagine, of no infrequent occurrence—should have been hung, drawn, and quartered as a traitor. But it is not within our province to inquire what mitigations of the doctrine prevailed in criminal practice: to this day, not only are all persons born within the United Kingdom *ipso facto* entitled to all the civil privileges conferred by the British character, but our law holds that they cannot divest themselves of that character by any act of theirs (*i*).

(*i*) Æneas or Angus Macdonald was born in the United Kingdom, but had lived in France from his early infancy, and came over in the affair of 1745 with a French commission. He was taken, and found guilty of treason, but pardoned on condition of leaving the kingdom, and continuing abroad during his life. Lee, C. J., informed the jury that "the only fact they had to try was

13. It remains to trace the relaxation of the severe rule which excluded from the same privileges the children of Englishmen born abroad. A perfectly logical doubt had arisen whether the king's child born abroad could inherit the crown, for if allegiance to a foreign prince were entailed by mere birth in his dominions, then surely one who owed such allegiance could not be a fit sovereign for England. This was met by the illogical statute 25 Edw. 3, st. 2, which, after removing by a declaration the doubt as to the heir of the crown, enacted, that "all children inheritors which from thenceforth should be born without the allegiance of the king, whose fathers and mothers at the time of their birth should be in the faith and allegiance of the King of England, should have and enjoy the same benefit and advantage, to have and bear inheritance within the same allegiance, as other inheritors; so always that the mothers of such children should pass the sea by the license and will of their husbands" (*k*). Lord Kenyon thought that this statute was meant to confer the complete English nationality, and not merely the right of inheritance (*l*): it seems to me, upon the old authorities, not to have been so interpreted; but the point is now of no importance. With regard to the children upon whom the rights, such as they were, were conferred, the necessity of the mother's original allegiance was very properly abolished by a dictum in *Bacon's case*, where it was said that the wife, though foreign by birth, "is *sub potestate viri*, and *quasi* under the allegiance of our king" (*m*). Still the

whether he was a native of Great Britain? If so, he must be found guilty." The principle obviously extends to the son of foreign parents born within the realm. 18 State Trials, 857.

(*k*) Sect. 5.

(*l*) 4 T. R. 308, in *Doe* v. *Jones*.

(*m*) Cro. Ch. 602. This was correct in principle, but if the statute had meant it there would have been no need to specify the allegiance of both parents. Indeed, the common law exception in favour of ambassadors' privilege was limited to the first generation, but then came the clause, 7 Anne, c. 5, s. 3, which enacted, that the children of all natural-born subjects, born out of the queen's allegiance, should be taken to be natural-born subjects to all intents, constructions, and purposes. These words, fairly construed, would have accomplished every reasonable purpose. The children of a British mother and alien father would have been excluded by the reason of *Bacon's case*, as by the marriage she would lose the character of a natural-born subject; and the child who came under this clause, being naturalized for all purposes, would be so for the purpose, amongst others, of transmitting the British character to his issue, and so on for ever, until in some manner that character had been forfeited by a person who would otherwise form a link of the chain. But by a narrow spirit of construction, something less than justice has been done to the expressions of this statute. It is not indeed to be regretted, considering the doubts which might have been raised, that the st. 4 Geo. 2, c. 21, s. 1, should have clearly established that there is no transmissive power in the mother, by declaring that the children, born out of the allegiance, of *fathers* who at the time of the birth of such children are natural-born subjects, are by 7 Anne natural-born subjects to all intents, constructions, and purposes (*n*). But the st. 13 Geo. 3, c. 21, s. 1, after a recital that naturalization had not been extended beyond the children of those born within the realm, extends it to the children of persons falling within the previous statute.

14. Thus stands the matter on the statute-book. The 13

children is said to have required that their mothers should also be English. Coke, *ubi supra*.

(*n*) The doubt was raised, even in spite of this statute, as to the foreign-born son of an alien father and English mother, but quashed without difficulty: *Doe* v. *Jones*, 4 T. R. 300. The incapacity to inherit, which provoked to the attempt, has since been removed by st. 7 & 8 Vict. c. 66, s. 3.

Geo. 3 still professedly naturalizes those within it "to all intents, constructions and purposes:" but as its recital is a parliamentary construction of the same words in 7 Anne and 4 Geo. 2, it is a question whether we are not bound by it to consider as excluded "the intent, construction and purpose" of standing as a natural-born subject in a second application of the same statute 13 Geo. 3 to their issue. If this be so, and the wives of successive English gentlemen, grandfather, father and son, should happen to present their husbands with heirs at Paris or Naples, no very improbable contingency, the third such foreign-born heir will find himself one morning not a British subject. He will probably not think proper to take up the foreign nationality, which in many countries he might claim from the accident of his birth, and hence will require the interference of parliament to save him from the consequences of bearing *caput lupinum*. It is said that of the most eminent lawyers in the country, five gave an opinion for, and five against, the right of one whose grandfather had been born out of the British dominions to inherit land (*o*). In my own opinion a court ought, in such a case, to admit the claimant in accordance with the plain words of the statutes, disregarding their restriction by an implied statutory construction: and in doing so, it would be countenanced by a decision of the Irish House of Lords. Godart de Ginckell, created Earl of Athlone in 1692, spent the latter part of his life on the continent, and it does not appear that any of his posterity had ever set foot on British soil; but in 1795, one who was the fifth in descent from him was admitted to sit in the Irish parliament as seventh earl (*p*). The statutes must, therefore,

(*o*) Report of Committee of House of Commons on Laws relating to Aliens (1843), *sub fin.*

(*p*) Report, &c., *ubi supra;* and Lodge's Peerage of Ireland, by Archdall, vol. ii. p. 157.

have been construed as not limiting to the first generation the power of transmitting nationality, but the decision may be open to remark on another ground. For though our parliament can confer the British character on one born abroad who may be willing to accept it, yet it can neither force the inconvenience of a double nationality on one who was never within its jurisdiction, and who chooses the citizenship of his native land, nor can it be presumed to have meant in any case to bestow the privileges without demanding the duties of a British subject. Now it is hardly possible but that some ancestor of the claiming earl must have so acted as to establish his Dutch character, and, if so, he must have lost his power of transmitting a British nationality at the same time with that nationality itself. I shall return to this point in Art. 24.

15. I have already mentioned that the great idea of Charlemagne, by which a direct personal tie should connect every subject with the monarch, took no permanent effect in France: and so little were the inferior landholders penetrated with the conception of an allegiance to their suzerain overriding that to their mesne lord, that even the establishments of St. Lewis are silent on the part which the vassal should take in a contest between his successive superiors. It was indeed in France that the feudal system arose out of the practice of personal commendation, but if France was the most feudal country of feudal times, it was because that system there retained the least of its origin, and was most emphatically a graduated subordination of lands, denuded of all personal ties except those which resulted from immediate juxtaposition in the scale of ownership. When thus the bond was so feeble between the king and the ultimate occupant of the soil, we do not wonder at finding that the duty of allegiance to the king was not held to arise necessarily and *ipso facto* from birth within the kingdom. But other causes also concurred in

this result. For early in the middle ages the revived study of the Roman law had taught men upon the continent to regard citizenship as a benefit to be conferred and not as a burden to be imposed, and the pride of a high-spirited people led them to look upon their nationality as a privilege, and on allegiance to their king as an honour. Yet the feudal principle, on which the relations of persons were governed by those of land, was so influential that birth within the kingdom was held to confer on the foreigner's son an inchoate right to the French character, though one which might be disclaimed. The disclaimer, if not express, was to be inferred from the language and conduct of the person, but if neither from word nor deed could an intimation of his intention be derived, he was deemed to have tacitly accepted the allegiance of the King of France. Correspondingly, and pursuant to the Roman principle that the freeman's child follows his father's condition, the issue of French fathers born abroad were accepted as French if they adopted that character, but not claimed as such if they preferred the allegiance of their native soil (*q*).

2. *Present State of the Doctrine of National Character.*

16. The option which, as we have seen, the French law has from an early period allowed to the child born in a country to which its father was alien, arose from the conflicting application to him of two principles, the feudal one of territorial allegiance, and the ancient one of an inherited status, under either of which he was allowed to range himself. Indeed it would have been no way consonant to the mediæval spirit, to hold that entire liberty of

(*q*) Much information on the old French law of allegiance will be found in 2 Knapp, 315 *et seq.*

choosing a nationality which was taught in the last century by Vattel and other publicists. What the latter said on this matter, we need not here cite; but, subject to the choice they reserved to the adult, any remaining influence of the feudal principle was altogether rejected by them in determining the *primâ facie* nationality of the infant. *Les enfants*, says Vattel, *suivent naturellement la condition de leurs pères, ... et l'on présume de droit que chaque citoyen, en entrant dans la société, réserve à ses enfants le droit d'en être membres . . . . . Le lieu de la naissance ne fait rien à cela, et ne peut fournir de lui-même aucune raison d'ôter à un enfant ce que la nature lui donne ; je dis de lui-même, car la loi civile ou politique peut en ordonner autrement pour des vues particulières* (*r*). The supposed contract between the members of the state in favour of their children was derived from the philosophy current in Vattel's age. To us it will be more satisfactory to base the rule on the probability that the child will be educated in the mental and moral habits of his father's country, so that natural fitness points him out as a member of that rather than of any other state, as well as on the hardship of separating the destiny of the child from that of his family by giving him any other nationality than his father's. This understood, and repudiating also the free choice of nationality, except in the case when the ancestral character competes with that sentiment which is always more or less inspired by one's native land, the following rule, based on that of Vattel, may be recommended as expressing the idea of modern publicists: *Legitimate children, wherever born, are regularly members of that state of which their fathers are members at the time of their birth, but may choose, if they prefer it, the nationality of their place of birth.*

17. This is the effect of the old French rule, except that

(*r*) Droit des Gens, l. 1, § 212, 215.

the presumption was there in favour of the place of birth; how far it is that of the English rule, as altered by statute, has been already discussed. It is also the rule of the Code Napoleon, but with three exceptions (*s*). One, that in favour of a French origin the father's nationality at the time of conception is preferred to that at the birth; that is, by the principle *infans conceptus pro nato habetur quoties de ejus commodis agitur*, every advantage which the child could derive from being born to a French father will also be secured to him, if the father lost the French character within the 180 days preceding the birth, which in article 312 are fixed as the shortest period of gestation. Another, that the privilege of claiming the French character is extended to the child born out of France to a father who at any previous time was French. And the third, that whenever the French character is claimed (*t*) by one who does not combine the two circumstances of birth in the territory, and to a father who was French at least within the 180 days, the claim must be supported by a formal declaration, and an actual domicile in France: though, when so supported, it will relate to the birth for all those whose situation includes either of the two circumstances just named, and is only treated as a novel acquisition on the part of those born abroad from fathers who had lost the French character prior to the 180 days. But inasmuch as this jurisprudence permitted the establishment in France of foreign families who chose to remain foreign from generation to generation, in order to escape the conscription, the law of 12th Feb. 1851 provided that the child born in France, to a foreign father himself also born in France, should be treated as French,

(*s*) See Code Civil, Art. 9, 10, with the decisions quoted in Rogron's notes.

(*t*) As to the time for making this claim, see Code Civil, Art. 9, and Law of 22nd March, 1849.

unless he repudiated that character within a year from attaining his majority (*u*).

18. The national character of illegitimate children is the subject of much difference. Since the condition of promiscuous issue was in the Roman law determined by the maxim *partus ventrem sequitur*, it might have been expected that the codes and authorities, which in the ordinary case support the Roman doctrine of a status inherited from the father, would here, to the same extent and with the same qualifications, adopt the nationality of the mother. And accordingly this is done by Heffter (*x*). But the 9th and 10th articles of the Code Napoleon, by omitting to specify birth *in matrimony*, empower the French father to transmit his nationality to his illegitimate, precisely as to his legitimate, children wherever born. This, however, does not proceed from ignoring altogether the distinction between legitimacy and illegitimacy in this matter. It is rather an instance of the leaning, noticeable in the French laws, to every consideration which may extend their own nationality: and the maxim *partus ventrem sequitur* is allowed its usual course when that end would not be effected by departing from it, so that the illegitimate child of a French mother by a foreign father is *primâ facie* French, though, if the father acknowledge him, he may accept the paternal nationality by preference (*y*). On the other hand, several treaties between Prussia and small German states absolutely assign the father's nationality to the issue whom he adopts, and some French writers have argued for the same rule (*z*). In the United Kingdom, as it is only by

(*u*) See the report on this law in Dalloz, 1851. These families amounted to a tenth part of some frontier villages, and concealed their foreign character when any of the rights of citizenship were to be enjoyed. The lesson shows that some such exception is necessary to the rule above suggested.

(*x*) Europäische Völkerrecht, 3rd edit. p. 109.

(*y*) See Rogron's notes to Cod. Civ. Art. 10.

(*z*) Fœlix, Droit International Privé, 2ème édit. p. 37.

statute that any born without the realm have been admitted to the benefit of allegiance, the illegitimate children of British mothers born abroad must be excluded, for no statute exists which can be construed in their favour. The illegitimate children of foreign mothers born here are of course British by their place of birth.

19. Foundlings of course belong everywhere to the country where they are found.

20. *Change of the Nationality of Origin.*—This involves two points, the acquisition of a new national character, and the loss of the old. The former, which is called *naturalization*, can only be accomplished by the supreme authority in the state which receives the alien into its membership. Nor, although the sanction of that authority has sometimes been given by general statutes passed in favour of all who should satisfy certain conditions, is it usual to give it otherwise than by an express intervention of the government in the case of each person. Again, as well in such general statutes as in such particular grants, it is usual to reserve certain privileges of natural-born, which it is not thought fit to extend to naturalized, subjects; and, from the number and nature of these reservations, a question often arises how far the grant really confers the national character of the adopting state. The true answer to this question, however, does not in any degree depend on the reservations, since, whatever their extent, they will be, if naturalization is intended, analogous only to the disqualifications which in most countries are imposed for some purpose or other on some portion of the natural-born subjects. The matter really turns on whether the relation of sovereign and subject is meant to be established; and so, whatever the terms used, and however various the privileges conferred, all the modes and degrees may be classed under the two heads of naturalization and denization, in the former of which the adopting state per-

manently aggregates the alien to its body, intending thereby to acquire as firm a grasp on his allegiance as on that of a natural-born subject, and in the latter only the permission is contained to establish a domicile in the territory, together with the grant of more or less limited rights. Thus the status of a denizen corresponds to what in some countries is called the *jus indigenatus*, and in France the enjoyment of the *droits civils* without the *qualité de Français*; and its original purport was no doubt to favour commerce by giving to foreign merchants the protection and conveniences of natives during their residence, and so far as might be required by its motive. Hence also its importance has diminished in modern times in proportion as, by the progress of humanity, the status of foreigners, as such, has improved. But the original purport of denization has not everywhere been so strictly followed out as to exclude political rights, as in England, for instance, denizens can vote, in respect of their tenements, in the election of members of parliament (*a*): which I notice to show the student how completely he must in fact, whatever may be said as to the idea, eschew the notion of testing state-membership by the rights enjoyed. The only question is, to which government is permanent subjection promised?

21. Such a general statute as before alluded to was that of 7 Anne, c. 5, for the naturalization of foreign Protestants, which for this purpose remained in force only three years. At present naturalization is conferred in the United Kingdom by a certificate of the Home Secretary under st. 7 & 8 Vict. c. 66, s. 8, and the oath of allegiance taken

(*a*) 2 Peckwell's Election Cases, 117; and Resolution of House of Commons, 22nd Dec. 1698, 12 Com. Journ. 367. Also in some of the United States of America, the suffrage is conferred on persons who by the laws of the Union are still aliens, notwithstanding that, by the constitution, naturalization is reserved to the Union: Wheaton's Int. Law, 6th ed. p. 628. See below, Art. 26.

thereupon; but such certificate is discretional, must except the capacity of becoming a member of the privy council or of either house of parliament, and may except any other rights and capacities. Before this act, an alien could only be individually naturalized by parliament.

22. That any one should be a member of two nations at once is inadmissible in principle, since a war between them would involve him in conflicting duties; and even in peace the notion would be incompatible with that absolute authority over subjects which, so far as any regular human interference is concerned, is contained in the idea of sovereignty, whether vested in a monarch or in the body of a republic. Thus naturalization always intends the transfer of subjection. But the same person may easily be claimed by two nations, when the one has naturalized him and the other does not relinquish him, and indeed some of the states which most readily adopt foreigners are among those which claim most strongly the perpetual allegiance of their own subjects. The idea of allegiance as a personal tie sanctioned, or liable to be sanctioned, by an oath, necessarily involved its perpetuity, at least until dissolved by the mutual consent of the sovereign and subject; and this, which is expressed in the maxim *nemo potest exuere patriam*, is still both the British and American (*b*) doctrine. But the opposite idea of a national character freely chosen by the person is expressed by the 17th article of the Code Napoleon, which declares the French character to be lost by naturalization in a foreign country, by accepting public employment from a foreign government without the sanction of the supreme authority in France, and by "every establishment made in a foreign country

(*b*) 2 Kent's Comm. 49. Secretary Webster's Argument in *Thrasher's case* (Wheaton, p. 123, *et seq.*) looks like a renunciation of allegiance, but Thrasher, as a resident, was bound not to conspire against the local government, besides that the attempt *exuere patriam* might forfeit his claim to protection against the sovereign of his choice.

sans esprit de retour," in which light, however, it is expressly defined, no establishment for commercial purposes shall ever be regarded. Similar provisions exist in many continental states, and are carried farthest in Russia, where the quality of a Russian subject is lost by unauthorized residence abroad, by voluntary expatriation without the intention of return, and by disappearance; the last being presumed of every person liable to the capitation-tax, who during ten years has not been heard of at the place of his domicile (*c*). Thus it must frequently happen that the Russian nationality is lost without acquiring any other.

23. If an agreement to sanction the change of nationality might have been expected in any case, that of a woman who marries a foreigner would have seemed the most likely. But there is none even there. The old English rule, which we have seen expressed by the dictum in *Bacon's case*, that the foreign wife is *quasi* under the allegiance, whatever else it meant, gave her no rights while she remained abroad (*d*). But by the st. 7 & 8 Vict. c. 66, s. 16, England has, in common with most continental countries, adopted the principle of the 12th article of the Code Napoleon, so that the foreign wife now acquires the British nationality of her husband (*e*): without, however, adopting the correlative principle of the 19th article, which turns over the French wife to the foreign nationality of her husband. Many cases may therefore be put in which the wife will be claimed at once by her husband's country and by that of her origin.

24. Any general rule for the change of nationality, could such be established, would obviate the difficulty foreshadowed in my remarks on the *Athlone Peerage case*,

---

(*c*) Révue Etrangère et Française, t. 3, p. 257.

(*d*) *Countess de Conway's case*, 2 Knapp, 364; *Case of Count de Wall's Representatives*, 6 Mo. P. C. 216.

(*e*) And without the option of refusing it: *Maria Manning's case*, 2 C. & K. 887, 19 L. J. (N. S.) M. C. 1.

and which at present stands thus :—A., an Englishman, emigrates to France or America, suppose, is naturalized there, and his posterity continue to reside there. They will of course be French or American, but, unless the British government consents to their ancestor's expatriation, the same posterity must be treated as British at least to the second generation, and perhaps for ever. The difficulty, however, may be got over in more ways than one. The most consistent, perhaps, with the principles of jurisprudence would be to hold that the acceptance of a foreign nationality at least incapacitates for transmitting the British to the issue, even if it leaves the acceptor entangled for himself with the conflicting obligations of a double allegiance. And this may be argued with great force from the exception, in st. 4 Geo. 2, c. 21, s. 2, of children whose fathers at the time of their birth would have been liable to the penalties of high treason or felony in case of their returning into the realm without the king's licence, combined with the st. 3 James 1, c. 4, ss. 22, 23, whereby promising obedience to any other prince, state or potentate was made high treason. Another method is to rest upon the remedial scope of the naturalization acts—and particularly on st. 13 Geo. 3, c. 21, s. 3, which appears to require that persons to be naturalized by that act shall reside within the realm, and take the oaths and make the declaration required by the st. 1 Geo. 1, c. 13 (*f*)—so as to hold that to the foreigner within their provisions there is merely an opportunity afforded of ranging himself under British allegiance by abandoning his native citizenship. The latter method would as well as the first, but not until the second generation, result in preventing the transmission of the privilege; for, by *Doe* v. *Acklam* (*g*), "the two

(*f*) Receiving the sacrament is now rendered unnecessary by st. 6 Geo. 4, c. 67.

(*g*) 2 Ba. & Cr. 779, 795.

characters of subject and subject by birth must unite in the father," so that, if the character of subject is not imposed on the father against his will, the option will not be offered to his son. But the first method has against it the decision of Sir James Wigram in *Fitch* v. *Weber* (*h*), where it was ably pressed by counsel; and the second is opposed by two *dicta*, neither however necessary to the case in which it was thrown out. One is that of the Lords of the Council in *Drummond's case* (*i*), who asserted that the naturalization acts do really impose a double subjection, and commended to the mercy of the crown any foreign issue within them who might be taken in war: the other is that of Sir James Wigram at the end of *Fitch* v. *Weber*(*k*), where he said, that the qualification required by the 3rd section of st. 13 Geo. 3, c. 21, did not apply to those whom he held to be *ipso facto* naturalized by the same act,—a *dictum* not very easy to reconcile with the words of the section itself.

25. We have next to consider the British empire as a collection of separate jurisdictions, governed by different laws, but united under one allegiance. Such an empire admits a variety of domiciles, but one national character, and the conditions of that one character must be derived from the jurisprudence of the dominant territory: accordingly it has been twice laid down by the Privy Council that the British character of an inhabitant of a colony must be decided by the law of England, though the rights to which, as British or alien, he will be entitled, depend on that of the colony (*l*). Of course, in construing the law of England on national character, it is not now the realm of that name, but the universal dominions of its sovereign,

(*h*) 6 Ha. 51.
(*i*) 2 Knapp, 295, 311—314.
(*k*) 6 Hare, 65.
(*l*) *Donegani* v. *Donegani*, 3 Knapp, 63; *Re Adam*, 1 Mo. P. C. 460.

to which the question of birth within or without the allegiance must be referred. Sometimes, to promote the settlement of colonies, the parent state confers the benefits of naturalization on aliens who emigrate to them: but this is no exception to the rule, for it is still by the law of the supreme government that the status of such emigrants is determined. Has, however, a new view been introduced by the st. 10 & 11 Vict. c. 83, which declares that the st. 7 & 8 Vict. c. 66 does not extend to the colonies, and validates all past and future colonial statutes for imparting naturalization within the respective colonies? The effect of this will probably be that of a naturalization unrestricted as to geographical limits—for it is difficult to understand a restricted one: there can be but one answer to the question, what government must protect him and answer for his acts abroad—but accompanied by limited internal disqualifications, as with regard to holding land situate in any other part of the empire than that in which he is naturalized. But I would not be understood to speak positively on the meaning of this act.

26. *United States of America.*—The American use of the term *citizen* is indistinct. A citizenship of a particular state is recognized, as well as one of the union; and the term is sometimes used to express the enjoyment of full internal political rights, so as to be denied to persons of colour, who even in many of the free states are not suffered to hold office or to vote for public officers. But it is only with the citizenship of the United States that we have in this place to do, and with that in the largest sense: for we are here considering the distribution of men between nations which have a recognized standing by each other's side, and all public relations with foreign countries are reserved to the union by its constitution; wherefore a slave or a person of colour, whatever his rights at home, is internationally a member of the body called the United States,

since that is the government under which he stands in relation to foreigners.

Now, as the British law of allegiance and alienage depends entirely on principles which existed, or on statutes which were passed, before the independence of America, it might be thought to apply there also, except so far as subsequently modified by the legislation of that country. The allegiance due to the crown from Americans was transferred to the union by the events of 1776—1783, and it was certainly one possible construction of the situation that, in analogy to the continued validity of the existing private law, the rules which previously governed the propagation of that allegiance to future generations remained applicable to the propagation of the subjection due to the Union. But for some reason which I do not find explained, it seems to have been considered that this was the case with such only of those rules as were drawn from our common and not from our statute law, the defects in which have since been supplied by a series of acts of Congress. First, then, every one is held to be a subject of the Union who is born within its jurisdiction (*m*). And, secondly, persons born out of the same territory who are citizens are, the children of American ambassadors, in pursuance of the English common law doctrine; and, under the acts of Congress of 1802, 1804 and 1855, persons whose fathers were citizens at the time of their birth, but so that "the rights of citizenship shall not descend to persons whose fathers never resided in the United States;" the children of naturalized fathers, who are minors at the time of their fathers' naturalization, if dwelling in the United States; and such wives of citizens as, being free whites, are not incapable of naturalization:

(*m*) 2 Kent's Comm. 39; Bouvier's Institutes of Amer. Law, 2nd edit. vol. i. p. 64.

but the citizenship of the widow and children is secured, if the father die after taking the preliminary steps to naturalization (*n*).

27. *Distribution of existing Populations in Cases of Cession.*—When Great Britain cedes a country, or acknwledges the independence of a colony, the persons whose allegiance is discharged are strictly those who are domiciled within the ceded limits, but any who may choose to transfer their domicile for that purpose will be allowed to retain their British character (*o*, *p*, *q*). This rule places the nationality of the infants of the territory in the power of their fathers, as it should do (*q*). Also, since all the rules as to domicile apply, a mere temporary continuance in the territory, or return to it, will not conclusively decide against the choice of the British allegiance (*p*, *q*). But the choice, from whatever posterior circumstances inferred, must be that which was made at the time of the treaty, no option to change it being afterwards allowed (*p*), unless, as is often done, a term in which to make the option be stipulated in the treaty itself. This is strictly in accordance with the common practice among states. The inhabitants of the ceded territory are said to be collectively naturalized in their new country, and have there all the rights of natural-born subjects, by the mere force of the cession of the soil, without the necessity of anything being expressed concerning the people (*r*).

(*n*) Kent, *ubi supra*, pp. 51—53; Bouvier, *ubi supra*, p. 65; Wheaton's Int. Law, 6th edit. p. 626.

(*o*) *Doe* v. *Acklam*, 2 Ba. & Cr. 779.

(*p*) *Doe* v. *Mulcaster*, 5 Ba. & Cr. 771; *Doe* v. *Arkwright*, 5 C. & P. 575.

(*q*) *Jephson* v. *Riera*, 3 Knapp, 130. In *Re Bruce*, 2 C. & J. 436, 2 Tyr. 475, the American nationality might therefore have been decided without going into Bruce's own acts. But they were rightly gone into, because his domicile and not his nationality was the true question: *Commissioners, &c.* v. *Devereux*, 13 Sim. 14; *Thomson* v. *Advocate-General*, 13 Sim. 153, 12 Cl. & F. 1.

(*r*) Wheaton, pp. 627, 631, 632.

CHAPTER III.

Domicile.

28. The distinctions of nationality which we have considered concern the relation between sovereign and subject, the former of which characters may be filled by the body corporate of a republic as well as by a monarch. But a state exists also in relation to a certain territory, within which one duty of sovereignty is to establish a legal order, and for that purpose to exercise jurisdiction. It is true that this double relation to persons and to the soil is not essential to the existence of a state, since nomadic tribes are mere aggregates of persons having no fixed residence, or property in land, nations without territories: yet they have governments and laws, and make war and peace. Feudalism on the contrary, confounding the conceptions of government and property, always tended to know no permanent relations but those which were derived from the tenure of the soil. But for the full development of man the state must indispensably be grounded in both personal and territorial arrangements. He needs to be impelled and constrained by forces both physical and moral, both immediate and slow in their operation. The protection of his property and person, the maintenance of that general security which is necessary to the continuous efforts and large combinations whether of mental or of industrial activity, demand a force which must be territorial, because it must be always ready and on the spot. And political

society, which is the true sphere of human existence, depends on ideas, the possession of which is not an accident of place. Neither the traveller, nor even the merchant who resides abroad, necessarily acquires foreign habits of mind, or loses those which birth and education have instilled into him; and the tendency of jurisprudence to assign him a citizenship independent of his casual abode or place of birth, does, as we have seen, but recognize the fact of his adaptation to one or other political society. Some of the most important aspects of the state may therefore be summed up in the aphorism, that it is related to the soil by the principle of what is now called order, and to persons by its political principle, on which order depends for its stability. And in this point of view, the industrial superiority of the modern to the ancient world may be compared with the greater prominence which, through the intermediate stage of feudalism, the territorial side of the idea of a state has acquired, and of which we shall see examples in the modification of the rules of international law and jurisdiction.

29. The separate relations of the state to the soil and to persons have their meeting-point in the idea of domicile or home. For while the maintenance of order compels in a thousand cases the exercise of jurisdiction over persons who are not generally the subjects of the sovereign before whose courts they are cited, in respect of the situation of property, or the place where sudden difficulties occur, there are many other purposes, having a peculiar connection with the person, for which jurisdiction cannot properly be exercised but in a place with which the person has some permanent ties, and which yet cannot without an equal inconvenience be reserved for the tribunals of his own sovereign. I forbear at present to particularize, because we shall see that there has been, and still is, much difference as to the cases which should be referred

to either class. Farther, we shall have to consider whether this relation of persons to their domicile does not extend itself beyond jurisdiction, so as even to affect the choice of the laws which must in certain cases determine rights. In one case this is obviously so, that in which different laws prevail in different portions of the same nation, as happens with England and Scotland. For such differences of laws, both being those of the same sovereign, can have relation only to the courts in which they are administered; and the jurisdiction of those courts can only be founded on the situation of things, the place of occurrence of events, and domicile, the last of which alone has a relation to persons; so that between English and Scotch, the international effect of domicile must be the sum of those effects which between English and French would arise either from domicile or from national character.

30. Domicile then is the legal conception of residence, and the two words differ no otherwise than as in all sciences common words, on becoming technical, are limited in meaning for the sake of precision. Such terms continue to hinge on the same central notion as in ordinary speech, but the circle of their application is more strictly defined: and if the language possesses another word originally synonymous, it is advantageous to use the one for the daily, the other for the scientific term; the one for the general, the other for the particularized conception. Yet this must be so done as not to impair the sense of the fundamental sameness, and thus, while we admit that residence is not domicile, unless accompanied by the circumstances under which the law will recognise it, we must not forget that after all that which in domicile the law does recognise is simply residence. Now residence is a simple conception, which may serve to fix others, but which cannot be made plainer itself by any amount of verbiage; wherefore no true definition of domicile is possible, nor

would it be just to the Roman emperors to represent them as having attempted one in that pathetic description of home so often and deservedly quoted. *In eo loco singulos habere domicilium non ambigitur, ubi quis larem ac fortunarum suarum summam constituit, unde rursus non sit discessurus si nihil avocet, unde cum profectus est peregrinari videtur, quo si rediit peregrinari jam destitit* (*a*). The modern attempts at defining domicile have not aimed at elucidating the meaning of the word, but at comprising in a formula all the conditions which the law demands for its recognition of the fact, and the most successful of them is, perhaps, that of Mr. Phillimore:—" a residence at a particular place, accompanied with positive or presumptive proof of an intention to remain there for an unlimited time" (*b*). No such attempt, however, can be perfectly successful, because domicile is not inferred solely from the circumstances which surround the person at the moment, but, as we shall see, the law presumes a domicile of origin, and is occupied with the changes to which that, or any other subsequently acquired, is subject. The nature of the case would admit of our summing-up in a formula the conditions under which *a change of domicile* will be inferred, but the resulting proposition would be either too cumbrous or too defective for utility.

31. Domicile is important as well in municipal as in international law. Thus, the jurisdiction of local courts, the right to exercise the suffrage or other political privi-

(*a*) Code, 10, 39, 7. The idea of residence is also well brought out by Lord Loughborough in *Bempde* v. *Johnstone*, 3 Ves. jun. 202: "domicile is the place where a man would be, if there were no particular circumstance to determine his position at the moment to some other place." The whole of this judgment is worthy of study for its principles; see, in p. 201, the statement that, " domicile is more a question of fact than of law,"—thus marking the broad distinction between domicile and national character; the latter of which, as it implies the *duty* of allegiance, must always be a question of law.

(*b*) Law of Dom. p. 13.

leges, the liability to serve offices or pay personal taxes, the right to relief under poor-laws, and many other points, are made in different countries to turn more or less on residence. Now the law of any country may prescribe certain conditions for the recognition of residence for those purposes, and even different ones for different purposes, but no such internal regulation can of its own nature, without an express enactment to that effect, bind the courts of such country as to the conditions under which they shall recognise residence in international questions; for wherever domicile is a necessary element in selecting the municipal law by which rights are to be determined, the question would be begged if a particular municipal law were selected to determine domicile. In this subject, therefore, we are thrown back upon the simple idea of home or residence, and can only refer to general jurisprudence for the considerations which may give it precision: but municipal laws, which, for any purpose, give the preference to any particular indication of a permanent establishment, are often cited in argument by way of analogy. Their weight, when so cited, must be in exact proportion to the probability that the legislator intended residence alone, unmixed with any other qualification, as the ground of the right or duty conferred or imposed. If it be clear that residence alone, and simply as such, was in his purview, any provision as to the circumstances under which it shall be presumed, will be tantamount to an opinion on domicile of high, but, if the municipal law do not relate to jurisdiction, not necessarily of binding authority. If it do relate to jurisdiction, its effect may be to determine conclusively one of the elements of fact on which the decision of the international case depends.

32. But what if the law of any country, as that of France does, forbids foreigners to establish a domicile

without the sanction of the government (c)? So far as such a law presents an impediment to the *de facto* establishment of a domicile, no difficulty arises: but if, as is also the case in France, foreigners are habitually permitted to become actually resident without obtaining the formal sanction, then such actual residence completely satisfies the idea of domicile as presented in this chapter, which is that of the home in fact, while how it may operate on the rights and obligations of the person, or on the effects of his acts, will have to be considered in connection with the principles of private international law hereafter to be discussed.

33. We have now to review such rules for ascertaining domicile as have a sufficient foundation in reason and authority.

Rule. I.—*Every one receives at birth a domicile of origin, which adheres until another is acquired: and so, throughout life, each successive domicile can only be lost by the acquisition of a new one.*

With regard to the great mass of mankind in civilized countries, this rule is but the simple expression of a fact. The only persons for whom it has not this character are those who, as the gipsies, or as certain outcasts from society, wander with no attachment to place, past or present; since even the soldier does not regard himself as having abandoned his home, because his duty obliges him to pass from land to land, and he therefore justly retains his original or his last domicile. For vagabonds, the rule is indeed arbitrary, but universally received, and indispensable, since no one can be permitted to withdraw himself altogether from the obligations which depend on domicile.

(c) Code Civil, Art. 13, on which see Merlin, Répertoire, Domicile, § XIII., and *Bremer* v. *Freeman*, 1 Deane, 192.

34. But though clear in principle, a difficulty may arise in applying the rule from a defect or equipoise of evidence. Thus, suppose a vagabond whose parentage and place of birth are totally unknown, so that no domicile of origin can be assigned him. Practically, such a person could hardly come under the law of domicile for any other purpose than that of jurisdiction, which would probably be exercised over him without scruple by any court within the territory of which he might be found. Or, take the case put by Lord Alvanley. "A man born no one knows where, or having had a domicile that he has completely abandoned, might acquire in the same or different countries two domiciles at the same instant, and occupy both under exactly the same circumstances; both country houses, for instance, bought at the same time. It can hardly be said, that of which he took possession first is to prevail (*d*)." This is the case of plural domiciles for the same purpose, which must be distinguished from that, before mentioned as possibly occurring in municipal law, of the use of the word domicile to denote equally places of which each has a significance only for some special purpose. Its conditions are the non-existence, or complete abandonment, of a previous home, the visible intention of an establishment somewhere, and a perfect balance of indications as to the place of that establishment. If it should arise in practice, we should necessarily, for some purposes, be driven to considerations independent of domicile, as Lord Alvanley, in the case of the man imagined by him, remarks, that for the distribution of his property on his death, "*ex necessitate* the *lex loci rei sitæ* must prevail:" though there may be other purposes, as that of founding jurisdiction over the person, for which either domicile might be available as such.

(*d*) 5 Ves. 791.

35. Rule II.—*The domicile of origin is generally that which the father has at the time of birth. It is the mother's, if the child be posthumous, or illegitimate and unacknowledged: if the parents are unknown, it is the place of birth, or that where the child is found.*

This rule is also universally received, and expresses the ordinary facts of an infant's home. When an illegitimate child is acknowledged and adopted, there appears to be no reason why in law, as in fact, its home should not be its father's. M. Fœlix arrives at this conclusion by extending to domicile the corresponding rule which we have seen holds between some countries as to national character, but the cases seem to be open to somewhat different considerations.

36. Rule III.—*The domicile of the unmarried infant, boy or girl, follows through all its changes that of the parent from whom it derived its domicile of origin. It also follows that of the mother or guardian after the father's death, and that of the guardian after the death of both parents.*

The latter part of this rule has been the subject of much controversy, as it has been thought that neither the mother nor the guardian ought to gain an advantage, in case of the child's death under age, by having removed its domicile to a country where the rules of succession are more advantageous to them. The impropriety of such advantage in any case will be discussed in speaking of the rules of succession. Supposing it established, which on the authorities it is very far from being, we should have to say that the succession of a fatherless minor is to be governed by the laws of that domicile which it had at its father's death; but as the proper abode of such a child is with its mother or guardian, we should only be falsifying the meaning of the word domicile did we deny the rule above stated.

37. Rule IV.—*Men and unmarried women, being of age,*

and men who have married, though under age, change their domiciles by changing their residence animo et facto (*e*).

It results from the preceding rules that to every one, on his becoming *sui juris*, a domicile is attributed by law. We now come to the mode in which, starting thence, the subsequent changes of domicile are traced. It is clear that the married minor must be treated as *sui juris* in respect of domicile, since on his marriage he actually founds an establishment separate from the parental home. For the rest, residence is neither changed by an unexecuted intention, nor by an absence during which the sentiments of home have not been transferred.

38. Rule V.—*The requisite* animus manendi *is an intention of residing in the new locality.*

From the necessity of the intention to reside, it follows that the mere being in the new locality, for however long a continuance, will not of itself be sufficient. But whether a certain length of continuance may not constitute so strong a presumption of such intention that the law will not allow it to be rebutted, is a question occasionally discussed among the tokens from which the *animus manendi* is inferred. A Scotch domicile has been retained, by an absence of the *animus manendi*, during an eight years' habitation in London (*f*).

Next, as the intention must be to reside, it will not be satisfied by a sojourn adopted for a limited or temporary purpose, with the design of returning on its accomplishment. This is strikingly illustrated by the case of political refugees, whose hope of a restoration, however distant its probability, is considered to preserve to them their native domicile (*g*). It must not be understood, however, that

(*e*) *De Bonneval* v. *De Bonneval*, 1 Curt. 864.

(*f*) *Munro* v. *Munro*, 7 Cl. & F. 842.

(*g*) *De Bonneval* v. *De Bonneval*, 1 Curt. 856. But the refugee acquires a domicile by remaining after his restoration has become possible, *Collier* v.

the acquisition of a domicile will be prevented by the vague thought of return or removal (*h*), for a true residence may aim at a terminable object, so that its duration be long and indefinite. An unhappy instance was once furnished by attendance on a Chancery suit: a better is that of the merchant in a foreign port, or the officer in foreign service, who hopes to enjoy at home the fortune he will have made abroad (*i*). Thus an English domicile would not be lost by the intention of spending a year or two in Italy for the sake of health (*k*), though if the necessity of a warm climate should cause one to remove his establishment to Naples, it would not be preserved by the indefinite hope of returning at some future period with a renovated constitution.

39. Rule VI.—*The requisite* factum *is a complete transit to the new locality.*

As an *animus manendi* is unintelligible unless it refer to some certain spot, the recent domicile must necessarily be retained, notwithstanding all appearance of its abandonment, as long as the person wanders from place to place, unresolved where to fix his abode (*l*); a case which must be distinguished from that above noticed, in which a regular course of life has been again adopted, but there is an equipoise of evidence as to its principal centre (*m*). The same reasons however do not apply to one who dies on a journey or voyage, having caused everything to be prepared for a permanent residence in the place of his destination, and

---

Rivaz, 2 Curt. 858; or even during his exile, by forming an attachment to its locality, *Heath* v. *Samson*, 14 Beav. 441.

(*h*) *Stanley* v. *Bernes*, 3 Hagg. 438, 465.

(*i*) *Bruce* v. *Bruce*, 2 Bos. & Pul. 229, note.

(*k*) *Whicker* v. *Hume* (Gilchrist's case), 13 Beav. 366, 398.

(*l*) *Bremer* v. *Freeman*, 1 Deane, 212.

(*m*) The rule of the Digest on this point was different, but is now definitively rejected. It was, *si quis domicilio relicto naviget vel iter faciat, quærens quo se conferat atque ubi constituat, hunc puto sine domicilio esse:* 50, 1, 27, 2. See Story, Conflict of Laws, s. 47. It was the case of *Munroe* v. *Douglas*, 5 Madd. 379.

the rule which makes him a domiciled inhabitant of the district which he has quitted was probably founded on the convenience of avoiding inquiries into the motive of an unfinished journey. The rule itself, however, is not so certain as might be desired, owing no doubt to the infrequency of cases which might call for a decision on it. It is maintained by Pothier, who says that *la volonté de transférer notre domicile dans un autre lieu doit être justifiée. Elle n'est pas équivoque lorsque c'est un bénéfice, une charge, ou un autre emploi non amovible, qui nous y appelle. En ce cas,* dès que nous y sommes arrivés *nous y acquérons domicile et nous perdons l'ancien* (*n*). It is also implied in what is said in *Craigie* v. *Lewin,* that, to consolidate the new domicile, when the transit is once complete, "length of time is not important; one day will be sufficient, provided the *animus* exists (*o*)." On the other hand, Sir John Leach, in stating the general rule, that "a domicile cannot be lost by mere abandonment," added the qualification, "unless the party die *in itinere* toward an intended domicile (*p*):" and Dr. Lushington said, in the case of the *Baltica,* "I have considered all the authorities on this subject, and I think the fair result is, with respect to a mercantile national character, that the party becomes clothed with a new character from the period when he first takes steps, *animo removendi,* to abandon his former domicile, and *animo manendi,* to acquire a new one (*q*)." But this refers to a trade domicile in war, and the incomplete *transitus* was in the particular case to a country the character of which the person could claim by descent, both of which circumstances, as it will appear by the next

(*n*) Introduction Générale aux Coutumes, s. 15.

(*o*) 3 Curt. 448. *Uno solo die constituitur domicilium, si de voluntate appareat.*

(*p*) In *Munroe* v. *Douglas,* 5 Madd. 405: and cited with approbation in *Forbes* v. *Forbes,* Kay, 354.

(*q*) Spinks, 267.

article, weaken the opinion as an authority for a general proposition on domicile: and the numerous authorities which declare that a former domicile is only lost by the acquisition of a new, and that the latter event can only happen by an acquisition in fact (*r*), must, when they express no exception to their doctrine, be held to support the rule stated at the head of this paragraph, which is its necessary consequence.

40. Rule VII.—*Except, perhaps, that the domicile of origin is regained* in transitu, *so that in its favour the only requisite* factum *is a complete abandonment of the late domicile.*

This exception, supposing the previous rule established, is commonly, though somewhat improperly, cited by the phrase "native allegiance easily reverts;" and its chief application has been in the prize courts. The liability of private property to warlike capture at sea has always depended not merely on the nationality, but also on the domicile of the owner: or it may be said that, for this purpose, domicile is the criterion of nationality. The motive, doubtless, lay in the assumption that the benefit of trade mainly accrues to that country from the ports of which it is carried on: whence only an actually subsisting residence for commercial objects could afford protection to the owner's property as against his nationality, for, when such residence was discontinued, nothing remained to take the case out of the general principle which exposed enemy's property, as such, to capture. With these considerations were combined the respect paid to the place of birth by the feudal principle of allegiance, and the recog-

(*r*) It would be unsatisfactory to cite a string of authorities, of no one of which it can be predicated with certainty that the generality of its language was meant to exclude an exception which there was no occasion to notice: but I may refer to Lord Cottenham's words in *Munro* v. *Munro*, 7 Cl. & F. 877—"the domicile of origin must prevail, unless it be proved that the party has acquired another *by residence*."

nised rule of international law, that a state to which allegiance has been transferred has not the right to protect the citizen against his former government, if by his voluntary act he again places himself within its power. All this might have been expressed by a proper provision for the cases in which domicile should or should not be the decisive consideration, without admitting irregularities in the rules by which domicile is itself determined; but the other method has been taken, and the exception above stated, which may sometimes have an anomalous effect on private rights, which are not within the reasons for it, is laid down by Story (*s*), and supported by the Scotch case of *Colville* v. *Lauder* (*t*). But I do not find any English authority for the exception, farther than for the purposes of the Court of Admiralty (*u*); and Sir John Leach, in the judgment already cited, expressly denies that, when another domicile is quitted, there is any difference between the resumption of that of origin, and the acquisition of a third (*x*). This, however, is of the less weight, because he holds the new domicile to be gained in either case *in itinere*, and because the instance before him did not need a decision on the point, for the indications of Dr. Munroe's intention, from the time he left India, did not point particularly to any country.

The subject of this article leads me farther to remark that the mercantile domicile which is influential in prize cases, and which does not fall within the scope of the present treatise, concerned as that is with private rights in time of peace, is subject to some other peculiar rules: as that one who has mercantile concerns in two countries is fixed with the character of each in transactions originating

(*s*) Conflict of Laws, s. 48.

(*t*) Morison, 14963, App., and 5 Madd. 384.

(*u*) *The Indian Chief*, 3 C. Rob. 12; &c., &c.

(*x*) 5 Madd. 404, 405.

in them respectively; and that, as the gist lies in the trade, which may be carried on without a counting-house, no fixed establishment, such as is commonly understood in domicile, is indispensable to it (*y*).

41. *Criteria of the* animus manendi.

We have now reached the criteria by which the *animus manendi*, required for the acquisition of a new domicile, is ascertained in the various combinations which human life presents for the consideration of courts of justice. Two leading classes of cases will readily be distinguished. In one, duty, business or pleasure attach a man to one or more spots different from his recent, and perhaps continuing domicile, from which, however, he has not entirely withdrawn himself. Against the latter, each of the connections so formed with other places must be separately weighed. Does any of them amount to a transference of the sentiments of home? In the other, the recent domicile is completely abandoned, there is no doubt of the intention not to return to it, but though settled habits of life have been contracted elsewhere, they exhibit a nice balance of attachment to several places, among which it is difficult to select the new *lar* and the *fortunarum summa.* It will not be necessary continually to advert to the distinction, for in each class the same criteria must be sought, but we shall not demand their presence in equal strength. The cases where the attachment to be appreciated is weighed against the prestige of a residence not wholly quitted will call for a stricter proof than we can obtain when, as the decision lies between localities otherwise equal, that one must prevail towards which the scale is inclined by however slight a weight of argument.

The first place is due to those criteria which the law will not allow to be rebutted, because they spring from the duty of residence in a certain place.

(*y*) *The Jonge Klassina*, 5 C. Rob. 297.

42. Rule VIII.—*The wife's domicile is that of her husband* (*z*).

Only if she take proceedings for a divorce, her actually separate residence will be noticed for the purpose of founding the jurisdiction, since the law which professes to grant her redress might otherwise stultify itself. And when a divorce has been decreed, be it even *a mensa et toro* only (*a*), or the husband has died, the wife regains the power of changing her domicile, but so that she retains the last matrimonial domicile until she has actually changed it *animo et facto*.

43. Rule IX.—*The domestic servant has his master's domicile.*

Domestic, that is, living in the house in his master's habitual service: so that this rule only states a fact. The particular circumstances of any other service must be taken into account as criteria of the *animus manendi*. The French code expressly includes in the rule workmen living in the house with their habitual employers (*b*).

44. Rule X.—*An office which requires residence confers a domicile in that place where its holder is bound to reside.*

Thus ecclesiastics are domiciled at their cures. Thus a service with the East India Company, or other Indian government, which requires residence in India, creates an Indian domicile (*c*): and when one who held such an employment returned to his previous home in Scotland, in hope "of not being called on to leave it again," the Indian domicile was nevertheless preserved by the constant liability to a recall (*d*). The case last mentioned, which

---

(*z*) *Bremer* v. *Freeman*, 1 Deane, 212.

(*a*) *Williams* v. *Dormer*, 2 Robertson, 505.

(*b*) Code Civil, Art. 109.

(*c*) *Munroe* v. *Douglas*, 5 Madd. 379; *Forbes* v. *Forbes*, Kay, 341.

(*d*) *Craigie* v. *Lewin*, 3 Curt. 435. Only this liability must not be so remote as to amount practically rather to the option, without the intention, was one of an officer in the Indian army, may be generalized into the proposition, that by entering the permanent military service of any government, a domicile in the territory of that government is acquired, and is retained notwithstanding a cantonment at a foreign station; for such cantonment is subject throughout to the contingency of abrupt termination, and the only lasting attachment is to the employing country. The same is true of a naval service, when the officer has his dwelling on shore in the territory of the government he serves (*e*); and, on principle, perhaps even without that circumstance, as the ships of a nation are equivalent to its soil. But if the employing nation include several jurisdictions, the native subject who enters its military or naval service retains, in general, the character of that subdivision to which he previously belonged (*f*); and this is the true meaning of what in a certain case appears to be said, namely, that naval employment cannot change the domicile (*g*). In that case, the person was Scotch by origin, as well as by residence during the intervals he passed on shore, and could not lose that character by a service which was not English but British: had he entered a foreign navy, his Scotch domicile would doubtless have been lost. On the other hand, the British service did not restrain the power he would otherwise have had to transfer his domicile to England, and it was necessary to examine his acts during the intervals of duty, in order to ascertain whether he had exercised it.

45. This rule is adopted by the Code Napoleon in a modified form only, to which also it was restrained in the

---

of returning, than to any real prospect of a compulsory return. *Forbes* v. *Forbes*, Kay, 359.

(*e*) *Ommaney* v. *Bingham*, 5 Ves. 757.

(*f*) *Dalhousie* v. *M'Douall*, 7 Cl. & F. 817.

(*g*) *Brown* v. *Smith*, 15 Beav. 444, 448, 21 L. J. N. S. Ch. 356.

ancient jurisprudence of France: namely, that a change of domicile is caused necessarily by the acceptance of an office requiring residence, and conferred for an indefinite period and without power of revocation, but not, unless there be independent proof of an intention to transfer the domicile, by a temporary or revocable appointment (*h*). It may however be questioned how far the tenure of the office can be of importance. Military service is terminable by the employing government, but, as we have seen, changes the domicile, and, on principle, if a private motive for removal need not extend to the whole future life, but will transfer the domicile so only it have a long and indefinite scope, then an indefinite residence imposed by duty ought to have the same effect, notwithstanding the chance of the duty being terminated by a revocation of the appointment. The case is quite distinct from that of military quarters in a country foreign to that of the service, which are not a residence even for the duration of the commission; and it is to such quarters, or to cases falling under one of the two next articles, that most of the instances mentioned by the jurists in support of the doctrine here opposed refer.

46. If the office require an occasional, but not a constant residence, the domicile is not thereby transferred. This was adjudged in the case of Lord Somerville, with regard to the parliamentary duties in London imposed by his election as a representative peer of Scotland (*i*).

47. Rule XI.—*But ambassadors and consuls retain the domicile of the country which they represent or serve* (*j*).

(*h*) Code Civil, Art. 106, 107; Pothier, *ubi supra*, 15; Merlin, Rép. Dom., § III. See *The goods of James Smith*, 2 Robertson, 332, where the language used tends the same way, but is not decisive.

(*i*) *Somerville* v. *Somerville*, 5 Ves. 750; and see Phillimore on Dom., p. 62.

(*j*) As to consuls: *Maltass* v. *Maltass*, 1 Robertson, 79; *Gout* v *Zimmermann*, 5 N. of C. 445.

The house of an ambassador is considered to be a part of his sovereign's territory. But as the same reason does not apply to the domicile of consuls, another ground must be sought for the rule; and it is supplied by the duty of these classes of public servants to act for the interests, and remain identified with the feelings, of the state by which they are accredited. Accordingly, the doctrine is confined to the retention of the home domicile by such ministers when sent out. If a government choose to employ in such capacity the services of one already resident in the foreign country, a frequent case with consuls and not unknown for ambassadors (*k*), the domicile is not changed by the appointment.

48. Rule XII.—*Of criteria which are not peremptory, the place of the wife and family prevails over that of business or occasional retirement, the merchant's town house over his country house (l), the landed proprietor's country house over his town house (l), and the place where the citizen exercises public functions over that where he does not possess them or neglects their exercise.*

These are about all the rules of comparison which can be laid down from English authorities, or which are applicable to English life. Some purely negative ones may be added, as that it is immaterial whether the residence be in a house or in lodgings (*m*), and that no description which a man can give of himself is of any force unless supported by facts (*n*); nor indeed, where the facts leave a doubt between two spots, have our courts much valued declarations of preference (*o*), or of an intention to return from the

(*k*) *Heath* v. *Samson*, 14 Beav. 441.

(*l*) 5 Ves. 789.

(*m*) *Whicker* v. *Hume*, 13 Beav. 395, 401.

(*n*) *Whicker* v. *Hume*, 13 Beav. 400.

(*o*) *Somerville* v. *Somerville*, 5 Ves. 750; *De Bonneval* v. *De Bonneval*, 1 Curt. 856.

one to the other of them (*p*). Such declarations "are undoubtedly admissible evidence," but are not entitled to the first degree of consideration (*p*).

49. But what if the rules of comparison thus furnished should, in some case to which several of them are applicable, lead to opposite results? Is it possible to establish a scale of precedency among these rules themselves? There is no more instructive instance of the mode of dealing with such cases than that of *Forbes* v. *Forbes* (*q*), where the rule preferring the landed proprietor's country house to his town house came into conflict with that preferring the place of the wife and family to those where the wife, whenever she went thither, "was a traveller and visitor only (*r*);" and where also the force of the former rule itself was considerably weakened by the evident insufficiency of the country house for the fortune of the testator, while his town establishment was suitable to his rank. Sir W. P. Wood held the residence of the wife and family to be decisive, and used language from which it may be inferred that in ordinary cases it would prevail over every other consideration; though "if some particular state of health required the wife to reside in a warm climate not agreeable to her husband, or the like, so that he was obliged to visit his wife away from home, he might still be domiciled at a residence of his own apart from her." But, had General Forbes not been a married man, the Vice-Chancellor would have attached no weight to the insufficiency of a country residence, which in the general's own judgment appeared to be a sufficient mansion for himself and his successors (*s*).

50. Another passage from the same judgment is worth

(*p*) *Anderson* v. *Laneuville*, 9 Mo. P. C. 325, 335.

(*q*) Kay, 341.

(*r*) p. 366.

(*s*) pp. 363—366.

citing. "If a party select two residences, in one of which he can reside all the year, whilst in the other his health will not permit him to do so; and he must from the first be aware that, should his health fail him, his days must be passed where alone he can constantly reside; there is an additional reason for concluding that he regards such place from the first as that which must be his home, a conclusion greatly fortified by his chief establishment being from the first fixed there."

51. Study at a university or other place of learning does not indicate an intention to transfer thither the domicile. Rather, as its probable duration is short, it implies the absence of such an intention. But if an academic life were adopted when the period of study was concluded, the case would be different, with which view the Roman law allowed the student to retain his former domicile for ten years, though we should now look more at the facts than at any fixed limit of time (*t*).

52. Rule XIII.—*An enforced sojourn does not change the domicile.*

The *animus manendi* which we have hitherto considered is either one freely adopted by a person *sui juris*, or at least, as in the case of a wife, one which results from duty, with which therefore the will is presumed to coincide. But if one is compelled to remain at a place against or without his will, this is neither residence nor domicile. Thus it has been decided that an Irishman retained his original domicile notwithstanding that he died in prison in England (*u*), and it appears to me that on the same principle a lunatic must retain the domicile which he had when he first lost his reason. In Lord Annandale's case, that domicile was in the same country where he continued

---

(*t*) Code, 10, 39, 2; *The Benedict*, Spinks, 314, 317.

(*u*) *Burton* v. *Fisher*, 1 Milw. 183.

during the lunacy, so that the judge was enabled to discard the lunacy from consideration without deciding on its effect (*x*); but I must confess that Mr. Phillimore believes that a lunatic would acquire the domicile of the committee of his person (*y*). The latter is indeed the modern French rule, because the uniformity of law in France has deprived the domicile of its effect on the distribution of property on death; but the old rule of that country, when its local customs varied as the laws of the component portions of the British empire do now, justly forbade the succession of a lunatic to be affected by any removal which might have taken place during the lunacy, and therefore without his will (*z*).

53. Rule XIV.—*Unless it be such as to exclude the prospect of return.*

"It is clear," says Mr. Phillimore, "in spite of two sentences passed during the time of the French revolution to the contrary, that the person banished for life (*déporté*), whether for a civil or political offence, loses his original domicile. It cannot be doubted that the same sentence would be passed in England with respect to persons transported for life (*a*)." The student should observe the difference between this case and that of the political refugee, whose residence is neither enforced, for he chooses the country of his sojourn, nor legally regarded as hopeless of return (*b*).

54. *Relation of Domicile to National Character.*—"All those who are domiciled in the territory" are enumerated by Heffter among the proper subjects of a state, as distinguished from those who are only subjects for certain

(*x*) *Bempde* v. *Johnstone*, 3 Ves. 198.
(*y*) On Domicile, p. 55.
(*z*) Code Civil, art. 108; Merlin, Rép. Dom. § V. No. IV.
(*a*) Law of Dom. p. 89.
(*b*) See above, Art. 38.

purposes (*subditi secundum quid*) (*c*); and similarly Mr. Secretary Marcy, in his note on behalf of the American government in Koszta's case, lays down that "foreigners may and often do acquire a domicile in a country, even though they have entered it with the avowed intention not to become naturalized citizens, but to return to their native land at some remote and uncertain period; and, whenever they acquire a domicile, international law at once impresses upon them the national character of the country of that domicile. It is a maxim of international law that domicile confers a national character: it does not allow any one who has a domicile to decline the national character thus conferred: it forces it upon him often very much against his will, and to his great detriment. International law looks only to the national character in determining what country has the right to protect (*d*)." Nevertheless it is certain that these doctrines are not generally admitted. Koszta's case did not need them, for not only had he taken the initiatory step towards naturalization in the United States, but the circumstances of his removal from Turkey had been such as distinctly to involve the consent of Austria to his expatriation. Neither do they appear needed by any motives of convenience. That indeed may require that the protection enjoyed in time of war by property embarked in commerce shall be founded on domicile; or that a government which permits foreigners to reside in its territory should protect them, whether in peace or war, in the enjoyment of all rights springing out of their residence, and in the performance of all lawful acts in or originating from the territory; but scarcely that one whose avowed intention it was not to be naturalized should, on account of domicile, be treated as naturalized when beyond the territory, and in matters having no concern with

(*c*) Europäische Völkerrecht, 3rd edit. p. 109.

(*d*) Wheaton's Int. Law, 6th edit. p. 132.

it. And, with regard to the extent to which these doctrines are accepted, not to mention the British claim to perpetual allegiance, they go far beyond the French rule, which makes the loss of French nationality a consequence of a foreign establishment adopted *without intention of return*,—a condition by no means necessary for the acquisition of a foreign domicile, and expressly repudiated by Mr. Secretary Marcy in the passage quoted,—and which also declares that a merely commercial establishment can never cause such loss of nationality (*e*). If a free choice of national character be permitted to adults, which Vattel thought that natural justice required, the French rule would seem to be the best expression of that principle: the renunciation of the old country ought at least to be complete.

55. *Domicile of a Corporation*.—This is a notional conception, introduced for purposes of jurisdiction and law, and named by analogy to the domicile which an individual has in fact. In the leading case of *Maclaren* v. *Stainton* (*f*), or *Carron Iron Company* v. *Maclaren* (*g*), Sir John Romilly in the first instance, and Lord St. Leonard's on appeal, held that a company "may, for the purposes of jurisdiction, be deemed to have two domiciles. Its business is necessarily carried on by agents, ... and the places of business may, for the purposes of jurisdiction, properly be deemed the domicile." But Lords Cranworth and Brougham, on the appeal, whose judgment therefore prevailed, held that a domicile for jurisdiction was not created by the agency of one who "had no concern whatever in any way with the management or direction of the affairs of the company," though employed in selling its goods. It is evident that the decision cannot be drawn

(*e*) Code Civil, art. 17. See above, art. 22.

(*f*) 16 Beav. 279.

(*g*) 5 H. L. Cases, 416.

from the meaning of the term domicile, but must turn on the juridical principles applicable to the duties of a body of persons acting through agents, so that the point must be deferred till these duties have been sifted from the international point of view.

CHAPTER IV.

IMMOVABLES.

1. *Introduction.*

56. WE have next to consider the principles on which the persons, whom we have classed by national character and domicile, are amenable to municipal laws and jurisdictions, either generally, or in reference to particular subjects of action. Now, in jurisprudence, the origin of rights naturally precedes the mode of enforcing them, or, in other words, the civil code is prior to the code of procedure. This order was indeed long inverted in our law, for, from the absence in it of clear expositions of principle, as well as from the singular distribution of powers among various courts, there was hardly any other mode of ascertaining whether a right existed, than by enquiring exhaustively whether it could be prosecuted under any of the known forms of remedy. Will trover lie? will trespass on the case lie? will chancery relieve? But the reproach in

question is gradually being removed from us, as well by the improvement of the English law itself, as by that of the institutional treatises which contain its elements; and, similarly, writers on the conflict of laws now usually consider on what law the creation of a right depends, before treating of the appropriate jurisdiction for its enforcement. But such was by no means the course first taken, and it will be found that many of the doctrines on the selection of a law have been deduced from positions which had been previously held on the subject of jurisdiction. The maxim by which the passage was made from rules of jurisdiction to rules of law was, that every jurisdiction decided according to its own law, or, as it was expressed, *paria sunt forum alicubi sortiri et statutis ligari: si ibi forum, ergo et jus.* Hence, if it could be determined to what jurisdiction any contention directly, or by the strict rule, belonged, the law of that jurisdiction was to be applied if the matter arose incidentally, or by a permitted deviation from the strict rule, in any other forum: and hence again the whole mass of provisions contained in the Corpus Juris on the forum for each kind of action, and which in the empire of Justinian could not possibly have contemplated a diversity in the laws of those forums, became at once available for determining questions of the conflict of laws, when in the middle ages such diversities arose. No doubt in the possibility of this last result lay one great temptation to the method itself, which was therefore partly occasioned by an overstrained reverence for the Roman law, and by a disposition to seek the solution of every difficulty in authority rather than in principle; yet the method was far from being wholly a mistaken one.

57. For, first, the departments of rights and remedies are not related to one another in private international law precisely in the same way as in municipal. In the latter, the authority of the sovereign to command is assumed:

the question of right is merely of what he has commanded, and that of remedy merely of the method he has prescribed for redressing disobedience to his commands. But in the former, the authority of the sovereign is the important element in deciding both the law which, in any case, imposes a duty, and the jurisdiction in which redress for the nonperformance of that duty must be sought. Thus, the grounds for asserting that title to immovable property must be made by the *lex situs*, and that immovable property can only be recovered in the *forum situs*, are so nearly similar, both propositions flowing from the territorial authority of sovereigns, that it is impossible to say which of them is logically prior to the other.

58. Secondly, a truth is embodied in the assumption that the municipal law to be chosen for a private international case is that of the jurisdiction to which the matter originally and properly belonged. Thus, in the first case put in Art. 3, the privilege which I should have enjoyed if sued in my native jurisdiction, where I became surety, is justly treated as a right vested in me, and therefore to be respected in courts where the law of the sovereign who gave that right would not, as such, be of force. Or, putting the same point in a more general light, it is a principle of private international jurisprudence that *rights which have once well accrued by the law of the appropriate sovereign are treated as valid rights everywhere;* and by means of this principle cognisance is taken every day of extra-territorial facts, and of persons not generally subject to the jurisdiction, which facts and persons could not otherwise be brought within the competence of the court. But then, as such a right was never a reality unless there was a jurisdiction to enforce it, this principle sends us back to the jurisdiction to which the matter belonged in its inception, in order to ascertain the appropriate sovereign whose law applies to it.

59. And, thirdly, certain matters, which municipal laws generally agree in grouping together for purposes of procedure, are in private international jurisprudence, on account of that general agreement, referred as a whole to the law of that jurisdiction to which they conventionally belong, although, if they were considered separately, the strict theory of sovereignty might refer them to different laws. This is in precise analogy to public international jurisprudence, in which a common usage, existing among all the populations to whose intercourse the system is applied, is accepted as a sufficient foundation for some rules which do not necessarily flow from the theory of sovereignty. An example is furnished, in the private department, by a movable succession on death, which is entirely regulated by the law of the deceased's domicile, only because that is conventionally the jurisdiction for its distribution, though it may be difficult to show theoretically why the several chattels which enter into it should not be distributed by the laws of their respective actual situations.

60. On all these grounds it appears to me necessary to examine first the rules of private international jurisdiction, before coming to the choice of the municipal law by which the merits of each cause must be decided: and in both these examinations the questions relating to the property in the soil will naturally stand first, because they depend entirely on the territorial aspect of the idea of a modern state, which is far less intricate than its relation to persons. Farther, the same simple connexion of immovables with the theory of territorial sovereignty, both with regard to jurisdiction and law, furnishes the means of presenting their private international relations in one view, before entering on the other parts of the subject, as will be attempted in this chapter.

2. *Jurisdiction.*

61. The right to the possession of land can only be tried in the courts of the *situs*. A trial elsewhere would be nugatory, as the officers of no other power could, without violating the national sovereignty, use force upon the spot to put or establish the successful litigant in possession. To a similar effect, each sovereign state is held internationally to have the eminent domain of its territory. This conception differs from the feudal one, in that it decides nothing as to the ultimate lordship of the soil between the sovereign person in the state, if any such there be, and his subjects, but asserts that as against foreigners the territorial sovereign enjoys the absolute ownership and disposal of the country. Whence it follows that only under his authority, or by his ministry, can possession be lawfully given or taken of any part of it.

62. The right of property in land can only be tried in the courts of the *situs*, for such property derives its only meaning and value from the right to possession. The Roman law, indeed, allowed the defendant to be sued at his domicile *in rem*, for the recovery of land situate in another province, as well as *in personam*: between the *forum rei* and that of the *situs* the plaintiff might choose (*a*). But that might well be in an empire subject to one supreme head, who could enforce throughout his dominions the process of any of his courts, and where the existence of an uniform law obviated the inconvenience which would now result from deciding on titles dependent on a strange jurisprudence, so that no analogy for our present guidance can be drawn from thence.

63. The same propositions are true, and for the same reasons, of all dismemberments of the property in land,

(*a*) Cod. 3, 19, 3.

and the right to their enjoyment: as of servitudes; rent-charges; the property in the surface as severed from that in the subsoil, or *vice versâ;* future estates, or particular ones limited in duration; rights of mortgage, pledge, or lien; the equitable ownership as severed from the legal, or *vice versâ;* and if there be any other real right in any way falling short of the entire dominion of the soil. But the equitable ownership must be understood as here spoken of only so far as the decree of a foreign court may affect to bind it directly. That cannot in any sense be done; but if a court, being competent in respect of the person or the obligation, enjoin a party to convey or deal with foreign land, it may be transferred or bound by his act done in obedience to such decree: and if there be a difference of opinion as to the competence, such as we shall hereafter see exists on many questions of personal international jurisdiction, it is of course the *forum situs*, and not that which pronounced the decree, which must decide whether the land is affected by the compulsory act.

64. In the mean time, as to the general principle of such compulsion, when such a special equity can be shown as would form a ground for compelling a party to convey or release English land, or any right therein, or for restraining him from asserting a title to such land or right, then the English chancery, if, according to its own rules, it have jurisdiction over his person, will similarly compel or restrain him as to land situate out of England, although a similar equity may not exist by the *lex situs*, provided only it be not absolutely excluded thereby (*b*). Such an exercise of authority is, in fact, supplemental to the *lex situs*, and is grounded on the supposition that every law intends the rights which it confers to be used conscienti-

(*b*) A similar doctrine prevails in the United States: *Massie* v. *Watts*, 6 Cranch, 148.

ously, of which, since the conscience is personal, the measure must be supplied, so long as the *lex situs* is silent, by that court which has personal jurisdiction; while, if the *lex situs* excludes the equity, then the right to hold the land free from it becomes one of the incidents of property, which, as we shall see, are decided for immovables by the law of their situation. This distinction, which is of essential importance, may be understood from the cases of *Exp. Pollard* (c) and *Martin* v. *Martin* (d). In the former, although the law of Scotland knows nothing of equitable mortgages, it was decided that the owner of a Scotch estate can be compelled in England to give effect to a pledge made by the deposit of its title-deeds: in the latter, that a purchaser's conscience is not affected by notice of an attempt made on valuable consideration to settle foreign lands, such attempt having been rendered ineffectual by the *lex situs*. There the law of Demerara, which gave the purchaser a good title notwithstanding notice, would have been absolutely contravened by holding him bound: but the Scotch law could not forbid the informal pledge of land by merely omitting to give a remedy in respect of it; and indeed, precisely in the spirit of *Exp. Pollard*, the court remarked in *Martin* v. *Martin* that, while the land remained in the ownership of the intending settlor, it would probably have been ready to decree a sale, in order that the price might be settled on the trusts which had been destined for the land.

65. For the rest, the claim to affect foreign lands through the person of the party must be strictly limited to those cases in which the relief decreed can be entirely obtained through the party's personal obedience: if it went beyond that, the assumption would not only be presumptuous but ineffectual. Thus, a bill will not lie for partition of lands

(c) Mont. & Ch. 239, 4 Dea. 27.

(d) 2 Russ. & My. 507.

beyond the jurisdiction (*e*), or to settle their boundaries (*f*); nor can any equity be enforced by sequestration of such land (*g*): nor, again, will the court try any question which, like the validity of a will of foreign land (*h*), does not involve a special equity between the parties, but is a general one affecting the land, and therefore solely dependent on the *lex situs*, on which law another tribunal than its own can only pronounce incidentally and not directly.

66. In pursuance of the proposition of Art. 64, thus explained and limited, the English chancery has, with regard to foreign lands, decreed an account of rents and profits between joint-tenants (*i*), enforced specific performance of contracts for sale (*j*) and agreements for the settlement of boundaries (*k*), foreclosed mortgages (*l*) and expressed its readiness to assist in their redemption (*m*), declared proprietors trustees (*n*), ordered reconveyances and releases of lands and interests in them fraudulently acquired (*o*), entertained bills for discovery of rents, profits and deeds on

---

(*e*) *Carteret* v. *Petty*, 2 Swans. 323, n., 2 Ch. Ca. 214; *Roberdeau* v. *Rous*, 1 Atk. 543.

(*f*) *Penn* v. *Baltimore*, 1 Ves. 444, p. 447; which is rather to be followed than *Tulloch* v. *Hartley*, 1 Y. & C., C. C., 114.

(*g*) When the English courts were held to have a superintendence over those of Ireland, sequestration of Irish land was consistently issued by the former: *Arglasse* v. *Muschamp*, 1 Vern. 135; *Fryer* v. *Bernard*, 2 P. W. 261. The latter case, however, supported by a dictum in 3 My. & Ke. 109, shows that colonial lands could not then, and that Irish lands cannot now, be sequestered here.

(*h*) *Pike* v. *Hoare*, 2 Eden, 182.

(*i*) *Carteret* v. *Petty*, and *Roberdeau* v. *Rous*, *ubi supra*.

(*j*) *Archer* v. *Preston*, cited in 1 Vern. 77: and see dictum in *Jackson* v. *Petrie*, 10 Ves. 165.

(*k*) *Penn* v. *Baltimore*, *ubi supra*.

(*l*) *Toller* v. *Carteret*, 2 Vern. 494.

(*m*) *Bent* v. *Young*, 9 Sim. 180, 190; *Beckford* v. *Kemble*, 1 S. & St. 7.

(*n*) *Kildare* v. *Eustace*, 1 Vern. 419.

(*o*) *Arglasse* v. *Muschamp*, 1 Vern. 75; *Cranstown* v. *Johnston*, 3 Ves. 170, 5 Ves. 277, a remarkable case, as the sale set aside was a judicial one in the *situs*; *Jackson* v. *Petrie*, 10 Ves. 164.

the ground of fraud (*p*), appointed receivers (*q*), and restrained by injunction the prosecution of suits commenced in the *situs* for the recovery of immovables (*r*).

67. The principles of this section show also that foreign land cannot be affected by the administrative act of any court: as by the appointment of assignees, syndics, curators, or administrators of the estate of any bankrupt, lunatic, infant, or deceased person. Such an appointment, though justified by the personal jurisdiction, and therefore valid for the other property of the individual, will be nugatory as to his foreign immovables. Nor can the person be obliged to supply the defects of such administrative act. In *Stein's case* (*s*), indeed, in which the court of session held that the English statutes of bankruptcy, and a commission thereunder, did not operate on the bankrupt's heritable property in Scotland, that tribunal took it for granted that they nevertheless imposed on him a legal obligation to execute the proper conveyances and do the necessary acts for transferring it to his assignees. But in *Selkrig* v. *Davies* (*t*), the House of Lords, on appeal from the same court, held that only a moral obligation to convey to the assignees was imposed, which might be justly enforced by withholding the bankrupt's certificate till he complied with it: and in a later case, Lord Wensleydale denied that

(*p*) *Angus* v. *Angus*, West's Rep. tem. Hard. 23.

(*q*) *Harrison* v. *Gurney*, 2 Jac. & Wal. 563; *Clarke* v. *Ormonde*, Jac. 108, 121.

(*r*) *Bunbury* v. *Bunbury*, 1 Beav. 318. From Lord Hardwicke's language in *Foster* v. *Vassall*, 3 Atk. 589, and the argument in *White* v. *Hall*, 12 Ves. 322, it might be supposed that the jurisdiction asserted in this paragraph only applied to lands in colonies under English law. But that it is not so limited appears expressly from Lord Alvanley's language in *Cranstown* v. *Johnston*, 3 Ves. 182, from which case *White* v. *Hall* is distinguished by the fact that the process of the local court had not been there abused, but there had been a decision of the local court on the very point.

(*s*) *Royal Bank of Scotland* v. *Cuthbert*, 1 Rose, 462.

(*t*) 2 Rose, 97; 2 Dow. 230, 246.

even the certificate can be properly withheld on this ground (*u*). There is a wide difference in principle between this case and that of Art. 64. Where there is a special equity affecting the person of an owner, in relation to his foreign land, and in favour of another person, the enforcement of such equity is a proper subject of personal jurisdiction. It falls expressly within the definition of Gaius: *in personam actio est, quotiens cum aliquo agimus qui nobis vel ex contractu vel ex delicto obligatus est, id est, cum intendimus* dare, facere, *præstare oportere* (*x*). But that a sovereign should claim to affect foreign land generally, through the compulsory intervention of the owner, merely on the ground of such owner's status as fixed by his ordinary authority over him, does not differ perceptibly from a claim to affect it directly.

68. The foreign codes, jurists and decided cases agree generally with the English law in maintaining the exclusive claims of the *situs* to the jurisdiction concerning immovables. But though none would permit an action for the recovery of land to be brought in a foreign forum, there is, perhaps, not quite the same universal consent in denying that land may be affected by the administrative justice of such a forum. Thus Stockmans asserts that a guardian, duly appointed by the personal judge of his ward, *auctoritatem et administrationem suam extra territorium prætoris, et in bona ubicunque locorum sita, exercet* (*y*): and other writers are quoted to the same effect. It may, however, be doubted whether anything more is meant by these expressions than what is distinctly said by John Voet: *quod tamen ex comitate magis quam juris rigore sustinetur; cum in casu quo pupillus immobilia habet sita in eo loco qui non subest eidem magistratui supremo cui pupillus subest ratione*

(*u*) *Cockerell* v. *Dickens*, 3 Mo. P. C. 98, 134.

(*x*) Inst. 4, 2.

(*y*) Decis. 125, n. 6, p. 262; cited in Story, s. 497.

domicilii, magistratus loci in quo sita sunt immobilia rebus in suo territorio existentibus peculiarem posset tutorem dare (z). And so Matthæus says that the guardian of an infant, or the curator of an estate appointed for the benefit of creditors, *nec tamen universorum negotiorum et bonorum administrationem consequitur, nisi cesset judex ejus territorii in quo prædia sita sunt;* that though the latter *silentio suo quodammodo approbare videatur curatorem a judice domicilii datum, vix tamen est ut curator ille prædia alibi sita proscribere ac vendere possit sine speciali permissu ejus judicis in cujus territorio sita sunt;* and that the same permission had best be obtained by the guardian, in case he desires to sell, for, though it was different in the Roman law, *id hodie minus tutum esse videtur, quia hodie singulæ provinciæ suam habent autonomiam* (a). If at least Stockmans meant to go farther than this, he is contradicted by a great consent of jurists (b).

3. *Principle of the* LEX SITUS.

69. *Communis et recta sententia est,* says Huber, *in rebus immobilibus servandum esse jus loci in quo bona sunt sita.* I shall not heap up other authorities to the same effect, because in the general proposition they would merely present an almost universal agreement of the jurists, while in particulars the same writers vary so much as to deprive their agreement in the general proposition of much of its value. This will be seen in the discussions we shall have to notice on the capacity of persons to convey land or devise it, on the proper forms of conveyance and testamentary disposition, and on other points.

70. It will be more interesting and useful to examine

(z) Ad Pand., lib. 26, tit. 5, s. 5.

(a) De Auctionibus, lib. 1, c. 7, n. 10.

(b) See particularly Boullenois, Observation xxxix. quns. 2, 4.

the reasons for the general proposition. The earliest notion, in accordance with the scholastic doctrine of occult qualities, seems to have been that the territorial law impressed its own qualities on the land. Thus Hertius, who shows a rather antiquated attachment to the scholastic mode of treating private international law, writes:—*rebus fertur lex cum certam iisdem qualitatem imprimit, vel in alienando, v. g. ut ne bona avita possint alienari, vel in acquirendo, e. g. ut dominium rei immobilis venditæ non aliter acquiratur nisi facta fuerit judicialis resignatio* (*c*). But then the statute of the domicile impressed its own qualities on the person, and what was to be done if the two classes of qualities clashed? For example: majority in A. is attained at 25, in B. at 21; can one domiciled in A. alienate land in B. at 23? Yes, says Hertius, for a statute is personal which says one is a minor till 25, but concerns things if it says that a minor shall have no power of alienation (*d*). Now, until some one will show that minority is something else than an abbreviated expression for a number of disabilities, of which that which respects alienation is one, this reasoning may be rendered thus, "that a personal statute uses words about persons, but the statutes which explain what those words mean are real." Such a method does not promise much, but it is perhaps as good as any which can be founded on the conception of statutes impressing qualities on persons and things.

71. Dumoulin and Huber, who are generally distinguished among the civilian jurists by preferring solid reasons drawn from the nature of things to formal ones depending on the words of statutes, or on their place in a systematic classification, here also strike out somewhat peculiar lines. Dumoulin, regarding, as usual with him, the Roman law as the common law of Europe, and

(*c*) De Coll. Leg., Sect. 4, § 6.
(*d*) De Coll. Leg., Sect. 4, § 5.

modern statutes or customs as merely introducing exceptions to it, seems naturally to have thought, if I may clothe his conclusions in the phraseology of an English lawyer, that all such exceptions, whether founded on the law of the situation or of the domicile, must be strictly pursued. Thus, in the case put above, if the subject of A. has no curator, his disability is exceptional, but the exception caused by the law of B. affects the land and is absolute, while that caused by the law of A. affects the person only while acting within the limits of A.—out of A. he can let his land situate in B., though in A. he could not execute the lease. But if a curator has been assigned him by the judge of his domicile, then his disability is an effect of the common law, and exists even when he attempts to act out of A. (*e*) Huber distinguishes between those provisions concerning land which the law of the situation does not permit even an owner *sui juris* to violate, such as an absolute prohibition of devise, or of selling the growing corn apart from the soil, with which the law of the domicile can never interfere, and the rules of status, which must always be subject to the law of the domicile; so that, in our instance, the subject of A. could not, wherever he might act, alienate his land in B., though the subject of B. who had attained twenty-three might alienate his land situate in A. This in truth is but an application by Huber of his principle that the fact of status must be referred to the domicile, but the incapacities attendant on the given status to the *lex situs* for immovable property, and to the *lex loci actus aut contractus* for other matters (*f*).

72. It is evident that the above systems agree in this, that they are only applicable to a commonwealth of nations in which the law is derived from one uniform source, such

(*e*) Conclusiones de Statutis, in Op. ed. 1581, t. 3, p. 556.
(*f*) De Confl. Leg., s. 12, 13.

as the Roman law has been for the continent of Europe: where consequently little else varies than the forms of transfer, the age of majority, and, generally, the provisions on which the existence of status depends; the modes and incidents of property, and those peculiarities of personal condition which constitute the meaning of any particular status, being pretty much the same everywhere. The feudal law of immovables is so different in all respects, whether we consider the estates or other modifications of enjoyment which it recognises, the forms by which they may be created or transferred, or the effects of marriage, minority or wardship, that if to a soil where it prevails we applied jurisprudence based on the Roman law, according to those international rules which as between the provinces of the latter would produce no inconvenience, we should only arrive at confusion, and often even at unintelligible results. To this cause, as well as to the intimate connection which feudalism established between the sovereignty of the territory and the lordship of the soil, we must attribute it that both in the British isles and in what are called the common law states of America, the doctrine that the *lex situs* governs immovables has always been carried out with a scrupulous consistency not easily to be found among the civilians who assent to the principle. But the excellent work of the late M. Fœlix may be quoted in proof of the progress which a similar consistency now makes even on the continent of Europe, under the influence of sound theories of public international law; while, considering the solidity of the reasons for it, it is much to be regretted that M. Demangeat, in editing the posthumous edition of that work, should have retrograded in this respect (*g*).

73. One of these reasons may be drawn from the inter-

(*g*) Droit International Privé, nos. 60, 93, &c.

national principle of eminent domain above explained, from which it follows that as no portion of the territory can be publicly alienated but with the assent of the sovereign expressed in a treaty, so also no foreigner can, as a private person, make title to any portion of the same district but with the assent of its sovereign expressed in his laws. Another reason may be found in the international principle which gives each sovereign the exclusive right to command within his territory; inasmuch as the laws which originate proprietary rights are in fact commands restraining all men other than the proprietor from any acts which might interfere with the latter's enjoyment of the thing owned, and inasmuch as such acts of interference, if done at all, must be done at the situation of the thing, that is, within the territory, where neither domicile, nor place of execution of any written instrument, nor any other pretext, can found an exemption from obedience to the commands of the local sovereign. Or again, and this is but the same principle presented in a different light, no court can be bound to respect a foreign law except in order to give effect to a right which has already been created by that law operating within its proper sphere: then indeed, as we saw in Art. 58, the common equity of civilized nations compels all tribunals to lend their aid to a right which has once well accrued. But no title can accrue to land by a foreign law, because no foreign legislator can at the spot use force to put the claimant in possession, and the force to execute its mandates is of the essence of municipal law.

74. It will be observed that all the above considerations relate to the title to or property in immovables, and some confusion may perhaps be saved if we keep our minds fixed on this conception, instead of speaking of things themselves as governed by this or that law. Persons are governed by laws, not things; and the laws of property

are merely addressed to persons in relation to their conduct about things. This must of course have been well known to great jurists in all ages, but the clearest thinkers are liable to be deceived by their own language, and of such error some instances perhaps may be found in what has been written on movables and immovables as governed respectively by the laws of the domicile and of the situation.

It is now time to enter upon the details, under their several heads, in doing which the nature of the subject will even more than usually limit our interest to the doctrines received in England.

4. *Extent of the Lex Situs as to Things and Rights connected with Immovables.*

75. The *lex situs* must determine what things are so annexed to the soil that they can only pass with it, for the same reasons which apply to the soil itself, since the territorial sovereign has the exclusive power to give possession of the fruits, fixtures and stock, no less than of the land (*h*). For the same reason also, if the law of its casual situation protects a chattel not annexed to the soil by requiring for its transfer the same forms which are used for immovables, or subjects it to the same course of succession, &c., that must prevail over the law of the place of contract or of the owner's domicile. Thus, when it was not fully settled that the sale of a negro was *turpis contractus*, it was held that no action lay on a contract made in England for the sale of a negro in a colony where he was an inheritance, and transferable by deed only (*i*).

76. A similar principle applies to the various incorporeal

(*h*) *Exp. Rucker*, 3 Dea. & Ch. 704.
(*i*) *Smith* v. *Brown*, 2 Sal. 666.

rights which may be regarded as dismemberments of the property in immovables, such as servitudes, charges, liens, trust and equitable estates, &c. To no such right can title be made otherwise than by the *lex situs* of the immovable in which it is claimed, because it is only through the jurisdiction of that *situs* that the enjoyment of the asserted right can be obtained. Thus a heritable bond affecting Scotch land, being not there a subsidiary security for a personal debt, but an integral portion of the value of the land dismembered from the residue thereof, does not pass by the creditor's English will, but descends to his Scotch heir (*k*); and the Scotch heir of the debtor cannot claim to be compensated out of the personal estate of his ancestor who was domiciled here (*l*).

77. If, however, a personal contract made in A. be secured by the pledge of land in B., and the former is void by the law of A., then the pledge will be void also, not by any direct operation of the law of A. on the land in B., but as a portion of an illegal transaction: the illegality of a contract being, as we shall afterwards see, determined for all jurisdictions by the *lex loci contractus*. Such cases have arisen on the grant of annuities in England, secured on land in Ireland, and void by the English annuity act (*m*); and they show how vain is the attempt to lay down any such general rule as that, when there are two securities in different countries for one debt, the immovable one will, as the *jus nobilius*, determine the character and incidents of the both. Each must stand on its own ground, and so a movable security will pass by the creditor's will made in the form prescribed in his domicile,

(*k*) *Johnstone* v. *Baker*, 4 Madd. 474, n.; *Jerningham* v. *Herbert*, 4 Russ. 388, Tam. 103.

(*l*) *Elliott* v. *Minto*, 6 Madd. 16; *Drummond* v. *Drummond*, in *Brodie* v. *Barry*, 2 Ves. & Be. 132.

(*m*) *Richards* v. *Goold*, 1 Moll. 22.

though the same debt be also secured by a Scotch heritable bond; and then if the debt be paid to the legatee, the Scotch heir, having no remedy, will have been indirectly affected by the will (*n*).

78. Lastly, questions respecting the title to an immovable will not be affected by its actual sale, as long as the purchase-money remains distinctly traceable, and liable to the equities which affected the land in the hands of the vendor. Thus, if by the *lex situs* a trader cannot give one of his creditors a preference by a pledge of land, the proceeds of the sale of such land, held by the trader's assignees in bankruptcy, will be free from any such attempted pledge, though it may have been contracted for at a place where a trader lies under no such disability (*o*).

5. *Incidents to the Property in Immovables.*

79. The incidents to the property in immovables are so clearly dependent on the *lex situs* that doubt has seldom arisen in England. It has however been decided, that if a mortgage debt be paid off by another than the mortgagor, without an agreement for the transfer of the security, the *lex situs* of the immovable decides whether the mortgage is *ipso facto* extinct, or remains capable of a subsequent transfer to him who paid the debt (*p*); also that the same law decides the liability of immovables to the debts of a deceased owner or to any class of them (*q*); also that English land, under what is called the mortmain act, cannot be devised for the establishment of a charity in Scotland (*r*); and that if an attempt be made to settle

(*n*) *Buccleugh* v. *Hoare*, 4 Madd. 467; *Cust* v. *Goring*, 18 Beav. 383.

(*o*) *Waterhouse* v. *Stansfield*, 9 Hare, 234, 10 Hare, 254.

(*p*) *Wilkinson* v. *Simson*, 2 Moo. P. C. 275.

(*q*) *Benatar* v. *Smith*, 3 Knapp, 143, note.

(*r*) *Curtis* v. *Hutton*, 14 Ves. 537. But money may be bequeathed by one domiciled in England for the purchase of lands in Scotland for charitable purposes: *Att.-Gen.* v. *Mill*, 3 Russ. 328, 2 Dow. & Cl. 393.

land in a manner not permitted by the *lex situs*, the conscience of the person designated as first taker will not be bound to give effect to the settlement out of the absolute ownership which, by an alteration of the *lex situs*, may be afterwards conferred upon him as such first taker (*s*). It is besides matter of daily experience that the capacity of aliens to take or hold land, and the consequences of an attempted transfer to them, depend in no degree on the domicile, either of the alien or of the transferor.

80. But among the incidents to property must be reckoned any restraint on alienation, whether general or special; and if special, whether directed against alienation in certain modes, as by will, or in favour of certain persons, as between husband and wife; and whether such restraint be total, or limited to a certain proportion of the value. And the conflict of laws arising out of provisions of this nature has occasioned much discussion on the continent, though there can be no doubt that here every such question would be decided by the *lex situs*, being identical in principle with the restraint on alienation in respect of its purpose established by the statute of charitable uses (*t*). Thus if husband and wife were precluded from mutual donations by the law of their matrimonial contract, we should hold such a preclusion inoperative as to English land, without being driven to the distinction between a general disability and a special one, and regarding the question as rather one of the incidents of the property than of any personal disability in the husband or wife to receive the conveyance. A somewhat less simple case may however be imagined, as, ought English land devised by one domiciled in France to be reckoned towards the proportion of his property of which the French law allows a testator to dispose? So far as the subject of this chapter is concerned, the property in im-

(*s*) *Nelson* v. *Bridport*, 8 Beav. 547. See below, Art. 85.

(*t*) See further, in Art. 89, as to the extent of this doctrine.

movables, we must answer that the English land would pass by the will; but the question remains, should the devisee be excluded from his share of the testator's movables and French land, except on condition of bringing the English land into hotchpot (*u*)? Or, since the Scotch law excludes an intestate's heir from sharing in the personalty without bringing the land into hotchpot, ought this rule to be applied to the heir of a Scotch intestate's English land? Such questions cannot arise in England, as our law fixes no disposable proportion, and attaches no condition to distribution on intestacy. But it is necessary to consider them, for the right understanding of a class of cases which does arise here, namely, those of Scotch heirs who, as we shall see in Art. 85, are put to their election by English wills. There is a seeming analogy, on which the two questions put above might be answered affirmatively; but the contrary opinion appears the truer, since one who has attempted to devise foreign land by an informal document may put his heir to election by the expression of an intention which he had the right to entertain, and might have carried out if he had used the proper means; while a law which fixes a disposable proportion, or distributes an estate with a hotchpot condition, has no authority to dispose of foreign lands, or therefore to impose an election on the foreign heir (*v*).

6. *Forms required for the Transfer of Immovables by the Owner.*

81. In spite of the general agreement among the continental jurists in favour of the *lex situs* as governing immovables, there is an equally general agreement among

(*u*) C. N. Art. 844.

(*v*) *Balfour* v. *Scott*, Mor. 2397, is right on either view, since the law which would have imposed the condition was not that which gave the benefit.

them in exempting the forms of their transfer from that rule, and subjecting them, either necessarily, or at the option of the transferor, to the *lex loci actus*. This is commonly grounded upon the principle that one who acts in any place is either necessarily subject, or at least may submit himself, to the laws of that place in respect of those acts (x). It will be seen, however, on reflexion, that this principle does not bear out the conclusion, for the question is not in what mode the *lex loci actus* obliges or enables the transferor to act, but in what mode he must act in order that the *lex situs* may give effect to his transfer. If the *lex loci actus*, to which it is true that he is personally subject, forbade or prevented his acting in that manner, the only result would be that he could not, while within its jurisdiction, transfer at all: such a prohibition or prevention could not found any positive authority for the *lex loci actus* to transfer by its own forms lands situate in another jurisdiction.

82. It will be readily imagined that an argument not soundly based in general jurisprudence could not have obtained so wide a currency, if it had not been countenanced by something in the particular system of law in which it has prevailed. The whole frame of continental conveyancing has always supposed public acts as the rule, and made but a comparatively sparing use of the private documents which constitute English titles. Now it is clear that an officer can perform a ministerial function only in

(x) *Est omnium doctorum sententia*, says Dumoulin in his 43rd consultation, *ubicumque consuetudo vel statutum locale disponit de solemnitate vel forma actus, ligari etiam exteros ibi actum illum gerentes. Cette opinion*, says Fœlix, *avait sa base dans les idées de la féodalité; on réputait sujet temporaire tout individu qui se trouvait dans le pays*: no. 83. I hold this temporary subjection to be a universal truth for governments feudal and not feudal, but, as shown in the text, it is beside the present question. For the rest, Rodenburg, John Voet, and Fœlix, are among a small minority who permit the form of the *lex situs* as an alternative: Paul Voet, Huber, Hertius, &c. are for the *lex loci actus* exclusively.

accordance with his own law, so that, although the land in any country may be transferable only by notarial act in a certain form, still it will be impossible for the notary of another country to draw up or pass a transfer in that form, if the form prescribed in his own country be different. Such a case amounts to the one just supposed, of the *lex loci actus* preventing a transfer in the mode demanded by the *lex situs;* and, to prevent the inconvenience of the strict consequence, namely, a disability to transfer while the owner remains within that jurisdiction, the rule has beên very naturally established that conveyances, even of immovables, are rendered valid by the *lex loci actus.* This, however, is merely a matter *comitatis gentium,* and the attempt to base it on juridical principle is seen at once to fail, when applied to the case of any one of those continental countries and England. An Englishman in France is personally, for the time, subject to the French law, but there is nothing in the French law which forbids or prevents his making there a grant or will of English land in our private form, nor anything in the English law which would enable it to give effect to a grant or will made there in the French form.

83. I say, *enable* it: for here another distinction must be pointed out. As between countries in which the law of immovables is the same in essential points, being derived from a common origin, it is a matter of choice, for the affirmative of which an obvious weight of convenience preponderates, whether the formal requisites of even private acts of transfer used in one of them shall not be recognized in another: the necessity of making as many wills as the jurisdictions in which the testator has land, and the ill effects of very natural mistakes in foreign formalities, are then obviated. Now, this is the case with those European countries in which the law of immovables has two common bases in feudal and Roman principles, developed

and blended through historical processes of which the operation was general in extent, and modified by the adoption of cognate codes. But the English law is free, as to immovables, from Roman influence, and even the feudal doctrines have been developed in it in a peculiar manner, so that it cannot possibly recognize a transfer which, made in a foreign form, might contemplate estātes, rules of succession, and other incidents of property, so strange to its system that even the words in which they were expressed might be incapable of an English interpretation. If, indeed, the law of some colony or daughter state should vary from ours in the forms of transfer alone or principally, there would be no impossibility in our accepting a will, for example, of land attested by one witness, by a comity extended to the *lex loci actus:* and it is probable that cases of this description may now exist, or some day arise, in the vast commonwealth of colonies and states which derive their law of immovables from an English parentage. But even then, as a conveyance in English form, requiring no public act, is possible everywhere, there could be little convenience, and might be much inconvenience, in departing from the strict juridical principle which requires a transfer in the mode prescribed by the *lex situs.*

84. That principle is firmly established in England and America, and I believe has never been questioned in either country as to conveyance *inter vivos.* That English land can only be devised or charged by a will made and witnessed as our law demands, was decided in *Coppin* v. *Coppin* (*y*).

85. It might be hastily concluded from this, that a will not made in the form of the *lex situs* could not put the heir of an immovable to his election, that being an indirect mode of devising or charging the immovable. But a will

(*y*) 2 P. W. 291.

which is valid so far as to confer a benefit, is valid also for the purpose of expressing the conditions on which the testator intends to confer it, and it has consequently been decided that an English will, or Scotch deed of trust and settlement, may put a Scotch or English heir respectively to his election or approbate or reprobate (*z*): nor is this at all inconsistent with *Nelson* v. *Bridport* (*a*), since there the *lex situs* did not at the time permit the first taker to give effect to the attempted settlement, and the property once fairly acquired was acquired with all the incidents, including the benefit of a subsequent amplification, which the *lex situs* attached to it.

86. To this head, of the forms of conveyance, belong all such provisions, as that an heir cannot be disinherited without naming the grounds of disherison, that a testator or assignor must live so many days after the date of his will or of an assignment *inter vivos*, &c. On all these questions the rule of the *lex situs* is as well settled in Scotland (*b*) and America (*c*) as in England, except so far as in America it may have been varied from by a decision quoted in the last edition of Story's Commentaries, but which I have not been able to refer to. It is said that in that case the assignment of a mortgage of real estate was held to be governed by the law of the state where made, and not that of the state where the property was (*d*), language, however, which may have been used rather of the assignment of the debt than of the security.

87. It must be farther remarked, that the questions dis-

(*z*) *Brodie* v. *Barry*, 2 Ves. & Be. 127; *Cunningham* v. *Gainer*, Mor. 617; *Dundas* v. *Dundas*, 2 Dow. & Cl. 349. In *Allen* v. *Anderson*, 5 Hare, 163, the will, in the then state of the English law, was not held to show an intention as to the after-acquired heritable bond; see 18 Beav. 391. See also *Johnson* v. *Telford*, 1 Russ. & My. 244.

(*a*) See above, Art. 79.

(*b*) Story, p. 728.

(*c*) Story, p. 727.

(*d*) *Dundas* v. *Bowler*, 3 McLean, 397, in Story, p. 728.

cussed in Articles 81—86 have lost much of their interest, even on the continent, from the extension of the system of transferring immovable property by entries in the public registers of the *situs*, since no one maintains that a form expressly imposed as an exclusive one by the *lex situs* can ever be dispensed with. By the law of 23rd March, 1855, immovable property in France is transferred *inter vivos* by a transcription in the *bureau des hypothèques*.

88. *Interpretation of Private Acts.*—If a deed respecting immovables use terms relating directly to the land, as in describing the measurement of the quantity sold, it must be taken to refer to the measures or other circumstances existing in the *situs* (*e*). If it use technical terms of limitation, having different meanings in different places, there is great doubt. Where the question has been as to the meaning of the word "heir," in a disposition of land subject to a peculiar custom of inheritance, as gavelkind, the interpretation has sometimes been according to that custom (*f*), and once has followed the general law in opposition to it (*g*). In a French case mentioned by Boullenois (*h*), the law of the disponent's domicile was held to decide whether technical words implied or did not imply substitution, and this is also Burge's general rule as to interpretation (*i*). We must, indeed, carefully bear in mind that interpretation does not raise questions of law but of fact; and certainly, in what is neither technical nor relates directly to the land, the domicile seems to afford the most probable clue, and has been followed as to the currency intended in portions charged on land by a marriage settlement (*k*).

(*e*) Fœlix, no. 93.

(*f*) 14 Viner, Heir, G. 5, pl. 3—6.

(*g*) 14 Viner, Heir, G. 5, pl. 1.

(*h*) 2 Observ. 510, 531. The father's domicile, and not the *situs*, was clearly the ground of the ultimate decision.

(*i*) Vol. 2, p. 857—8.

(*k*) *Phipps* v. *Anglesea*, 5 Vin. 209. See also *Lansdowne* v. *Lansdowne*, 2 Bl. 60.

7. *Capacity of the Owner to transfer Immovables.*

89. I have considered in Art. 80, the restraints on alienation by owners *sui juris*, arising out of the tenure of the land. They graduate into another class of restraints, those arising out of an incapacity of the owner. If we conceive status as that peculiar condition of a person whereby what is law for the average citizen is not law for him, then restraints on alienation resulting from marriage belong to status, and are properly ranked with the latter class, whether we suppose the case of a woman passing by matrimony under the power of her husband, or, though that point was considered in Art. 80 with the former class, the case of a husband and wife precluded from mutual donations. But the peculiarities of condition existing under local laws are innumerable, and mostly adapted to the systems of law in which they respectively exist, so that, as remarked in Art. 73, it is simply impossible to apply them to rights given by other systems: wherefore it was necessary, without regard to the true definition of status, to reserve for this section such incapacities only as are universally recognized, as those arising from minority and lunacy. Now, upon these it is quite possible to follow exclusively the law and the jurisdiction of the *situs*, but the principle of territorial sovereignty by no means demands our doing so, but gives us the alternative of Huber's doctrine, mentioned in Art. 71. Thus, for example, although by the *lex situs* majority may be fixed at 21 for those personally subject to it, yet that alone does not show that for the conveyance of land within its jurisdiction it does not accept any earlier, or require any later, majority which the personal law of the owner may prescribe. Nor, again, is there any principle to prevent the *lex situs* from accepting, as a *res judicata*, a sentence in which the owner of immovables has been found lunatic by his personal judge.

If the *lex situs* has an express provision on either point, it is conclusive: if not, analogies and arguments must be sought, which can only be discussed in connection with the general topics of personal law and jurisdiction, for which, therefore, I reserve the authorities, stating in the meantime that I know of no English decision. It must farther be observed here, that the acceptance of a foreign judgment of lunacy or minority would only conclude the capacity of the person, and not necessarily lead to recognizing the authority of foreign curators over the land, contrary to the doctrine of Arts. 67, 68: also, that the system of Huber, if admitted in principle, is applicable between two given countries as to any incapacity resulting from a status which they may both recognize, though generally applicable only in respect of such universally allowed incapacities as minority and lunacy.

8. *Transfer of Immovables, and Creation of Rights in them, by Force of Law.*

90. The doctrines under this head belong principally to succession *ab intestato*, marriage, and prescription.

On the first point there is no doubt but that the *lex situs* declares the rules of inheritance: but opposite answers have been given to the question—since all rules of inheritance suppose the legitimacy of the heirs, by what law must their legitimacy be decided? One is that of the civilians, who consider legitimacy as a universal status, to be determined everywhere and for all purposes by the personal law of the claimant: the other that of the feudists, who, while admitting the universality of the personal status of legitimacy for all other purposes, yet, in determining the succession to land, review all the facts relating to the alleged marriage of the parents and to the birth of the offspring, and appreciate them according to the law of the *situs*, just as if they had all occurred within its jurisdiction. On the latter opinion a variety may be engrafted, by demanding in addition a legitimacy existing by the personal law of the claimant, so that a failure by either law is fatal to his succession. It is this last variety which, on the opinion of the judges, but against the great authority of Lord Brougham, was declared by the House of Lords to be the law of England in the case of *Birtwhistle* v. *Vardill* (*l*), in which one born in Scotland of parents then domiciled there, and who afterwards married there, was held not entitled to succeed as heir to English land. For the exception thus introduced into the general doctrines on legitimacy, two reasons are given: one drawn from the supposed conflict of the real and personal statutes, and expressed by D'Argentré in the words, somewhat tinged with feudal pride, *nullus princeps legitimat personam ad succedendum in bona alterius territorii* (*m*): the other special, from the particular provisions supposed to be contained in the English law of inheritance.

91. On the question of conflict, the matter appears to stand thus. A bastard does not inherit, not because his bastardy is regarded by any law as a positive blemish which should disable him, but because the law, at least for the purpose of inheritance, professes ignorance whose son he is: it is therefore a question of the legal evidence of sonship, and determinable (as we shall see all questions of evidence are) by the *lex fori*, which, for immovables, must be the *lex situs*. But the evidence demanded of sonship is birth in wedlock, and the fact of wedlock is referred by all laws to a single decision, drawn generally from the law of the place where, if at all, it was contracted. Thus, the *lex situs* may by no means claim to appreciate itself every

(*l*) 5 Ba. & Cr. 438, 9 Bl. N. R. 32, 2 Cl. & F. 571.

(*m*) Art. 218, gl. 6, n. 20.

detail in the history of the case, but only steps in in order to refer the decision to the law of the alleged marriage.

92. Nor does the doctrine of *Birtwhistle* v. *Vardill* appear to be at all more firmly based in the peculiarities of English law. The statute of Merton merely states our law, which no one disputes, and is totally silent as to the limits of its own application. But the whole science of private international jurisprudence is based on the assumption that laws have limits of application not expressed in their own tenour, some of which result from the limited authority of the legislators, and others from those maxims of jurisprudence, by which, since they are founded in natural right, all legislators intend their enactments to be interpreted. If, indeed, any statute does express the limits of its application, such expression will bind the courts of that sovereign power whence it proceeds, whether consonant or not to the result which would have been derivable from juridical principles; but so completely is such an expression absent from the statute of Merton, that the argument based on it might be used of any other, to the extent of destroying this whole branch of legal science. So also Lord Coke's dictum, that the heir must be *ex justis nuptiis procreatus*, does not decide, but opens, the question what is lawful wedlock: and, as Lord Brougham, after remarking this, proceeds—"Is there any greater reason for being bound by the law of the country where the marriage contract was made, in deciding whether or not the wedlock was lawful, than there is for being governed, in ascertaining the legitimacy of the issue of the marriage, by the law of the country where that issue was born, more especially when it was also the country where the marriage was had? But can the court stop short, according to its own principle, at the mere fact of the marriage being according to the *lex loci contractus?* Do not the principles on which their decision proceeds demand this further in-

quiry,—Were the parties able to marry by the *lex loci rei sitæ?* and thus a door is opened to the farther examination of how far a preceding divorce of one of the parties was sufficient to dissolve a previous English marriage. All such difficulties are got rid of by holding the *lex loci contractus* and *nativitatis* as governing the validity of the contract and legitimacy of its issue; but they are not to be got over in this way by any argument which does not with equal force apply to holding that the legitimacy of the issue is a question equally to be governed by the *lex loci contractus* and the law of the birthplace."

93. In fact the argument of the judges, as expressed by Chief Baron Alexander, does not itself accept the English law, contained in Coke's dictum and the statute of Merton, as final in the case of a foreign-born heir; but adds to it the requirement that he shall be legitimate by the law of his birthplace. Now the use of international principles is not to add to municipal laws, but to fix their mutual limits; and it must be thought strange that the judges who refused them for the latter purpose should have resorted to them for the former. If our municipal law had not originally a declarator of legitimacy, then it knew that status only as the synonym of birth in wedlock, wherever the latter words may occur in particular statutes or maxims. Thus it says that the eldest son born in wedlock shall be the heir, and either to accept or to refuse the foreign law as ascertaining the person who answers to that description is intelligible: to reject it from that function, to treat the question as one of mere English law, and then to say that the claimant, besides being the eldest son born in wedlock, must also be legitimate in some other sense by his personal law, is scarcely intelligible. There appears to be no escape from these inconsistencies and confusions of thought but in admitting the universal status of legitimacy, ascertained by the appropriate law, as

the proper international evidence of birth in wedlock, whenever that question depends on foreign facts. The opposite view, says Lord Brougham, "makes a man legitimate or illegitimate according to the place where his property lies or rights come in question; legitimate when he sues for distribution of personal estate, a bastard when he sues for succession to real; nay, legitimate in one country, where part of his land may lie, and a bastard in some other where he has the residue. So in like manner all who claim through him must have their rights determined by the same vague and uncertain canon, a circumstance which I nowhere find adverted to below. All the learned judges proceed upon the case being one of an inheritance claimed by the party himself. But what if he were dead years ago, and another claimed an estate in England to which he (the alleged bastard) never had been and never could have been entitled, an estate for example descending from a collateral who took it by purchase after the death of the alleged bastard? Then the pedigree of the claimant must be made out through legitimate persons, and the question of legitimacy is raised as to one who is not himself claiming any land, who never did or could claim any land; and it is not raised in respect of any right in him to inherit, any right to be called the heir to any land. I apprehend this shows strongly the necessity of taking another view than the learned judges seem to have deemed sufficient for getting over the difficulty of the case, and of admitting that there is a status of legitimacy which is personal, and, travelling about with the individual, must be determined by the law of his country (*o*)."

94. The House of Lords, sitting as a Scotch appeal court, has applied these doctrines to Scotch lands by its judgment in declarations of bastardy, which is in fact the

(*o*) 9 Bl. N. R. 73, 2 Cl. & F. 584.

only manner in which they can be so applied, since no one there questions but that the status determined in this *præjudicialis actio* applies to inheritance as well as to every other matter (*p*); and in the *Strathmore Peerage* it applied them directly to the succession to a Scotch title, which of course depends on the same principles as that to a Scotch immovable (*q*). We shall have to revert to these cases when on the general subject of illegitimacy, since in some the parent's marriage was, and in one it was not, celebrated in the country where the child was born. They all agree in that the law held under the circumstances to be the personal law of the claimant prevailed over, or rather was adopted by, that of Scotland, even where the title to a Scotch hereditament was directly or indirectly concerned.

95. Marriage, in the absence of express agreement, operates everywhere as the legal creation of certain mutual rights, present or prospective, of the husband and wife in each other's immovable property: in many foreign countries by the various systems of dowry and community, and at home, and in those countries of which the law has an English source, by the doctrines of dower and tenancy by the curtesy, and by the husband's present rights in his wife's freeholds and chattels real. There has been much discussion abroad for many centuries whether these rights are to be determined by the *lex situs*, the opinion of those, with D'Argentré (*r*) at their head, who wrote in provinces where the Roman jurisprudence had least encroached on the feudal principles of real property; or by the law of the matrimonial domicile, and that, either as the personal law of the parties prevailing, as in a question of status, over

(*p*) *Patrick* v. *Shedden*, 6 Bl. N. R. 487; *Munro* v. *Saunders* (al. *Rose* v. *Ross*), 6 Bl. N. R. 468.

(*q*) 6 Bl. N. R. 487.

(*r*) Art. 218, gl. 6, n. 33, 34, 41.

the law of the things, or, which was the opinion of Dumoulin (*s*), as introduced by the tacit consent of the parties into the matrimonial contract. Many of the authorities will be found collected by Story (*t*), and they need not be farther referred to here, since there is no doubt but that in England the *lex situs* would prevail (*u*), as it does in America. "If," says Story, "persons who are married in Louisiana, where the law of community exists, own immovable property in Massachusetts, where such community is unknown, upon the death of the husband the wife would take her dower only in the immovable property of her husband, and the husband upon the death of the wife would take as tenant by the curtesy only in the immovable property of his wife (*v*)."

96. Our law has nothing analogous to the usufruct which that of Rome gives to the father in the property of his unemancipated child, but it may be interesting to know that, after long and earnest disputes on this point also, the best modern opinion is that such usufruct is personal-real, that is, that it must be given by the *lex situs*, and yet that even the *lex situs* cannot give it to a father who by the law of his domicile has not the *patria potestas* over his child, the usufruct being regarded as incapable of existing otherwise than as an accessary of the *patria potestas* (*x*). Hence an English father would not enjoy such usufruct in his child's immovables, though situate in a country where the *patria potestas* with such accessary is found.

97. The acquisition or extinction of title to any land or servitude by prescription must necessarily depend on the *lex situs*, not only from the general principles which attach

---

(*s*) T. 2, p. 963; t. 3, p. 555.

(*t*) Sect. 450—452.

(*u*) This was decided as to dower in *Jephson* v. *Riera*, 3 Knapp, 130, 149.

(*v*) Sect. 454.

(*x*) Merlin, Répertoire, Puissance Paternelle, sect. 7, no. 1.

immovable rights to its province, but because there is no conflict, the *situs* being the only proper forum for the determination of such rights, and the conflict in other cases of prescription being introduced by the claim of the *lex fori* to regulate that question as incident to procedure. The same remark applies to charges on land, though, if their amount be also personally due, the prescription of the *situs* will not affect the collateral securities. So also, in the personal actions which may be brought in any forum on contracts to convey immovables, the term of limitation existing where the subject of contract may be situate cannot prevail over that which the general principles on obligations, hereafter to be explained, would point out.—An isolated point, under this section, is the lien for the price of supplies necessary for the management of an estate; which it depends on the *lex situs* to give or refuse to him who furnishes them (*y*).

9. *Effect and Evidence of the Contract of Sale.*

98. By the French law, before the enactment of 1855 above referred to, the property in land was transferred by the contract of sale (*z*). In such a case, there is of course no room for a personal action against the vendor for specific performance, such as mentioned above in Arts. 64 and 66, for the only possible action is a real one for the recovery of the land, which has become the purchaser's though the vendor may detain it. But what if any law, like the English, so subdivides the property into an equitable and a bare legal one that the former is transferred by the contract of sale, yet so as to leave room for the suit

(*y*) *Sayers* v. *Whitfield*, 1 Knapp, 133, 148. See also *Scott* v. *Nesbitt*, 14 Ves. 438.

(*z*) Code Civil, Arts. 1138 and 1583. See above, p. 76.

for specific performance in order to obtain the transfer of the latter? A question arises, how in either case must the contract be evidenced, in order that in the one case the entire, and in the other the equitable, dominion may pass by it from the moment of sale. In the former instance, the answer is plain: for if the contract passes the entire property, it is in fact simply a conveyance, and its sufficiency must depend on the *lex situs*, as that of any other conveyance. And this answer is given by Fœlix (*a*) with regard to the French law which existed when he wrote. But in the latter some confusion may arise from the continuing operation of the contract as a contract no less than as a conveyance. Now we shall hereafter see that in the general conflict between the *lex loci contractus* and *lex fori* on solemnities, contracts must ordinarily be fortified by all the proofs required by either, since they will otherwise fail, either by the *lex loci contractus* as never having been originally binding, or by the *lex fori* as not sufficiently evidenced. The latter part of the proposition is strictly applicable to our case, with the observation that in it the *lex fori* is the *lex situs*, since it is only in the *situs* that the question whether the land is bound can be tried; and thus we conclude, for example, that English land cannot be transferred in equity by a foreign contract which does not comply with the statute of frauds (*b*).

99. But is the former part equally applicable, so that English land could not be transferred in equity by a contract satisfying that statute, but not also satisfying forms imposed by the *lex loci contractus?* I apprehend that the reason here fails, for though we grant that a person not

---

(*a*) Droit International Privé, no. 60.

(*b*) Thus also a disposition of a heritable jurisdiction in Scotland, executed in England after the English form, was not sustained even against the grantor, to oblige him to grant a more formal conveyance: *Dalkeith* v. *Book*, Morison, 4464.

bound at the time and in the place of contracting cannot become so *ex post facto* by the accident of the forum, yet the land, in our case, is not bound through any binding of the person, but by an independent operation of the *lex situs* on the right of property. We have seen that all dismemberments of the property in land are themselves immovable subjects of property, and, as such, alienated by the forms of transfer prescribed by the *lex situs.* The more obvious instances are dismemberments in duration, as successive estates, or in value, as charges; but the equitable dominion, entire both in duration and value, yet severed from the legal dominion, is but another kind of dismemberment; and the contract of sale, evidenced according to the law of the situation, is the appropriate form for its conveyance, and, as such, immediately and necessarily efficacious. Hence also it appears necessary to conclude that even the remedy by specific performance could be pursued in our chancery in such a case, notwithstanding the absence of the form of contracting required in the place of contract. If not entitled *ex contractu* to a conveyance of the legal estate, the purchaser would at least be entitled to it as equitable owner: and this appears to be the opinion of Burge (*c*).

(*c*) Vol. 2, p. 865. A similar question may now arise in France, for the law of 1855 reserves to the purchaser all such rights as he previously had against the vendor. *Le consentement réciproque reste la loi des parties :* Report of the Commission on this Law, n. 23.

CHAPTER V.

Jurisdiction on Obligations.

100. Having treated of the property in immovables, which exhibits in its simplest form the relation of sovereignty to the soil, it will be convenient to take obligations next, as showing most simply its relation to persons. For as in the former we considered laws which protect a proprietor's enjoyment by forbidding the interference of others generally, and which therefore did not involve a tie between the sovereign who issued them and any particular person, but only between him and the soil owned, so in obligations, which are the rights acquired by one person of directing through the agency of justice the conduct of another, we have to consider only the causes for which the defendant, as a definite individual, may be subject in the matter in question to the commands of a particular sovereign. Having thus examined the jural results of sovereignty from the two most distinct points of view, we shall be better able to enter on the remaining investigations of our subject; and these considerations will oblige us in this chapter, as well as in that on the international law of obligations, to discard all reference to the status of the parties, who will be presumed capable to act or contract by every law applicable or conceivably applicable to

their case. The question of jurisdiction must precede that of law, for the reasons given in Arts. 57 and 58.

1. *History and Principles.*

101. The Roman rules of jurisdiction on obligations must first be detailed, not only on account of the influence they have had on the subsequent development of jurisprudence on this subject throughout the world, but because they are still, as such, acted on in those parts of the continent which have not codified their laws, or which, having codified them, have not inserted in their codes express provisions on the matter; also because they have furnished the principles for those treaties which have been concluded between certain states, and especially between Prussia and small German states, for settling certain points of private international law. The following sketch of the Roman system will follow throughout the authority of Savigny, in the eighth volume of his great work on the modern Roman law, as well for the interpretation of the ancient sources, as for the facts of the present practice; but important variations from his views will be noticed, both for their historical interest, and since, from the nature of continental law, so far as it is neither codified nor fixed by treaty, any opinion on the true interpretation of the Corpus Juris may, and at times does, become influential on the daily judgments of courts.

102. In the empire of Justinian, then, obligations, of whatever nature or wherever contracted, might be put in suit in the *forum rei*, the personal forum of the defendant. This was, for an Italian, either that of the *civitas* or *respublica* of which he was a *municeps* (*a*), or that of the one

(*a*) *Civis* is only used of the Roman citizen, in opposition to *latinus* and *peregrinus:* but *municeps* is used of every municipal citizen, whether of a *municipium* or of a *colonia*, either being a *civitas* or *respublica.* A *colonia* however is not included in *municipium.*

in which he was domiciled, the choice lying with the plaintiff. The reason was that Italy was entirely divided into *civitates* having original jurisdiction, of one of which every Italian was a member by municipal citizenship, a relation which involved subjection to the jurisdiction of the community, although he might be domiciled in another such *civitas* or in a province, a relation which involved subjection to the local jurisdiction. This is certain in principle, but it is likely that an express statute existed, though no trace now remains of it, which prevented a plaintiff from choosing the former, or *forum originis* (*b*), against a defendant domiciled elsewhere, except when he might be actually found within its territory.

103. But, since the provinces did not contain *civitates* with original jurisdiction (at least until in late times something of the kind arose in the authority of the *defensores*), being subject to the imperial governors, the personal forum of a provincial was only that of his domicile, except so far as he had a *forum originis* at Rome, through the edict of Caracalla which extended the Roman citizenship to all the free subjects of the empire. The Roman citizenship had been long before enjoyed by all Italians, through the *lex Julia*, so that for such of them as did not belong immediately to Rome, but primarily to some other Italian *respublica*, there existed a double citizenship, besides a domicile possibly different from either. For this case, as well as for that of the provincials after the time of Caracalla, express texts of the Corpus Juris show that they could not be sued at Rome, in virtue of their citizenship, unless actually there (*c*); which is the ground for presum-

---

(*b*) This, citizenship as opposed to domicile, is the Roman meaning of *origo*, which has therefore nothing to do with what we now call the domicile of origin in opposition to an acquired domicile.

(*c*) And even then with many exceptions, constituting collectively the *jus domum revocandi*.

ing, as noticed in the last article, that a similar protection existed against all drawing of defendants to answer out of their domicile on the ground of citizenship.

104. In the modern Roman law, existing as it does on a soil the juridical relations of which have descended from those of the provinces, and where also feudalism has counterbalanced the civic element introduced through the *defensores* in the later imperial times, the *forum domicilii* remains, but the *forum originis*, in its ancient sense, has disappeared. For "in Germany the cities have indeed for many centuries past formed an important element of the constitution, as well in the empire as in the particular countries, yet only an isolated one, standing by the side of others generally more important, so that it was never there possible to think of the whole state as running out into nothing but municipal territories and communities. And as with Germany, so it was in this respect also with other modern states: at most in Italy are circumstances still partially found which, however incomplete, not only remind us of the condition of the Roman empire, but are even to be regarded as in fact remains of it (*d*)." But this must be understood with the reservation of what will be afterwards said, on the introduction by codes of a jurisdiction founded on nationality.

105. But besides the *forum rei*, the Roman law allowed the plaintiff, and allows him as still practised, the option of suing in the proper jurisdiction of the obligation, for which *forum contractus* and *rei gestæ* are modern terms applied more widely than to the particular cases they would seem to indicate. "This jurisdiction," says Savigny, "is to be considered as founded in the several following cases:—

I. At the place which has been specially fixed on by the will of the parties as that of the fulfilment of the obli-

---

(*d*) Savigny, v. 8, p. 90.

gation, whether it have been so fixed on through express words (as in the famous law *contraxisse unusquisque in eo loco intelligitur in quo ut solveret se obligavit* (*e*)), or through the nature of the transaction to which the obligation is to lead, that being such as is only possible at a single place (as in a contract for the sale or lease of land or houses, which implies the delivery of possession).

II. In default of a fixed place of fulfilment, the jurisdiction can be founded on the circumstance that the obligation arises from the transaction by the defendant of affairs connected with a determinate spot. (Here belong the following cases. The *tutela* over persons not *sui juris*, as also every kind of *curatela*. Farther, the care of another person's affairs; whether of all his affairs, a general agency or attorneyship, or of a certain class of them, as the management of a manufacture or of a commercial undertaking; and whether in consequence of a contract—*mandatum* or *operæ locatæ*, or proceeding from the will of one side only—*negotiorum gestio* (*f*). Lastly, one's own regular banking or commission business—*argentaria*. . . . . In most cases this special ground of jurisdiction does not come prominently into view, because the transaction of such affairs coincides with the domicile: they can however be separated, and then this ground of jurisdiction is practically exhibited (*g*).)

III. The jurisdiction is farther founded on the place where the obligation arises, when that coincides with the defendant's domicile. (The practical importance of this is felt when the defendant changes his domicile after con-

(*e*) Dig. 44, 7, 21.

(*f*) Which would give rise to an obligation *quasi ex contractu*.

(*g*) Pp. 217, 218. *Argentarium ubi contractum est conveniri oportet:* Dig. 5, 1, 45, i. e., he must suffer himself to be sued. By mistranslating this, some have denied for this case the right of the plaintiff to choose the personal forum, which is, however, expressly recognised in Dig. 2, 13, 4, 5.

tracting the obligation, and so becomes liable to two jurisdictions in respect of it.)

IV. Also the place where the obligation arises, though out of the defendant's domicile, can found the jurisdiction, when through the circumstances an expectation is reasonably grounded that the obligation will also be fulfilled in the same place. (For which purpose the nature of the obligation must be looked at. The shortest stay will do for an inn-bill; a stay at a watering-place will do for the contracts of daily life, but not for those of commerce; the setting up of a business of any duration will suffice to found the expectation that the wares there contracted to be sold will be delivered there (*h*).)

V. When none of the above suppositions holds, the forum of the obligation is at the defendant's domicile. (As in contracts by travellers not falling under IV.: in the liability of the *dos* to be sued for at the husband's domicile, though the marriage contract may have been made elsewhere: and when a manufacturer sends round an agent to get orders, for the contract is then fulfilled at the seat of the manufacture by the sending the article, as is shown by the fact that from that moment the Roman law placed the article at the risk of the buyer, although the property, requiring delivery for its change, did not pass till its arrival (*i*).)

106. All these cases, so different in character as they seem, and so arbitrary as their copulation appears, yet may be referred to a common principle. It is universally the place of fulfilment which determines the special jurisdiction, whether expressly fixed on (I.), or resting on a tacit

---

(*h*) Pp. 221—223. *Durissimum est,* says Ulpian, *quotquot locis quis navigans vel iter faciens delatus est, tot locis se defendi. At si quo constitit, non dico jure domicilii, sed tabernulam, pergulam, horreum, armarium, officinam conduxit, ibique distraxit, egit: defendere se eo loci debebit:* Dig. 5, 1, 19, 2.

(*i*) Pp. 224—226.

expectation (II.—V.). In both cases must a free submission of the defendant to this jurisdiction be presumed, unless excluded by an express declaration to the contrary (*k*)."

107. This *forum contractus*, for so it is commonly called notwithstanding that the obligation may have arisen *quasi ex contractu*, serves generally only for those actions which aim at the fulfilment of the obligation, and not for those which seek its dissolution, or to recall that which has been done in pursuance of it: unless indeed the dissolution have a common origin with the obligation, as when it is claimed through a contract collateral to that which created the latter (*l*).

108. The *forum delicti* is a conception foreign to the older Roman law, but placed in the imperial times on a level with that of contract, so that the plaintiff could choose between it and the personal forum. It does not rest on presumptive submission, but on the mere breach of the law, so that it needs none of the accompanying circumstances, which, as guides to the expectation of the parties, are required for the forum of contract, where that is not expressly fixed on (*m*).

109. But the special forum of the obligation can only be made use of when the defendant is either personally present there, or possesses property there, in which latter case the plaintiff can obtain the *missio in possessionem*. It might be thought that Justinian removed this restriction by the 69th novel, but the language of that law is vague, and it does not seem to have been so interpreted or acted on even in ancient times. "The great preponderance of modern

---

(*k*) *Nisi alio loci ut defenderet convenit:* Dig. 5, 1, 19, 2. The whole passage in inverted commas is translated from Savigny, v. 8, p. 226—228; except that the illustrations in parentheses are taken from his separate developments of the several heads.

(*l*) Savigny, v. 8, p. 241. But Linde unconditionally denies the application of the *forum contractus* to its dissolution.

(*m*) Savigny, v. 8, p. 239.

practice has sided with this opinion, so that thus the jurisdiction of the obligation cannot be made available against an absent person through the mere requisition of a foreign tribunal" (*n*).

110. Of the opinions opposed to the above system of Savigny, that which has made itself most influential in practice is the view, commonly diffused in the middle ages, by which the place of contracting the obligation (*locus celebrati contractus*, or *ubi verba proferuntur*), and not that of its destined fulfilment, was supposed to determine the special jurisdiction in the Roman law. The texts on which this view chiefly rested are *at ubi quisque contraxerit* (*o*), which was regarded as furnishing the rule, the concluding part of the same citation—*contractum autem non utique eo loco intelligitur quo negotium gestum sit, sed quo solvenda est pecunia*—being regarded as merely an exception for the case of an express contract to pay money in a certain spot: and *proinde et si merces vendidit certo loci, vel disposuit, vel comparavit, videtur, nisi alio loci ut defenderet convenit, ibidem se defendere* (*p*). The former, however, is identical in effect with the law *contraxisse*, mentioned in Art. 105 (I.); and the latter is not a law at all, but a suggestion of Ulpian as to what might be thought at first sight, which he immediately corrects by the remarks cited in the note to Art. 105 (IV.). But in modern times, the opinion that the place of fulfilment furnishes the true Roman forum of the obligation has gained ground both in theory and practice, though there has been much discussion whether, when that place has not been expressly fixed on by the parties, its jurisdiction is founded on their tacit expectation, or on laws obligatory without the intervention of their will. The

(*n*) Savigny, v. 8, p. 245. Foreign, that is, to his domicile; nationality being rejected by Savigny as a ground of jurisdiction.

(*o*) Dig. 42, 5, 3.

(*p*) Dig. 5, 1, 19, 2.

Prussian code however, following the Roman law as understood when it was compiled, and several treaties concluded by Prussia with small German states, prescribe the *forum celebrati contractus*, but reserving to the plaintiff his choice of the defendant's personal forum, for every case in which a fulfilment at a certain spot has not been stipulated for (*q*): and Linde still maintains the *forum celebrati contractus* as in the common law of Germany competent concurrently with the so called *forum solutionis* (*r*).

111. To the Roman system, however, there has always existed on the continent one great exception. The *forum contractus*, whether *celebrati* or *solutionis*, was not received in France, from the vigour with which the feudal system flourished there. The seigneurs had patrimonial rights of administering justice, and in the royal courts the emoluments of justice were, on account of the venality of their offices, considered as forming for the judges a kind of property. Consequently the trial in his domicile, being no longer the privilege of the defendant so much as that of the judge, could not be waived by the former, either through his submission when sued elsewhere, or through his previous consent in contracting; and both the seigneurs and the royal courts were authorized to reclaim their justiciables, even when the tribunal seised of the cause had jurisdiction over the subject of litigation, and was only incompetent by reason of the domicile of the parties (*s*). Now the rule of the *lex loci contractus*, as governing obligations, was drawn from the common rules of jurisdiction, on the maxim *si ibi forum ergo et jus*: and it is expressly on this ground of the non-applicability in France of the common doctrines of jurisdiction, that Boullenois re-

(*q*) Allg. Ger. Ordn. 1, 2.

(*r*) Lehrb. des Deutsch. gem. Civilprocesses, 7th edit. s. 91.

(*s*) Henrion de Pansey, De l'Autorité Judiciaire en France, 3me édition, t. 1, pp. 370, 371.

jects altogether the *lex loci contractus* as a principle, and betakes himself to a separate consideration of the motives of decision for each of the cases ordinarily included under it (*t*). To the same source must probably be referred the general disposition of the old French jurists to postpone the law of the place of contract, considered as a rule, to any special tests by which the intention of the parties can be inferred; and of which, in anticipation of the discussions on law to be gone into hereafter, an instance may be given from Dumoulin. The rule of the Digest by which the vendor of land was, in the absence of expression, required to procure such a number of sureties, and who would warrant the title in such an amount, as might be prescribed by the local custom,—that being taken as the interpreter of his contract,—was during the middle ages universally understood to refer to the custom of the place of sale. Another interpretation, one would have thought at least equally obvious, would refer it to the custom of that place where the land sold is situate. Dumoulin however does not question but that the place of sale is meant, only he says that the rule will not apply to a vendor and purchaser of one country who may casually contract in another, because the law of their common domicile is binding on them, as that of which they were both aware, and which neither intended to reject (*u*).

112. But the principle of the *forum contractus* was introduced into France, to a modified extent, by the ordinance of 1673, which, in commercial matters, gave the plaintiff a similar choice to that which he now has in the same matters by Art. 420 of the *Code de Procédure Civile*, which runs thus:—*Le demandeur pourra assigner, à son choix, devant le tribunal du domicile du défendeur, devant celui dans l'arrondissement duquel la promesse a été faite et la*

(*t*) T. 2, p. 456.
(*u*) T. 3, p. 554.

marchandise livrée, devant celui dans l'arrondissement duquel le payement devait être effectué. In order to understand the extent to which this relaxation is carried, we must examine the rules which govern the competence of the tribunals of commerce, to which alone it refers, in respect of the subject of litigation. They are then competent as to all engagements and transactions between merchants, shopkeepers and bankers (*x*): as to the purchase of goods bought for the purpose of reselling or letting them, whether with or without having worked upon them; as to every business of manufacture, commission, carriage by land or water, contracting, agency (*y*), auctioneering, or public spectacles; as to all operations of exchange, banking, brokerage, or of public banks; as to bills of exchange, and remitments of money from place to place, between all persons whatsoever (i. e. traders or not) (*z*): as to a number of other specified matters, apparently intended to exhaust all that relates to shipping and the employment of ships in trade (*a*): in actions against factors, and shopkeepers' clerks and servants, with reference to their employment as such; as to the notes made by persons accountable to the public revenue (*b*): and as to bankruptcies (*c*). To this extent then redress may be had in France, whatever the personal forum of the parties.

113. Also the Code Napoleon has reintroduced the principle of national character as determining the personal forum (*d*), and has added the novel conception of a per-

(*x*) Code de Commerce, Art. 631.

(*y*) This word appears to translate both *agence* and *bureau d'affaire.*

(*z*) Art. 632.

(*a*) Art. 633. *Entreprise de construction* in this article has been decided to mean the building ships only, and not making a canal: and the article has also been held to refer only to marine and not to fluviatile navigation. See the cases in Rogron's notes on it.

(*b*) Art. 634.

(*c*) Art. 635.

(*d*) Art. 15.

sonal forum of the plaintiff (*e*), on the ground that a subject is entitled to demand justice of his sovereign: by which means the French courts, other than those of commerce, are now open to all actions on obligations in which either the plaintiff or defendant is a French subject, or a foreigner who, with the authorization of the French government, has established his domicile in France, wherever the obligation may have arisen or is to be fulfilled. Farther, though this has formerly been much disputed, an overwhelming weight of decisions now leaves no doubt that a domicile in fact, of either party, though not authorized by government, will at least found the personal jurisdiction, though it may not conclude the personal law (*f*).

114. But what if neither party fulfil these conditions, and the matter is not within the competence of the tribunals of commerce? The Code Civil then contains no provision giving the *forum contractus* any wider recognition than it had before, except perhaps in Art. 111, which empowers persons (foreigners are not distinctly mentioned) to elect a domicile in France, expressly, for the purposes of the special instrument containing the election. Now even in the old jurisprudence it might have been said that the reasons given above for denying the *forum contractus* as to those who were justiciable in a French domicile, did not apply to foreigners over whom no French judge had a right of jurisdiction, and from whose creditors justice might sometimes be hopelessly withheld if not done them in France. But the practice, though not constant, tended to reject that consideration (*g*): and under the Code Napoleon, according to Fœlix, it stands thus. The defendant may give the court competence by his submission, either through appointing in the contract a place of payment in France,

(*e*) Art. 14.

(*f*) Fœlix, no. 152, with Demangeat's note.

(*g*) Fœlix, no. 149.

or through an election of domicile under Art. 111 of the Code Civil, or through not pleading to the jurisdiction *in limine litis*. But the court cannot entertain the cause without such submission, nor is it bound to entertain it even by such a submission, but may declare itself incompetant *proprio motu* (*h*). And this has been held also on the similar provisions contained in the codes of the Two Sicilies and Belgium, though in Rhenish Prussia, where the Code Napoleon has also been received, the *forum contractus* is admitted (*i*). M. Demangeat, however, shows that by the most recent French decisions jurisdiction has to a certain extent been assumed, even over recalcitrant defendants, on the ground of the *locus celebrati contractus*, or the *locus delicti*, being in France (*k*).

115. Next, to consider on principle the several forums which have been traced historically, those of the defendant's domicile and nationality seem to be reasonably founded in the general authority which their respective sovereigns exercise or claim over him, and the protection which he enjoys or may claim from the same sovereigns. If indeed, for domicile, these considerations are weakened by the question how far it alone can give claim to protection, beyond the territory, and in matters having no concern with it (*l*), yet in the same case they are fortified by the presumption of habitual presence, which nationality does not carry with it, while it is obviously just that every one should furnish to his creditors some place where he may be always expected to meet their claims. Indeed the Roman rule, supposed to have restricted the *forum originis*

(*h*) Fœlix, no. 155.

(*i*) Fœlix, nos. 151, 166.

(*k*) Note tc the 3rd edition of Fœlix, no. 151. Where a criminal tribunal can award damages for the crime it punishes, the foreigner who sustains the injury has always been allowed to claim them: Fœlix, no. 165.

(*l*) See above, Art. 54.

to the case of the defendant's actual presence, appears a very reasonable one: but for rejecting that forum altogether, on account of the change of circumstances, when the division of the civilized world into independent states presents a condition of things so nearly analogous to the ancient Italian *civitates*, sufficient cause does not appear to have been given.

116. For a personal forum of the plaintiff, founded on domicile or nationality, the reason assigned appears inadequate. Granted that justice is the sovereign's debt to his subjects, the question remains whether it is justice to call on any one to answer, at a distance both from his home and from the seat of the transaction in question. Something may be said for giving up the principle of suit in a determinate forum altogether, as antiquated. And, indeed, now that locomotion is frequent and easy, and the occasions are surprisingly multiplied on which men contract obligations abroad, one is led to meditate on a remark of Lord Camden, who said, in sustaining a colonial suit, though one had been previously commenced in England for the same matter,—"As to the inconvenience, considering the difficulties of administering justice between parties occasionally living under the separate jurisdictions, I think the parties ought to be amenable to every court possible, where they are travelling from country to country: and we must then endeavour to correct the mischief of these double suits as much as we can, by allowing in each country the benefit of all the other proceedings in the other part of the king's dominions." Nor will the rights of the litigants be in general affected by the choice of a forum, since they depend on the law to be applied, and it is agreed by all that the law appropriate to each case should be selected on principles common to every tribunal. On the other hand, there is the harshness of suing where proofs cannot easily be furnished, and where it may be

vitally inconvenient to a party to be compelled to sojourn; considerations which to most lawyers but English will appear decisive. And as long as these considerations are allowed to maintain the principle of suit in a determinate forum, they tell entirely for the defendant, who must be presumed not liable till he is proved to be so.

117. With regard to the peculiar forum of the obligation, it is true that the reasonable expectation of the parties ought not to be disappointed (*m*). The whole system of private international law rests on the extension of this protection to all such expectations, wherever and by whomsoever formed, a principle which is closely related to that of Art. 58. But there seems an impropriety in supposing that the expectation of contracting parties is directed towards any one jurisdiction. In the first place, they usually expect the voluntary fulfilment of the obligation, and not its compulsory fulfilment, or redress for its non-fulfilment. Or, if they do look on each other with mutual suspicion, they would probably desire that any and every court should be ready to help them to their rights. But how do these become rights? only through the law which imposes a duty as the result of the contract, and that must be the law of the sovereign who has the authority to command the contracting person at the time of his contract, the sovereign, namely, of the *locus celebrati contractus*. It does not from this follow that the same place must necessarily furnish the *forum contractus*, for there can be no suit till there is a breach, and, if the *locus celebrati contractus* be not the place of fulfilment, no breach may occur while the party is within the territory, and therefore subject to the commands, of its sovereign. But it follows, by the principle of Art. 58, that, the duty of fulfilling the obligation having been once well imposed, a breach should be re-

---

(*m*) See above, Art. 106.

dressed when it occurs by the tribunal of every other sovereign who both can, and reasonably can, do so: and this is true of the tribunal of the place of fulfilment, though the defendant be not present there, provided he have property there through which the breach can in fact be redressed, because he ought to have been there, either personally or by an agent, to fulfil his obligation, and such redress is therefore reasonable. If the place of fulfilment be founded as the *forum contractus* on the mere expectation of the parties, it is extremely difficult to give any reason why its judge may not render a valid personal sentence *in absentem:* so that in Savigny's system the condition of the defendant's presence or possession of property figures as a condition narrowing the principle (*n*).

118. The student may perhaps hesitate at its being said in the last paragraph, that the sovereign of the *locus celebrati contractus* has the authority to command the contracting person at the time when he binds himself. It is however universally received, both in the theory and practice of international law, that authority to command is vested in the territorial sovereign, as to all those who whether permanently or temporarily are found within his geographical limits. Thus persons, foreign both in nationality and domicile, are in all countries daily made amenable to criminal jurisdiction for offences there committed: nor was it ever imagined that for this purpose the authorization of their own governments is necessary. Thus also in private law the same principle is implicitly admitted by those who maintain that a jurisdiction is founded by delict, that is, now, considering the modern French practice noticed above, by every authority on the subject. And the command which imposes the legal duty of fulfilling a contractual or quasi-contractual obliga-

(*n*) See above, Art. 109. He calls it a *beschränkende bedingung*.

tion, thereby exposing to suit to redress the breach of that duty, is essentially of no different nature from the command which enjoins redress of an injury. So close and natural has their connexion always seemed, that in the ancient forms of action of the English law many a claim of a contractual or quasi-contractual nature could be prosecuted in trespass on the case, the form of which the idea was taken from delict. The non-performance of a contract is in truth an injury.

119. Nor does the proposition at all interfere with that allegiance which subjects, wherever they may be, owe to their own sovereign. The permanent and temporary subjections are concurrent. If they should be at variance, the moral duty may often lie with the conduct prescribed by the former. But as long as the latter continues, and in a state of peace, the permanent sovereign is debarred from enforcing his commands by the immediate employment of physical force on a foreign soil, and can only attack the property his subject may have left at home, or threaten his person on his return; while the temporary sovereign can touch the person, though, if he does so without reasonable cause, redress may be claimed by the government which owes protection in return for allegiance.

2. *English Doctrines.*

120. On approaching the English law on this subject, we enter at once on a different line of thought. Partly from the small influence of the Roman law, still more, probably, from the early subjection of the whole country to the immediate authority of the *curia regis*, the idea of one or more determinate forums for each action did not here arise. We know nothing at common law either of the *forum rei* or of the *forum rei gestæ*, England forming, in the superior

branches, but one undivided jurisdiction. There were, however, rules of venue, that is, of the locality in which that single jurisdiction should cause a question of fact to be tried by jury; and these rules, though originally intended merely to portion out business as to which the competence of the court was undisputed, reacted on the competence by limiting it to actions for which the rules enabled a venue to be assigned. Hence our great classification of personal actions, with a view to the question of competence, is into local and transitory: the former arising from causes which could not have transpired elsewhere than in the place of their actual occurrence, such as trespasses to land; the latter from facts which it is supposed might have taken place anywhere, as personal injuries and breaches of promise. Transitory actions at common law were entertained against, and at the suit of, any British subject or alien friend, if only the defendant happened to be in England at the right moment, so that process might here be served upon him, wherever the cause of action really arose (*o*): for, if it arose abroad, a venue in England was assigned it, this being possible because the venue for transitory causes of action arising even in England is arbitrary. But, inasmuch as the venue of a local cause of action is not arbitrary, to such actions it was farther necessary, besides personal service on the defendant within the realm, that the cause should have occurred in England (*p*).

(*o*) *Rafael* v. *Verelst*, W. Blackstone, 1055, an action on a personal injury committed in the dominions of an independent Indian sovereign. *Mostyn* v. *Fabrigas*, Cowp. 161, on an injury in a colony.

(*p*) *Doulson* v. *Matthews*, 4 T. R. 503, overruling some expressions of Lord Mansfield in Cowp. 180, and reinstating the authority of *Skinner* v. *East India Company*, cited in Cowp. 167. It will farther be observed that, as to the arbitrariness of the venue, I speak of the principle. There are certain rules about changing it, both in local and transitory actions, which do not interfere with its reaction here described on the competence.

121. The latter restriction of local actions, depending as it does on the venue, has not been removed: and the rule is so stringent that an action will not lie here on a covenant, which is transitory, and though that covenant was to pay rent in London, if the land be in Ireland, and the burden of the covenant have come to the defendant as assignee of the lease, which is a local fact. It is said that the plaintiff's right then depends on privity of estate, and not on privity of contract, as it would have done if the original lessee had been defendant, in which case the action would have lain (*q*). But what if the cause of action arose among savages, where there are no local courts? Would redress, though not to be had elsewhere, be refused against one who was domiciled, or owed allegiance, here? Lord Mansfield would not have refused it, and perhaps this part of the doctrines he laid down in *Mostyn* v. *Fabrigas* (*r*) has not been overruled. On the other hand, that restriction which depended on service within the realm has been removed for "causes of action which arose within the jurisdiction, and in respect of the breach of a contract made within the jurisdiction," whatever the nationality or domicile of the defendant, except he be a British subject residing in Scotland or Ireland; and for all other transitory actions, if the defendant be resident within the jurisdiction; provided always he know of the writ, or wilfully elude process (*s*).

122. This jurisdiction, when once it has attached on a foreigner by the commencement of a suit against him in this country, is strictly enforced by retaining him here. For the statute 1 & 2 Vict. c. 110, which abolished arrest on

(*q*) *Barker* v. *Damer*, Carthew, 182; *Way* v. *Yally*, 2 Salk. 651, 6 Mod. 194.

(*r*) Cowp. 180, 181.

(*s*) St. 15 & 16 Vict. c. 76, s. 2, 17, 18, 19.

mesne process in general, still permitted it, by sect. 3, in case of there being "probable cause for believing that a defendant is about to quit England," the cause of action amounting to £20 or upwards. Under this a defendant will be arrested and held to bail, if it appear likely that he will not otherwise "be forthcoming in order to be taken into execution," supposing judgment to go against him (*t*); notwithstanding that he may be only returning, after a temporary sojourn here, to his domicile out of the jurisdiction, and that the cause of action also arose abroad (*u*); unless he have been entrapped into England by the fraud of the plaintiff (*x*).

123. The personal authority of the court of chancery was originally founded on service of the subpœna, now replaced by that of the bill, within the jurisdiction, for which purpose the affidavit of service must show where it was made (*y*), and attachment will not issue for non-appearance on service made abroad, even though the defendant afterwards come within the jurisdiction (*z*), though in one such case it was granted because the defendant's solicitor had acknowledged the service and promised appearance (*a*). Also the service was always required to be personal, unless made at the defendant's dwelling-house, the original process being there produced to some one whose duty it would be to communicate it to the defendant; but such dwelling-house need not be his domicile strictly so called, nor need the defendant, when service is made, be either

---

(*t*) *Larchin* v. *Willan*, 4 M. & W. 351, 353. As to what prospect of a speedy return will prevent the arrest, see *Atkinson* v. *Blake*, 1 Dowl. N. S. 849, and *Hitchcock* v. *Hunter*, 10 L. J., N. S., Q. B. 87.

(*u*) *Lamond* v. *Eiffe*, 3 Gale & Dav. 256, 12 L. J., N. S., Q. B. 12.

(*x*) *Stein* v. *Valkenhuysen*, 27 L. J., N. S., Q. B. 236.

(*y*) *Davis* v. *Hole*, 1 Y. & C., Ch. 440.

(*z*) *Fernandez* v. *Corbin*, 2 Sim. 544; *Hackwood* v. *Lockerby*, 3 W. R. 440.

(*a*) *Nichol* v. *Gwyn*, 1 Sim. 389.

domiciled or actually present within the jurisdiction (*b*). Hence the justiciables of the court were all persons casually within its territory (*c*), and those who might happen to have dwelling-houses, though not necessarily domiciles there; while those domiciled in the jurisdiction, but not having a dwelling-house in it, as might easily happen to one who had quitted this country without establishing himself elsewhere, or who was at the moment travelling, and, while at home, lived in lodgings, were not justiciable.

124. Nothing has been done to restrain the wide extent which this gives the process in some directions, but much has been done to widen the narrow extent it had in others. The statute 5 Geo. 2, c. 25, established a process against a defendant in any suit in equity who might be believed on just ground to be gone out of the realm, or otherwise absconding, in order to avoid service; and it is not confined to parties domiciled, or even having dwelling-houses, or commonly residing, within the realm. The 31st order of May 1845, *in pari materia*, is limited to persons who have been within the jurisdiction at some time not more than two years before process is issued. And the statutes 2 & 3 Will. 4, c. 33, and 4 & 5 Will. 4, c. 82, enabled equitable process in suits respecting land, or any charge, lien, judgment or incumbrance thereon, or concerning any government or other public stocks or shares, to be personally (*d*) served, by direction of the court, in such part of the United Kingdom, or the Isle of Man, as the defendant should be then "residing" in: and, with regard to defendants in such suits not residing within the United

(*b*) *Davidson* v. *Hastings*, 2 Keen, 509, 513.

(*c*) So much so, that even a foreign wife, who has separate property, can be restrained from leaving England to rejoin her husband abroad, until she gives security to abide the event of the suit: *Moore* v. *Meynell*, Dick. 30; *Pannell* v. *Tayler*, T. & R. 96, 103.

(*d*) If the defendant secreted himself to avoid service, the court might, by sect. 2 of the second statute, order substituted service.

Kingdom, empowered the court to direct personal service (*e*) in such manner as it should specify, or, if the court should think fit, service on "the receiver, steward, or other person receiving or remitting the rents of the lands or premises, if any, in the suit mentioned."

125. After these provisions, which rested fairly on the ground of jurisdiction over the subject of suit, the statutes 3 & 4 Vict. c. 94, and 4 & 5 Vict. c. 52, empowered the court of chancery to alter "the forms and mode of proceeding in" it; and among the orders made under this authority is found the 33rd of May 1845, by which the court may in any suit direct personal service to be effected anywhere. The practice under this order may be seen detailed in Smith's Chancery Practice (*f*), and, being a matter of municipal law, need not be gone into here. Only it must be remarked that, though the exercise of the power thus taken is discretionary, some very large principles have been laid down as to the use of that discretion. "The material question," it has been said, "in judicial proceedings is whether the defendant has due notice of the proceedings, so that he may be enabled to come in and make his defence, and not whether he receives that notice at Boulogne or Dover. Although it does not appear why the bill was not filed in Ireland," where the defendant resided, and service was ordered, "there is no ground to suppose that the defendant is in a worse position by having it filed here (*g*)." The last words can only mean that it was *possible* for the defendant to come over to England and watch the cause, and produce his proofs here: it is another question whether it was *equally convenient* for him to do so, and whether he ought to have been obliged to do so, in

(*e*) See note (*d*), p. 108.

(*f*) Pp. 249, 255, of the sixth edition.

(*g*) *Whitmore* v *Ryan*, 4 Hare, 612, 617, 618.

a matter concerning dealings which do not appear from the report to have had their seat in England.

126. "The ordinary practice of courts of equity in England," said Lord Redesdale, "when one party is out of the jurisdiction and other parties within it, is to charge the fact in the bill that such a person is out of the jurisdiction, and then the court proceeds against the other parties notwithstanding he is not before it. It cannot proceed to compel him to do any act, but it can proceed against the other parties, and, if the disposition of the property is in the power of the other parties, the court may act upon it (*h*)." The rights of the absent party are always reserved, but, as his interest may nevertheless be practically affected, the allegation of his being out of the jurisdiction will not be received without proof (*i*), even though its truth be admitted by the parties who appear (*j*).

127. The jurisdiction of chancery however is not wholly based on obligation, even in the widest sense. It has a power of ordering, independent of any special equity affecting the parties through their own acts; and it may probably be laid down as a principle, as it is certainly demanded by the very nature of sovereignty, that this power will not be exercised as to persons domiciled abroad, and as to their conduct abroad, even though process have been served upon them here. Thus a foreign creditor cannot be restrained from suing in his own country, notwithstanding a decree for administration here of which he might take the benefit (*k*). There are also certain special restrictions on the jurisdiction with regard to the subject

---

(*h*) *Smith* v. *Hibernian Mine Company*, 1 Scho. & L. 238, 240.

(*i*) *Dibbs* v. *Goren*, 1 Beav. 457; *Hughes* v. *Eades*, 1 Hare, 486; *Moodie* v. *Bannister*, 1 Drew. 514, 520.

(*j*) *Egginton* v. *Burton*, 1 Hare, 488, note.

(*k*) *Carron Company* v. *Maclaren*, 5 H. of L. 416, 441.

matter: as that discovery will not be granted in aid of the defence to a suit in a foreign court (*l*).

128. The jurisdiction *in personam* over corporations presents some difficult questions, which have recently occupied the court of chancery. Many such bodies, as municipalities and hospitals, are clearly connected with specific spots: in the case of others, as railway companies, the operations of which may be equally connected with spots in different jurisdictions, it is usual on the continent to fix their domicile for jurisdiction in their statutes; "and if," says Savigny, "this has been neglected, the judge must seek to reason out their centre of operations by methods of art (*m*)." Now this is entirely satisfactory for litigation internal to the body, which it would be unreasonable to allow in any casual jurisdiction determined by a member, who yet must have joined it with notice of its nature: indeed, the records of the company being kept at its principal seat, a litigation relating to them must in general be ineffectual elsewhere (*n*). But what if the litigation be external, as on an obligation contracted by the corporation in the course of its dealing, particularly if its statutes have not fixed its jurisdiction, for of such a provision those who deal with it might be taken to have notice? Or what if the court be called on to exercise its authority independently of any special equity to which the body has made itself liable?

129. The last case arose in *Maclaren* v. *Carron Company*, where it was sought to restrain a Scotch manufacturing company from taking proceedings in Scotland as creditors of an estate, after an English decree for adminis-

---

(*l*) *Bent* v. *Young*, 9 Sim. 180, commenting on *Crowe* v. *Del Rio*, p. 185, note, and on a supposed opinion of Lord Redesdale to the contrary.

(*m*) Syst. d. heut. Röm. Rechts, v. 8, p. 66.

(*n*) *Sudlow* v. *Dutch Rhenish Railway Co.*, 21 Beav. 43. *Lewis* v. *Baldwin*, 11 Beav. 153, was so peculiar a case that it cannot be said to be inconsistent with the principle.

tering it made in a suit to which the company had not been a party (*o*). The case was considered at the Rolls without reference to domicile properly so called, but to the question whether the agency, which the defendants had in England for selling their goods, was a dwelling-house of their body for the purpose of serving process under our technical rules mentioned above in Art. 123 (*p*): this being decided in the affirmative, the injunction was farther sustained upon the merits, which were treated as between acknowledged subjects of the jurisdiction. But, on appeal, the questions of jurisdiction and domicile were held to arise upon the merits, on the ground noticed above in Art. 127. It was absolutely necessary to fix a centre of the company's existence, in order to ascertain whether it was subject to the general authority of the court. Now, notwithstanding that, on universal principles, the company might have furnished against itself a forum here, for the contracts of sale made through its English agency—for this is clearly the case of IV. and not of V. in Art. 105—yet such forum could not be carried beyond the purposes of the agency which created it, and the general subjection which for an individual is founded on domicile was rightly held to exist for the defendants in Scotland alone.

130. It is sufficiently apparent that by the rules of jurisdiction we have been considering, allowing in many cases a wide liberty as to the forum, and, besides, not the subject of universal or even general agreement, suits may often be brought in different countries for the same matter, which each of the respective forums may think itself entitled to entertain. Must then all these suits go forward together, or may any of the tribunals restrain by injunction the parties before it from proceeding elsewhere, or make their abandonment of the foreign proceedings, or their submis-

(*o*) See above, Art. 55.
(*p*) 16 Beav. 287.

sion to its own order in conducting them, a condition of their receiving any benefit from its own process? To answer this, let us suppose first that none of the suits has yet proceeded to sentence: it would then seem that any forum, which under the circumstances had the means of doing complete justice, might reasonably interfere to stop or prevent suits in forums where complete justice could not be done. There is no room for the objection that authority would thus be assumed over an independent jurisdiction, for it is not the foreign judges whom the injunction would attempt to restrain, but the parties who *ex hypothesi* are, or are considered by the court to be, its own justiciables (*q*). Accordingly our chancery habitually grants injunctions against proceedings pending abroad, without waiting for the matters in question to be settled by its own decree, if and so far as it sees that it will itself be better able to settle them. Thus, in *Bushby* v. *Munday*, the reason given was that "this is a case which must be fully investigated and finally decided here," and an exception was made of that part of the Scotch proceedings which sought relief against Scotch land, the plaintiff in England being put on terms to submit to such steps in Scotland as would secure his lien on it to the defendant, in case he should succeed in establishing here any demand on the bond in question (*r*). In this case the lien on the Scotch land would have been obtained only through judgment in a personal action, but where the foreign land itself is the subject of suit, still, if circumstances make it on the whole better that the determination should take place here, the defendants will be restrained from prosecuting the proceedings abroad, the plaintiffs undertaking to submit to and carry into effect any order which our court may thereafter make with regard

(*q*) As to this, see Art. 127.

(*r*) 5 Madd. 297, 309.

to those proceedings: that is, the determination will be had here, the foreign suit being kept on foot as a means of giving it effect against property which the English tribunal could not touch. This was done in *Beckford* v. *Kemble* (*s*), where foreclosure in Jamaica of land there was restrained on the ground that a decree leading to, though not for, redemption had been made here before the bill was filed in the West Indies; and in *Bunbury* v. *Bunbury* (*t*), where both real property in Demerara and personal property were in question, this being the proper forum for the latter, and the title to both depending to some extent on the same questions.

131. Nor, again, is it necessary that a better determination should be obtainable here than in the country of the foreign suit. If the court in which that suit is pending have powers insufficient to do complete justice, the injunction will issue, notwithstanding that in the same foreign country another court may exist having similar powers and opportunities with our own chancery (*u*). And if a decree has already been pronounced here, or is pronounced at the same time that the injunction against the foreign proceedings is granted, then there is reason *a fortiori* for preventing the continuance of another litigation on a matter already provided for (*x*).

3. *Extraterritoriality.*

132. We have hitherto considered only actions *in personam* against private citizens or bodies. We have now to

(*s*) 1 S. & St. 7. This case goes to the verge of the principle. Nothing but the mortgage was in question, and the original bill in the situs was prior to the original bill here, the suit restrained being a supplemental one.

(*t*) 1 Beav. 318.

(*u*) *Portarlington* v. *Soulby*, 3 My. & Ke. 104.

(*x*) *Wharton* v. *May*, 5 Ves. 27, 71; *Harrison* v. *Gurney*, 2 Jac. & W. 563; *Beauchamp* v. *Huntley*, *Clarke* v. *Ormonde*, Jac. 546.

consider at once certain exceptions to the above rules, which have to be made in the case of diplomatists, and the extent to which the rules may apply against sovereign persons or bodies. These matters are grouped together under the name of extraterritoriality (*exterritorialité*), because they were treated on the principle of a fiction, by which the residences of ambassadors, and those which sovereigns might occupy while abroad, were treated as forming part of their own territory, and not of that in which they actually lay. So far was this fiction carried that the ambassador's residence formerly furnished in most countries an asylum from justice, and large franchises were enjoyed even by the quarter of the city in which it stood: but these privileges have been generally restrained, whence any exception which extraterritoriality may cause to rules either of law or of jurisdiction must rest on its own footing, and cannot be satisfactorily deduced from a fiction now far too wide to represent the actual facts, although the term may be retained for conveniency of classification. Moreover, the privileges in question were never so largely allowed in England as in some countries, whence also foreign rules on the subject can be the less used here for argument by analogy.

133. To take then the simple point of jurisdiction on obligations, we should have to say, from the continental point of view, that the *forum rei* (if any) of any person within the exception of extraterritoriality is that of his own country, for, as we have seen in Art. 47, ambassadors retain their home domicile, while sovereigns cannot be personally subject to foreign powers: and that for such persons there is no *forum rei gestæ*. From the English point of view, the result will now be the same, inasmuch as such persons in England are not amenable here, while our writ at common law might easily be served, and the court of chancery would no doubt, in the exercise

of its discretion, order service of its process abroad, in a proper case, on a British ambassador resident at the court to which he was accredited. From either point of view, the persons, natural or juristic, within the exception are independent governments; those sovereign persons in foreign states who for public international purposes are identified with their respective governments, though their power at home may not be unlimited; and the diplomatic servants who, being foreigners, represent their governments abroad. The privilege also extends to the families and suites of ambassadors, but so that as to these it is that of the ambassador (*y*), and may be waived by him for those to whom he would else communicate it (*z*), while for himself he cannot waive it, it being as to him the privilege of his government (*a*). In England these general propositions would receive their interpretation from the statute 7 Anne, c. 12, which, on the occasion of the arrest of the Russian ambassador, declared the persons, goods, and chattels of ambassadors and other public ministers of foreign princes or states, and of their domestics and domestic servants, to be free from process (*b*): also that no merchant or trader within the bankruptcy laws could take any such benefit from the service of such a functionary (*c*).

134. The reason of these exemptions is not that a case cannot arise in which, on strict principles of law, parties

---

(*y*) So that, if the ambassador do not claim it for the defendant, the domesticity (statute 7 Anne, c. 12, s. 3) and *bona fides* of the service will be very strictly considered: *Fisher* v. *Begrez*, 2 C. & M. 240. See also *Heathfield* v. *Chilton*, 4 Burr. 2015.

(*z*) By French court of cassation, in Fœlix, 3rd edit., v. 1, p. 392.

(*a*) Vattel, l. 4, s. 111.

(*b*) Sect. 3. Bynkershoek (de Foro Leg., c. 4) denies that the goods and chattels of a foreign government are protected from process, but Huber, Fœlix, and the uniform tenour of modern decisions, are against him. See the decision of the court of cassation, that there can be no process of garnishment (*saisie-arrêt*) against the French debtor of a foreign government: Dalloz, 1849, 1, 1.

(*c*) Sect. 5.

deemed extraterritorial would be amenable, for even a government may by its agents commit an injury within the jurisdiction; nor that civil process against them would necessarily be without effect, for even a government might have property within the jurisdiction capable of being reached by the sentence; but to avoid the danger of provoking war by wounding the dignity of a foreign state. Also ambassadors ought not to be impeded by private suits, which might moreover be got up by the governments with which they resided, from transacting the public business entrusted to them. So far is this carried that Bynkershoek considered that a sovereign who should personally commit licentious and criminal acts against individuals, in a foreign land where he had been received as a friend, though amenable to justice on principle, ought rather to be sent out of the country, as is done in the case of ambassadors similarly delinquent, or even punished by popular tumult rather than judicially (*d*).

135. But a foreign sovereign, and *a fortiori* an ambassador, may sue here, since jurisdiction, being the legitimate employment of force, depends only on the person against whom it is exercised (*e*). Only the government which so sues must be recognised by our own, as no corporate existence could else be attributed to a body of persons calling themselves a government; and such recognition, being notorious, need not be proved to the judge (*f*). And such a plaintiff will be open to a principle applicable to all who sue where they would not otherwise be amenable, that, having sought equity, they have submitted themselves to do it: *qui non cogitur in aliquo loco judicium pati, si ipse ibi agat, cogitur excipere actiones et ad eundem*

(*d*) De Foro Legatorum, c. 3.

(*e*) *King of Spain* v. *Machado*, 4 Russ. 225; *Hullet* v. *King of Spain*, 1 Dow & Clark, 169.

(*f*) *City of Berne* v. *Bank of England*, 9 Ves. 347.

judicem mitti (*g*). Hence, if suing in equity, the plaintiff will be liable to a cross-bill (*h*); if at law, to a bill of discovery in equity (*i*): and, in any case, the court may put him on terms (*k*), and he will be exposed to process for the recovery of costs in which he may be condemned (*l*). For this reason, a foreign government can only sue "in the names of some public officers who are entitled to represent the interests of the state, and upon whom process can be served on the part of the defendants (*m*)."

136. And even in other cases than those of Art. 135, the exemption from suit stated in Art. 133 must be understood only of really hostile proceedings, and not of those where, by the rules of pleading observed in the English court of chancery, it may be necessary to make some one a defendant either for his own advantage, or at least without threatening him with loss. Upon this I will give Lord Langdale's words:—"There have been cases in which, this court being called upon to distribute a fund in which some foreign sovereign or state may have had an interest, it has been thought expedient and proper, in order to a due distribution of the fund, to make such sovereign or state a party. The effect has been to make the suit perfect as to parties, but, as to the sovereign or state made a defendant in cases of that kind, the effect has not been to compel or attempt to compel such sovereign or state to come in and submit to judgment in the ordinary course, but to give the sovereign an opportunity to come in to claim his right, or establish his interest in the subject matter of the suit. Coming in to make his claim, he

(*g*) Paulus, in Dig. 5, 1, 22.

(*h*) *King of Spain* v. *Hullet*, 1 Cl. & F. 333.

(*i*) *Rothschild* v. *Queen of Portugal*, 3 Y. & C. 594. See also *Queen of Portugal* v. *Glyn*, 7 Cl. & F. 466.

(*k*) *Hullet* v. *King of Spain*, 1 D. & Cl. 174.

(*l*) Even if a new action be required to recover them: Fœlix, n. 217.

(*m*) *Colombian Government* v. *Rothschild*, 1 Sim. 94.

would, by doing so, submit himself to the jurisdiction of the court in that matter; refusing to come in, he might perhaps be precluded from establishing any claim to the same interest in another form. So where a defendant in this country is called upon to account for some matter in respect of which he has acted as agent for a foreign sovereign, the suit would not be perfect as to parties unless the foreign sovereign were formally a defendant, and by making him a party an opportunity is afforded him of defending himself instead of leaving the defence to his agent, and he may come in if he pleases: in such a case, if he refuses to come in, he may perhaps be held bound by the decision against his agent" (*n*).

137. A more complicated case is that in which the foreign character entitling to the exemption is combined with subjection here. It has been decided that no suit can be maintained against a foreign sovereign who is also a British subject, for acts done in virtue of his authority as sovereign, notwithstanding that process may have been served upon him while exercising in this country his rights as such subject (*o*). But is such a person "liable to be sued in the courts of this country, in respect of any acts and transactions done by him, or in which he may have been engaged, as a British subject?" (*p*) The affirmative was held by Lord Langdale, and we may admit, as implied by Lord Brougham, "that, supposing a foreign sovereign, being also a naturalized subject in this country, had a landed estate in this country, and entered into any transactions respecting it, as a contract of sale or mortgage," then "a court of equity in this country might compel him

(*n*) In *Duke of Brunswick* v. *King of Hanover*, 6 Beav. 39.
(*o*) S. C. 6 Beav. 1, 2 H. of L. 1.
(*p*) S. C. 6 Beav. 57.

specifically to perform his contract (*q*)." For strict law would support the jurisdiction, and we should probably think our dignity as much involved in maintaining as his in repelling it.

138. It is universally agreed that an ambassador appointed from among the subjects of the state to which he is accredited remains subject to its jurisdiction in private matters, and, if any inconvenience is suffered thereby, the government which appointed him has but its own choice to blame. But here again the same distinction exists as in the case of the sovereign-subject. Such an ambassador is exempt from the jurisdiction in every thing which directly relates to his ministry (*r*): and an opinion has been expressed by Lord Campbell, that a British subject who is neither a sovereign nor an ambassador is equally exempt from British jurisdiction, in respect of what he has done by the authority of a foreign government's instrument of state, for acting under which he has had the sanction of the sovereign of this kingdom (*s*).

139. The privileges of extraterritoriality do not extend to consuls, if not expressly secured to them by treaty, unless in any special case a diplomatic commission may be combined with their ordinary functions, which are only to protect the commercial interests of their countrymen. Indeed the residence of a consul has such a character of continuance that it may even found a *forum rei* for the obligations contracted by him, though, as we have seen, it does not change his domicile for most purposes (*t*). And

(*q*) *Duke of Brunswick* v. *King of Hanover*, 2 H. of L. 24.

(*r*) Vattel, l. 4, s. 112.

(*s*) In *Duke of Brunswick* v. *King of Hanover*, 2 H. of L. 26. The dictum refers to what had been done by the Duke of Cambridge, but the only possible generalisation of it appears to be that given in the text.

(*t*) Above, Art. 47.

hence the consuls who have been placed by treaty on the footing of those of the most favoured nation, of which number are the British consuls (*u*), enjoy in France an exemption from *arrest* on obligations not contracted by them in the way of commerce (*x*), an exemption which implies of itself that they may *be sued* there on their general obligations (*y*). But in *Mountflorence* v. *Skipwith* the court of cassation held a foreign consul not justiciable in France, at the suit of another foreigner, and on a non-mercantile obligation (*z*).

(*u*) Treaty of January 15th, 1787.

(*x*) The type-treaty is the convention concluded with Spain on March 13th, 1769.

(*y*) Fœlix, nos. 218, 221.

(*z*) Merlin, Rép., Étranger, § II. I have more particularly mentioned these details, on account of the short and indistinct notice of the status of consuls in France, cited in *Bremer* v. *Freeman*, 1 Deane, 204.

CHAPTER VI.

PRINCIPLES OF THE INTERNATIONAL OBLIGATION OF LAW.

140. AT this point, when we are about to commence a detailed investigation of the international law of obligations, as based on the causes for which a definite individual may be subject in a definite matter to the commands of a particular sovereign, it will be well to pause, in order to consider some of the theories which have been entertained on the mutual limits of the authority of laws.

1. *Theories of the Reality and Personality of Statutes, and of the Comity of Nations.*

141. The term "statutes," which is classical in this subject, was originally used of the by-laws of the imperial and other free towns, in Italy and elsewhere, and was thence extended to the unwritten customs and written *coutumiers* of the feudal jurisdictions. But the common law of all those towns and countries was that of Rome, to which therefore the statutes were exceptions, the existence of which occasioned some difficulty, because in the empire legislation was confessed to be an exclusively imperial prerogative, while in France there had been for

many centuries a total cessation of all exercise of legislative power. To account for the statutes, two methods were therefore entered on. One, more common in Italy and in early times, was evidently induced by the legislation which, however contrary to theory, actually took place in the cities. It consisted in admitting the statutes to have the proper force of law, but only through a resort to some curious argumentative shifts. Thus, inasmuch as the Venetians made their wills with only two witnesses, while the Roman law required five, one doctor trusted that they had received some forgotten dispensation from the successors of Justinian; while another argued that since by the Roman law a parent could with two witnesses divide his property between his children, a city, which was the parent of her subjects, might authorize them to distribute their substance with no more elaborate formality (*a*). When it is remembered that Venice, at the time these apologies were made for her, did not acknowledge the authority of the emperor, it will be understood how severely the difficulty of regarding the statutes as laws must have been felt in the imperial towns, such as Florence or Milan. The other method, more common in the feudal districts, and appropriate to their condition, seems to have denied the force of law to the statutes, and regarded them as what in fact in those districts they purported to be, customs which men chose to follow there. Hence their authority was not generally their own, but derived from the intention of the parties, to which a clue was afforded when the circumstances made it probable that they meant to conform to any particular custom. Of the effect which this had in different directions abundant instances may be furnished from Dumoulin. Thus in Art. 71 we have seen that, according to him, a custom, the nature of which is

---

(*a*) Bartolus, ad Cod. 1, 1, 1.

such that it cannot operate through the will of the parties, must be construed very strictly, as in derogation of the common law (*b*): in Art. 111, that the custom to which the parties were supposed freely to conform was not always that which those who gave to customs the force of law considered to govern the transaction: and again, where Dumoulin perceived in the custom the choice of the parties, he extended its effect, through the mediation of that choice, to matters which by its native vigour it could not reach, as in his opinion that the custom of the matrimonial domicile regulated, in the absence of express agreement, even the foreign immovables of the spouses (*c*). In precise accordance with this appears to have been the meaning of Henry Boich, when he said that a personal custom was one *per quam jus nascitur ex contractu* (*d*).

142. Such were the statutes, in the conceptions current during and at the close of the middle ages: and at the same time an attempt was made to classify them by their contents, as disposing of persons or things, of which we see a rough sketch in the following crude rules of Bartolus:—*Mihi videtur quod verba statuti seu consuetudinis sunt diligenter intuenda. Aut illa disponunt circa res, ut per hæc verba, "bona decedentis veniant in primogenitum;" et tunc de omnibus bonis judicabo secundum usum et statutum ubi res sunt situatæ, quia jus afficit res ipsas, sive possideantur a cive sive ab advena. Aut verba statuti seu consuetudinis disponunt circa personas, ut per hæc verba, "primogenitus succedat;" et tunc, aut ille talis decedens non erat de Anglia, sed ibi habuit possessiones, et tunc tale statutum ad eum et ejus filios non porrigitur, quia dispositio circa*

(*b*) An instance of this will be given from Bartolus also in the next paragraph.

(*c*) See particularly Dumoulin's 53rd consilium, v. 2, p. 963, of the 1581 edition.

(*d*) Apud D'Arg., Comm. in Brit. Leg., Art. 218, gl. 6, n. 14.

personas non porrigitur ad forenses; aut talis decedens erat Anglicus, et tunc filius primogenitus succederet in bonis quæ sunt in Anglia, et in aliis succederet de jure communi (*e*). The last clause of this citation, in which a statute asserted to be personal is restrained in operation apparently on the ground of its being an exception to the common law, reminds us of the doctrine of Dumoulin, in which, as we have seen, the personal statute is restrained by the double limitation of affecting only its own subjects, and with regard to things within its own territory.

143. Thus stood the matter till late in the sixteenth century. A statute which had persons for its principal object was personal, and applied to all who were domiciled within its limits: those which had things for their principal object were real, and applied to property situate within their limits. In distinguishing these, the foolish attention of Bartolus to the words of statutes was generally repudiated, and provisions as to the status of persons fell into the former class, but the chief motive of a law was so vague a criterion that the latter class remained in truth totally undefined, but with a general tendency to confine its extent. When however the states of modern Europe were establishing a continually increasing separation from a common imperial system, the intrinsic authority of law was more boldly claimed for the customs, and with the necessary effect of restraining their operation to narrower limits. This we have seen, in Art. 90, in the language of the Breton D'Argentré, who also vehemently opposed Dumoulin's doctrine of the tacit matrimonial contract (*f*). His position naturally led him to be forward in this movement, since the independence of customs was in the spirit

(*e*) Ad Cod. 1, 1, 1.

(*f*) *Ubi supra*, n. 33, 34. To Boich's definition of a personal statute, partly cited above, he subjoins, *addo ego, et si ex statuti dispositione et potestate obligatio nectitur in personam.*

of that local independence a certain amount of which Brittany was struggling to maintain. In the same author we meet with the third, or mixed, class of statutes, which afterwards grew so vastly in importance, but in which he states that the real character predominates, as in the prohibition of donations and bequests between man and wife, so far as it applies to land, and in statutes which make the rights in a suit for partition depend on the noble or villein status of the parties (*g*); and with the distinction between a status affecting the person universally, as *infamatio*, and an inability imposed with regard to some special act on a real subject, which last is not to be judged by the law of the domicile (*h*).

144. It was not long after this that a still more powerful impetus was given in the same direction, through the elaboration by Grotius of his theory of territorial sovereignty, which seemed at first sight to strike at the root of all extraterritorial application of personal or mixed statutes. But as it was quite impossible that this could be suffered, jurists were led to inquire how the adoption in any case of a foreign law could be reconciled with the plenary of authority of sovereigns within their respective geographical limits; and the earliest formal answer is that of Huber, expressing the doctrine of an international comity in three maxims, which have become classical.

I. *Leges cujusque imperii vim habent intra terminos ejusdem reipublicæ, omnesque ei subjectos obligant, nec ultra.* II. *Pro subjectis imperio habendi sunt omnes qui intra terminos ejusdem reperiuntur, sive in perpetuum sive ad tempus ibi commorentur.* III. *Rectores imperiorum id comiter agunt, ut jura cujusque populi intra terminos ejus exercita teneant ubique suam vim, quatenus nihil juri aut potestati*

(*g*) *Ubi supra*, n. 5, &c.
(*h*) *Ubi supra*, n. 16, &c.

alterius imperantis ejusque civium præjudicetur (*i*). But the doctrine that foreign laws are only to be admitted by a comity, limited by the rights and authority of the admitting state and its members, tells us indeed nothing, since it is just these rights and this authority of which the extent is in question. Thus, can one who is of age in the country of his domicile devise land situate where he would still be a minor? Huber answers, Yes (*k*): a decision which many in England and America would reject, as derogatory to the territorial authority of the sovereign of the land. Nay, more: by referring to the rights of the individual citizens of the forum, the doctrine opens the door to very un-juridical reasonings founded on their supposed interests. Thus, relying on the principle that *mobilia sequuntur personam*, you mortgage a chattel to me, without delivery, but in a country where delivery is not necessary to complete my title: a claimant under you by a posterior title anticipates me in taking possession, at a place where that is necessary to the title: can I establish my priority by a suit in the latter place? No, says Huber: because the right acquired in the country of the forum, by the occupation of the possession, cannot be taken away by a foreign law (*l*). Now he does not mean that a claim resting on foreign law can never compete with one resting on the *lex fori*, else in the former case the devisee could not compete with the minor's heir *ab intestato*: and, not meaning this, it seems to be reasoning in a circle to set up the posterior legal claim, which, if the first mortgage was valid, cannot be to more than the right which remained in the owner. Yet I believe that legal claim was what Huber meant, and that the supreme court of Louisiana misunderstood him,

---

(*i*) De Confl. Leg., s. 2.
(*k*) Ibid. s. 15.
(*l*) Ibid. s. 11.

when it came to the same decision expressly on the ground of the interest of the citizens of the forum, in considering which it fancied that he had led the way (*m*). It will complete the picture of how little is to be expected from Huber's third maxim, when I add that Story, who adopts it, appears to dissent from this result which the Louisiana judges have extracted from it (*n*).

145. In truth however the free reception of a foreign law does not infringe the principle of territorial sovereignty, since it is simply by the authority of the territorial sovereign that it is received. His code may not lay down the precise cases for such reception, but he must be taken as cognisant of that general understanding, by which his own and all other judges enforce foreign laws in accordance with the principles of private international jurisprudence. It is a question of interpreting his meaning, and the principles of such interpretation must be sought beyond the text to be interpreted, in that science of law to the ideas of which no legislator intends to run counter. It is admitted on all hands that if the municipal law of any country contain provisions on cases of collision, they must be followed by its judges, however opposed to general theory: a reservation which clearly shows that it is only by the tacit approbation of the local legislator that the theory is ever adopted. Since then the principle of independent sovereignty did not destroy this branch of jurisprudence, and that of comity led to no clear results of its own, merely smoothing the way for those which might be otherwise obtained, men still tried to make what they could out of the old distinctions of real, personal, and mixed statutes. Now many questions arose in working them out.

146. First, were those statutes alone personal which de-

(*m*) *Olivier* v. *Townes*, 2 Martin, N. S. 93.

(*n*) Sect. 390.

fined the status of the person, or also those which defined the juristic consequences of that status, the rights and limitations arising out of it? For example, a statute which fixes the age of majority is certainly personal: but is one which fixes the incapacities of a minor also personal? Hertius, as we saw in Art. 70, took the negative side, and he has been followed in modern times by Meier, Mittermaier, and Wächter: but the majority of authors have always repudiated the distinction. "If we look closely at the thing," says Savigny, "we find no other difference than that many personal conditions are denoted by particular names, and others are not. . . . . . A major we name him who possesses the fullest capacity to act which can be reached by age; it is thus a name for certain juristic effects, for the denial of previous limitations of capacity. In the same way we name a minor him who does not yet possess that full capacity, for the denial of which condition it is a name. Now when a law establishes certain grades of capacity even among minors, without using particular names for them, no ground can be seen on which these grades of capacity should not, as well as the commencement of full capacity, be judged according to the law of the domicile (*o*)."

147. Secondly, the mixed statutes were frequently defined as relating to acts. *Si lex actui formam dat, inspiciendus est locus actus,* says Hertius, putting this on a level with *quando lex in personam dirigitur,* and *si lex directo rei imponitur,* as the third member of the classification (*p*). Now did this class comprise those which related to the substance of the act, as Hertius, notwithstanding his expression *actui formam dat,* with the majority, understood; or was it limited to the external ceremonies of acting, as John Voet thought? For the former opinion spoke the

(*o*) Syst. d. heut. Röm. Rechts, v. 8, p. 136.

(*p*) De Coll. Leg., Sect. 4, § 10.

difficulty of saying to which of the first two classes the statutes relating to the substance of the act belonged. Thirdly, in one point of view the mixed class, with its whole consequence of the *lex loci actus aut contractus*, threatened to vanish, since there is hardly any law which may not be argued to relate principally either to persons or to things. But then, mixed statutes being also defined as those which concern at once both persons and property, the third division arose again, and with a prodigious development, since most laws relate to persons in their conduct about things.

148. I pass over the distinctions of pure personal statutes and personal-real, and the subdivision of pure personal into personal-universal and personal-particular, as also various other questions, in order to point out wherein the weakness of this whole theory, which never even wore the appearance of leading to a general agreement in practical results (*q*), appears to me to have lain. It considered laws in a manner entirely beside the only character in which they can originate rights, namely, as commands or prohibitions addressed *to* persons, and took them as ordering *about* persons and transactions. Now it makes little difference whether such order was imagined to have a sort of sacramental operation (as probably was, though vaguely, the first notion), making the minor a minor, or the land subject to primogeniture, all the world over, and for all intents and purposes; or whether it was held to operate extraterritorially through comity. The cases in which a right is fairly entitled to extraterritorial consideration, are

---

(*q*) So hopeless was it to ascertain the extent of a statute's application by referring it to its class, that Paul Voet and Bouhier classify real and personal statutes by the extent in which they are applied, which reduces the whole system to a means of registering the rules practically received from motives of convenienc: P. Voet, de Statutis, s. 4, c. 2, n. 5; Bouhier, Obs. sur la Coutume de Bourgogne, c. 23, n. 59.

those in which the correlative duty was imposed by a sovereign who could lawfully command at the time; and no progress could be made towards a satisfactory enumeration of these cases by a method which did not go upon the authority to command or prohibit conduct, but to regulate a personal status, a piece of land, or the form of a transaction.

2. *Principles of the Law Common to the Parties, and of the Law of the Defendant.*

149. The distinction of real and personal statutes has been illustrated from continental authorities, because, though never totally unknown here, yet neither was it ever of much importance in English law: a circumstance probably to be attributed to the fact that our juristic system had already acquired a fixed character entirely unlike that of the continent, before the period when that distinction attained its full development abroad. Hence also the current English decisions bore to a considerable extent the impress of that continental period which preceded D'Argentré, and when, as we have seen, the mixed class of statutes was not well distinguished from the personal. Thus the fact of marriage, as one relating to status, would in the strict theory of statutes be referred to the law of the domicile, as the personal law: but it was always referred in England to the *lex loci contractus*, not only for the form of the ceremony, but also for the capacity of the parties and the consent of parents or guardians required, in accordance with a practice of the canonists which dates from the period when the *lex loci actus* was not yet well distinguished from the *lex domicilii*. How far this may have been altered by recent English decisions, we shall hereafter have to consider. Thus too it was always admitted in England that a movable succession was governed on

death by the law of the testator's or intestate's domicile, but without its clearly appearing whether this went on the *lex loci actus*, the domicile being the place where (in continental phraseology) the succession was opened, or on the *lex domicilii* combined with the maxim *mobilia sequuntur personam*. But the principles which are the subject of the present section, and which are especially operative when the natives of civilized countries meet and act either in regions where no law is established, or where, as in the Levant and in India, legal systems exist totally foreign to their habits and ideas, have, from the enterprise and colonizing activity of the English nation, received in our jurisprudence a consideration at least as full as any they have obtained elsewhere.

150. In a highly cultivated condition of society, many circumstances concur to familiarize men with the conception of law as springing essentially from enactment by sovereign authority. Interests are so complicated that the introduction of new rules is no longer freely entrusted to judicial decision, but demands the interference of the legislative power, whether that be vested in a monarch or in a parliament. Also the execution of all judgments is secured by the ubiquitous and regular force of the supreme executive, whence even those decisions of which the ground cannot be directly referred to the legislature are seen to derive their binding authority from the sovereign body in the state. But it may be safely said that legislation never commenced the juristic history of any people. In few instances is it even its earliest known phase, and, where the memory of previous stages has perished, we may be sure that the people whose genius for law permitted the introduction of a code cannot have previously lived without legal rules. The historical origin of law must always have been a national persuasion or conscience of that which is jurally right, that is, not only morally right, for

no people has aimed at the authoritative suppression of all which is morally wrong, but also proper to be enforced by man on his fellows. This persuasion varies from people to people, with their apprehension of moral principles, the circumstances to which they have to apply those principles, and their more or less stringent views of the extent to which moral obligations ought to be enforced by men on each other. But, prior to legislation, no other warrant than this persuasion itself, such as it exists among any people at any time, can be sought or found for its own enforcement. The exposition of this common law is at first entrusted either to popular courts, or to judges and lawyers, who in such case are the depositaries of the national conscience in jural matters. It is even through them that important changes are first made, as in *Taltarum's case*, and in that practice of conveyancers which, contrary to the express words of the statute *de donis*, prevents the creation of an estate tail by the word *issue* in a deed: both striking instances, since they show that the productive and alterative vigour of the common law long survived the commencement of legislation. But the age of legislation has fully arrived when changes are so contested that they can no longer be effected by a silent revolution of public conviction, when whole departments of social life arise of which the jurist class cannot be presumed to know the details, and the declining vigour of the common law becomes unequal to create those new institutions, as for example that of bankruptcy, which do not aim at mere justice between man and man, but deal comprehensively with extensive interests by way of disposition and mutual compromise. Correspondingly, the authority by which the law is executed is often in the earlier stages vested in special powers or bodies within the state, whose close connexion with the people, or with sections of it having a distinct existence for jural purposes, cannot be mistaken. Thus, when the sheriff executed the law declared by the freeholders in the county court in which he had himself been chosen, or the officers of a trade that declared in the court of its guild which also elected them, the source of the law was not the less obviously the common conviction of a number of men forming a certain society. But the centralization of the executive, no less than the substitution of prospective legislation for the development of law by judgment on foregone facts, conduces to give to law an external character. Now when rights are considered as proceeding from an external enactment by sovereign authority, the necessity that in a very artificial state of society each such authority should have definite geographical limits assigned to its activity, leads to the conception of private rights as dependent on the law of the place where they originate, since at that place the local sovereign alone can issue the commands which are requisite to create them. But the idea which lies historically at the root of private rights, namely, that they are sufficiently created by a common conviction in any organized body of men of that which ought to be law, does not limit the application of a national law by any considerations of place. The nomad tribe carries its institutions with it in its wanderings; different laws may coexist on the same soil by the agglomeration of unmingled races, as happened in Europe with what are called the personal laws during the dark ages, and as is the case now with regard to the British and native laws in India; and according to the same idea the mutual dealings of fellow-citizens in a foreign country, or concerning foreign things, may have their effect according to the common law of the parties, as well as though they acted at and in relation to their home.

151. These principles are exemplified in the mutual dealings of Christians in Mahometan countries. Not only did the Turks never think of displacing the private juris-

prudence of the Greek empire in its application to the conquered people, but they have never claimed to subject the private affairs of Christian foreigners within their states to laws so little applicable to them as those of the Koran, leaving them rather to the operation of those laws which, as expressing the common sentiments of the parties, are naturally of force in their mutual dealings. It is true that the immunities of Christians in Turkey neither have nor could have rested solely on legal principles, for the enjoyment of their own laws could not have been guaranteed to them without freeing them from the ignorant and corrupt local administration of justice, a privilege which of course no foreign power could otherwise obtain for its subjects than by treaty. But the legal principles in question are presupposed in the capitulations which have been made between Turkey and the Christian governments, for these merely give to the latter certain rights of jurisdiction over their subjects, but express nothing as to the laws by which the jurisdictions so created shall proceed. Thus when a British ambassador or consul hears a cause between Englishmen in Turkey, he applies the English law to the case, because it is common to the parties as persons without reference to place, and not from any Turkish declaration or enactment respecting the law which shall bind foreigners on Turkish soil. In the same manner, after the cession of Gibraltar to Great Britain, but before British courts were established there, the Spaniards, French, Genoese, and Dutch had each their own consuls in the town, who, there being no regular Spanish tribunal in it, determined the differences between the members of their respective nations, and, doubtless, according to their respective laws (*r*).

(*r*) Chalmers's Opinions, edit. 1858, p. 186. Had there been a Spanish court at Gibraltar, it would have continued to administer justice by Spanish law till the conquerors changed the law.

152. Another example is furnished by the settlement of British subjects in a newly discovered country, where principle alone can decide what law is to be followed, during the silence of the sovereign who may enact it. It has been determined by the privy council on appeal from a colony, "that if there be a new and uninhabited country found out by English subjects, as the law is the birthright of every subject, so wherever they go they carry their laws with them, and therefore such new-found country is to be governed by the laws of England; though, after such country is inhabited by the English, acts of parliament made in England without naming the foreign plantations will not bind them (*s*)." Upon this Blackstone remarks that "such colonists carry with them only so much of the English law as is applicable to their own situation and the condition of an infant colony, such, for instance, as the general rules of inheritance and of protection from personal injuries. The artificial refinements and distinctions incident to the property of a great and commercial people, the laws of police and revenue (such especially as are enforced by penalties), the mode of maintenance for the established clergy, the jurisdiction of spiritual courts, and a multitude of other provisions, are neither necessary nor convenient for them, and therefore are not in force. What shall be admitted and what rejected, at what times and under what restrictions, must in case of dispute be decided in the first instance by their own provincial judicature, subject to the revision and

(*s*) *Anon.*, 2 P. W. 75. See also *Blankard* v. *Galdy*, Sal. 411. And even acts passed by the British parliament after the settlement, and neither including the particular plantation nor the plantations in general, might be, and sometimes were, tacitly adopted by the colonists, notwithstanding the existence and activity of a colonial legislature, of which acceptance usage was evidence: opinions of P. Yorke, Att.-Gen. (Lord Hardwicke), alone (1729), and with C. Wearg, Sol.-Gen. (in 1724); Chalmers's Opinions, edit. 1858, pp. 208, 229.

control of the king in council (*t*)." And this is in substance true, but the distinction is not that vague one between what is more or less artificial, nor is it a mere discretion which the colonial judicature exercises. The settlers take with them all those laws which concern private rights between man and man, and the colonial tribunals must enforce them; for such laws were common to the parties as fellow-citizens in their homes, and they are presumed to have that common opinion of their equity which in the absence of enactment, and since some such laws are necessary, is both a sufficient, and the only possible, ground for their obligation: and this it is which is meant when these laws are said to accompany Englishmen as their birthright. They do not take with them the public department of law, even so far as its contents may affect property, because that department finds its expression in institutions such as those mentioned by Blackstone of revenue, police, and an established church, which from the nature of the case cannot exist in any society where they have not been instituted. It cannot even be asserted as a universal proposition, that they take with them those laws which lay down the definition and punishment of crime (*u*). Nor again into a colony founded as here supposed can those laws be tacitly carried which, like those of bankruptcy, though essentially private, belong to the *justitia attributrix* and not to that *expletrix*, that is, dispose of interests, and not simply do right between party and party on the ground of property or obligation (*x*). Nor those which affect private rights from no motive of private

(*t*) Comm. v. 1, p. 108.

(*u*) Opinion of R. Henley (Lord Northington) and C. Yorke, Attorney and Solicitor General, in 1757: Chalmers's Opinions, edit. 1858, p. 209.

(*x*) It is matter of notoriety that a simple charter of justice does not introduce the bankrupt laws into a colony, and supplemental charters have been granted to remedy the defect.

justice, but from a reference to supposed public benefit, as in the case of the statute of charitable uses. For the community formed by the settlers does not in any manner continue or represent the person of the mother-country, so that, even were the circumstances the same, the same views of public policy should be attributed to it, in a way analogous to that in which the settlers continue the chain of the legal principles which are applicable to them as individuals. A leading case on this is that in which Sir W. Grant decided that the statutes of mortmain did not extend to the conquered island of Grenada, though passed previous to the conquest, and though the English law generally had been introduced into the island (*y*). The case of a conquered colony differs from that of a settled one, and turns upon the intention of the authority which introduced the English law, an intention which in the particular case, judging from the grounds of policy on which the English statute was based, Sir W. Grant held could not have extended to the introduction of that statute into the island. In a settled colony, it is only a question of what laws the people going there are subject to, not of the implied introduction by authority of any laws beyond those. But Sir W. Grant intimated that the decision would have been the same had Grenada been a settlement (*z*), and so the case is taken by Lord Brougham (*a*).

153. The establishment of the British in India presented originally a case similar to that of European merchants resident in factories in the Levant, and, as the latter have always been governed by their own laws and not by the Turkish, so the former were from the first regulated by the English laws, since there never could be a

---

(*y*) *Att.-Gen.* v. *Stewart*, 2 Mer. 143.

(*z*) *Ib.* p. 159.

(*a*) In *Mayor of Lyons* v. *East India Company*, 1 Moore, P. C. 273, 1 Moore, I. A. C. 271.

thought of applying to them either the Mahometan or the Gentoo jurisprudence which they found in the country. But afterwards, and indeed long since, although a titular sovereign reigned till lately at Delhi, and no official change was made in those relations which the Company once had with him as the delegated administrators of certain of his provinces, yet it became the established doctrine of our lawyers that the British crown enjoyed the sovereignty of the soil in what was even then called British India. No exact account can be given of the mode in which, or even of the time when, this view began to be adopted: it appears to have resulted from a silent accommodation of theory to fact (*b*). It had certainly not been adopted in 1773, when the act was passed which empowered the king to erect the Supreme Court at Calcutta, for the preamble of the thirteenth section recites that sufficient provision had not been made for the administration of justice in such manner as the state of the Company's presidency at Fort William in Bengal would require, *so long as the Company should continue in possession thereof* (*c*). The erection of the Supreme Court was therefore not an act of territorial sovereignty, still less the yet earlier erection of the mayors' courts at Calcutta and Madras (*d*); and in their first administration of English law to British subjects in India, these tribunals must accordingly have proceeded on the same principles which have been already pointed out as governing the case of the Levant factories. I will therefore quote the provisions of the statute passed under this earlier state of things for the guidance of the Supreme Court of Calcutta, as being a legislative acknowledgment of the natural obligation of laws as between persons,

(*b*) Lord Brougham, in 1 Mo. P. C. 275, 1 Mo. I. A. C. 274.

(*c*) St. 13 Geo. 3, c. 63.

(*d*) Bombay was British territory, acquired from Portugal on the occasion of Charles II.'s marriage with Catherine of Braganza.

when unaffected by the sovereignty of the soil. "The inheritance and succession to lands, rents and goods, and all matters of contract and dealing between party and party, shall be determined in the case of Mahomedans by the laws and usages of Mahomedans, and in the case of Gentûs by the laws and usages of Gentûs; and, where only one of the parties shall be a Mahomedan or Gentû, by the laws and usages of the defendant: and in order that regard may be had to the civil and religious usages of the natives, the rights and authorities of fathers of families and masters of families, according as the same might have been exercised by the Gentû or Mahomedan law, shall be preserved to them respectively within their families; nor shall any acts done in consequence of the rule and law of caste respecting the members of the said families only be held and adjudged a crime, although the same may not be held justifiable by the laws of England (*e*)." If we examine the details thus enumerated, the matters of contract and dealing between persons belonging both to the same law, and the authority of heads of families, fall clearly under the principle of the law common to the parties. The rule propounded on matters of contract and dealing between persons whose laws are different appertains to the principle of the law of the defendant, as that which his conscience at least cannot refuse, and to which the plaintiff submits himself by dealing with him and in-

(*e*) St. 21 Geo. 3, c. 70, ss. 17, 18. Thus the supreme court of Bombay cannot enforce restitution of conjugal rights between Parsees: *Ardaseer Cursetjee* v. *Perozeboye*, 6 Moore, Indian Appeal Cases, 348. On the same principles, the English law had been recognised as the measure of right between the English in India by the charter of 1661, which empowered the old company to judge by it persons belonging to or living under them in their factories; the charter of 1683 had empowered the same company to erect judicatures which should proceed by the law merchant and equity: East India Company's Charters, pp. 75, 121. And so it was decided that British subjects carried their law of marriage with them to Madras: *Lautour* v. *Teesdale*, 8 Taun. 830.

stituting the suit. And a passage is made from the one doctrine to the other by the rule of inheritance and succession, which may be either regarded as founded in the deceased's individual identification with his own law, in regard to the disposition of his property which he would desire, or in the circumstance that that would in the great majority of cases be the common law of the claimants.

154. Another point here essential to observe is, that in this stage of our occupation of India, in which all laws were personal and none founded in the sovereignty of the soil, there could be no territorial law of inheritance affecting the land as land. And accordingly the British in India were free to apply to the lands owned by them either the modes of transfer and rules of succession which prevail in England for realty, or those which we here use for personalty, either being equally personal to themselves, and, from our strange subdivision of the subjects of property, equally personal to them in respect of immovables. This freedom of choice was originally exercised by regarding land as a chattel, and as passed by instruments used for the conveyance of chattels, a view which is said to be still held at Madras (*f*); and although in Bengal the lands of British proprietors came early to be treated as inheritable in the manner of an English fee-simple, yet the English conveyance by lease and release, and the exclusive devise of such lands by a will executed in accordance with the English statute of frauds, though both adopted in Bengal, are expressly held not to have been necessary consequences of the mode of inheritance (*g*). And if we regard all that was done with respect to land, whether at

---

(*f*) 1 Moore, P. C. 247, 1 Moore, I. A. C. 246.

(*g*) *Gardiner* v. *Fell*, 1 Jac. & Wal. 22; and Lord Brougham in 1 Mo. P. C. 249, 1 Mo. I. A. C. 248.

Madras or in Bengal, not as the selection by the British from among laws which had been personal to them at home, but as the establishment of new laws personal to them there, as the members of a distinct community, including other Europeans besides British subjects, in the same mode in which the common law of England itself was formed, we shall have in these facts a yet stronger instance of the way in which laws may become obligatory among a people without the aid of any sovereignty, other than that which in virtue of its common convictions the mass exercises over individuals.

155. When however it came to be held that the British monarch is sovereign of the soil of Bengal, by a change unaccompanied by any express introduction of the English law, the case of the British in India became less analogous to that of the Levant factories than to that of settlers in a new country taken possession of for the British crown: to a colony obtained by conquest there could be no resemblance, since that retains its own laws, with their territorial validity, until they are altered by the conquering power. It was accordingly of importance to ascertain whether this caused any change in the laws concerning land, and that it did not do so was decided in *The Mayor of Lyons* v. *The East India Company* (*h*), as well by the point there directly ruled, that the incapacity of aliens to hold English land does not extend to our Indian possessions, as by the interpretation there given to *Gardiner* v. *Fell* (*i*), by which it appears that not even the necessary conformity of a will of land in Bengal to the then English form would have resulted from our acquisition of the sovereignty of the soil. There can be no doubt that all this was correct in principle, since it is not by the mere fact

(*h*) 1 Moore, P. C. 175, 1 Moore, I. A. C. 175.

(*i*) 1 Jac. & Wal. 22.

that two countries have a common sovereign that the laws of one concerning immovables are introduced into the other. It is only through the legislative power which it confers that the sovereignty of a country can be made to affect its laws; and there had been no British legislation as to the law to be observed in India, besides that which I have already cited from the statute of the 21st of George the Third. Here therefore is the true distinction which, notwithstanding some analogy, exists between British India and a colony formed by settlement. The European and native communities in the former already possessed common laws, concerning land as well as other things, previous to the establishment of our sovereignty, which therefore could not change them by any tacit operation. The colonists in the latter bring with them the English law, as "their birthright" our lawyers call it, to a virgin soil, but to which the territorial character of laws recognized by all old and advanced countries is immediately assumed to apply, so that on that soil the law which is personal to its sovereigns becomes at once territorial. Thus the then English laws on the inheritance and transfer of real estate, as well as those of contract, would become territorial now in a newly occupied South Sea island, as they formerly did in our American plantations.

156. The principles of this section are however of rare application in Christian and settled states, for in these the views of law on which they rest may be sunk without inconvenience in the conception of private rights as created by a territorial authority external to the conscience of the persons whom it binds. The latter conception indeed can only become the basis of a system of private international jurisprudence, on the supposition that none of the territorial laws which it considers differs so widely from the others of them, as to shock the conscience of any of the

nations to whose members the system may cause it to be applied. In other words, the extraterritorial acceptance of rights founded on territorial laws can only exist as between countries which resemble each other in the leading characters of their civilization, and none of which departs in any considerable degree from the average standard of those characters. We could not, for instance, recognize polygamy in Christian Europe or America, on the ground that the plural marriages were contracted in Turkey and by Turks. In this manner, the principle of the law of the parties marks as it were the limits of this department of legal science. It is when the conditions fail for applying its ordinary rules, from a contact with places where no law has yet been enacted, or with populations not within the jural community it supposes, that this principle, suppressed in general, emerges to supply the defect with all the force which it possessed in the infancy of law. The following cases however still mark its occasional employment even in Christendom (*k*).

157. While the general law of this country provided but one ceremonial of marriage, and that of a Christian character, the validity of marriages celebrated in England between British Jews was nevertheless tried by their own ritual observances (*l*). The marriage of English-born subjects, apparently also domiciled in England, celebrated at the Cape of Good Hope soon after its conquest from the Dutch, was held valid by English law, the conflict between that and the Dutch law being on the age at which the consent of parents or guardians would cease to be necessary (*m*): the *lex loci contractus* being in the same case asserted, in oppo-

(*k*) The law of the defendant was the rule, in the system of personal laws which arose among the barbarians on the soil of the Roman empire.

(*l*) *Lindo* v. *Belisario*, 1 Hagg. Cons. 216.

(*m*) *Ruding* v. *Smith*, 2 Hagg. Cons. 371.

sition to the *lex domicilii*, as the true rule for such a conflict (*n*), and the decision being grounded on the presumption that, the conquerors not having up to the date of the marriage sanctioned the continuance of the Dutch law otherwise than by the capitulation in favour of the conquered, they could not mean it to be of force between themselves. British troops in hostile occupation of a foreign country, as also the British who accompany them, carry their law of marriage with them (*o*): and Lord Stowell thought it probable that they would do so also if in friendly occupation of a foreign country (*p*). The privilege of marrying in an ambassador's chapel by the laws of his nation does not rest on the fiction of local extraterritoriality alone, but requires that at least one of the parties shall be of that nation (*q*). Hither also must be referred the dicta occurring in several cases of contest between the assignees of an English bankrupt and his English creditors who had obtained possession of his property by the judgments of foreign courts, from which it would appear that, on account of the common subjection of such parties to the law of this country, the assignees can sometimes in those cases recover under circumstances which might not give them a right against foreign creditors (*r*). Similar questions have also been raised on the right of fellow-citizens to arrest each other, or seize each other's goods, in civil suits

---

(*n*) *Ruding* v. *Smith*, 2 Hagg. Cons. pp. 390—392. Such was the avowed view of the court: at the same time, the intimation, in p. 389, that the decision might have been the same on the marriage in Holland of English persons not domiciled there, shows how much Lord Stowell was inclining towards the *lex domicilii* as the rule; a maxim which, in some of the reasons for it, is closely allied to the principle of the law common to the parties.

(*o*) *King* v. *Inhabitants of Brampton*, 10 East, 282.

(*p*) *Burn* v. *Farrar*, 2 Hagg. Cons. 369.

(*q*) *Pertreis* v. *Tondear*, 1 Hagg. Cons. 136.

(*r*) *Hunter* v. *Potts*, 4 T. R. 182, 194; *Sill* v. *Worswick*, 1 H. Bl. 665, 693; *Philips* v. *Hunter*, 2 H. Bl. 402, 406. These cases will be more particularly considered in their proper place.

abroad, if unable to do so at home, which is denied by Peckius (*s*), but asserted by John Voet (*t*): and on the operation of statutes of limitation on claims mooted between parties who were both subject to those statutes during the whole term of prescription (*u*).

158. On the other hand, it has been decided that the British law cannot be invoked in cases of collision between British and foreign ships on the high seas, not only by the owners of the former as promoters of the suit (*x*), but not even against them as filling the character of defendants (*y*). Nor again, with regard to acts committed on the high seas, can the defendant invoke the protection of his own law (*z*). But there is in these cases the peculiarity that a general law maritime exists, to which the municipal law of any country is regarded as only introducing exceptions; so that, if such municipal law be not common to the parties, in which case it would certainly apply though the tort was committed beyond the territory, it is natural to fall back on the general rule rather than to appeal to the principle of the law of the defendant. It does not follow that that principle would be inoperative in torts committed beyond the empire of any geographical law, maritime or other, though Story says of this case, as well as of that

---

(*s*) De Jure Sistendi, c. 8.

(*t*) Ad Pand. l. 2, t. 4, n. 45. And this is the English doctrine: *De la Vega* v. *Vianna*, 1 Ba. & Ad. 284. But J. Voet admits that the plaintiff would make himself liable in damages at home.

(*u*) Story, s. 582, 582 b. An important topic, to which we shall have to return: see *Huber* v. *Steiner*, 4 M. & Sc. 328.

(*x*) *The Zollverein*, Swabey, 96. In the case of *The Girolamo*, 3 Hagg. Adm. 169, the collision took place in a river within British territory.

(*y*) *The Dumfries*, Swabey, 63, 125.

(*z*) *The Nostra Signora de los Dolores*, 1 Dodson, 290. This is not inconsistent with *General Steam Navigation Co.* v. *Guillon*, 11 Mee. & Wel. 877, for there the defendant was not protected by the French law as owner, but was shown by the French law not to be owner; but it is inconsistent with the dicta in *The Vernon*, 1 W. Rob. 316.

of maritime torts, which he does not distinguish from it, that "in cases of torts, committed on the high seas and in other extraterritorial places, by the subjects of one nation upon vessels or other movable property belonging to the subjects of another nation, ... the most that can with any probability be stated is that, in the absence of any general doctrine to the contrary, either each nation would, in respect to the case when pending in its own tribunals, follow its own laws; or would apply the rule of reciprocity, granting or refusing damages according as the law of the foreign country, to which the injured ship belonged, would grant or withhold them in the case of an injured ship belonging to the other nation. The rule of reciprocity is often applied in cases of the recapture of ships from the hands of a public enemy" (*a*).

3. *Various Modern Theories.*

159. "Grotius," I have said elsewhere, "rested his international theory on the position that rights originate in the law natural, and are anterior to political society; that states are formed by individuals relinquishing portions of these rights, and that from the sovereignty so created flows in its turn the institution of positive law. But then, since it could not be said that individuals ever relinquished rights except mutually, each in favour of his fellow-citizens, it seemed to follow that private rights against the members of foreign societies depend still on the law of nature, precisely as those of independent governments, between which positive law has no place. The generality however of this conclusion was restrained by the territorial character of political society. In certain modes pointed out by the law of nature, nations have acquired *dominium*

(*a*) Sect. 423 h.

and *imperium*, the property in and the rule over the tracts of land they occupy; whence it is *natural* (*b*) that within those tracts their respective laws should be observed. Nay, more; it is not natural that any others should be there observed. For the law of nature does not enjoin, but permits, what are called the natural modes of acquiring property, so that they may be abrogated by the positive laws enacted in virtue of territorial *imperium* (*c*); and that men have designed so to abrogate them appears from the fact of their disuse. The Roman jurists indeed and their modern copyists enumerate some natural modes of acquisition as still in force between individuals, but they are not really such. They have been introduced by custom, and, simple as they are, the truly natural modes are simpler still (*d*). Wherever therefore civil government exists, men do, both by right and in fact, contract with reference and in subjection to the positive law of the place of contract; and every jural question which can arise out of their contract, including expressly the capacity of parties, must be decided by that law. Only in places yet unoccupied, as at sea, or in newly discovered countries, or when two persons who happen at the moment to be in different territories contract by letter, can their dealings be now regulated by the law of nature; but in those cases they are still governed by that law alone" (*e*).

160. It was impossible that this system could become practical, not only because, even in the cases which it submits to positive law, it dismisses all considerations of national character, domicile, place of execution of contract, and situation of thing dealt with, each of which is often

---

(*b*) Grotius, de Jure Belli ac Pacis, l. 2, c. 11, s. 5.

(*c*) Ibid. l. 2, c. 3, s. 5.

(*d*) Ibid. l. 2, c. 8.

(*e*) Ibid. l. 2, c. 11, s. 5. Papers read before Juridical Society, 1855-8, p. 174.

made, by a common jural sense of mankind, to override that single point of the actual place of contracting to which exclusive weight is attributed by Grotius; but also because it resigns to the sway of a vague law natural, which can amount in practice to little else than the judge's private opinion of what is equitable, those innumerable transactions of commerce in which all the parties do not happen to be at the critical moment within the same jurisdiction. Indeed we have here the result of the territorial theory—the local authority, which arises even from temporary subjection, imposing a duty on the party who obliges himself—crudely combined with a sense of the contract as something common to the parties who deal with one another, so as to deny such operation of the local authority where both parties are not subject to it by bodily presence. We have seen how Huber attempted to complete this system as it were from the outside, by adding the doctrine of comity; an attempt which could only lead to perpetuating the old war of real and personal statutes, because comity might be a reason for receiving any rules on this subject, but could hardly point out which to receive. But in more recent times the internal method of completing the system has again been entered on, namely, by trying whether the principle of the territorial character of positive law cannot be made to yield some more satisfactory results than Grotius drew from it. The most remarkable of these efforts is Savigny's, which refers the question of capacity to act to the law of the domicile, as the territorial law of the person, without farther explanation of the reason; and, where the capacity to act is granted, seeks for each case a law which shall not only be common to the parties with reference to the subject, but shall also be so common to them in its character of a territorial law; so that while the separate subjection of each party to the law under which he obliges himself is left very much out of sight (*f*), great subtlety is displayed in extending the other Grotian element, the subjection of both parties to the same law *qua* territorial law, beyond the case in which alone Grotius perceived it, that of their both acting within its geographical limits.

161. The foundation then of Savigny's system is the conception of a jural relation (rechtsverhältniss), comprising all the circumstances and events which have to be considered in the determination of the case. Thus, to give his own example: "two brothers are subject to the *patria potestas;* one makes a loan to the other; the borrower repays it after the father's death, and the question is whether he can recover the sum so repaid as repaid in error. The several elements of the jural relation were, the *patria potestas* over both brothers, a loan by one to the other, a *peculium* which the debtor had received from the father. This combined jural relation has farther developed itself through the father's death, the succession to his estate, the repayment of the loan" (*g*). Next, "every jural relation which comes before us for judgment necessarily has its origin in juristic facts, which must always be thought of as having taken place in past time, more or less remote. Then, since changes in positive law can enter during the interval since the origin of the jural relation, we have besides to determine from what point of time the rule which governs the jural relation must be taken" (*h*). For all jural relations are governed by rules of law, which again belong to juristic institutions: as "the institutions brought into play in the example just given are, the father's acquisition through his children, the old

---

(*f*) Not totally, as he admits it, both in principle and practice, when a foreigner is sued in the *locus delicti* on the obligation arising from the tort. See also note (*i*), page 151.

(*g*) Syst. d. heut. Röm. Rechts, v. 1, p. 8.

(*h*) Ibid. v. 8, p. 4.

peculium and particularly the *deductio* into it, the passing over of the deceased's rights of action to the heirs, the confusion of rights and liabilities by their meeting in the heirs, the *condictio indebiti* (action to recover money unduly paid). To simplify our conceptions, a natural distinction lies in this, that we can first construe the juristic institutions separately from each other, and then combine them at our will, while on the contrary the jural relation is given by the occurrences of life, and so appears immediately in its concrete combination and complication. But on farther consideration we recognise that all juristic institutions exist in connexion with a system, and that they can be fully comprehended only in the whole co-ordination of that system" (*i*).

162. Now the rules of law which govern jural relations are subject to changes of two kinds; in time, when the positive law of any country is altered, and in place, when the relations in their development come into connexion with countries having different positive laws (*j*). But from the remarks just cited it is plain that, notwithstanding such changes, Savigny can only regard the relation and the in-

---

(*i*) Syst. d. heut. Röm. Rechts, v. 1, p. 10. At the same time, Savigny admits that the most natural and earliest view of bilateral obligations is to consider separately the obligations of the two parties, determining from his own person the law and jurisdiction to which each is subject as defendant, the unity of the jural relation being a scientific invention to meet complicated cases; and he quotes in proof of this the very common Roman habit of concluding a contract of sale by two separate stipulations, for the delivery of the article and for the payment of the price: ib. v. 8, p. 202. Now this admits the separate subjection of one party, independently of that of the other, quite as much as though it were of the *lex loci celebrati contractus* it was asserted, and not merely of the *lex domicilii.*

(*j*) This connexion of private international jurisprudence with the jurisprudence relating to a change of municipal law, which Savigny has pointedly brought out and formalised, had however been for some time previous clearly apprehended on the continent, in consequence of the importance of the "transitory questions" which arose whenever a code was substituted for an older legal system.

stitutions bearing on it as wholes; whence arises his principle, "that in the case of each jural relation that law must be sought, to the empire of which the relation belongs or is subject according to its peculiar nature." This principle is applicable to both descriptions of change, and when applied to change in place, the empire in question may be farther defined as "that in which the relation has its seat" (*k*). I have detailed this at greater length than may appear necessary to the English reader, for the sake of fairness, having already expressed my dissent from the view of law as governing cases instead of expressing commands to persons; in order to give, as nearly as possible in the words of the original, a philosophy which is similar to the old theory of mixed statutes and *locus regit actum*, differing perhaps only in this, that it undertakes to give an account also of what was referred to the reality of statutes.

163. The application of Savigny's principle rests on a very wide, but not unlimited, admission of the will of the parties as decisive; which will may be expressed by a tacit submission, as in cases of contract to the law of the place of fulfilment, and in the acquisition of immovable property to that of its situation (*l*). In the former case, this conclusion is referred to an expectation of the parties that their rights will be decided by that law, similar to the expectation on which the same place is based as the special forum of the obligation. With Savigny, these two expectations are co-ordinate (*m*), for he rejects the doctrine that each court should *prima facie* apply its own law (*n*), and therefore sees no other ground for the choice of a law

(*k*) Syst. &c. v. 8, pp. 28, 108.
(*l*) Ibid. p. 110.
(*m*) Ibid. pp. 203, 204.
(*n*) Ibid. p. 126 *et seq.*

than in the expectation directed thereto. In the older view, the expectation as to jurisdiction is the fundamental one, that as to law being deduced from it on the maxim that each court will *prima facie* apply its own law; so that, where the *forum contractus* was not received, the *lex loci contractus* was but weakly held (*o*). Upon either view, no difficulty could arise from the plaintiff's choice of the jurisdiction, for he could not be allowed to choose the law, and, in respect of law, the special forum was pointed out as the only one to which the intention was directed in the special matter, that of the defendant's domicile being merely a general forum. And either way again, the disputes between the so called forums *celebrati contractus* and *solutionis*, noticed in Art. 110, must affect to at least the same extent the law of the contract, to which, for Savigny, and most of those who agree with him in preferring the latter forum, the five rules of jurisdiction given in Art. 105 are at once applicable.

164. But a third opinion, arising out of the disputes last mentioned, must not remain unnoticed, namely, that the *lex loci celebrati contractus* must govern, notwithstanding that the true forum is that *solutionis*. This rests on a correct interpretation of the Roman texts referred to in Art. 110, combined with an incorrect one of the famous law: *si fundus venierit, ex consuetudine ejus regionis in qua negotium gestum est pro evictione caveri oportet* (*p*). It is however clear that the place of sale is only here intended

(*o*) Arts. 56 and 111, above. *Aut*, says Dumoulin, *statutum loquitur de his quæ meritum scilicet causæ vel decisionem concernunt, et tunc aut in his quæ pendent a voluntate partium vel per eas immutari possunt, et tunc inspiciuntur circumstantiæ voluntatis, quarum una est statutum loci in quo contrahitur, et domicilii contrahentium antiqui vel recentis, et similes circumstantiæ—aut, &c.*: t. 3, p. 554.

(*p*) Dig. 21, 2, 6. See above, Art. 111. A precisely similar interpretation must be given to the equally famous passage *id sequamur quod in regione in qua actum est frequentatur*: Dig. 50, 17, 34.

under the supposition that that place was either, as Dumoulin argued, the domicile of the parties, or else, as may seem probable, the situs of the land, or again, which is the most probable supposition of all, that all those three places coincided. The law in question does not treat of the conflict between these, but asserts local customs generally, as interpreters of contracts within their proper spheres, in opposition to an exclusive reference to the common law.

165. To me the whole matter appears in the following light. We must always look at the time when the duty correlative to every right arose, and to the territorial law to which at that time the party on whom the duty is imposed was subject. Then the principle applies that *rights which have once well accrued by the appropriate law are*, by comity, if you please, though it is a comity almost demanded by a sentiment of justice, *treated as valid everywhere.* This has been carried out in Chap. IV. as to immovables, in which discussion corporeal chattels might have been throughout included, if the theory were not in their case relaxed for convenience. For obligations, the law which imposes the duty on each party is that to which he was territorially subject at the time of becoming obliged, that is, the *lex loci actus*, or *celebrati contractus.* But it does not follow from this that every question which can arise even on express contracts must be determined by the law under which they were entered into, not only because the reason of the case may cause that law in some particulars to adopt another one, but also because many duties arise from the combination of the contract with facts committed or omitted subsequent to its inception, which facts, by the same principle, must operate according to the law under which the party stood when he committed or omitted them. Before however entering into the particulars, I will collect some of the chief authorities for the much disputed general proposition that the obliga-

tion arises by the law of the place of contracting, and not by that of fulfilment.

166. First, then, it will be interesting to the reader to have the words of Bartolus, because they have been classical for five centuries, and open the way to a consideration of the details (*q*). *Et primo quæro quid de contractibus. Pone contractum celebratum per aliquem forensem in hac civitate: litigium ortum est, et agitatur lis in loco originis contrahentis: cujus loci statuta debent servari vel spectari? Distingue: aut loquimur de statuto aut de consuetudine quæ respiciunt ipsius contractus solemnitatem aut litis ordinationem, aut de his quæ pertinent ad jurisdictionem ex ipso contractu evenientis executionis. Primo casu inspicitur locus contractus. Secundo casu aut quæris de his quæ pertinent ad litis ordinationem, et inspicitur locus judicii: aut de his quæ pertinent ad ipsius litis decisionem, et tunc aut de his quæ oriuntur secundum ipsius contractus naturam tempore contractus, aut de his quæ oriuntur ex post facto propter negligentiam vel moram. Primo casu inspicitur locus contractus: et intelligo locum contractus, ubi est celebratus contractus, non de loco in quem collata est solutio. Secundo casu, aut solutio est collata in locum certum; aut in pluribus locis alternative, ita quod electio sit actoris; aut in nullum locum, quia promissio fuit facta simpliciter. Primo casu inspicitur consuetudo quæ est in illo loco in quem est collata solutio: secundo et tertio casu inspicitur locus ubi petitur. Ratio prædictorum est quia ibi est contracta negligentia seu mora.* Among the examples of these principles, Bartolus gives the following. *Aut quis vult petere restitutionem ex læsione contingente in ipso contractu tempore contractus, et inspicimus locum contractus: aut ex læsione contingente post contractum ex aliis negligentiis, ut mora, et inspicimus locum ubi est illa mora contracta, ut ex prædictis apparet, et sic si*

(*q*) They occur in his commentary on the Cod. 1, 1, 1.

esset in loco judicii inspicimus locum judicii. For the sake of clearness, I have omitted the citations from the *Corpus Juris* which Bartolus interweaves as authorities with his own sentences: but the reader will recollect that it is as much on them, as on their own intrinsic reasonableness, that the latter are meant to repose. Most of the citations relate to the choice of a forum, and have been already given in that connexion. Others of them merely declare that the price of goods sold without a price being named should be that of the place of delivery, or, if no place of delivery be stipulated, that which rules where the action is brought: a question purely internal to any body of law, and not one of the conflict of laws at all.

167. In this passage Bartolus enunciates the following principles: that *litis ordinatio*, the mode of procedure, depends on the law of the forum: that the solemnities necessary to contracts, and the obligations which result at the time of contracting from the nature of the contract itself, depend on the law of the place of celebration: that those which result from the combination of a posterior fact with the original contract depend on the law of that place where the posterior fact occurs: that the nonperformance of the contract by the omission or delay of one of the parties is to be regarded as such a posterior fact, and its juridical consequences deduced accordingly: that if the parties stipulate for the performance of their contract at a certain place, it is by the law of that place, as that where the omission to perform is committed, that the obligations flowing from nonperformance must be ascertained: and that if they name no place of performance, or stipulate for several in the alternative, so as to leave the choice to the promisee, the obligations flowing from nonperformance must be ascertained by the law of the forum, whether the promisor's domicile, or any one of the stipulated places of performance, have been chosen as the forum by the plaintiff.

168. Again, *qui in loco aliquo contrahit,* says Grotius, *tanquam subditus temporarius legibus loci subjicitur* (*r*). Of the three maxims of Huber cited in Art. 144, the two first are to a precisely similar effect; and from them Huber deduces the following rule: *Cuncta negotia et acta, tam in judicio quam extra judicium, seu mortis causa sive inter vivos, secundum jus certi loci rite celebrata, valent etiam ubi diversa juris observatio viget, ac ubi sic inita quemadmodum facta sunt non valerent. E contra, negotia et acta certo loco contra leges ejus loci celebrata, cum sint ab initio invalida, nusquam valere possunt; idque non modo respectu hominum qui in loco contractus habent domicilium, sed et illorum qui ad tempus ibidem commorantur.* He then subjoins his exception, *si rectores alterius populi exinde notabili incommodo afficerentur;* and, after an example or two of the rule, adds *idque non tantum de forma sed etiam de materia contractus affirmandum est.* Similarly it is said by Hertius: *Ratione actuum subjiciuntur cujusque generis personæ, etiam advenæ sive exteri, vel transeuntes vel negotiorum suorum causa ad tempus in civitate commorantes, quatenus nimirum ibi agunt, v. g. contrahunt vel delinquunt* (*s*).

169. Lastly, the mention of "a contract made within the jurisdiction," though only for founding the *forum contractus,* in st. 15 & 16 Vict. c. 76, s. 18, leads to the conclusion that for such contracts our law also should prevail, according to the intimate connexion between law and jurisdiction in such cases, noticed above in Art. 163. The Austrian code expressly chooses the *locus celebrati contractus* as that of which the law shall govern, except the parties have demonstrably looked to another (*t*).

170. The detailed application of these principles to the international law of obligations must be reserved for the

(*r*) L. 2, c. 11, s. 5.

(*s*) De Coll. Leg., s. 4, § 4.

(*t*) Sects. 36, 37.

next chapter. Only here the general subject of the international force of private law must be completed by observing that the laws which prescribe the modes of judicial procedure are commands addressed, not to the party, but to the judge; whence it follows that the latter is bound by those of the sovereign from whom he holds his commission, and that no circumstances can found for the parties a right to have the procedure determined by any other rule than the *lex fori*. This principle is that of the *litis ordinatio* in the citation from Bartolus, and has been universally received; though, as we shall see, great difficulty often arises in its application, in deciding whether a particular question belongs to the nature of the right or the method of the remedy.

CHAPTER VII.

INTERNATIONAL LAW OF OBLIGATIONS.

1. *Formal Requisites of Obligations.*

171. *The formal requisites demanded for a contract by the law of the place where it is made are sufficient for its validity everywhere.*

For the law of that place imposes a duty on the party who obliges himself, the right correlative to which will thenceforth be respected and aided, even where the same facts would not have caused it to arise.

I am not aware that this rule has been impugned (*a*), for even those who hold the law of the place of fulfilment to be the general one on obligations do not press its exclusive adoption for their solemnities, on the ground of their maxim *locus regit actum:* indeed, the extreme inconvenience of an opposite course is obvious. The English cases commonly cited in support of the rule are those on marriage, which, however, have no reference to the special

(*a*) The Prussian code establishes the rule *locus regit actum* in general, I. 5, s. 111; but with the exception that "in all cases where immovables, their property, possession or use, are the subject of a contract, the law of the situation of the thing must be observed:" I. 5, s. 115. See my remarks to a similar effect in Arts. 98, 99.

subject of obligation, and would prove too much if alleged for the maxim just mentioned, which our doctrines on the form of acts relating to immovables, as well as some others, show not to be generally received in England.

172. But a difficulty arises in carrying out the rule, when the *lex fori* demands evidence which by the *lex loci contractus* is unnecessary, or rejects evidence which by the latter is admitted. As the *lex fori* is an imperative direction to the judge in questions of procedure, one opinion, and I think the better, is, that while he recognises the possibility that the right may have been sufficiently created by the law of the place of contract, he must yet declare that the fact of its creation has not been so proved to him that he can enforce it. Another opinion is that of Boullenois, who deemed the mode of proof, as whether by oral or written testimony, to be a part of the *vinculum obligationis*, and therefore to depend on the law of the place of contract (*b*). Savigny's view appears to be intermediate. "The authority of merchants' books as evidence," says he, "must be decided by the law of the place where they are kept . . . . . . it is indissolubly bound up with the form and effect of the transaction itself, which here must be regarded as the predominating consideration. The stranger who intermixes himself with the merchant of a place where such books are evidence subjects himself to its local law" (*c*). The same reasoning would clearly apply to all rejection of evidence by the *lex fori* in the interest of the defendant, as in pursuance of the principle that no one can be a witness in his own cause: but Savigny so earnestly enforces everywhere the necessity that each tribunal shall respect those of its municipal laws which have a moral

(*b*) Traité des Loix, t. 2, p. 459.

(*c*) Syst. d. heut. Röm. Rechts, v. 8, p. 355. And so, he says, it has been decided at Cassel.

ground, that he would doubtless refuse oral evidence where the *lex fori* demands written for the express purpose of preventing perjury. We may therefore suppose that he would have agreed with *Leroux* v. *Brown* (*d*), where the fourth section of the statute of frauds prevented the enforcement in England of an agreement which had been sufficiently solemnized by the *lex loci contractus*. Only as that case was put on the broad distinction between rules of procedure and others, without reference to the motives of the former, we may suppose it to adopt the first of the above three opinions. And besides that a law of procedure, however motived, is imperative on the judge, the fear of perjury lies so much at the root of all rules of evidence that it must be very difficult ever to disprove their moral end. In *Leroux* v. *Brown* the court appears also to have thought that the seventeenth section of the statute of frauds, as not being a rule of procedure, would not apply to foreign transactions.

173. *The formal requisites demanded for a contract by the law of the place where it is made are necessary for its validity everywhere.*

For if that law impose no duty, the *lex fori*, in the attempt to do so, would bear the same relation to the foregone fact on which alone it could operate, that a new statute bears, in the ordinary change of municipal jurisprudence, to the events which have taken place before its enactment. Also, if the principal contract be rendered ineffectual by this rule, any collateral security given on foreign land must fall with it, though sufficiently created by the *lex situs* (*e*).

(*d*) 12 C. B. 801.

(*e*) *Richards* v. *Goold*, 1 Mol. 22. The case there referred to of *Bifield* v. *Taylor*, Sm. & Ba. 111, would have been a direct decision for the rule of Art. 171, in the case of a conflict between the *lex loci celebrati contractus* and *solutionis*, if the advocates of the latter had not withdrawn their contention, on the opinion of the court appearing to be for the former. The annuity was covenanted to be paid in London, but the pleadings obliged

174. The first objection to this rule is that of those who hold the maxim *locus regit actum* to be an exception, made for convenience to the law of the place of fulfilment. They of course consider that the parties may waive this exception, by contracting in the forms of the latter law (*f*).

175. The next doubt takes a wider scope, by admitting the parties to waive, not an exception from the proper law, but that law itself, namely, by contracting in the forms of their common domicile. If a contract so made were asserted as universally valid, the opinion might be rested on the principle of the law common to the parties, and would no longer appear as a permission to waive the proper law, but as a peculiar instance of the proper law. But the jurists who have maintained it have generally removed it from this ground by confining the validity of these contracts to suits in the common domicile (*g*), in which form the opinion must be objected to as breaking in on the intercommunity of law, which is the principle of private international jurisprudence. Accordingly, though an error of pleading prevented a decision on it, it would appear from *Benham* v. *Mornington* (*h*) that the bond of a British peer, made in France to another Englishman,

---

the court to hold that the covenant was executed at Dublin, and the question was on the necessity of a memorial registered pursuant to the English annuity act.

(*f*) This appears to be the just extension to contracts of Rodenburg's doctrine that, in wills, the form *loci actus* may be waived for that *rei sitæ* (De Jure quod oritur e Statutorum Diversitate, tit. 2, c. 2, s. 3; see also tit. 3, c. 3); and the just application to them of Savigny's doctrine that the form *loci actus* may always be waived for the proper one of the transaction (Syst., v. 8, p. 358).

(*g*) P. Voet, de Statutis, s. 9, c. 2, n. 9; Hertius, s. 4, § 10, non valet 6; Boullenois, t. 2, p. 459; Fœlix, n. 83. On the other hand, J. Voet appears to allow the widest liberty of choosing the forms of acts, so that it can hardly be doubted but that he would have held a contract thus made to be valid everywhere: ad Pand., l. 1, tit. 4, p. 2, n. 15.

(*h*) 3 C. B. 133.

must fulfil the requirements of French law by having *bon* or *approuvé* written on it by the hand of the obligee.

176. Another objection formerly made was to the necessity of foreign stamps, on the ground that no court is bound to respect the revenue-laws of a foreign jurisdiction. This exploded doctrine will be noticed in speaking of the legality of contracts, but is not really in point here, for the question is not whether our respect for foreign revenue-laws shall restrain us from imposing an obligation, but whether an obligation arose in the country of the agreement when it was made, since we cannot otherwise impose one here. Thus in *Alves* v. *Hodgson* (*i*), an action on a promissory note made in Jamaica, but payable in London, failed for want of the Jamaica stamp: in *Clegg* v. *Levy* (*k*), an agreement of partnership made at Surinam between the plaintiff and defendant was not received in answer to the action, as it had not the Surinam stamp: "I agree," said Lord Cranworth, in *Bristow* v. *Sequeville*, "that if for want of a stamp a contract made in a foreign country is void, it cannot be enforced here" (*l*). These authorities overrule the opposite dicta in *James* v. *Catherwood* (*m*) and *Wynne* v. *Jackson* (*n*).

In the New York case of *Ludlow* v. *Van Rensselaer* (*o*), a promissory note made in France and payable at New York was held good, though wanting the French stamp, on the alternative ground that either stamps depend on the *lex loci solutionis*, or that no regard should be paid to

(*i*) 7 T. R. 241.

(*k*) 3 Camp. 166.

(*l*) 5 Exch. 279.

(*m*) 3 Dow. & Ry. 190.

(*n*) 2 Russ. 351. Story (s. 260, note) is probably right in referring the informality in the French bills in this case to the want of a stamp: but, whatever it was, it must have been a defence at law, so that the case is good independent of the dictum.

(*o*) 1 Johnson, 94.

foreign revenue-laws. Both these mistakes are expressly corrected in the Louisiana case of *Vidal* v. *Thompson* (*p*).

177. *A law existing at the place of contract, by which a certain description of evidence is made necessary to support an action, is equivalent to one requiring certain solemnities as preliminary to the contract* (?)

For a legal right is nothing else than the power of invoking the law against another, which, in the case supposed, does not exist by the *lex loci contractus:* it is therefore vain to say that the *lex fori* contains no such rule of evidence, for the foundation of every procedure must be an obligation, and by the only law which could impose one no obligation exists. This reasoning has the authority of Story (*q*). But it has not been as yet adopted by the English courts, since in *James* v. *Catherwood* (*r*) a loan, and in *Bristow* v. *Sequeville* (*s*) the payment of money to the use of another, were allowed to be proved by receipts which in the respective countries where the advances were made would not have been evidence for want of stamps. The ground of disregarding foreign revenue-laws was taken in the former case, but repudiated in the latter. It is possible therefore that the former might have been differently decided if the evidence needed had not been a stamp, but in *Bristowe* v. *Sequeville* Lord Cranworth adopts the view that questions of evidence, like others of procedure, are in all cases governed by the *lex fori,* and not by the *lex loci contractus.* I cannot however think that his lordship's view was correct. The special force of a rule of evidence is to exclude, not to admit, testimony of a certain character, every kind being *prima facie* receivable. We therefore give full effect to the *lex fori* if we

(*p*) 11 Mar. 23.
(*q*) Sect. 260, note.
(*r*) 3 Dow. & Ry. 190.
(*s*) 5 Exch. 275.

admit no evidence which it rejects, without accepting, merely because it does not reject it, proofs of which the real tendency is not to establish but to create an obligation. Or the point may be put thus: Read the evidence, if you please, but read it for what it is worth. The point we have to try is whether there was an obligation in the *locus contractus*, to the law of which you submitted yourself (*t*); and to this your evidence does not go, for it only proves the transaction as a fact, which is not enough.

178. *If there are several parties to a contract, the solemnities which must be satisfied by each are generally those of the place where he engages himself.*

In applying this, it will be recollected that if I become a party to a contract, through an offer or assent contained in a letter, the place where I engage myself is that whence the letter is dispatched, even though, in the case of an offer, my obligation be not complete till it has been accepted elsewhere: this is a question of fact. *Acebal* v. *Levy* (*u*) was an action on a refusal to receive nuts ordered by the defendants in London from the plaintiff in Spain. It failed, and properly, for want of a sufficient memorandum under the statute of frauds, the defendants having promised in England, by letter dispatched thence, and therefore under English law. The vendor's assent, which was given in Spain, would have been necessary, no doubt, to complete the defendant's obligation: but it could not by itself create it, when the statute of frauds prevented the existence of any inchoate obligation which the vendor's assent might complete. Suppose the plaintiff in *Acebal* v. *Levy* had omitted to tender the nuts, after having sufficiently assented to the bargain by the law of Spain: in an action for the non-delivery, the Spanish courts should,

(*t*) See the citation from Savigny in Art. 172.
(*u*) 10 Bing. 376.

I think, hold such an one free, for the failure of consideration, the other party not being bound by English law to pay the price.

179. The doctrines of the last article have been much disputed. The opinion of Grotius, that only the so-called law of nature can avail in the case of a contract concluded by correspondence, has been already noticed: it is also adopted by Hertius (x). Others compare the person who writes the first letter with one who travels to the place where his correspondent gives the assent, and there concludes the contract orally: but then as this scientifically determined *locus celebrationis* is not in their system sufficient to regulate even the material contents of the obligation, unless on the condition of its being also the place of fulfilment, still less can it serve to found an application of the maxim *locus regit actum*, the reasons for which, whether drawn from a temporary subjection to the local law or from the convenience of the parties, require an actual and not a constructive presence (y). Hence the contract is considered as concluded, for the purpose of determining its formal requisites, by each party at his own domicile: a conclusion which would support the decision in *Acebal* v. *Levy*. The Prussian code lays down that for the formal requisites of contracts concluded by correspondence, if different laws prevail in the domiciles of the parties, that shall be followed by which the contract will be supported (z).

(x) De Commeatu Literarum, s. 16—18. Unless the recipient of the first letter declare his assent before witnesses: *hoc quippe facto, contractus isto loco protinus suam firmitatem, et simul formam, nanciscitur:* s. 19.

(y) Casaregis, de Commercio, Disc. 178, n. 1, 2, 9, 10, 62—64; Savigny, v. 8, pp. 237, 257. Story, not perceiving this distinction between the solemnities and matter of a contract, supposes Casaregis to decide even the former by this constructive *lex loci;* and therefore objects to *Acebal* v. *Levy*, supporting himself by cases which, both the English and American ones, refer only to the *vinculum obligationis:* s. 285.

(z) Allg. land. Recht, I, 5, s. 113, 114.

180. *But when a contract to which there are several parties is evidenced by a single instrument, the necessary form of that instrument is determined once for all by the law of that place where it begins to have an operation.*

This is the case in bills of exchange. The requirement of special forms in them may be instanced from stamps—from the law of Germany, where the draft must contain the words "bill of exchange," or their equivalents in any language in which it may be penned (*a*)—and from that of France, where a bill of exchange is only such if drawn from one place on another (*b*). Now the bill is constituted by the drawing and putting in circulation alone, and is thenceforward the evidence of a complete obligation, even though it never should be indorsed or accepted: for the drawer guarantees its acceptance no less than its payment. Consequently the stamp or other form of the place of drawing will be both necessary and sufficient, in whatever country the draft be afterwards negotiated or accepted.

Thus in *Snaith* v. *Mingay* (*c*), the Irish stamp was held sufficient on a bill drawn in Ireland with blanks for the sum, time of payment, and drawee's name, and which, after being there signed and indorsed by the drawer, had been sent by him to a correspondent in England with authority to fill it up. It was remarked by Justice Bayley that if the drawer had died, and afterwards the blanks had been filled up and the bill negotiated to an innocent indorsee, the drawer's executors would have been bound. Conversely, an acceptance on a blank stamp will not do, if the bill be afterwards drawn on it in a country where a different stamp is required; for the acceptance relates to the drawing and not *vice versa* (*d*): nor therefore is the stamp

(*a*) Art. 4 of law mentioned below in Art. 181.
(*b*) Code de Commerce, Art. 110.
(*c*) 1 M. & S. 87.
(*d*) *Abrahams* v. *Skinner*, 12 A. & E. 763.

of such country of blank acceptance at all necessary. The British legislature has acted on this doctrine in assuming a right to impose a stamp on bills drawn in Great Britain and Ireland and payable abroad, while on the other hand bills drawn abroad will not require the British stamp, though accepted or made payable here (*e*): only now, by stat. 17 & 18 Vict. c. 83, s. 5, a stamp is required on foreign bills presented for payment in England, so that the effect of the general principle is now restrained to exempting foreign bills from the British stamp-laws when presented for acceptance here (*f*).

181. It must be observed that the rule of Art. 180 only relates to the forms necessary to the validity of the instrument, and that, if the liability of any of the parties to it can be separated from this question, that will still have to be decided by the rule of Art. 178. Thus the invalidity of a particular indorsement leaves the existence of the bill of exchange itself untouched, and the indorser will therefore not be chargeable unless the law of the place of indorsement be satisfied. Now if that law do not expressly impose a stamp on the indorsement of bills, the stamp which it may impose generally on the bill will not be made necessary by the indorsement within the jurisdiction, because such stamp, as we have seen in Art. 180, will depend on the place of drawing (*g*). But now, by stat. 17 & 18 Vict. c. 83, s. 5, a stamp is imposed on the indorsement of bills in England; and it may be a question whether, if a foreign bill be sufficiently stamped where drawn, but an

(*e*) *Boehm* v. *Campbell*, Gow. 56, 8 Taun. 679.

(*f*) *Sharples* v. *Rickard*, 2 H. & N. 57. I must therefore dissent from *Hamelin* v. *Bruck*, 15 L. J., N. S., Q. B. 343, where it was thought that an English stamp was necessary on a bill drawn abroad for a larger sum and accepted here for a smaller. The foreign stamp which covered the greater sum should have covered the less, and at any rate the place of acceptance could not affect the question.

(*g*) *Holdsworth* v. *Hunter*, 10 B. & Cr. 449.

indorsement made upon it here be invalid for want of this stamp, that will discharge subsequent indorsers in other countries, who may be presumed to have relied on the validity of all the previous indorsements. This case has been foreseen and provided for by the 85th article of a uniform law on bills of exchange, drawn in 1847 at a congress of the north-German governments, enacted by the national assembly at Frankfort in 1848, and since successively adopted, with some variations, by all the states of the confederation. The whole article is worth quoting, and runs thus:—"The differences arising upon the fulfilment of the essential conditions of a bill of exchange drawn in foreign countries, or in any other contract of exchange made abroad, ought to be adjudicated according to the laws of the country whence the bill has been drawn and the engagement taken. Nevertheless, if the clauses inserted in foreign bills accord with the requirements of the German law, the objection, that they are deficient according to the law of that country, cannot be urged against them to the effect of invalidating the subsequent indorsements inserted in Germany. In the like manner, the clauses contained in such bills, according to which a German binds himself towards another German in a foreign country, are effectual if they accord with the requirements of the German law" (*h*).

182. If the actual place of drawing (and so, now, of indorsing) be disputed, with the view of showing that the bill, as improperly stamped, is not receivable as evidence, the judge, and not the jury, must decide where it was drawn or indorsed (*i*). And as it is a serious offence to misdate a bill for the purpose of evading the stamp-laws, very stringent proof of such an act will be required, and the bill will do, if it may have been drawn in any

(*h*) This translation is borrowed from Levi's Commercial Law, v. 2, p. 73.

(*i*) *Bartlett* v. *Smith*, 11 M. & W. 483; *Bennison* v. *Jewison*, 12 Jur. 485.

part of the country at some place in which it bears date (*k*). Also a party to a bill cannot be estopped from taking advantage of its not being duly stamped (*l*).

183. All the above cases refer to stamps. But others may arise. Thus, with reference to the French law mentioned in Art. 180, Pardessus points out that the draft of one London merchant on another should be valid and negotiable in France (*m*), and we should hold the draft of one Parisian merchant on another invalid and not negotiable in England.

2. *Material Contents of Obligations.*

184. After the formal requisites, there comes the general question of the *vinculum juris*, or legal tie, arising between the parties to a contract: its extent, duration, and modifications. What rights of either against the other does this tie include? Does it carry with it an inherent liability to dissolution? and, if so, when or on what conditions will it be dissolved? And are the rights which it includes subject to receive any and what modifications during its continuance? In order to answer these queries, the rights which flow from a contract have been variously subdivided, some being said to be of its essence, some of its nature, and others merely of its obligation in a narrower sense of that word. And doubtless such a classification may sometimes be of use, especially in countries where the principal kinds of contracts are accurately enumerated by the law, and many regulations made about them. But in proportion as men enjoy a freedom of making any engagement, however modified, which may suit their own

(*k*) *Abraham* v. *Dubois*, 4 Camp. 269; *Biré* v. *Moreau*, 2 C. & P. 376. Or, now, in the United Kingdom; st. 17 & 18 Vict. c. 83, s. 4: but this clause does not seem to meet the case of a bill drawn in one foreign country and dated in another.

(*l*) *Steadman* v. *Duhamel*, 1 C. B. 888.

(*m*) Droit Comm., s. 1485.

desires, it is impossible to carry out the above or any other minute classification of the rights which result from contract, considered in themselves. More may be learnt by attending to their origin, and hence it is that no distinction is really so fertile, or throws so much light on this subject, as that which in the passage cited in Art. 166, is drawn by Bartolus, between the rights which immediately flow from and at the instant of the contract, and those which arise from non-performance, delay, or any other posterior fact. The same distinction appears to have been present to the mind of Mævius, though in the following passage he has intimated it less clearly, because without an express reference to time: *Cave autem in hac materia confundas actuum et contractuum solemnia, necnon effectus ab ipsis causatos, cum eorum onere et accidenti extrinseco, quod contractus subsequitur sed non ex ipsis contractibus est. Id dum multi ignorant, aut non discernunt, forenses maximopere læduntur et gravantur: in his enim, quia non spectant ad formam modumque contrahendi, contractum autem extrinsecus subsequuntur, non sectamur statuta loci contractus* (*n*).

185. Every lawful dealing between parties which gives rise to a legal tie or obligation is a contract, a term opposed to tort or delict, which is the unlawful fact of one person binding him by a legal tie or obligation to another. Here lawfulness is opposed to unlawfulness, and a dealing between parties to a fact proceeding from one side. You may also be bound to another by your own sole but lawful act, and this is an obligation *quasi ex contractu.* Now men contract by agreement, by consent, or by fact. The obligation of an agreement arises from promise, which may be oral, written, or inferred from acts, and, if express, need not distinctly enumerate every thing which it includes,

(*n*) Ad Jus Lubicense, Quæst. Prel. 4, n. 18.

Thus a party to a bill of exchange promises by his signature to do all that which as drawer, acceptor, or indorser he may have to do: a promise the details of which are far more complicated than appears in the simple words of the draft. The obligation of a consensual contract is imposed by the law on the relation in which the parties have placed themselves by their consent. Thus the pecuniary rights of a husband and wife, who marry without settlement, do not flow from any mutual promises, but from the matrimonial relation in which the consent interchanged in the ceremony has placed them. If the law permits them to vary their mutual pecuniary rights by special arrangement, the nuptial contract is consensual as to all those pecuniary rights which the parties may have left to the general law, and an agreement as to all which they have promised each other in derogation of it. Lastly, when parties enter into a particular dealing without agreement, they institute a contract by fact, as in the loan of money when no terms are stipulated as to interest, or the time and mode of repayment. In contracts by fact, as in consensual contracts, the obligation is measured by the law; but, as in agreements, it is not an indefinite series of obligations proceeding from one general relation which is in question, but a limited obligation arising out of a certain transaction.

186. Now what has been said as to the formal requisites of contracts applies equally to agreements and consensual contracts. In contracts by fact, and in obligations *quasi ex contractu*, there can of course be no question of solemnities, farther than as rules of evidence may have an operation equivalent to them, as was discussed in Arts. 172 and 177; in such cases, as in delicts, there is nothing to be considered but the proof of the transaction and the obligation imposed thereon by law.

187. In agreements, the next point to the form is the

interpretation. Even if the parties express their intentions at length, as in the exuberant provisions of an English marriage settlement, there may be obscurity in their language. If, as in a bill of exchange, they do so by a few words depending for their development on known laws and customs either openly or tacitly referred to, we may have to ask whether this law or that usage was intended to be incorporated with the contract. Then, when all which was contemplated in the agreement is ascertained, it will usually be found that the transaction places the parties in fresh relations which had not been foreseen, and we ask by what law the rights and duties incident to those relations are to be determined. This last branch of the inquiry is that which in the other kinds of contract, and in delicts, is made without any previous question of interpretation. Nothing was contemplated, or at least, as in a loan when no terms are stipulated, it does not appear what was contemplated, but the lawful or unlawful fact placed the parties in new relations, and we ask what law decides their rights under them. So too in the consensual contract of marriage, when celebrated without settlement, the consent of the parties being directed to the establishment of a personal relation, quite heterogeneous from the pecuniary rights which result from it, and there being no proof that those pecuniary rights were in the particular instance considered by the parties at all, there can be no question of interpretation, but simply one of law.

188. Interpretation is a question of fact. *Prima facie*, the law of the place of contract will furnish the most proper clue to the meaning of the parties. If they have used words which there are technical, or have mentioned coins, weights, or measures which have a different value there and elsewhere, it is the value or technical sense of that place which they are most likely to have contemplated. Whatever they have not mentioned, yet cannot but have

contemplated, they most likely meant to follow according to the law of the same place, or the usages there prevailing. Yet these are but presumptions, and therefore liable to be rebutted. If the agreement expressly stipulate for a performance elsewhere, the usages and technical language of the place of execution, at least in all that relates to the execution, are more likely to have been present to the minds of the contractors than those of the place of contract. Still more will this be the case if the place of execution be also the domicile of both parties: and it is conceivable that the law of their common domicile might, even without the circumstance of a stipulated performance there, afford a safer guide to their meaning than that of the merely casual place of contract. On all these points, the greatest writers on this branch of jurisprudence have abstained from laying down sweeping presumptions of law which might be applicable to every description or example of agreement.

189. Care however must be taken to bear in mind the true scope of this inquiry, that the latitude allowed in it may not result in setting the whole subject at sea. There is no question here of introducing wholesale the laws of any particular country, by an implication that the parties contracted with reference to them. There is no question of introducing any thing into the agreement at all, but only of developing what was actually intended by the words used. Sometimes that only requires the meaning of the words to be explained: sometimes it needs more. Thus if a bill of exchange is expressed to be payable on a certain day, and at a certain place where certain days of grace are allowed, the acceptor meant to reserve for himself that grace. The intention cannot indeed be elicited by the dictionary from any particular words he has used, but he has sufficiently indicated it by the general form of the instrument, well known in commerce to convey that mean-

ing. He intended to bind himself to payment on a certain day, which day is sufficiently indicated by naming one earlier than it by the known interval of grace. Thus also "usances," if such a term occur in the bill, are to be interpreted as referring to the custom of the place of payment (*o*). But by what law the damages shall be measured in case he does not pay, or by what law it shall be decided whether he has a right of set-off against the assignees of a bankrupt holder, are not questions of interpretation, since it does not appear from the bill that these contingencies were considered when it was made. By attending to this, and to the distinction between agreements and consensual contracts, the student will see that this doctrine of interpretation leads to no such result as, for instance, that by marrying without express nuptial contract, the spouses tacitly apply the law of the place of marriage to immovable property situate elsewhere. We have already remarked how far all law is originally founded on the existence or presumption of a common intent, or persuasion of justice, among the members of the community where it exists: but to apply that presumption, as a juridical argument, to the case of every individual, would be to obliterate the boundary between the law and the will of the party.

190. The place of payment of a bill of exchange is a matter of interpretation no less than the time, and, on the same principles, must be referred to the law or understanding prevalent where the bill is accepted. Here however an attempt has been made to establish a universal rule, for Lord Brougham has said "the general rule is that where the acceptance is general, naming no place of payment, the place of payment shall be taken to be the place of the contracting of the debt." But I cannot

(*o*) Pardessus, Droit Comm. s. 1495. And whether months are lunar, &c.

suppose it was intended to apply this rule even when the existence of a different one in the country of the acceptance may be proved: and the application of the rule in the particular case to Scotland, where, his lordship said, "it appears—and it is rather singular that it should be so—that where a bill is accepted generally, it shall be deemed payable at the place at which the acceptor is domiciled when it becomes due," should rather be taken as overruling that point of former Scotch law, than as a refusal to interpret the place of payment with reference to the custom of the country of the acceptance (*p*). The time and place of payment, determined either as here explained, or by any other principle, will apply to the drawer and indorsers no less than to the acceptor, since they guarantee payment at the time and place indicated by the tenour of the bill.

191. On this head, of interpretation, I may also refer to what has been said in Art. 88, and the authorities there cited.

192. The meaning of the parties being ascertained, it is next necessary that it be lawful, both in respect of the thing promised to be done, and of the consideration for the promise. The legality of the former should, on principle, depend on the law of that place where it is to be performed. For one sovereign cannot enjoin the performance of any act in the territory of another. If I in England promise to do that in France which is there permitted, an obligation arises by English law, not as though the sovereign authority here could command me to do any

---

(*p*) *Don* v. *Lippmann*, 5 Cl. & F. 1, 12, 13. The old Scotch rule was evidently based on the maxim *actor sequitur forum rei*. To the general rule propounded there appear two serious objections, that the obligation on the bill is not identical with that as a security for which it is given, and that the holder of the bill may be unable to ascertain where the latter obligation was contracted.

thing in France, but because it can command me at least to make good by an equivalent the expectation I have raised. But if I in England promise to do that in France which is not there lawful, the respect due to an independent power forbids our law to contemplate the actual performance of my promise, and no obligation arises, because I cannot be considered to have raised any expectation. And this general rule, that the legality of an undertaking is to be referred to the place of execution, has, subject to the limitations to be mentioned in Art. 196, the common support of the jurists (*q*). If no place of performance be stipulated, either expressly or by necessary implication, the legality of the thing promised will depend on the law of the place of contract, as that of the state where the undertaking is primarily to be executed. These principles are illustrated by a bond executed at New York, and conditioned for the faithful management of a lottery in Kentucky. Lotteries are legal in the latter state, illegal in the former: and an action on such a bond has been sustained at New York, the law of that place being held to impose an obligation on a promise made there to do that which would have been prohibited by its own provisions, though permitted in the place of performance (*r*).

193. The English authorities on the same subject go less directly to the point. In *Heriz* v. *Riera* (*s*), an agreement was made in Spain between a merchant who had concluded a contract with the Spanish government and an

(*q*) It falls in with the rule of the *lex loci solutionis*, for those who refuse the *lex loci contractus:* only, when there is no fixed place of execution, they must have recourse to the contrahent's domicile.

(*r*) *Kentucky* v. *Bassford*, 6 Hill, 526. The general doctrine is stated in the American case of *Cambioso* v. *Maffet*, 2 Wash. 104: "if the contract of a foreigner is to be completed in, or has a view to its execution in, a foreign country, and is repugnant to the laws of that country, he is bound to take notice of them."

(*s*) 11 Sim. 318.

officer of the same government, by which the latter was to share in the profits of the contract. The agreement was, from the public character of the officer, invalid by the law of Spain; but the bill, which was filed against the merchant for an account by the English administrators of the officer, alleged other promises to the same effect made by the merchant after he had left Spain. The court held that there was no sufficient evidence of these later promises, but I submit that even had they been proved, they would have been void by the law of Spain as the country of performance. Again, the statute 6 Geo. 1, c. 18, gave to two English companies a monopoly, but for England only, of insuring marine risks in partnership. Another company having its place of business in London was held capable of insuring marine risks by its agent at Glasgow (*t*). It was argued that the agent promised that a policy should be granted in London, in which case the promise would have been void by the law of its place of performance: and such probably was the real nature of the transaction. But Lord Lyndhurst avoided contravening the international doctrine, by a supposition that the policy promised by the agent might be granted in Scotland.

194. The legality and sufficiency of a consideration should depend on the law of the place of contract (*u*); since the promisor will not be bound if the consideration do not, from its nature or value, support his promise by that law to which he is subject; while, if bound in the place of contract, he will be held so everywhere, by the principle of the international validity of rights which have once well accrued. This rule may be supported by two cases in which the question regularly arose between the

(*t*) *Pattison* v. *Mills*, 1 Dow. & Cl. 342; S. C., *sub nom. Albion Insurance Co.* v. *Mills*, 3 Wils. & Sh. 218.

(*u*) Here the supporters of the *lex loci contractus* and *lex loci solutionis* are of course at variance.

place of contract on the one hand, and, on the other, that of stipulated payment, or the *situs* of the thing to which the contract related. In the Massachusetts case of *M'Intyre* v. *Parks* (x), a mortgage of Massachusetts land was sustained, which had been contracted for in New York as a security for the price of tickets there sold in a Delaware lottery: and in the English case of *Wynne* v. *Callander* (y), bills of exchange having been given in England for money here lost at play, and afterwards French bills substituted for them in France, the effect of which was to continue the English contract with a new and foreign place of payment, Lord Gifford ordered the latter bills to be delivered up without requiring any information as to the French law. In *Quarrier* v. *Colston* (z), money won at play, and lent for the purpose of play, where that is lawful, was held recoverable in England: a decision consistent with the rule, and valuable as showing that the *lex fori* did not interfere on the ground of turpitude, though there was not in the case a place of stipulated payment distinct from that of contract. A case equally indecisive, and for the same reason, is one where by the usury law of the state where the loan was made, and was to be repaid, the principal was recoverable; by that of the state where it was secured by mortgage, the rate being the same, the whole was vitiated; and the former prevailed (a).

195. But one English case contains a dictum in which an opposite view is taken to the one here maintained. I mean *Robinson* v. *Bland* (b), an action on a bill of exchange, payable in England, but accepted and given in

(x) 3 Met. 207. Though lotteries are not allowed in New York, the sale there of tickets in a Delaware lottery was in this case held to be good by New York law.

(y) 1 Russ. 293.

(z) 1 Ph. 147. See Art. 196, as to the principle of turpitude.

(a) *De Wolf* v. *Johnson*, 10 Wheat. 367.

(b) 2 Burr. 1077.

France, for money partly lost there in gaming, and partly lent at the time and place of play. Lord Mansfield thought that the bill, being payable here, was subject to our law as to the vice of the consideration. It was not necessary to decide the point, as by the death of the acceptor there had ceased to be an obligation in France: a debt of honour, during the life of the debtor, could then have been recovered in that country in the court of the marshals of France. Yet questions about the consideration belong most essentially to the *vinculum obligationis* of Boullenois, and the obligations resulting at the time and according to the nature of the contract of Bartolus, which those great authorities refer expressly to the place of contract as distinguished from that of performance.

196. Nevertheless, no state may hold transactions legal which it considers to be contrary to the law of nature, or hurtful to the purity of morals, notwithstanding that an opposite view may be taken of them elsewhere (*c*). "It is a maxim," said Lord Wynford, "that the *comitas inter communitates* cannot prevail in any case where it violates the law of our own country, the law of nature, or the law of God." I should prefer to say that comity, rightly understood, cannot violate, because it is a part of, the law of this as of every country: but the other members of the sentence furnish a real help towards settling the limits of comity. No state can be justified in directing its tribunals to enforce obligations which it holds to be founded in wrong. It may countenance foreign rights which it would not originate, where the diversity of laws does not depend on an opposition of deep-seated moral ideas, but on a difference in the circumstances of two countries, or on those errors of judgment which the legislator will excuse

(c) The exception here asserted in favour of the *lex fori* is allowed by all, whether advocates of the *lex loci celebrationis* or *solutionis*.

in his fellow-man. But when the claim is held by us to be subversive of the fixed principles of our nature, and to tend towards the promotion of vice, we must reject it, as well from the duty of keeping ourselves clear of guilt, as for the evil example which its recognition would give to our citizens.

197. There is no doubt great difficulty in drawing the line between the foreign laws which, on these principles, may and may not be admitted. The fundamental maxim of private international jurisprudence, that a right which by the appropriate territorial law has once accrued shall thenceforth be universally recognised, can only be fully carried out between nations which possess common ideas on all the topics with which law is conversant. Whether between any two nations the jural intercommunion which the maxim would establish be in the main possible, is a question of degree, depending on the number and importance of their differences on social matters. It need hardly be said that rights flowing from the Mahomedan law of marriage could never be enforced in a Christian country: there are questions on which even Christian countries diverge so widely from each other that their laws on them cannot be mutually received. Thus specific performance will not be granted here of a contract between husband and wife to "facilitate" proceedings for divorce, and to place the custody of a child with the mother, contrary to our law (*d*). And it was doubted in *Robinson* v. *Bland*, though, as we have seen, the latest decision is in the affirmative, whether gaming debts, contracted where play is lawful, could be recovered in England. We have seen also that the exception of turpitude is not held in America to extend to lotteries.

198. But this exception has been agitated with the greatest warmth when slavery has been concerned. *Smith*

(*d*) *Hope* v. *Hope*, 22 Beav. 351, 3 Jur. N. S. 454.

v. *Brown* was an action for the price of a Virginian slave sold in London (*e*). The declaration failed to show the situation of the slave at the time of the contract, and it appeared that slaves in Virginia were *ascripti glebæ*, but the court seems to have thought that but for these objections the action would have lain. Property however in man was not then regarded in England as contrary to the law of nature, for a lord's property in his villein was noticed by the court in the argument, so that the decision, even had there been one, could not be considered as binding now. The doctrine was much discussed in *Forbes* v. *Cochrane*, an action in tort for harbouring escaped slaves on board a British ship of war, but which went off on the ground that such a ship was for such a purpose the same as English soil (*f*). In *Madrazo* v. *Willes*, it had been decided that the subjects of a state which permits the slave-trade cannot be lawfully interfered with in carrying it on (*g*). The great American case on this subject is *Greenwood* v. *Curtis*, where a cargo was sold on the coast of Africa for slaves, and partly paid for in them, then a balance struck in bars, an African currency, and a promissory note immediately given for the amount in slaves (*h*). Justice Sedgwick held, and apparently with reason, that the whole transaction was one bargain for slaves, and that therefore no action could be sustained for the balance struck nominally in bars; but the majority of the court considered that the form of such balance showed a primary sale of the cargo for money, on which the plaintiff was allowed to recover, as separable from the agreement for slaves. The case was one for the application of the law of nature only, as it would be absurd to talk of any African

(*e*) 2 Sal. 666.
(*f*) 2 B. & Cr. 448.
(*g*) 3 B. & Al. 353.
(*h*) 6 Mass. 358.

law on the subject, so that it was not at all parallel to *Smith* v. *Brown*, where the Virginian law was in question. It has been held in argument by Chief Justice Shaw that, upon a note given in a slave-state for the price of a slave, a suit might be maintained in Massachusetts (*i*): but we may say with Story—and, in England, with a more confident doubt—that "this doctrine, as one of universal application, may admit of question in other countries, where slavery may be denounced as inhuman and unjust, and against public policy" (*j*).

199. It will be understood that, in cases falling under Arts. 192 and 194, the taint of illegality is not confined to the mere stipulation for the performance abroad of acts there prohibited, or to the consideration branded by the strict letter of the law of the place of contract, but extends to all those dealings which have a necessary, though remote, connexion with the offence. This belongs indeed to the general principles of law, and not in any peculiar sense to international jurisprudence. The internal jurisprudence of every country must contain full details on the kind and degree of that connexion with an illegal object which will vitiate a contract not directly aiming at it: and the same ancillary protection should be thrown with an impartial hand round those foreign laws of which we admit the obligation within their proper territories. Hence, by the law of whatever country the illegality of an act or of an agreement be determined, it will affect transactions connected therewith, and other agreements depending on the primary one, to the same extent as in any ordinary violation of municipal law, though the contracts so impugned may have been made in other jurisdictions than the primary one, and may not be illegal in their immediate places of contract or execution. Thus no re-

(*i*) In *Commonwealth* v. *Aves*, 18 Pick. 215.

(*j*) Sect. 259, note.

covery should anywhere be suffered on a contract, made in one country, to insure a ship in a violation of the navigation or customs laws of another: such an insurance would be subsidiary to the breach of a foreign law. In *Waymell* v. *Read*, the vendor of lace at Lisle, who had packed it in a peculiar manner to facilitate its being smuggled into England, was unable to recover the price (*k*): but in *Holman* v. *Johnson* (*l*) and *Pellecat* v. *Angell* (*m*), the price was recovered of goods which had been sold and finally delivered abroad, the vendor being no way concerned in smuggling them into this country, though he was aware they had been purchased with that object. In all these cases the mere agreement was to be executed as well as made abroad, but in the first it had an inseparable connection with the performance of an illegal act in England. It is very doubtful whether the mere knowledge of the unlawful purpose should not in the latter cases have been held to amount to an equally inseparable connexion with it (*n*), but what is important for us to remark is, that the doctrine of internal law on the point, such as it was understood to be, was applied to these foreign contracts. On the principles of this article also, our courts refuse to take cognizance of any claims arising out of loans made, or expenses incurred, to assist insurgents against governments at peace with ours, until such insurgents have been recognised by Great Britain as

---

(*k*) 5 T. R. 599: S. P. *Clugas* v. *Penaluna*, 4 T. R. 466; and *Biggs* v. *Lawrence*, 3 T. R. 454. In the latter case however the court relied much on the British character of the plaintiff, a circumstance which did not exist in the other cases, and on its opinion that the agreement was to be considered as made in England.

(*l*) 1 Cowp. 341.

(*m*) 2 Cr., M. & R. 311.

(*n*) However, in *McIntyre* v. *Parks* (see above, Art. 194), the vendor knew that the purchaser's object was to resell the lottery tickets in Massachusetts.

a new state, though the pecuniary part of such transactions may have its seat entirely in England (*o*).

200. With the doctrines of Arts. 192 and 199, substantially coincides the position often taken, that contracts lawful where made are yet to be held illegal, if the parties have made them there rather than elsewhere for the express purpose of evading a prohibition decreed by the law of the country where they would naturally have been entered into. At least, that position, known as the *in fraudem legis* principle, appears to be true so far only as it is coextensive with what is here delivered. If my contract be illegal where it is to be executed, or be inseparably connected with some act illegal where it is to be performed, it will not be valid though I go elsewhere to make it. In any other case, I only use my right by contracting where I please.

201. It remains to notice an exception which has been made to the doctrine of international legality here delivered. It has been said that no state is bound to give effect to the revenue-laws of another: and this maxim has received the support of many distinguished jurists, especially in former times, when monopolies of trade were so commonly aimed at by states that, but for the fact that all were equally culpable, we could not wonder that they did not enlist the ordinary sentiments of justice in their support. At present however the maxim is mentioned by most writers with deserved reprobation (*p*). It

---

(*o*) Expenses; *Macnamara* v. *D'Evereux*, 3 L. J., Ch. 156: loans; *Jones* v. *Garcia del Rio*, T. & R. 297; *De Wütz* v. *Hendricks*, 9 Moore, 586, 2 Bing. 314; *Thompson* v. *Barclay*, 6 L. J., Ch. 93; *Thompson* v. *Powles*, 2 Sim. 194. And the court will take judicial notice of whether the insurgents have been recognised; *Taylor* v. *Barclay*, 2 Sim. 213: though at *nisi prius* evidence has been admitted on that point; *M'Gregor* v. *Lowe*, Ry. & Moo. 57, 1 C. & P. 200.

(*p*) Pothier, Traité du Contrat d'Assurance, n. 58; Kent, Commentaries, v. 3, pp. 263—267; Story, s. 257; &c. But Kent and Story admit the is one of the constant marks of a barbarous age that the duties of humanity are conceived to be limited to compatriots: and such was the character of the jurisprudence which allowed smugglers to contract for the breach of the laws of friendly states, provided by them, in the exercise of an undoubted authority, as specially necessary to their and their citizens' pecuniary interests. In *Boucher* v. *Lawson* (*q*), it was held that an action would lie in England on a contract to smuggle gold out of Portugal; and Lord Hardwicke remarked that the contrary opinion "would cut off all benefit of such trade from this kingdom, which would be of very bad consequence to the principal and most beneficial branches of our trade." If the principal branches of our trade had really corresponded to this conception of them, England must for ever have wanted the might which alone could give to such a doctrine the colour of right. In *Lever* v. *Fletcher*, Lord Mansfield held it lawful to insure a ship in England against loss to be occasioned by embarking in prohibited trade with a Spanish colony, although the noble lord noticed in his judgment the additional fact that such trade was "illicit by the treaty of Paris" (*r*). Now it is a principle that, as expressed by Lord Stowell, "every treaty is a part of the private law of the country which has entered into that treaty, and is as binding on the subjects as any part of their municipal laws" (*s*), so that the contract approved in *Lever* v. *Fletcher* did not more tend to the performance on Spanish soil of an act there illegal by Spanish law, than it was directly contrary to the law of England, not to men-

complete establishment of the maxim in American practice, and I am obliged to repeat here the similar English cases, not being able to cite any which directly overrules them.

(*q*) Ca. t. Hardwicke, 85.

(*r*) 1 Park, Mar. Ins. 506; 1 Marsh. Ins. 56.

(*s*) In *The Eenrom*, 2 Rob. 6.

tion the bad faith of supporting our own subjects in the breach of our own treaties. It is only with pain that such decisions can be mentioned. In *Planché* v. *Fletcher*, recovery was had on the insurance of a ship which, with the knowledge of the underwriters, cleared out for a false destination, in order to evade certain French custom-duties and English lighthouse-dues (*t*). The case has been questioned on the ground of the latter (*u*), and I may include the former in the reasons of my dissent.

202. In *Sharp* v. *Taylor* an account was decreed between partners, of the profits made in the employment of a ship which had been registered in the United States by a fraud on the ship-registry laws of that republic (*x*). "Will the courts of this country," said Lord Cottenham, "refuse to administer justice between joint importers of any article of commerce upon proof that, in the production or exportation of such article, some fiscal law of the country of produce had been violated? During the French war the greater part of the foreign trade of this country was carried on in despite of the fiscal regulations of other countries, some of which were not at war with this country; and there are still instances existing of the same kind; but the parties to such transactions have not, upon that ground, been denied the ordinary administration of justice in matters growing out of such transactions. The cases do not support any such proposition. (See *Pellecat* v. *Angell*, and the cases there cited.)" (*y*) It must always be recollected that much discretion is reposed in a court of equity, in the exercise of which it may see fit to interfere in respect of the profits between parties

---

(*t*) 1 Doug. 251.

(*u*) 1 Marsh. Ins. 462.

(*x*) 2 Ph. 801.

(*y*) Ib. p. 816. See Art. 199, as to the cases referred to by Lord Cottenham.

equally at fault, and it cannot therefore from *Sharp* v. *Taylor* be concluded that an unexecuted contract in defiance of the revenue laws of the place of performance would now be enforced in England. The reference to what happened during the great war may be illustrated from *Simeon* v. *Bazett* (*z*), in which the underwriter was held liable on an insurance effected against the enforcement of the continental system by Prussia, on traffic with her; Prussia, though she had acceded to that system, not being then at war with us. The system, however, was so essentially hostile, that no court could reasonably treat the relations arising out of it by the rules of a nominal peace, and it would be difficult therefore to draw from this case a precedent for countenancing a violation of foreign laws under ordinary circumstances. It is however unfortunate that in his judgment Lord Ellenborough should have dismissed the licence from the British government, under which the traffic was carried on, as rendered immaterial by the absence of open war with Prussia: a dictum which gives a colour for treating the case as an authority in a state of virtual as well as nominal peace. A court which was not disposed to coincide with the doctrines of *Boucher* v. *Lawson* and *Lever* v. *Fletcher*, and yet hesitated to draw itself the line within which justice demanded the extension of comity to foreign laws, might have found in that licence a justification for the course actually pursued in *Simeon* v. *Bazett*.

203. One application of the doctrine of the legality of contracts is to stipulations for a certain rate of interest, or for compound interest, on the loan or forbearance of money. The classical text of the Digest is from Papinian: *cum judicio bonæ fidei disceptatur, arbitrio judicis usurarum modus ex more regionis ubi contractum est constituitur, ita*

(*z*) 2 M. & S. 94. Affirmed, *sub nom. Bazett* v. *Meyer*, 5 Taun. 824.

tamen ut legi non offendat (*a*). This obviously relates to judicial interest *ex mora* in the nature of damages; and, even for that, expresses merely the general principle, without reference to the case of a contract made in one place, to be fulfilled in another, and sued on in a third. It has however been drawn into the controversy on stipulated interest, and with reference to such conflict. By the repeal of the British usury laws, the subject has lost much of its interest here, but is still sometimes necessary to be considered in foreign contracts. Now if the interest agreed on exceed that of the place of stipulated payment, the parties at least can never be taken to have imported voluntarily into their contract a law which would defeat it. Nor will it always be found reasonable to decide the question of usury by the law of the place of repayment. If I lend money in New York to a merchant who intends to employ it in Louisiana, where he resides, but for my own convenience stipulate for its repayment at New York, would it be just that I should be limited to the New York rate of interest? Usury laws exist for the protection of the borrower, from whom no greater sum is to be extorted than the profit which the law conceives he may have made by the employment of the capital advanced; but what necessary connexion is there between the place of repayment, and the probable place of employment of the loan? It is clear that a more reasonable rule would be given by the domicile of the borrower, as it is at his home, or at his place of business, that he is most likely to use the sums he has borrowed. The case is not different when a rate of interest is stipulated in case of the non-performance of an obligation; as if a bond, a promissory note, or a bill of exchange, specifies the interest to be paid in case it should not be discharged at the appointed date. This interest is

(*a*) 22, 1, 1.

not indeed primarily intended by the parties to be paid at all, for on the contrary the fulfilment of the obligation at its maturity is intended, and the interest is a compensation to the creditor in case the expectation so raised should be defeated. Therefore, if the parties have been silent on its amount, the court, granting interest *ex mora*, may justly measure the compensation by the damage; that is, by the rate of the place of stipulated repayment, where it is presumable that the creditor would have employed the money, had he duly received it. But, if the parties have chosen to refer themselves expressly for such compensation to the higher rate of the debtor's domicile, the latter cannot complain of having to give for his use of the creditor's money what he may be presumed to have made of it, nor can the creditor be deemed to act hardly if he refuse to accept the security on any other terms. In all that has been said, the place where the loan is made or the forbearance occurs may be substituted for the debtor's domicile, since that also is a place in which he may have employed the money: and thus we are led to the conclusion that, from the motives of usury laws, the most onerous stipulations may be justified which are allowed either by the law of the debtor's domicile, or by that of the place of the actual transaction, but not by that of the place of repayment, which has in this matter only the technical value arising from the famous law *contraxisse*.

204. The rate of judicial interest *ex mora* has properly no concern with the subject of the legality of contracts on which we now are; but, because they are not well distinguished in the cases, and in order to bring together the whole doctrine of interest, I may refer to what was said incidentally in the last paragraph, as fixing its just measure by the law of that place in which the fulfilment of the obligation was promised. The non-fulfilment is a new fact posterior to the contract, the effects of which must be de-

termined from its own nature and appropriate law. Now on the one hand, the omission which constitutes such fact must be taken to occur where the performance ought to have been, and therefore under the empire of the law of that place; and on the other, its nature is to cause damage to the creditor, the amount of which is fairly measured by the interest of the spot where he hoped to receive the money.

205. The above system agrees with that of Fœlix, except that in conventional interest he allows the parties a latitude of choice which would altogether exclude the operation of usury laws on the subject (*b*). Savigny on the contrary would limit all interest to the measure of the *lex fori*, on account of the moral end of usury laws, since it is admitted that no judge may violate the moral sense of his own legal system. No doubt it is in a supposed interest of morality that such laws exist, but the question remains, what particular interest of morality? and, if it be the protection of the borrower, cases may arise in which that will allow a foreign rate of interest to be recovered. But, so far as the *lex fori* does not oppose, Savigny agrees with Fœlix in admitting a claim to conventional interest not lawful in the proper seat of the obligation, because he acknowledges no operation of law on the contract otherwise than by the voluntary subjection of the parties, which is not conceivable with reference to a law which would defeat their engagement (*c*). Story's conclusion is that "interest may be validly contracted for at any rate not exceeding that which is allowed in the place of payment or performance: and in the absence of any express contract as to interest, the law of the same place will

(*b*) No. 109.

(c) Syst. d. heut. Röm. Rechts, v. 8, pp. 276, 277.

furnish the rule, where interest is to be implied or allowed *ex mora*" (*d*).

206. The English cases repudiate the limitation of interest to the measure of the *lex fori*. Thus, where there was a simple conflict between that and the *lex loci contractus*, no place of fulfilment appearing distinct from that of incurring the obligation, the latter law was followed both in the old cases of *Dungannon* v. *Hackett*, *Lane* v. *Nichols*, *Harvey* v. *East India Company*, and *Ellis* v. *Loyd* (*e*); and in the later one of *Bodily* v. *Bellamy* (*f*). The next step is made by *Stapleton* v. *Conway*, where there was nothing foreign about the whole transaction but the situation of the immovable property on which a security was given, and which thus brings the matter to this point, that the place of contract prevails over both the forum, and the place (if any) of such security (*g*). The subdivision, as it may be called, of the place of contract commences in *Ranelagh* v. *Champante*, where a bond was executed in England, conditioned for the repayment in Ireland of advances made there. According to two reports, Irish interest was allowed, which appears to be the just decision (*h*): but by another, the English rate only was allowed, "because the bond was executed here" (*i*). The latter report was adopted by Lord Hardwicke in *Connor* v. *Bellamont*, and appears to have been the ground of his converse decision in that case, allowing Irish interest on a bond given in Ireland for a debt contracted in England (*k*).

(*d*) Sect. 296.

(*e*) All in 1 Eq. Ca. Abr. 288, 289.

(*f*) Burr. 1094.

(*g*) 1 Ves. Sen. 427.

(*h*) 1 Eq. Ca. Abr. 289, and Pre. Cha. 128.

(*i*) 2 Vern. 395.

(*k*) 2 Atk. 382. His lordship also went on a security having been given on an Irish estate, which argument may be answered from his own decision in *Stapleton* v. *Conway*, *ubi supra*.

This however may be considered to have been set right by Lord Cottenham's dictum in *Fergusson* v. *Fyffe*, who, with reference to an alleged agreement to pay compound interest on the balance of an account stated, said that its legality depended on the place where the debt was contracted (*l*): so that to the place of executing the security, if different from that where the advance is made, we need probably pay no farther attention. So far then the cases agree with the principles of Arts. 203 and 204; but now, if the debtor's domicile, or the place of the actual transaction, differ from that of stipulated repayment, it must be confessed that the English authorities support the rate of interest of the latter. Thus, in *Thompson* v. *Powles*, the vice-chancellor said of a loan negotiated in England by a foreign government, that "in order to hold the contract to be usurious"—that is, as transgressing the English rate—"it must appear that the contract was made here, and that the consideration for it was to be paid here. It should appear at least that the payment was not to be made abroad, for, if it was to be made abroad, it would not be usurious" (*m*). It is however difficult to see why it should have been more improper to pay the interest in London than to an agent of the fundholder abroad, the real transaction, either way, being a foreign investment.

·207· But in America a different ground has been taken, and the decisions there are consistent with what I have suggested as the reasonable rule. In *Depau* v. *Humphreys*

(*l*) 8 Cl. & F. 121, 140. It is true that this was only a dictum (except, for which purpose it is not here used, in excluding the *lex fori*), for the agreement, if any, was made where the debt was contracted.

(*m*) 2 Sim. 194, 211. The circumstances of *Harvey* v. *Archbold*, 3 B. & Cr. 626, seem to have amounted to a commission by the bankrupts to the defendants to borrow money for them at Gibraltar. In *Dewar* v. *Span*, 3 T. R. 425, and *Exp. Guillebert, re Trye*, 2 Dea. 509, every circumstance combined to point to the English law. There is also an anonymous case which decided that British subjects lending money abroad were not, as such, bound by our usury laws: 3 Bing. 193.

a New Orleans firm had given at New Orleans to their New York creditor a promissory note payable at New York, which, for the forbearance, was to bear interest at ten per cent., the legal rate at the former place, that of the latter being seven (*n*). It was sustained by the court of Louisiana, on the ground that interest depended on the *lex loci contractus celebrati* and not on the *lex loci solutionis*, and "that the circumstance of the place of payment differing from that in which the lender parts with his money ought to have no influence in the fixation of the rate of interest." In *Chapman* v. *Robertson* a New York merchant while in England had contracted to borrow £800 from an English merchant, on the security of his bond and of a mortgage of his land in New York, both which he was to execute on his return. This was done accordingly, and in a suit for foreclosure Chancellor Walworth said, "I have arrived at the conclusion that this mortgage, executed here and upon property in this state, being valid by the *lex situs*, which is also the law of the domicile of the mortgagor, it is the duty of this court to give full effect to the security, without reference to the usury laws of England, which neither party intended to evade or violate by the execution of a mortgage upon the lands here" (*o*).

208. The meaning of the parties being ascertained, and found to be lawful, an obligation to fulfil it is imposed, and must therefore be measured, by the law to whose commands they are temporarily subject; that namely, for each, of the place where his promise is made. This is obviously true for the immediate rights of action, as is also a similar proposition for those arising from delict, and for contractual obligations arising by fact, all which must depend

---

(*n*) 8 Mar. N. S. 1.

(*o*) 6 Paige, 627, 633. *De Wolf* v. *Johnson*, 10 Whea. 367, is S. P. with *Stapleton* v. *Conway*, *sup.*, p. 192. *Jacks* v. *Nichols*, 1 Seld. 178, is a clear case.

on the law of the place where the person to be charged acted. But it is no less true for the subsequent rights of action. If I become surety for a loan which is to be repaid elsewhere on a future day, no action can be brought against me till default has been made, yet whether it will then be necessary first to exhaust all remedies against the principal debtor will depend on the law of the place where I became surety: for the conditions under which I am to be called on belong essentially to the obligation imposed on me by that law, which consists of a potential liability to suit, to become actual at a future period, and cannot from the first be defined without stating the conditions on which its actuality is to depend. The jurisprudence which binds the contractor in the inception of his contract determines the nature and extent of the liabilities he incurs, and, if any of them are conditional, the circumstances in which they are to arise: and though those circumstances may afterwards occur within another jurisdiction, they can have no other legal effect than by relation to the contract, or therefore than was traced out for them in the beginning by the law which then bound the contractor.

209. Thus, in marine insurance. There is much variation in the laws which regulate general average, both as to the interests which are liable to contribute, and the losses for which it may be claimed. The holder of a respondentia bond is not liable to contribute in England, in Denmark he is so: and in England general average is founded on the sacrifice of part to save the rest, while in some other countries it extends to all cost or loss voluntarily incurred to escape danger, as by putting into port from stress of weather, or by the destruction of tackle through putting on a press of sail to avoid being driven on shore. Will then the underwriter of an insurance effected in England be liable to reimburse a contribution exacted in a foreign port, but which would not have been due by English law?

In *Walpole* v. *Ewer* (*p*) the point was decided against the insurer of a respondentia bond on the cargo of a ship bound to a Danish port: but this has been overruled by *Power* v. *Whitmore* (*q*), in which the underwriter of cargo was held not liable for a general average which in England would not have been struck. The later decision is in accordance with the maxim of the *lex loci contractus*, for the promise was made in England, though it was a conditional one on events which happened abroad. The same doctrine is also firmly established in America, where the insurer will only be held liable for losses which may be incurred in accordance with the law of the place where the insurance was made (*r*).

210. These cases illustrate the difficulty which attends any system of private international jurisprudence based on the supposed intention of the parties to act or contract with reference to any particular law. Was the insurer most likely to think of his own law, or of that of the port of destination for which he effected the insurance? The balance of probabilities is so nice that it might be inclined either way by the judge's own turn of mind, and in *Walpole* v. *Ewer* Lord Kenyon held the underwriter *bound* to know the law of the port of destination, which, according to *Power* v. *Whitmore*, he is not even *supposed* to know. Such instances may induce us to be cautious in the implication of agreements beyond what it is ascertained that the parties actually had in view. That indeed should be ascertained with care, as in *Newman* v. *Cazalet* (*s*), where the underwriter was held liable on

(*p*) Park on Insurance, 8th edit., p. 898.

(*q*) 4 M. & S. 141.

(*r*) *Schmidt* v. *United Insurance Company*, 1 Johns. 249; *Lenox* v. *Un. Ins. Co.*, 3 Johns. Ca. 178; *Shiff* v. *Louisiana State Ins. Co.*, 6 Mar. N. S. 629.

(*s*) Park on Insurance, 8th edit., p. 899.

proof that averages struck in the particular foreign court, in the mode then in question, had been often submitted to by English insurers; and the case was accordingly distinguished in *Power* v. *Whitmore*, as depending on the special agreement considered to have been proved in it. But though the principle of this distinction is certainly just, it may be doubted whether in *Newman* v. *Cazalet* the special agreement was sufficiently proved, as the evidence, so far as it tended to establish any thing, pointed much rather to its being a general custom of English insurers to submit to the law of the port of destination.

211. Another instance is furnished by the mutual rights of partners, since they flow from the contract of partnership, and not from the transactions which give them their immediate occasion. The contract of partnership could not indeed be fully defined otherwise than by enumerating the duties which in any event are to be performed by the partners to one another, and these are therefore regulated once for all by the local law of the partnership (*t*). The same reasoning holds for companies, the questions between the shareholders in which must everywhere be decided by the law of that country from which they derive their incorporation or their statutes (*u*). But the liability of a partner to third persons, on the dealings of his copartner, depends on the local law of those dealings: for the jurisprudence of the partners' country "can no more affect the rights of those who contract with them in a different country, than particular stipulations between the partners could" (*x*). A proposition perhaps rather too large. It seems, however, to be on this ground that Story, putting the case of a partnership *en commandite*, of which the

(*t*) *Vanzeller* v. *Vanzeller*, 15 Jur. 115; *Baldwin* v. *Gray*, 4 Mar. N. S. 193.

(*u*) *Sudlow* v. *Dutch Rhenish Railway Company*, 21 Beav. 43.

(*x*) *Baldwin* v. *Gray*, 4 Mar. N. S. 192, 193; a Louisiana case. See below, Art. 223.

general partner orders goods from a house in a country where limited liability is not allowed, asks with great hesitation whether, on an insolvency of the partnership, the *commanditaires* will be liable to the vendors beyond the amount of their subscriptions (*y*). The truth is that the directors or other managing members of a firm or company are the agents of the other members, to pledge their credit to the extent agreed on between themselves: a case which includes that of an ordinary English partnership, in which all the members are agents for each other to an unlimited extent. And, secondly, these directors or managing members may act through extraneous persons expressly employed by them. The question then of the liability of partners to third persons depends at least on a single, sometimes on a double, application of the doctrine of agency, which we will now pause to consider.

212. And, first, let us suppose a principal carrying on a business in a foreign country through an agent expressly employed there for that purpose: then in all the contracts which the agent makes, or the acts which he does, in the course of such business, it is universally admitted that the case is the same as though the principal were there present, and made or did them himself. He is indeed constructively present, and that too through his own free will, in the agent's person; so that there can be no question of the extent of the latter's authority to bind him, but only of the substance of the obligation, as depending on the interpretation of what has passed between the agent and the third person, and the effect of the local law thereon. Thus, in the Louisiana cases of *Malpica* v. *M'Kown* (*z*) and *Arayo* v. *Currell* (*a*), the pretension was rebutted that the liability of a shipowner, who employed his vessels in the carrying

(*y*) Sect. 320 a.
(*z*) 1 Louis. 248.
(*a*) Ib. 528.

trade between foreign ports, in respect of losses incurred by passengers and freighters, or torts committed against them by the captain, depended on the law of his own domicile, and not on the local laws of the contracts made with the plaintiffs. There might of course be a question, supposing the voyage to commence under one law and terminate at a port subject to another, whether the true local law of the contract is that of the former place, where the agreement is made by the master of the ship, or other representative of the owner, who receives the passengers or goods, or that of the latter, where the agreement is to be completely fulfilled. But that was not at issue in those cases, nor was the master's agency to contract for the carriage disputed; but the point was whether the obligation of that contract was to be measured by the same rule, which would clearly have had to be applied if the owner had made it at the same place in person.

213. Next, let us suppose an agent contracting or acting out of the course of the business in which he is employed, and that a claim is made on the principal, by those with whom the agent has so dealt, as bound to ratify and adopt the dealing. Such claim may of course be sustained on the ground of private instructions from the principal, if the existence of any which the agent followed can be proved: but what if it be rested on a law empowering agents to act in emergencies for the interest of their principals? A law to that effect in the principal's domicile had him for its subject when he there took the agent into his service, and therefore imposed such potential liability on him from the first, wherever the dealing by the agent, which was the condition for actuating the liability, may have afterwards occurred. Or, it may be said that such a law was tacitly accepted by the principal, as that which was to govern his employment of the agent. But a law to the same effect in the place of the agent's subsequent dealing makes nothing

to the principal's intention, as to which the latter place is quite casual: nor has it the principal for its subject, he not being present there, either in fact, *ex hypothesi*, nor constructively, since the agent's authority for the particular dealing is the very point in dispute.

214. "Thus, the English law does not allow the master to hypothecate the vessel, at least expressly, unless in a foreign port where personal credit is unattainable; but entitles him to pledge the absolute personal responsibility of his constituents for the amount of necessary repairs, furnishings, &c.: while on the other hand the French law authorizes him to hypothecate the vessel, &c., but not to bind his constituents personally, at least not beyond the eventual value of the ship and freight, &c., on her return: and it is quite clear that the merchants and artisans of the respective countries must contract with the shipmasters of each other, according to the powers respectively inherent in those offices. . . . . . The clear result is that the transactions must be held to have reference to the master's implied mandate, according to the law of his own country" (*b*).

215. Let us now take a case where the principles of Arts. 212 and 213 appear to be complicated. The agent acts out of the business for which he is employed, and without private instructions, so that the third party with

(*b*) Brodie's Supplement to Stair's Institutes, v. 2, p. 956. The leading English case to this effect is *The Nelson*, 1 Hagg. Adm. 169. The American authorities to the same effect are collected by Justice Story, in his judgment in *Pope* v. *Nickerson*, 3 Story, 478. The same jurist, in his Conflict of Laws, s. 286 b, adds, "but it is far from being certain that foreign courts, and especially the courts of the country where the advances or supplies were furnished, would adopt the same rules, if the lender or supplier had acted with good faith, and in ignorance of the want of authority in the master." For this he cites Emérigon, Contrats à la Grosse, c. 4, s. 8, § 3, a passage which refers solely to a concealed restraint by the owner on the master's legal authority, as to which see below, Art. 217—and *Malpica* v. *M'Kown*, which refers to the wholly different case of Art. 212.

whom the agent so deals can have no claim on the principal but under the law of the latter's domicile. But suppose the dealing in question to affect the interests of a fourth party, with whom the agent had previously dealt in the course of the business he was employed in, and so therefore as to bind his principal according to the local law of that previous contract. Thus a vessel, owned in Massachusetts, and being on a voyage from a port in Spain to a port in Pennsylvania, is compelled by stress of weather to put into Bermuda, where the master sells both her and the whole cargo; and the action is by the shippers against the owners to recover the amount of their consignment. Surely the law to be applied is that either of Spain or of Pennsylvania, for the owners must be taken to have contracted in the one country to carry the goods to the other. Yet the circuit court of the United States determined that the liability of the owners was governed by the law of Massachusetts (*c*).

216. As the judgment in this case was delivered by Justice Story himself, the reader will expect a more particular account of it. The learned judge entirely ignored the distinction drawn in Arts. 212 and 213, and, referring to the cases of *Malpica* v. *M'Kown* and *Arayo* v. *Currell*, said "they appear to me to proceed upon false principles, and to be at war with the current doctrines of the common law. The decisions proceeded upon the ground that there is no difference in the legal result, whether a contract is made in a foreign country by an agent, or by the principal himself personally in that country. Assuming the general rule to be so, to what cases does it properly apply? Certainly to those, and to those only, where the agent possesses full authority to make the particular contract" (*d*). Here I pause, in order to bring into strong

(*c*) *Pope* v. *Nickerson*, 3 Story, 465.
(*d*) P. 481.

contrast a passage from the earlier part of the same judgment. "It is not denied that the master was duly authorized to take the present shipments on board for the voyage" (*e*). In the mean time, the learned judge had cited from the Digest the words: *cum interdum, ignari cujus sint conditionis vel quales, cum magistris propter navigandi necessitatem contrahamus, æquum fuit eum qui magistrum navi imposuit teneri ut tenetur qui institorem tabernæ vel negotio præposuit . . . . . . Omnia enim facta magistri debet præstare qui eum præposuit, alioquin contrahentes decipientur:* supposing that their point was removed by the exception which yet, in connexion with the admission of the master's authority to take the shipments, seems to clench the matter against the owners: *non autem omni ex causa prætor dat in exercitorem actionem, sed ejus rei nomine cujus ibi præpositus fuerit, id est si in eam rem præpositus sit* (*f*). But the laws of Spain and Massachusetts limited the responsibility of the owners for the torts of the master and mariners to the value of the vessel and freight, a restriction which did not exist in Pennsylvania: and accordingly said Story, "if the ship is owned and navigated under the flag of a foreign country, the authority of the master to contract for and to bind the owners must be measured by the laws of that country, unless he is held out to persons in other countries as possessing a more enlarged authority" (*g*). And is he not so held out, by being sent among them for the purpose of conducting a particular business in their territory? If a Massachusetts bank established a branch in Spain, would not the cashiers be held out as possessing authority to bind the partners by Spanish law? I do not perceive what difference the flag makes, since the contract for

(*e*) P. 473.
(*f*) 14, 1, 1. From Ulpian.
(*g*) 3 Story, 475.

carriage was neither made nor to be fully executed on the high seas. An argument for confounding the case with that of Art. 213 might have been drawn from the words of Ulpian next following those last quoted: *ut puta si onus vehendum locatum sit, aut aliquas res emerit utiles naviganti, vel si quid reficiendæ navis causa contractum vel impensum est, vel si quid nautæ operarum nomine petent.* But in illustrating the consequences of agency, it was not necessary for the Roman jurist to distinguish that created by the principal from that created by the law, the importance of the distinction arising only under a conflict of laws such as did not exist in the Roman empire. In the former description of cases, the third person deals with the agent as with the principal: in the latter, he deals with him expressly as agent.

217. Another distinction often taken on this subject is between the general powers incident to an employment, and those to which the agent may be restricted by the private instructions of his principal. It is perfectly sound, only the student may be misled by the terms sometimes used, as though such general powers were referred to the general law maritime, or to the Roman law, as supposed to be common ones, to which exceptions may exist by municipal laws, or by private instructions compared to municipal laws. This however is not the meaning, nor would it be sound. By whatever municipal law the principal's liability may have to be determined, it cannot be farther restricted by special terms concealed from the person who deals with the agent knowing him to be an agent: and in this, the Roman and general maritime laws figure only as the municipal laws of the countries which adopt them.

218. By some laws, as of Massachusetts, all acts done by an attorney after the death of his principal are nullities. "By the law of Louisiana, if an attorney, being

ignorant of the death or of the cessation of the rights of his principal, should continue to act under his power, the transactions done by him during this state of ignorance would be valid. There is no doubt that an authority given to an agent is to be executed according to the law of the place where the business is to be transacted. But this may well be admitted to be the rule while the authority is in full force, without making the law of that place the rule by which to ascertain whether the original power of attorney is still subsisting. Some of the cases already alluded to may be thought to furnish an analogy unfavourable to the validity" (*h*) of the acts so done under it in Louisiana, after the death of the principal in Massachusetts. It would seem that the principal created against himself an obligation in the country where he employed the agent, to be pursued however against his heirs by the law under which they take his succession.

219. These principles on agency afford perhaps the best insight into contracts made by correspondence. The comparison of a letter with a messenger is familiar in this subject, and will be made still clearer by observing that a messenger is exactly analogous with, in fact is, an agent employed by his principal to transact a particular business in the country into which he is sent. Now when the formal requisites of a letter for binding the writer, as with regard to the necessity of signature or the statement of the consideration, are in issue, these are comparable to the question discussed in Art. 213 on the disputed authority of an agent: and the decision there given, in favour of the law of the principal's domicile, as that of the agent's employment, coincides with that of Art. 178, referring the formal requisites of a letter to the place from which it is sent. But when the letter is established as

(*h*) Story, s. 286 d.

against its writer, the contract concluded by it is one of the place where the assent is given by the correspondent, just as in Art. 212 we saw that a principal contracts through an agent in the place where the agent contracts.

220. These conclusions are chiefly operative in the contract of sale, where the warranty of title or quality involved, and the rights of rescission and of lien for unpaid purchase-money, depend on the *lex loci contractus:* only here the farther question arises, which is perpetually meeting us on international obligations, between the places of final assent as that of celebration, and of delivery as that of fulfilment. In general these are the same, for the order comes from the purchaser, and is assented to by the vendor, who executes it by delivery to a carrier who is the purchaser's agent. But they may be different, as when the negotiation is opened by an offer from the vendor, or when the delivery is by agreement not to be complete till the goods reach the purchaser. These topics were much considered in *Orcutt* v. *Nelson*, an action in Massachusetts for the price of wine and spirits ordered, by a letter written in that state, from a dealer in Connecticut, and delivered in the usual manner to the carrier as the purchaser's agent (*i*). The difficulty arose from a Massachusetts statute invalidating the sale of spirituous liquors, and not only was the contract sustained as one of Connecticut, but it was said that the result would have been the same even had a delivery in Massachusetts been contracted for (*k*): an opinion which may be justified on the ground that it was not the delivery, but the sale, at

(*i*) 1 Gray, 536. The facts were more complicated than here stated, but were reduced to this form by an interesting discussion, involving the principle that the ratification of a change in an order so relates to the original order as to incorporate the change with it.

(*k*) *Ubi supra*, p. 543. With reference to the application of Art. 199 to this case, it was stated that there was here no fraudulent view to a resale of the liquors in Massachusetts: p. 541.

which the statute in question struck. A case in which the *locus contractus* of the sale was not that of delivery is furnished by *Territt* v. *Bartlett*, which arose in Vermont on a similar law of that state, the liquor having been delivered at New York in pursuance of a contract made by the vendor in person while travelling in Vermont: and the judgment was, on similar principles, against the validity (*l*).

221. We have seen in Art. 193 that the legality of an insurance depends on the law of the place of business of the insurers, where the policy is granted, and the promise contained in such policy is to be executed by payment, if occasion arise, of the amount insured. But suppose the contract for the policy is made by correspondence, the proposals coming from a client in another country, the law of which forbids the insurance by foreign companies, or by such foreign companies, of property there situate; and that the policy is either despatched to such client by post, or delivered to him at his home by the company's agent. This case has happened when New York mutual insurance companies have insured in Ohio or in Canada West, and their liability has been sustained at New York (*m*). "When the application," said Justice Johnson, "was received and approved by the company, and the policy executed and put in course of transmission to the insured, the contract was complete, and both parties became bound, so that if a loss had occurred before its actual receipt by the insured, the company would have been responsible. . . . . . The validity of the contract is therefore to be determined by the law of New York. Here it was made, and here it was

(*l*) 21 Vermont, 184.

(*m*) *Hyde* v. *Goodnow*, 3 Comstock, 266—policy sent by post to Ohio: *Western* v. *Genesee Mutual Insurance Company*, 2 Kernan, 258—policy delivered by agent in Canada West.

to be performed" (*n*). But it appears that the New York company cannot recover in Canada West on a note given there for the premium, as might have been expected, the legality of the consideration for such note depending on the law of the place where it was made (*o*).

222. Let us now apply these results as to agency to the case of a partnership *en commandite* suggested by Story, as mentioned in Art. 211. The general partner may, on the principles of Art. 220, so act as clearly to subject himself to the law of the country in which the goods are sold, as by giving the order through an agent of his established there for that purpose, and there receiving the goods. This is taking the case most strongly against the *commanditaires.* But even so, before the principles of the same article can be again applied to show that they also subjected themselves to the same law through the general partner as their agent, the authority given by them to him must be strictly examined: and since that authority, if they have not held themselves out as partners in the place of the sale, can only be deduced from the terms of their copartnership, it seems impossible to set it up at all without at the same time importing the limit to which the liability was restricted.

223. Suppose however a partnership of liability unlimited by any definite amount of subscription, but existing in a country where its members are liable only for a proportionate share of each debt contracted by it. Will this restriction follow it, in contracting where partners are liable *in solido?* No, for there is here an unlimited mutual

(*n*) 2 Kernan, p. 262. But Justice Marvin appeared to think the law of Canada West would have been important, if it had been before the court on proper proof, on account of the difference of the principles applicable to the foreign operations of corporations and natural persons, noticed below in Art. 224.

(*o*) *Genesee Mutual Insurance Company* v. *Westman* (*Western?*), imperfectly stated in 2 Kernan, 259.

agency of the partners, to contract for one another according to the local law of each transaction: or, supposing the contract to be made by an agent not a member of the firm, he is the agent for all the partners, each of whom subjects himself through him to the local law (*p*). If, on the contrary, liability *in solido* be the law of the country of the partnership, and liability for a proportionate share that of the place of the particular contract, it seems difficult to give to the creditor a larger right against the partners than that for which he contracted, so that they will be responsible for their virile parts only (*q*). These principles apply also to part-owners of vessels used in trade.

224. But as corporations are persons in law, there can never in their case be any question of separate liability on the part of their members, supposing the corporate power of acting to be at all recognized extraterritorially. As to this, the following opinion has been expressed by Justice Denio of New York:—" In respect to contracts made in another state, a corporation stands upon a different footing in some respects from individuals. As to the latter, the citizens of each state are entitled to all privileges and immunities of the citizens of the several states. This is secured by the national constitution. But corporations are not citizens in the sense of that provision. They are beings existing only in contemplation of law, and have no other attributes than such as the law confers upon them; and as the laws of a country have in general no extra-territorial operation, a corporation cannot challenge, as a matter of right, the privilege of dealing in a country not under the jurisdiction of the sovereignty which created it. Any of the states of the Union may, as this and several of the other states have done, interdict foreign corporations

(*p*) Story, s. 322. *Ferguson* v. *Flower*, 4 Mar. N. S. 312.
(*q*) *Baldwin* v. *Gray*, 4 Mar. N. S. 192.

from performing certain single acts, or conducting a particular description of business, within its jurisdiction. But in the absence of laws of that character, or in regard to transactions not within the purview of any prohibitory law, and not inconsistent with the policy of the state as indicated by the general scope of its laws or institutions, corporations are permitted by the comity of nations to make contracts and transact business in other states than those by virtue of whose laws they were created, and to enforce those contracts, if need be, in the courts of such other states. It is of course implied that the contract must be one which the foreign corporation is permitted by its charter to make; and it must also be one which would be valid if made at the same place by a natural person, not a resident of that state. (*Silver Lake Bank* v. *North*, 4 Johns. Ch. 370; *Bank of Augusta* v. *Earle*, 13 Pet. 519; *Mumford* v. *American Life Insurance and Trust Company*, 4 Comst. 463.)" (*r*)

225. In promissory notes and bills of exchange, there is a conflict of laws as to the conditions necessary to call into play the guarantee of the drawer or indorser, namely, as to the necessity and form of a demand and protest, and as to what is sufficient notice of dishonour. "By the common law," says Story, "the protest is to be made at the time, in the manner, and by the persons prescribed in the place where the bill is payable. But as to the necessity of making a demand and protest, and the circumstances under which notice may be required or dispensed with, these are incidents of the original contract, which are governed by the law of the place where the bill is drawn. They constitute implied conditions, upon which the liability of the drawer is to attach, according to the *lex loci contractus*; and, if the bill is negotiated, the like responsi-

(*r*) In *Bard* v. *Poole*, 2 Kernan, 504.

bility attaches upon each successive indorser, according to the law of the place of his indorsement; for each indorser is treated as a new drawer" (*s*). I cannot altogether agree with this doctrine. There is, no doubt, a sound distinction between the events on the occurrence of which the drawer or indorser undertakes to pay, and the notice given to him of their occurrence: but the making a demand and protest, when necessary by the law of the place of payment, should, I think, rank among the former no less than the dishonour itself; since, if these formalities be omitted, the drawer may be impeded in the exercise of his remedies against the acceptor. Besides, if the necessity of demand and protest were determined by different laws for the drawer and the several indorsers, it might easily happen that one of those parties was made liable without being able to recover over from a previous one. A sounder rule therefore is that given elsewhere by the same author. "If a protest of a bill of exchange, made in another state, is required by the laws of that state to be under seal, a protest not under seal will not be regarded as evidence of the dishonour of the bill" (*t*). But the sufficiency of the notice after completion of the protest, if any, may well be tested by the law of the place of drawing or indorsing, as a condition implied in the contract, and which a regard for the contractor's own security does not refer to any other law. The latter point is indeed well settled in America. One of the most recent authorities for it may be cited, because it at the same time asserts one of those exceptions which afford the clearest insight into rules, inasmuch as they spring out of their principles. I will give it in the words of Chief Justice Ruggles.

226. "The defendant indorsed the notes for the accom-

(*s*) Conflict of Laws, s. 360.

(*t*) Story, Conflict of Laws, s. 260 a; citing *Tickner* v. *Roberts*, 11 Louis. 14; and *Bank of Rochester* v. *Gray*, 2 Hill, N. Y. 227.

modation of the maker. This appears from the fact that the notes came from the possession of the maker and not of the indorser, and were first negotiated in New York (the place where they were made payable), and apparently for the benefit of Carew, the maker. So long as they remained in Carew's hands, there was no liability on the part of the indorser. The indorser's contract therefore must be regarded as having been made in New York, where the notes were delivered to Ryckman (who passed them to the plaintiff), and the indorsement first became effective. The law of Michigan (where the indorsement was made) has, therefore, no application to the case. The contract having been made in New York, the law of New York governs the case as to the sufficiency of the notice" (*u*). In truth, the accommodation-party to a bill of exchange or promissory note makes that party to whom he lends his signature his agent for putting the instrument in circulation, and his own contract with those to whom it is negotiated must consequently be judged on the principles of agency, which refer it to the place where the circulation commences.

227. *Rothschild* v. *Currie* was an action, on the dishonour of a bill drawn in France, against the payee who had indorsed it in England (*x*). A delay in the notice arose solely from an inevitable delay in the protest, which was dispatched to the defendant immediately on its completion, so that in my view the plaintiff rightly recovered. The argument however, passing lightly over the necessity of the protest, which in England is not required on inland bills, appears to have turned mainly on the sufficiency of the notice as from the date of the dishononr, a point on which, if the English law had been held to rule, the plain-

(*u*) *Cook* v. *Litchfield*, 5 Selden, 279, 290.
(*x*) 1 Q. B. 43, 4 P. & D. 737.

tiff must have failed. And the court, taking the same view of the stress of the case, selected the French law for reasons to which I cannot assent, for they followed Pothier in considering that every question about a bill must be decided by the law of the place where it is payable, as that of the performance of the contract. Now even were this in general a true interpretation of the principle of the *lex loci contractus*, yet the place where the bill is payable is not that of the performance of the drawer's and indorser's contracts, since it is not there that they contract to pay, but in the respective places where they become parties to it, only on the occurrence of such events in the place drawn on as, by actuating their potential liability, may give occasion to a demand to be made on them where they severally affixed their names (*y*). Story, determining the necessity of a protest by the *lex loci contractus* of the drawer or indorser, has objected to *Rothschild* v. *Currie* (*z*). In the New York case of *Aymar* v. *Sheldon*, the necessity of a protest for non-payment, one for non-acceptance having been made, was determined against the indorser by the law of the place of indorsement: and the court looked in the face the probable consequence of its judgment, that the defendants might have to pay without recourse against the drawers, which it said was their fault for not having indorsed specially (*a*).

228. We have now to consider the acceptor's contract. If the bill be payable in the place where it is accepted, his obligations will of course be governed by the law of that place; and any equitable defence, or right of set-off, which he may by it enjoy against the holder, he cannot be deprived of on account of the bill having originated elsewhere. Thus, in *Burrows* v. *Jemino*, it was held that the

(*y*) See the judgment in *Allen* v. *Kemble*, 6 Mo. P. C. 321.

(*z*) On Bills, s. 296, note.

(*a*) 12 Wendell, 439.

question whether an acceptance is avoided by the acceptor not having sufficient effects of the drawer in his hands at the time of the acceptance, must be decided by the law of the place of acceptance: and, the acceptance having been vacated by a court of that place, he was held discharged in England (*b*). Nay, the drawer and indorsers, as the acceptor's sureties, may use in their own countries the same pleas which he might found on the law of his acceptance. Thus, in *Allen* v. *Kemble*, bills having been drawn and indorsed in Demerara, and accepted payable in London, the assignees of the bankrupt holder obtained in Demerara a judgment against the drawer and indorser for the full amount due on the securities, notwithstanding that the acceptor had a right of set-off against the plaintiffs by English law, which right could also have been made available in the colony in proceedings against the acceptor—the objection to its validity in the actual suit being that by the Roman-Dutch law, which is that of Demerara, compensation only takes effect in cases of mutual debts between the parties to the action: but on appeal to the Privy Council the set-off was allowed (*c*). The same case throws light on the question between the places of acceptance and payment, when these are different: for the bills, though drawn payable in London, were addressed to the drawee in Scotland, and there accepted by him payable in London. The latter therefore, said Lord Kingsdown, "being fixed as the place of payment, they are payable by the drawee according to the law of England: a different law is imported as regards the acceptor, but not as affects other parties" (*d*).

(*b*) 2 Strange, 733.

(*c*) 6 Moore, P. C. 314. Lord Kingsdown said (p. 323) that the case must be decided according to the law of Demerara, by which was perhaps intended that that law itself would treat the appellants as sureties, liable only for what was due from their principal, though it must be confessed that this ground does not appear in the judgment.

(*d*) 6 Moore, P. C. 322.

That is, the place of payment is completely substituted for that of acceptance, as to all questions which depend on the law of the acceptor's contract, and which, as we have seen, sometimes mediately affect the drawer and indorsers; but the contracts of the latter parties, so far as they are independent of that of the acceptor, depend still on their own laws. Thus, if in *Allen* v. *Kemble* those parties had been able to claim a set-off against the assignees by the Roman-Dutch law, it would certainly have been allowed without reference to the law of England.

229. It is impossible to exhaust the particular kinds of contracts. The instances given will enable the reader to form an opinion on those cases which have not yet come before our tribunals, or at least are not contained in their reports. But the following cases, which have mostly not been already mentioned, may be usefully brought together, as well for illustrating continental views of the matter, as because some of them which sound very foreign may find application in our system of equity. To the law of the contract belong every peremptory exception, for these only determine various forms and degrees of imperfect validity, and therefore cannot be referred to the laws of procedure, the more so as any attempt to distinguish them from the question of validity could only be carried out through such sharply defined thoughts and expressions as are often wanting in modern legislation (*e*): but not herein the exceptions arising from the *senatus consultum Macedonianum* and *sc. Velleianum*, because these do not turn on the imperfection of the obligation in itself, but on the imperfect capacity of the parties, by the laws of whose domicile they must therefore be decided. Also every action by which a contract can be defeated: as the nullification of a sale for lesion above half the value, or through the *redhibitoria*

(*e*) Savigny, v. 8, p. 270; opposing Fœlix, n. 100.

actio, or the *actio quanti minoris:* and every restitution against a contract producing an obligation, even when such restitution rests on minority, because, from the gradual development of that institution in the Roman law, it cannot be regarded as a simple consequence of incapacity, but as a remedy defeating the obligation as such (*f*). In sales, warranty, the right to rescind either for simple change of mind or for non-accomplishment of conditions, and the risk of the articles perishing before delivery: in partitions, warranty: in general contracts, the real or personal nature of the obligation; whether co-contractors, co-sureties, or co-heirs of a contractor are liable *in solido* or *pro virili parte;* which party must pay the fiscal dues; and accessory obligations, as the giving security (*g*). Also all questions arising out of farming-leases, the place of execution, of which the law is decisive, being the situation of the immovable (*h*). To the accidental consequences of a contract, which produce their juristic effect according to the law of the place where the events which occasion them occur, belong *restitutio in integrum* founded on non-performance, the duty of reinvestment of monies repaid, and the confirmation or ratification of a null, defective, or rescindible contract (*i*). The *lex loci contractus* governs an agreement for discharging a mortgage on a foreign immovable (*j*).

230. The last point on the material contents of obligations is the consequences arising from their breach, as to which the main principle is that the creditor must be reinstated in the same position in which he would have stood had the contract been duly executed in time and place. Let us consider these two points separately, and first as to time. We have already seen that interest *ex mora* is allowed

(*f*) Savigny, p. 272. See also pp. 164, 165.

(*g*) Fœlix, n. 109.

(*h*) Fœlix, n. 109, with Demangeat's note: Savigny, p. 281, who in the same place asserts the same law for the vendor's right of repentance.

(*i*) Fœlix, n. 109.

(*j*) *Campbell* v. *Dent*, 2 Mo. P. C. 292, 307.

at the rate of the place of stipulated performance, or of that where performance ought to have been made, since it is there that the creditor has really missed the use of his money, and the rate of that place therefore measures the damage actually incurred. To the authorities cited on this in Art. 206, may be added the opinion of Savigny (*k*), and a case showing that the interest on damages from a tort is measured by the rate of the *locus delicti*, the principle being similar, for it must have been there that the means of the injured party were cramped by the loss (*l*). The same result follows from the principle which we saw in Arts. 166 and 167, that the nonperformance of a contract is a new fact, producing its juristic effects according to its own local law. For the place of such nonperformance is that where performance ought to have been, as has been expressed by Lord Langdale. "The nonpayment of the money when the bill becomes due is a breach in England of the contract which was to be performed in England . . . . and I think that the law of England, that is, the law of the place where the default has happened, must govern the allowance of interest which arises out of that default" (*m*). From this point of view also the doctrine is carried a step farther than it is taken by regarding the amount of damage as a matter of fact. For if the law of the place of default, as such, determines the juristic consequences of the breach of contract which has been committed there, then it will be for that law to say whether interest *ex mora* shall be given at all (*n*).

231. And so clear is this that discussions have seldom been raised about it except on the question where a par-

---

(*k*) System, &c., v. 8, p. 282.

(*l*) *Ekins* v. *East India Company*, 1 P. W. 395, 2 Bro. P. C. 382.

(*m*) *Cooper* v. *Waldegrave*, 2 Beav. 282, 285.

(*n*) See *Montgomery* v. *Bridge*, 2 Dow & Clark, 297; where however a conflict between the places of contract and performance did not arise for consideration.

ticular obligation ought to have been performed, which is one of municipal as much as of international law. I might perhaps say, never; but for an opinion of Lord Wynford, expressed indeed only at *nisi prius*, in an action on a Scotch judgment, rendered for the balance due to an agent in Scotland from his principal in England. The question was whether the interest which the judgment had allowed could be sustained; and his lordship said, in disallowing that part of the claim, "as the contract (for the employment of the agent) was made in England, although it was to be executed in Scotland, I think it ought to be regulated according to the rules of the English law" (*o*). Story approves the decision, but on the ground that, though the agent's services are to be performed in Scotland, yet the principal was to pay the commission in England (*p*): a ground perhaps not inconsistent with Savigny's reference of the contract of agency to the place where the *defendant* transacts affairs connected with it (*q*). Advances are generally considered to be repayable where made, and therefore to carry the interest of that place (*r*): but they have been held in Louisiana to carry the interest of the domicile of the principal for whom they are made, a rule which the court said accorded with the general mercantile opinion (*s*). In the great case of *Consequa* v. *Fanning*, it was decided that the consignee of goods, who is to sell them and remit the proceeds, performs his contract by putting the money on board the proper conveyance, even though the goods were

(*o*) *Arnott* v. *Redfern*, 2 Ca. & Pa. 88.

(*p*) Sect. 292, note.

(*q*) See above, Art. 105 (II.). So a factor is subject, as to the amount of his remuneration, to the law of the place of his employment: *Pennant* v. *Simpson*, 1 Knapp, 399. Yet that amount may carry the interest of the place where the principal has to pay it.

(*r*) *Grant* v. *Healey*, 3 Sumner, 523, decided by Justice Story. See his Conflict of Laws, s. 287.

(*s*) *Ballister* v. *Hamilton*, 3 Louis. Ann. 401; cited in Story, s. 284 b.

delivered to his agent by the consignor at the latter's place of business (*t*). But in both the higher and lower courts it was allowed that the rate of interest, in case of the consignee's default, depended on the place where his repayment would have been complete.

232. Next, to take the question of place alluded to in Art. 230. The creditor cannot call on the defendant to remit the amount of his debt to the country of the forum (*u*): on the contrary, such sum only will be adjudged as, on being remitted to the country where the debt ought to have been paid, will produce that amount there (*x*). But what if the question of place become complicated with one of time, by a variation of the rate of exchange between the date when the debt fell due, and that when the action is brought? It is the latter period at which the exchange must be taken, for the only fixed element is the amount owing in the place where the debt is payable, increased of course from time to time by such interest as may there accrue on it: what is due elsewhere fluctuates from forum to forum and from moment to moment, being always the sum which on being remitted will produce that amount (*y*).

233. In the last article, it has been assumed that the effect of considering the exchange will be favourable to the debtor. But what if in the forum it require a larger

(*t*) 17 Johnson, 511, reversing Chancellor Kent's decision in 3 Johnson, Ch. 587.

(*u*) *Ekins* v. *East India Company*, 1 P. W. 395, 2 Bro. P. C. 382; *Delegal* v. *Naylor*, 7 Bing. 460.

(*x*) *Scott* v. *Bevan*, 2 Ba. & Ad. 78.

(*y*) As to the precise time for taking the rate of exchange, Lord Tenterden, in *Scott* v. *Bevan* (2 Ba. & Ad. 85), referred generally to that current "at the commencement of the action, or for some time before or afterwards;" but the note to the same case (p. 86) states that under an act of the Jamaica legislature, as to the recovery there of English debts, the colonial practice has fixed the day on which the execution is lodged, which seems more correct in principle. In *Bertram* v. *Duhamel*, 2 Mo. P. C. 217, it was said, "at the time the judgment is recorded."

sum than the nominal amount of the debt, in order to produce, by remittance, the true amount in the place where the debt is due? There is no reason why the same principle should not still be applied, the hardship to the debtor being only apparent, for it is but nominally that the sum he would have to pay would exceed that justly due from him: nor can there be any suspicion that the English courts would hesitate to apply the principle (*z*). But the usual state of the exchange between Europe and America makes the question to be of most importance in the recovery of debts due to the former in the latter quarter of the globe. The courts of New York and Massachusetts allow no recovery but at the par of exchange, in any case except on bills of exchange: but in the circuit court of the United States the actual rate is allowed, as we have seen that it is in Jamaica (*a*).

234. The question of commission, when the debt is received by an agent, obviously depends on similar principles to that of exchange, and is thus treated by Lord Eldon. "Where a debt is contracted in Jamaica, and is therefore *prima facie* to be paid there, it is obviously reasonable that, if the creditor lives in London, and his agent makes a demand upon the debtor where he resides, and he there pays the whole, he has paid the creditor when he has paid the agent; and the expense of the transmission of the debt is between the creditor and his agent, the contract of the debtor being satisfied. But upon a security made payable in London, the creditor is in London to receive so much money, and . . . . . . the person who undertakes to pay must pay that money in England without deduction (of agent's commission): otherwise he does not make good his contract" (*b*).

(*z*) See *Cash* v. *Kennion*, as cited in the next article.

(*a*) Story, s. 311 a. As to Jamaica, see above, note (*y*), p. 218.

(*b*) *Cash* v. *Kennion*, 11 Ves. 314, 315, 317.

235. To apply this to the damages on bills of exchange, we must observe that the acceptor promises to pay where the bill is made payable, or, if no place of payment is named, at the known place of business from which he dates his acceptance (*c*). He will therefore be liable to such interest *ex mora* as is given in that place (*d*). Also, failing payment by the drawee, the drawer and indorsers promise to pay, each in the place where he became a party to the bill, a full compensation to the holder. Now the holder may if he pleases have recourse to re-exchange: that is, he may, from the place where the bill should have been paid by the drawee, draw another bill on the drawer or any of the indorsers, for the amount of the former one, increased by costs, and by the exchange, at the time of receiving the notice of nonpayment (*e*), of the place on which he draws on that on which the old bill was drawn. Thus if a bill be drawn in London on Amsterdam, and be indorsed at Paris, the holder may on its dishonour draw a new bill on the indorser for such a sum that, when negotiated at Amsterdam according to the current rate of exchange between that place and Paris, it may immediately produce to him the amount of the former bill with his costs: or he may redraw on the drawer, for a sum to be similarly ascertained by the rate of exchange between London and Amsterdam. The amount for which the holder

(c) But see Art. 190. In America, payment of a promissory note, which carries no place of payment on its face, is demandable at the maker's then residence or place of business when it becomes due, even though the maker have changed his residence or place of business since the making, so it be still in the same state where the note was made: if the maker have no establishment in that state, or none known to the payee, the place of making is that of demand: *Anderson* v. *Drake*, 14 Johnson, 114; *Hepburn* v. *Toledano*, 10 Mar. 643. And the observance of these rules is necessary to charge the indorsers: *Jacks* v. *Nichols*, 1 Selden, 178, 186. See also *Peck* v. *Hibbard*, 26 Vermont, 698, 702.

(*d*) *Cooper* v. *Waldegrave*, 2 Beav. 282.

(*e*) *Denston* v. *Cairns*, 13 Johnson, 322.

may so redraw is clearly that of the debt which at the time of the notice of dishonour is due to him from the drawer or indorser in the place of drawing or indorsing: it is that which if then paid him there would place him in the same position as if he had been duly paid the first bill in the place on which it was drawn. This then is the amount for which he must sue the drawer or indorser.

236. But if in the place of drawing or indorsing there exist a rule for determining such amount by a fixed proportion to that of the dishonoured bill, "in lieu of interest, charges of protest, and all other charges incurred previous to or at the time of giving notice of non-acceptance or non-payment" (*f*), such rule is binding as a part of the local law of the drawer's or indorser's contract. Thus in Maryland the damages on bills on Europe are fixed at 15 per cent., in Pennsylvania at 20, and in New York at 10. Suppose a bill drawn in Maryland on England, and successively indorsed in the other states named: the holder, on its dishonour, for every 100 dollars of its amount may sue his immediate indorser in New York for 110, the previous indorser in Pennsylvania for 120, or the drawer in Maryland for 115. And if the suit be brought elsewhere, it must be as for a debt of such respective amount due in the state of the drawing or indorsing, on the computation pointed out in Arts. 230—233 (*g*). And the sum

(*f*) Revised Statutes of New York, in Bouvier's American Law Dictionary, Art. Damages on Bills of Exchange; where also the other fixed rates here mentioned will be found. It was determined by a very narrow majority that the old New York rate of 20 per cent. was not inclusive of the exchange: *Graves* v. *Dash*, 12 Johnson, 17. And the same holds now, if the bill be expressed in foreign money, when the exchange "at the time of the demand of payment" will be added, besides the 10 per cent. "upon the principal sum specified in the bill:" but if the bill be expressed in United States money, the exchange will not be reckoned: Bouvier, *ubi supra*, New York.

(*g*) So that the rate of interest will also be that of the place of drawing or indorsing: *Gibbs* v. *Fremont*, 9 Exch. 25. But see *Pecks* v. *Mayo*, 14 which each indorser can recover over from the drawer or any previous indorser will be correspondingly limited, so that though the first indorser pay 120 dollars in Pennsylvania, he will only receive 115 from the drawer in Maryland (*h*).

237. *Delicts.*—Every authority which traces the force of a contract, or of an obligation *quasi ex contractu*, to the local law under which the agreement or the act is made or done, must of course be of equal avail to trace the obligation arising from a delict to the local law under which it is committed. The same conclusion follows from the generally recognised *forum delicti*, combined with the considerations which in all cases assert the law of the proper jurisdiction as that which must be applied if the cause emerges elsewhere. Thus we have seen that the interest given by way of damages depends on the *locus delicti* (*i*); and in *Caldwell* v. *Vanvlissengen*, a Dutchman was held liable for the infraction in England of an English patent (*k*), a case however the point in which, inasmuch as the *locus delicti* was there also the forum, is of less value than the broad terms in which the principle was laid down. Natural justice, said Sir George Turner, required the provisions of the stat. 32 Hen. 8, c. 16, s. 9, which enacted "that every alien and stranger born out of the king's obeisance, not being denizen, which now or hereafter shall come in or to this realm or elsewhere within the king's dominions, shall, after the 1st of September next coming, be bounden by and unto the laws

---

Vermont, 33, where after two arguments the court decided by a majority that the indorser of a note was liable to the interest of the place where it was made payable, forgetting that the amount due in that place is fixed once for all when the note is dishonoured, the subsequent delay occurring where that sum should then have been paid by the indorser.

(*h*) Story, s. 314.—See, on this article, *Francis* v. *Rucker*, Ambl. 672.

(*i*) *Ekins* v. *East India Company*, 1 P. W. 395, 2 Bro. P. C. 382.

(*k*) 9 Hare, 415. See particularly pp. 425, 426.

and statutes of this realm, and to all and singular the contents of the same."

238. But we shall expect to find that the view by which private international jurisprudence is based on the freely willed subjection of the parties, and not on the territorial authority of law, is incompatible with the conception of an obligation so deeply imprinted by the *lex loci* of a delict that it may be enforced elsewhere. Accordingly Savigny refers delicts entirely to the *lex fori*, being farther influenced thereto by the stringent moral end of the laws which redress them. I fail however to see clearer proofs of such an end in the redress of most torts than in that of a breach of contract: and, were this difficulty got over, though it is true, as before remarked, that the morality of a legal system must prevent the admission of foreign claims which might subvert it, it requires to be explained how it can confer the right of extending its own penalties to acts which have been committed in the empire of another law. "This question," says Savigny, "has been in no class of obligations so frequently mooted, doubted, and disputed, as in those flowing from seduction and adultery. . . . . If then such a claim is urged before a court which stands under the French law, it must be rejected, even when the intercourse has taken place at a spot of which the law permits and favours such a claim" (*l*). So far the doctrine may be admitted, as demanded by the excluding force here, and in Art. 196, attributed to the morality of a jurisprudence. The investigation to which the suit would lead cannot be made where the law regards it as too foul.

239. But it is more questionable, when the same jurist proceeds to say that "conversely must such a claim be admitted by the court of a spot of the latter kind, even

(*l*) Syst. d. h. Röm. Rechts, v. 8, p. 279. The *lex fori* was repudiated in *Cope* v. *Doherty*, as inapplicable to torts: 4 K. & J. 367, 384.

when the intercourse has taken place at a spot under the French law. And what holds here for the extreme opposition of unconditional rejection or admission, must be similarly asserted when the several local laws diverge in a less degree, as in the conditions or scope of the claim. The decisions of the courts on this question are very various. For the forum, which will in general (*m*) coincide with the defendant's domicile, the superior court of Stuttgart has pronounced: for the *locus delicti*, the supreme court of appeal of Munich, and two judgments at Jena. . . . It follows from the above principles that in such cases an important power will often be placed in the hand of the plaintiff, who often has the choice of several jurisdictions, and so can determine which of several local laws shall be applied. But this is the inevitable result of the peculiar nature of this class of laws. Also the danger for the defendant is diminished by the very restrictive conditions to which the special forum of every obligation is bound" (*n*).

240. With respect to the actual place of a delict, "it has been determined in Ohio that an action on the case, for diverting water from the plaintiff's mill situated in Ohio, might be sustained in the courts of that state, although the act of diversion took place in another state" (*o*). Yet the legal character and consequences of an act must certainly depend on the jurisprudence of the country where it is done, and not on that of any spot to which its consequences may extend. The damage is not an injury, unless it results from conduct prohibited by the law which governs the agent.

(*m*) Observe, not always, so that this is not Savigny's reason.

(*n*) That is, the alternative of the defendant's personal presence or possession of property there, as necessary for the *forum delicti* as for the *forum contractus*. See above, Art. 109.

(*o*) *Thayer* v. *Brooks*, 17 Ohio, 489, thus shortly stated in the 7th edition of Story's Conflict of Laws, s. 554.

3. *Transfer of Obligations.*

241. If an obligation be not assignable in its inception, it is clear that no private attempt to assign it, to which he is not a party, can give a title against the debtor. And even its public assignment by the bankrupt law of the creditor's domicile will not enable the assignee to sue on it, in a country where choses in action are not assignable, otherwise than in the creditor's name (*p*).

242. If an obligation be assignable in its inception, the assignee may sue on it, and in his own name, even in a forum by the proper law of which choses in action are not assignable; for the promise or duty of the debtor was, from the first, to the contingent series of assignees no less than to the original creditor. This is equally true, whether the original assignability existed by the peculiar law of the obligation, as in the case of Irish judgments made assignable by an Irish statute (*q*), and in that of a Scotch bond (*r*); or by the terms of the obligation, notwithstanding that no effect would be given them by its peculiar law, as when a note is made payable to order in a country where notes are not negotiable, and is indorsed in another country where they are nogotiable (*s*). For, in the last case, the maker must be considered as having waived by his original contract the privilege he might have had of being sued only at the option of the payee, and the right of the latter is excluded by his own negotiation made in a country where that is effectual. And what is thus true of the general question of assignability is equally so of the conditions under which it exists. Thus if a promissory note

(*p*) *Jeffery* v. *McTaggart*, 6 M. & S. 126.

(*q*) *O'Callaghan* v. *Thomond*, 3 Taun. 81.

(*r*) *Innes* v. *Dunlop*, 8 T. R. 595.

(*s*) *Lodge* v. *Phelps*, 1 Johns. Ca. 139, 2 Caines, Ca. in Error, 321. But, *per curiam* in the same case, the maker may use against the assignee all the defences which by the law of the place of making he could have had against the payee.

is made payable to bearer, in a country where a *bona fide* transfer for value confers a good title to a stolen note, the maker's liability to a bearer who satisfies the large conditions thus implied is a part of his contract from the first, and if the note be stolen and transferred *bona fide* for value in another country, it will not be necessary to inquire what the effect of such transfer would be by the law of the latter locality (*t*). On the other hand, if the maker, by the law of the place of making, may set up any equitable defence against a *bona fide* indorsee which he could offer against the payee, he will retain the same faculty notwithstanding an indorsement in a state where such is not the law (*u*).

243. Suppose that the obligation is assignable, but that there is a conflict of laws as to the proper form of an assignment, or as to its substantial validity. Between the original creditor and the assignee, the general principles as to contracts show the just rule to be the law of the place of assignment: and that rule imposes no hardship on the debtor, whose interests are equally liable to be affected by an assignment under any law. Thus where a bill of exchange, drawn in the state of New York on Massachusetts, in pursuance of a written authority and promise to accept by the drawee, was purchased in the former state by a banker there, and made payable to his cashier, in an action in Massachusetts against the drawee the banking-law of New York was referred to, apparently for the purpose of showing that on such an assignment of the defendant's promise the banker could sue in his own name. But in the same case the previous question, whether the defendant's promise was negotiable at all, was decided by the law of Massachusetts, where it was given (*x*).

244. There is a conflict of laws on the necessary form

(*t*) *De La Chaumette* v. *Bank of England*, 2 Ba. & Ad. 385.

(*u*) *Ory* v. *Winter*, 4 Mar., N. S. 277. See also *Lodge* v. *Phelps, ubi supra.*

(*x*) *Barney* v. *Newcomb*, 9 Cushing, 46, 53, 54.

of indorsing promissory notes and bills of exchange, an indorsement in blank not being allowed in France (*y*). The point between the places of making and indorsement did not arise in *Trimbey* v. *Vignier*, in which both had been done in France, and the court accordingly, while rejecting the *lex fori*, did not explain whether it rested its judgment for the defendant on the law of France as that of the original contract, or as that of the attempt to assign it (*z*). But the principles above maintained would command the universal assent of foreign jurists, on the ground that *locus regit actum*, and are supported also by the cases which decided that foreign notes were made negotiable here by the English statute 3 & 4 Anne, c. 9: since the law which can confer negotiability may also prescribe the form of negotiation (*a*). Also, if the holder of a negotiable security dies, and a personal representative is duly appointed to him in his domicile, so as to be the legal transferee of the security in the place of the asserted transfer, our principles would show that the latter, or his indorsee, can sue the foreign drawer or maker, without taking out administration either in the forum or in the country of the

(*y*) Code de Commerce, Arts 137, 187.

(*z*) 1 Bing. N. C. 151, 4 M. & Sc. 695. If we remember that the maker's promise was always a negotiable one, the following remarks of Chief Justice Tindal, though valuable for their general principles, seem applicable to the French law in either character. "We think the French law on the point above mentioned is the law by which the contract is governed, and not the law which regulates the mode of suing. If the indorsement has not operated as a transfer, that goes directly to the point that there is no contract upon which the plaintiff can sue. Indeed, the difference in the consequences that would follow, if the plaintiff sues in his own name or is compelled to use the name of the former indorser as the plaintiff by procuration, would be very great in many respects, particularly in its bearing on the law of set-off:" 1 Bing. N. C. 160, 4 M. & S. 705.

(*a*) *Pollard* v. *Herries*, 3 Bos. & Pul. 335; *Splitberger* v. *Kohn*, 1 Star. 125; *Milne* v. *Graham*, 1 Ba. & Cr. 192; *Bentley* v. *Northouse*, M. & Mal. 66: overruling *Carr* v. *Shaw*, Bayley on Bills, 6th edit., p. 28. Of course our law could not have given effect against the maker to an indorsement here of a note not negotiable where made.

original contract. And this, in cases where the two latter coincide, as indeed they usually would, has been decided by the supreme court of the United States (*b*), as well as by the latest judgment of the court of Maine, overruling its former doctrine on the point (*c*).

245. It must here be observed that though a contract be illegal, yet if benefit be actually derived from it, either through the debtor's sense of honour preventing him from setting up the illegality, or by any other means, an assignment of that benefit, made even prospectively, to a person whose conduct has not been tainted with the original illegality, even though he may be cognisant of all the circumstances, will be supported as between the assignor and assignee. This is a rule of municipal law also, a leading case on the principle of which is *Thomson* v. *Thomson* (*d*), and it is the same principle that Lord Cottenham considered himself to follow in *Sharp* v. *Taylor* (*e*): but I mention it here because, in an important American case, it has been applied to the assignment of a contract which was void itself as made to promote insurrection in a foreign and friendly state, under the doctrine of Art. 199 (*f*). The conduct of the assignee was here untainted by the illegality, because the Mexican insurrection was complete, by the achievement of acknowledged independence, before the assignment, though the Mexican government did not discharge the claims on it till afterwards. It seems almost superfluous to remark that an assignment, however good between the parties to it by its own local law, or unconnected with the illegality affecting the con-

---

(*b*) *Harper* v. *Butler*, 2 Peters, Sup. Co. 239.

(*c*) *Barrett* v. *Barrett*, 8 Greenleaf, 353; supporting the doctrine of Story, s. 359, in opposition to *Stearns* v. *Burnham*, 5 Greenl. 261.

(*d*) 7 Ves. 470.

(*e*) 2 Ph. 801. See above, Art. 202.

(*f*) *McBlair* v. *Gibbes*, 17 Howard, 232. See also Chief Justice Taney's remarks in pp. 268, 269.

tract assigned by its local law, cannot avail to give the assignee a claim upon that contract against the original debtor which the assignor could not have enforced (*g*).

4. *Extinction of Obligations.*

246. The primary manner in which an obligation may terminate is by its due fulfilment, or, failing that, by satisfaction of the damage: as to which there is only to be said that, in case of dispute as to the fact, it must, like any other fact, be proved by such evidence as the *lex fori* admits in general, without requiring such special evidence as that law may require of the fulfilment or satisfaction of obligations contracted in its own sacramental forms. Thus, if in A. payment of a debt contracted in writing can only be proved by written evidence, or in B. that of a debt contracted under seal only by evidence under seal, yet payment of a debt contracted in A. in writing, or in B. under seal, may be proved elsewhere by witnesses: and, conversely, payment of a debt contracted by sealed writing out of A. and B. may be provable in either of those countries by witnesses, though not by such witnesses whose testimony is inadmissible in the forum on grounds unconnected with the mode of contracting the obligation. The *locus contractus* must be also the forum, in order to necessitate any special mode of proving the payment; and the *lex loci contractus* must coincide with the *lex fori*, in order only to justify it. These principles can cause no difficulty to any

(*g*) Yet in *Thatcher* v. *Morris*, 1 Kernan, 437—an action in New York against the contractor in a Maryland lottery, for the prizes drawn by tickets bought by the plaintiff after the drawing—the marginal note, countenanced by some expressions of Chief Justice Gardiner which are probably insufficiently reported, attributes the plaintiff's failure to his not showing that he purchased the tickets in a state where lotteries are lawful. The true point, as taken by Justice Allen, was in what state the defendants' promise to the plaintiff's vendor was made.

one who reflects that the obligation is by universal jurisprudence actually extinguished by the payment; and that neither, on the one hand, if the *lex loci contractus* shuts its eyes to the fact of its extinction, can that justify the judges of a different forum in doing the same thing; nor on the other, if the *lex fori* chooses to fence round with peculiar peril what may be called its own sacramental forms of contracting, is it bound to make defendants pay twice out of respect to the sacraments of a foreign law, though certainly from comity it may do so. But these truths have been strangely perplexed, by confounding the case with the totally distinct one of an obligation dissolved without being fulfilled or satisfied, so that the law of the place of payment has been brought into the discussion (*h*).

247. Supposing then that the obligation is neither fulfilled nor satisfied, it may be dissolved by the consent of the parties, or by the free act of the creditor; either of which, being a new contract or quasi-contract, will be subject, as to its formal and material requisites, to the rules investigated in the first two sections of this chapter. And this is the true application to the subject of the principle that *unumquodque dissolvitur eodem modo quo colligatur*.

248. Farther, all contracts carry with them from the beginning a liability to dissolution upon the happening of more or fewer contingencies, of which a certain lapse of time is always one, the right of either of the parties to rescind the contract, either generally within a limited period, or on the occurrence of certain conditions, may furnish another, and so on. Now this liability is a part of the *vinculum juris* existing between the parties, and to take the obligation without it would be, while nominally referring to the proper law of the contract, to take in fact a more stringent tie than that law ever created. "If," said Lord

(*h*) Story, s. 351 a, 633.

Brougham, expressing the views both of this and of the last paragraph, "a contract for sale of a chattel is made, or an obligation of debt is incurred, or a chattel is pledged in one country, the sale may be annulled, the debt released, and the pledge redeemed, by the law and by the forms of another country in which the parties happen to reside, and in whose courts their rights and obligations come in question; unless there was an express stipulation in the contract itself against such avoidance, release or redemption. But at any rate this is certain, that if the laws of one country and its courts recognise and give effect to those of another in respect of the constitution of any contract, they must give the like recognition and effect to those same foreign laws when they declare the same kind of contract dissolved. Suppose a party forbidden to purchase from another by our equity, as administered in the courts of this country (and we have some restraints upon certain parties which come very near prohibition); and suppose a sale of chattels by one to another party, standing in this relation towards each other, should be effected in Scotland, and that our courts here should (whether right or wrong) recognise such a sale because the Scotch law would affirm it; surely it would follow that our courts must equally recognise a rescission of the contract of sale in Scotland by any act which the Scotch law regards as valid to rescind it, although our own law may not regard it as sufficient. Suppose a question to arise in the courts of England respecting the execution of a contract thus made in this country, and that the objection of its invalidity were waived for some reason: if the party resisting its execution were to produce either a sentence of a Scotch court declaring it rescinded by a Scotch matter done in *pais*, or were merely to produce evidence of the thing so done, and proof of its amounting by the Scotch law to a rescission of the contract, I apprehend that the party relying on the contract could never be heard to say: 'The contract is English, and the Scotch proceeding is impotent to dissolve it.' The reply would be, 'Our English courts have (whether right or wrong) recognised the validity of a Scotch proceeding to complete the obligation, and can no longer deny the validity of a similar but reverse proceeding to dissolve it—*Unumquodque dissolvitur eodem modo quo colligatur*.' Suppose, for another example, which is the case, that the law of this country precluded an infant or a married woman from borrowing money in any way, or from binding themselves by deed; and that in another country those obligations could be validly incurred: it is probable that our law and our courts would recognise the validity of such foreign obligations. But suppose a *femme coverte* had executed a power, and conveyed an interest under it to another *femme coverte* in England; could it be endured, that where the donee of the power produced a release under seal from the *femme coverte* in the same foreign country, a distinction should be taken, and the court here should hold that party incapable of releasing the obligation? Would it not be said that our courts, having decided the contract of a *femme coverte* to be binding when executed abroad, must, by parity of reason, hold the discharge or release of the *femme coverte* to be valid, if it be valid in the same foreign country?" (*i*).

249. As a first instance of the liability to termination inherent by the *lex contractus*, I may mention merger in another cause of action, the occurrence of which will therefore be determined by the law of the former cause (*k*).

250. Another instance is furnished by the prescription of the *lex loci contractus*, which belongs entirely to what

(*i*) In *Warrender* v. *Warrender*, 9 Bligh, N. R. 125.

(*k*) *Bryans* v. *Dunseth*, 1 Mar., N. S. 412.

may be called the modality of the obligation (*l*). The opinion which refers this question to the *lex fori*, as one of procedure, rests on two fallacies. First, "the argument that the limitation is of the nature of the contract supposes that the parties look only to the breach of the agreement. Nothing is more contrary to good faith than such a supposition" (*m*). But this is to confound the interpretation of the contract with the operation on it of the *lex loci contractus*. After the detailed exposition already given of the difference between these, in Arts. 187—189, I need only add that I am not acquainted with any writer on this subject who has treated them as identical in theory, though of course many questions arise in practice as to the points which belong to each. Secondly, "it is said that by the law of Scotland"—the *lex fori*, which it was proposed to apply as governing the remedy—"not the remedy alone is taken away, but the debt itself is extinguished . . . . . . I do not read the statute in that

---

(*l*) Hertius, de Coll. Leg., s. 4, § 65: Savigny, v. 8, pp. 273, 274; who cites on the same side a judgment given in 1843 by the court of revision at Berlin, as well as numerous recent German writers: and the uniform current of modern French decisions, alleged by Fœlix, n. 100, and by Demangeat, in his note on that passage in the posthumous edition. On the other side are P. Voet, de Stat., s. 10, c. 1, n. 1, 2: Huber, de Confl. Leg., s. 7: and Story, with a positiveness quite unusual with him, s. 576 *et seq*. The older French authorities will be best seen in Fœlix, n. 100, as the effect of what is said by Boullenois and Pothier is a little overstated by Story on his side. That French jurists should assert the law of the debtor's domicile was likely, as the *forum contractus* was not originally received in France: it is therefore at least as much as we could expect, when we find Boullenois, Pardessus and Troplong maintaining the prescription of the place of execution *named by the parties*, in doing which they clearly lead the way to the present French acceptance of the European doctrine, to which Fœlix himself inclines in principle. It will be considered in the next paragraphs how far the American doctrine is received in Great Britain.

(*m*) Lord Brougham, in *Don* v. *Lippmann*, 5 Cl. & F. 16. The debt is similarly said to be left existing by the English statute, and by others *in pari materia*.

manner . . . . . . The debt is still supposed to be existing and owing (*n*)." There is however little or no meaning in saying that a debt subsists which cannot be recovered. The law may preserve a memory of the circumstances out of which it arose, in order to justify the late creditor in retaining its amount if he can get it, but in the mean time he has no right, for a right is only a faculty of putting the law in force. There is nothing therefore at bottom, in any statute of limitations, but an essential modification of the rights created by the jurisprudence in which it exists, and which is therefore incapable of a just application to rights created by the jurisprudence of another country. The rule here advocated is also, as Savigny remarks, the most reasonable, because it excludes both the arbitrary power of the plaintiff to choose between competing forums that which allows the longest term of prescription, and the arbitrary power of the defendant to defeat his creditor by removing his domicile to the forum which allows the shortest term, and avoiding, while it runs, personal presence in the special forum of the obligation.

251. The *lex fori* has however been established as the Scotch international rule on prescription by two decisions of the highest authority. In *Campbell* v. *Steiner* the court of session had declared for the *lex loci contractus*, but, on appeal, Lord Eldon moved the judgment of the House of Lords in favour of the *lex fori*, because it had been ruled that, where the merchant creditor resided in England and his debtor in Scotland, the latter might plead the Scotch prescription (*o*). His lordship unfortunately did not perceive that in most of the cases which he thus described the *locus contractus* would coincide with the *forum*. In *Don* v. *Lippmann* a similar judgment was

(*n*) See note (*m*) in preceding page.

(*o*) 6 Dow. 116, 134.

moved by Lord Brougham (*p*), and an opinion to the same effect has been expressed by Lord Cottenham in the Scotch case of *Fergusson* v. *Fyffe* (*q*).

252. The English cases are *The British Linen Company* v. *Drummond* (*r*), and *Huber* v. *Steiner* (*s*). In the former, Lord Tenterden inclined to the *lex fori*, on the authority of Huber and (as alleged) of John Voet, but with a hesitation grounded on the old Scotch law, as it stood before the appeal in *Campbell* v. *Steiner*, which was not quoted to him. The point was not pressed to a decision, but, had it been so, and the whole literature of the subject presented to his lordship, it is probable that, sitting as an English judge, he would have held the general consent now arrived at in Europe to outweigh the decision of the House of Lords on that Scotch appeal. He actually considered himself to follow the general European doctrine as opposed to the particular Scotch, and we may suppose that, on an international question, he would have been prepared to do the same, had he known that each was the reverse of what he thought it. In the latter case the *lex fori* was adopted, chiefly it seems on Story's authority, from whom also a distinction, not arising on the facts, was cited with approval. It was, that the prescription of the *lex loci contractus* will extinguish the claim, if "the parties are resident within the jurisdiction (of that law) during all that period, so that it has actually operated upon the case:" then this part also of the *lex loci contractus* would go *ad valorem contractus, ad decisionem litis.* It would be intelligible that the law of any country, in which the parties have both been domiciled during the whole period of prescription fixed by it, should be held to extinguish

(*p*) 5 Cl. & F. 1.
(*q*) 8 Cl. & F. 140.
(*r*) 10 Ba. & Cr. 903.
(*s*) 2 Scott, 304, 2 Bing. N. C. 202.

the right, on the ground of its having had them both for its subjects (*t*): but I do not understand why this should be asserted of the *lex loci contractus* more than of any other law; nor how the question, whether the *lex loci contractus* is effectual to mould the essence of an obligation, can depend on subsequent events, when the efficacy of that law cannot be sustained at all except on principles which exhaust it at the moment of contracting, although indeed, which is an entirely different matter, that law, if it be efficacious, may create at that moment obligations dependent on subsequent conditions. The whole subject is still open for the higher English tribunals.

253. In the cases of merger and prescription, we have had to consider the manner in which the *vinculum juris* is moulded by such general provisions of the law which creates it, as are immediately applicable to the particular obligation itself. But the same law may contain general provisions concerning debtors personally subject to it by domicile, under which they may obtain certificates discharging them, as bankrupts or insolvents, from all personal liabilities. Suppose the debtor either to be at the time of the contract domiciled in the *forum contractus*, or, for that appears to make no difference, to become domiciled there during the continuance of the obligation, and then to obtain his discharge in that forum under its law of bankruptcy. Suppose also that, through another change of domicile, or through happening to be, or to possess goods, in a country where the principles on jurisdiction

(*t*) See above, Art. 157. In *Ruckmaboye* v. *Mottichund*, 8 Moore, P. C. 4, 5 Moore, I. A. C. 234, the principle of the law common to the parties was held not to include terms of prescription, so that the English term was applied between Gentoos, notwithstanding the rules contained in the Indian charters of justice, as to which see above, Art. 153. The reason given was that the question was one of procedure, but the weight of the authority was, as usual, impaired by the ignorance that a serious doubt existed. "It has become almost an axiom in jurisprudence," &c.

are lax, he is yet sued on the obligation: will the discharge be available? It is not indeed such an extinction of the obligation by the *lex loci contractus* as those we have dealt with, but it is a discharge of the debtor by the authority of the same law, or sovereign, which, or who, bound him: and if that authority is recognised for the latter purpose, why not also for the former? The plaintiff cannot object that the exercise of discharging authority founds a plea which is *ex post facto* as regards his right, because the exercise of such authority must be considered as always reserved by a sovereign whose code includes a law of bankruptcy, whenever he imposes an obligation on a contract. It has accordingly long been settled by the English cases that an obligation is extinguished by a discharge of this nature under the laws of the country of the contract (*u*). Of course, to have this international effect, the discharge must be a complete one from the debt in the country where it is given, and not merely protect the person from incarceration, or exempt special classes of effects from seizure, as tools or wearing apparel (*v*).

254. There does not now exist in the United States any general bankruptcy law, and those which have been established in many of the several states have been adjudged to impair the faith of contracts, contrary to the constitution of the Union. Hence it was a great question how far discharges of obligations, under such laws existing in the countries where they were incurred, could be received, and an inclination was shown, the history of which is traced through the cases by Story, to limit their reception by the condition of the creditor also being a domiciled

---

(*u*) *Ballantine* v. *Golding*, 1 Cooke's Bankruptcy Laws, p. 347, 5th edit. It was thought an open question in *Pedder* v. *Macmaster*, 8 T. R. 609; but again decided in *Potter* v. *Brown*, 5 East, 124, which has been followed by *Quelin* v. *Moisson*, 1 Knapp, 265, note.

(*v*) *Exp. Burton*, 1 Atk. 255.

subject of the sovereign authority which gave the discharge, in which case it would be sustained on the principle of the law common to the parties (*x*). In the recent case of *Peck* v. *Hibbard* it has however been fully laid down, on a review of the decisions, that the discharges in question, when granted by jurisdictions foreign to the Union, will be held universally valid therein: but that, when granted under the insolvency laws of the states of the Union, they will not be held valid against plaintiffs whose title accrued before the date of the defendant's application for the discharge, unless such plaintiffs were at that date citizens of the same state with the debtor, in which case the constitution of the Union cannot interfere between them: while even the latter discharges will be held valid against plaintiffs taking, as by the indorsement of a promissory note, after the date of the defendant's application (*y*).

255. As between the members of the Union, then, this case settles the law as laid down in *Braynard* v. *Marshall*, where, though both the maker and payee were citizens of the state where the note was made and the discharge obtained, the maker was still held liable to the citizen of another state who had taken by indorsement previous to the proceedings in insolvency (*z*). And it is hard to see how any other conclusion could have been arrived at, under the constitution of the Union, interpreted as proscribing discharges of bankrupts. "The promisor," said Chief Justice Parker, "became, immediately upon the indorsement, the debtor to the indorsee, who was not amenable to the laws of New York, where the application

(*x*) Story, s. 340.

(*y*) 26 Vermont, 698. The promissory note in the case was payable where made, but the validity of the discharge was expressed to be founded on the law of that place as the place where it was payable.

(*z*) 8 Pickering, 194.

was made for relief under the insolvent law" (*a*). But, as a wider doctrine of public law, applicable beyond the United States, the same case has followed the strictures made on *Braynard* v. *Marshall* by Story, who, observing that the indorsement does not create a new contract between the maker and the indorsee in the place of the indorsement, justly contends that the maker's discharge by the original *lex loci contractus* of the note must avail him against the holder under a negotiation effected in a foreign country (*b*).

256. But will effect be given internationally to a discharge by the bankruptcy law of any other country than that of the contract, as if the debtor, not being domiciled in the *forum contractus*, becomes bankrupt in the jurisdiction to which he is personally subject, and is afterwards sued in the *forum contractus*, or elsewhere? There seems to be no juristic principle which compels an affirmative answer, and Story very positively gives a negative one (*c*): but the case is eminently one for the application of comity, between those nations which have instituted such discharges in their respective systems of law. They cannot mutually object to their justice, though in other countries these discharges may be considered as impairing the faith of contracts: and, when their international validity has once been established to this extent, for which there appear to be precisely the same motives which recommend such discharges to the public opinion of trading countries at all, the maxim that they are granted by the jurisdiction of the debtor's domicile becomes a part of the knowledge with which men are presumed to contract. And there

(*a*) P. 197. See also *Donnelly* v. *Corbett*, 3 Seld. 500; *Scribner* v. *Fisher*, 2 Gray, 43.

(*b*) Conflict of Laws, ss. 344, 345. These strictures were extended by Story to the case even as it actually arose under the constitution of the Union.

(c) Sect. 342.

seems to be some advance towards the establishment of this comity. In the older cases, it was held that *when the plaintiff was a British subject,* and the debt was contracted here, a discharge under a foreign bankruptcy was unavailing (*d*): and in applying this rule, an Irish bankruptcy (*e*) was held a foreign proceeding here, as an English bankruptcy was in the application of a similar rule in Scotland (*f*). Next, a discharge under a Scotch sequestration was held in England to bar an English debt, on the ground that it was founded on an act of the parliament of the United Kingdom, an authority competent with regard to English plaintiffs and transactions (*g*). Finally, it was determined by the Privy Council, on appeal from the supreme court at Calcutta, that the certificate under an English bankruptcy barred an action for a debt contracted by the bankrupt at Calcutta, although the creditor was resident at Calcutta and had no notice of the commission of bankrupt (*h*).

257. I have in the last paragraph considered the suit as not brought in the forum of the discharging law: but there is an obvious connexion between the question there discussed, and that of what debts the bankruptcy law is to be considered in its own forum as intended to discharge. Story appears to suppose that, in the absence of express words, such a law is only meant to discharge debts con-

---

(*d*) *Smith* v. *Buchanan,* 1 East, 6. Why this repeated reference in these cases to the plaintiff's nationality, which seems contrary to the equal footing on which we treat alien friends, if the judges felt themselves strong on the discharging law not being the *lex contractus?*

(*e*) *Lewis* v. *Owen,* 4 Ba. & Ald. 654. And so was a Scotch *cessio bonorum: Phillips* v. *Allan,* 8 Ba. & Cr. 477, where, *semble,* it would have been different if the plaintiff had accepted a share under the *cessio.* Yet see *Exp. Burton,* as cited in Art. 253.

(*f*) *Rose* v. *McLeod,* 4 Shaw & Dunlop, 311; overruling *Royal Bank of Scotland* v. *Cuthbert,* 1 Rose, 486.

(*g*) *Sidaway* v. *Hay,* 3 Ba. & Cr. 12.

(*h*) *Edwards* v. *Ronald,* 1 Knapp, 259.

tracted under it; and clearly lays down that, if it attempts to do more, even its *res judicata* may be held of no authority abroad (*i*). But in *Sidaway* v. *Hay* the presumption that parliament intended a Scotch sequestration to discharge English debts, merely because it was competent to entertain such an intention, goes beyond Story's interpretation of the *prima facie* meaning of the law: and in *Edwards* v. *Ronald*, inasmuch as our parliament does not, though it might, legislate on the private law of India, the assumption that our bankruptcy laws intend a discharge of all debts, wherever contracted, appears almost undisguised. The 200th section of the Bankrupt Law Consolidation Act, 1849, declares the certificate a discharge to "the bankrupt from all debts due by him when he became bankrupt, and from all claims and demands made provable under the bankruptcy." The latter words seem to refer to claims and demands made provable by the act, but debts contracted abroad and to foreigners are provable, and therefore within the reason of the rule. And the weight of authority appears to be in favour of attributing to such laws the widest intention to discharge of which their expressions will admit (*j*).

258. It will be understood that international effect cannot be given to any discharge obtained under a law which in such an application would be palpably unjust, even though existing in the *locus contractus*; as if some bankruptcy law should provide for a distribution of the debtor's effects, without any notice which could by possibility reach his foreign creditors (*k*). Such a law was held, in the case cited in the note, to be intended only for opera-

(*i*) Sect. 348.

(*j*) See *Lynch* v. *M'Kenny*, 2 H. Bl. 554; *Murray* v. *De Rottenham*, 6 Johns. Ch. 52; *Marsh* v. *Putnam*, 3 Gray, 551; *Journeay* v. *Gardner*, 11 Cush. 355; *Le Feuvre* v. *Sullivan*, 10 Moore, P. C. 1, 13.

(*k*) Story, s. 351, citing with approval the language of Chief Justice Parker in *Prentiss* v. *Savage*, 13 Mass. 24.

tion within the jurisdiction: at least, whatever the intention, it could only be allowed to operate there. Again, it is not necessary that the domicile to found a bankruptcy should be that strictly so called, on which, for instance, succession on death would depend: but similar remarks would apply to a discharge which should be granted on an unreasonably slight connexion with the jurisdiction.

259. Thus much for dissolubility inherent in the obligation. There are some other topics which belong almost equally to the material contents of obligations, as involved in the interpretation of the contract, and to their extinction. "A tender and refusal, good by the *lex loci contractus* either as a full discharge, or as a present fulfilment of the contract, will be respected everywhere. Payment in paper money, bills, or in other things, if good by the same law, will be deemed a sufficient payment everywhere. And on the other hand, where a payment by negotiable bills or notes is by the *lex loci* held to be conditional payment only, it will be so held even in states where such payment under the domestic law would be held absolute" (*l*). In all this however the *locus solutionis* must be understood, since the debtor cannot compel his creditor to accept an arbitrary mode, any more than an arbitrary time or place of payment.

(*l*) Story, s. 332.

CHAPTER VIII.

Movables.

260. Corporeal chattels are entirely within the reasons which have been given in Chap. IV. for answering by the *situs* all questions of the property in, and jurisdiction with regard to, land. No other sovereign can lawfully use force to change or maintain their existing state of possession, and it is therefore a matter of mere fact that the forum of the situation of every corporeal chattel must conclusively determine on its property (*a*). Can any reason be given why in so doing it should apply any law but its own? None which will not equally be of force as to the property in land. On the other hand, the protection which the local power accords to the rights of ownership draws with it the just claim to regulate them. It is indeed true, as said by the court in *Philips* v. *Hunter*, that " the country where the proprietor resides, in respect to another species of protection afforded to him and his property, has a right to regulate his conduct relating to that property. This protection afforded to the property of a resident subject which is situated in a foreign country is not imaginary, but real. The executive power of this kingdom protects the trade of its subjects in foreign countries, facilitates the recovery of their debts, and if justice be delayed or denied, the king by the intervention of his ambassadors demands

(*a*) " In a legal view," says Lord Kames, " a movable situated within a certain territory is subjected to the judge of that territory, and every action claiming the property or possession of it must be brought before that judge. Warrant for execution must be granted by the same judge, as no other judge has authority over it:" Principles of Equity, b. 3, c. 8, s. 3.

and obtains redress" (*b*). But the occasional protection thus afforded has only to be named, in comparison with the continual protection on which the enjoyment of property depends, to show how little it can weigh in determining the law to be applied. It is moreover a protection, not against the justice of the country to which the proprietor sends his ships or his merchandise, but against the possible failure of that justice, and therefore presupposing its course as the rule. To that course indeed the proprietor must in general be taken to submit himself, as to the chattel which he acquires within its jurisdiction, or which he dispatches thither. Or even if the circumstances are not such that a submission can be presumed, the territorial sovereign authority is always recognised as competent to operate on the property of the individual chattel, provided it does so in pursuance of general and reasonable laws, and not by an arbitrary act directed against particular persons, or by judicial processes not so framed as to afford a fair prospect of justice. Thus an American ship, captured by pirates, whose capture is universally allowed not to change the ownership, and afterwards stranded within a Spanish port, was regularly sold there by the Spanish officer as a derelict: and the title so acquired was held at New York to be good (*c*). Why then, if the territorial sovereignty may judicially transfer the property in an individual chattel, shall not its general laws on the transfer of property in chattels be of force with regard to such as are found within its jurisdiction? The existence of any sufficient reason is altogether denied by Savigny (*d*).

261. But the actual dicta of the majority of jurists, at

(*b*) 2 H. Bl. 406.

(*c*) *Grant* v. *McLachlin*, 4 Johnson, 34. These proceedings are quite ordinary, and always supported.

(*d*) System d. heut. Röm. Rechts, s. 366.

least until recent times, are thus correctly expressed by Lord Rosslyn in terms which run precisely counter to the principles here advanced. "It is a clear proposition," said his lordship, "not only of the law of England, but of every country in the world where law has the semblance of science, that personal property has no locality. The meaning of that is, not that personal property has no visible locality, but that it is subject to that law which governs the person of the owner. With respect to the disposition of it, with respect to the transmission of it, either by succession or the act of the party, it follows the law of the person. The owner in any country may dispose of his personal property. If he dies, it is not the law of the country in which the property is, but the law of the country of which he was a subject, that will regulate the succession. For instance, if a foreigner having property in the funds here dies, that property is claimed according to the right of representation given by the law of his own country" (*e*).

262. The general adoption of the law of the owner's domicile for corporeal chattels has been founded on two reasons, thus given by Story. "Some are of opinion that all laws which regard movables are real; but at the same time they maintain that by a fiction of law all movables are supposed to be in the place of the domicile of the owner. Others are of opinion that such laws are personal, because movables have in contemplation of law no *situs*, and are attached to the person of the owner wherever he is; and, being so adherent to his person, they are governed by the same laws which govern his person, that is, by the law of the place of his domicile" (*f*). The latter reason has been extended to rights of action, by the aphorism *nomina creditoris ossibus inhærent;* and both are summed up in the maxim *mobilia sequuntur personam.*

(*e*) In *Sill* v. *Worswick*, 1 H. Bl. 690.

(*f*) Sect. 377.

263. Let us however examine the true motives by which these fictions have been suggested. In the first place, the reader will observe that the propositions quoted are asserted of movables, whereas we set out with considering only corporeal chattels. The latter alone are strictly subjects of property: the former include also incorporeal rights of action, lucrative or active obligations, with regard to which, when we speak of property in them, we only mean in whom the power of enforcing them is vested, by the original creation of the rights, or by their voluntary or involuntary assignment. These have been classed with the true subjects of property, on account of the importance which attaches to them as part of the fortune or means of the creditor. Indeed, this conception of a person's fortune as an entirety is forced upon us in numberless cases, as bankruptcy, administration on death, and others involving what are called *universitates juris*, in which the corporeal chattels must be dealt with as forming one mass with the active credits, a mass too which continually tends to include immovable property, hitherto more or less excluded from it in most countries by the system of feudal law, or from considerations referring to the supposed interest of the state. Now it would be intolerable that in these cases the several corporeal chattels and active credits should be administered on principles varying with the casual situation of each of the former, and with the true seat of each particular tort or contract that might be involved in the latter, rather than on one uniform rule for the whole body of rights dealt with: and hence the necessity of considering together rights which must be distinguished in a scientific classification. It is thus impossible to apply to movables, at least in every case, principles as strict as those by which we dealt with immovables, for whatever principles are employed must often serve for rights of personal action as well as for rights of property

in things corporeal, and therefore, if strictly drawn from either, could apply only by an imperfect analogy to the other: nay, whichever of these classes of movable rights be taken as the typical species, it would be improper to select our principles from a consideration of it alone, and not also with a view to their application to the other species. Now when once it is recognised that rights of property and of action are, for many purposes of transmission and administration, to be grouped together in the character of wealth, the only point of union which can furnish a common rule for them is to be found in the person of the owner whose wealth they constitute. They are so grouped together round the person of their owner, for more or fewer of these purposes, in every system of law which exists among civilized men: and therefore, when they are similarly dealt with in international law, it can only be from his domicile that the rules to be applied to them must be derived (*g*).

264. These considerations show at once the foundation and the limits of the *lex domicilii* as applied to movables. Their results are very well expressed by Fœlix, though it is to be regretted that he has taken the vague notion of a more or less intimate connexion with the owner's person as the framework of his classification, when the particulars he enumerates show plainly enough that the true distinction is between the cases in which a man's property is considered as an entirety, and those in which the single articles which compose it are considered; the *lex situs* being allowed to prevail in the latter cases, from the absence of any sufficient motive to the contrary. *La règle*, says Fœlix, *suivant laquelle les meubles sont régis par la loi du domicile de celui à qui ils appartiennent, repose sur le rapport intime entre les meubles et la personne du propriétaire, sur*

(*g*) See Art. 59.

une fiction légale qui les répute exister au lieu du domicile de ce dernier. De là il suit que cette règle ne peut s'appliquer qu'aux circonstances ou actes dans lesquels les meubles n'apparaissent que comme un accessoire de la personne; par exemple, en cas de succession ab intestat, *de dispositions de dernière volonté ou entre-vifs (tels que les contrats de mariage exprès ou tacites). La règle est sans application à tous les cas où les meubles n'ont pas un rapport intime avec la personne du propriétaire: par exemple, lorsque la propriété de meubles est réclamée et contestée, lorsqu'on invoque la maxime qu'en fait de meubles possession vaut titre; lorsqu'il s'agit d'exercer un droit de gage, des priviléges ou des voies d'exécution sur les meubles, d'en prohiber l'aliénation, d'en prononcer la confiscation ou de déclarer une succession mobilière en déshérence au profit du fisc, ou enfin d'interdire l'exportation des meubles. Dans tous ces cas, il faut appliquer la loi du lieu où les meubles se trouvent effectivement: car la dite fiction cesse par le fait. Par exemple, la convention conclue en pays étranger, par laquelle le propriétaire d'un objet mobilier qui se trouve en France accorderait le privilége de gage (Art.* 2073 *et suiv. du Code civil) sur cet objet, n'aurait pas d'effet en France, si ce gage n'a pas été livré au creáncier (Art.* 2076), *quoique cette condition ne fût pas exigée par la loi du domicile du propriétaire* (*h*).

265. It is nevertheless true that the *lex domicilii*, as governing the transmission of the property in movables, has not by the jurists of former times been generally restrained within these limits, but has been applied to the alienation of individual chattels also, in all the latitude expressed in the citations given above from Story and Lord Rosslyn. The practical point at issue is commonly whether the sale is complete without delivery. For by the Code Napoleon, the property is transferred by the

(*h*) No. 62.

contract of sale (*i*), while by the English law, and that of many colonies and American states based on ours, the purchaser is only bound to take possession within a reasonable time, or, if the goods be at sea at the time of the sale, within a reasonable time after their arrival in port: if he complies with this condition, his title is superior to that of subsequent purchasers and creditors who by greater diligence may have anticipated him in taking possession. But the law of Louisiana, as the Prussian (*j*), and some others which are founded on the Roman, awards the property to the one who first gains the possession on a lawful title, without regarding the priority of the titles, or whether laches is imputable to the claimant who has been outstripped.

266. The preference of the *lex domicilii* of the alienor in these cases appears to have been founded on a feeling, expressed thus by Lord Kames: "the will of a proprietor, or of a creditor, is a good title *jure gentium*, that ought to be effectual everywhere" (*k*). And this maxim has thus far a true foundation, that the feudal principles, which contributed so much to exclude the operation of foreign laws on the transmission of land, did not extend to chattels; so that there was in their case no jealously guarded positive law, proceeding on motives of a public character, to interfere with the will of a foreign proprietor, properly expressed and authenticated. It is farther true that the absence of such motives encouraged a laxity in examining private dispositions of chattels, to such an extent that in many countries the conception of property in them was almost entirely dropped, as we know that in England, and the case was the same in France, a chattel could not be specifically recovered, but only a personal

---

(*i*) Art. 1138.

(*j*) But not for the Rhenish province, which is under the Code Napoleon.

(*k*) On Equity, b. 3, c. 8, s. 4.

action lay for its value. But it is not true that any such maxim was ever formalised in private law as that the mere will of a proprietor, however authenticated, made a good title. That it never could have been so appears from several considerations. The nations which alone could have been disposed to adopt such a maxim, as having abandoned the Roman requirement of delivery of possession, were those which at the same time abandoned, as just pointed out, the conception of title to chattels altogether, reducing the rights existing with regard to them to the description of personal rights. Moreover, the whole question of what modes of acquisition were natural, or *juris gentium*, and what of positive institution, belonged to the publicists, who discussed it for the purpose of regulating the acquisitions of territory by states, and was never, at least for any practical purpose, transported into the domain of modern private law (*l*). The feeling however which lies at the bottom of Lord Kames's maxim, that the interests of commerce require great freedom of disposition to be allowed to proprietors, was certainly operative in producing a tolerably wide international recognition of the validity of an alienation made in the manner prescribed, not only in the alienor's domicile, but even in the place of sale (*m*): and in fact, notwithstanding the reiterated assertions by jurists of the *lex domicilii* for movables, it is the forms of the place of sale which have been most usually employed, and on which by the same jurists the most stress has been practically laid. These in

(*l*) See, as to this question, Grotius, as referred to in Art. 159.

(*m*) Thus Story says, that to maintain the *lex situs*, as to the necessity of delivery on a sale of chattels, "would most materially impair the confidence which the commercial world have hitherto reposed in the universal validity of the title acquired under a bill of lading:" s. 394. When bills of lading and dock warrants are regarded as negotiable representatives of the chattels to which they relate, the maxim *locus regit actum* becomes applicable at once to their transfer by indorsement or otherwise.

fact are the forms which it is easiest and most obvious to follow, and they had for them the continental maxim *locus regit actum*.

267. Of late years however the current has set very strongly, even in commercial countries, towards enforcing the *lex situs* on the title to chattels. We have seen the French doctrine in the words of Fœlix. The courts of Louisiana enforce it also, in sales made under the dominion of the English law. The cases where this has been done are those of ships or goods sold, in Virginia for instance, and afterwards, but before delivery, attached at New Orleans by creditors of the vendors (*n*); and of the same goods sold by each of two partners, the earlier sale made at a place under the English law, but possession first taken at New Orleans under the later (*o*). The last-mentioned case is also varied, as the domicile of the firm is either at New Orleans or in the place of the earlier sale. Similar decisions to these of Louisiana have been made too in Massachusetts, where delivery is also thought essential, though without express reference to the topics of international jurisprudence involved (*p*). And Savigny says expressly, "when a Parisian sells at Paris to a Parisian his movables then happening to be at Berlin, the property is only transferred by delivery. But when, conversely, a Berliner sells at Berlin to a Berliner his chattels at Paris, the mere contract immediately transfers the property. The same result exactly will follow, if in these examples we put Cologne for Paris. For the application of this rule it will suffice that the existence of the chattel in the place

(*n*) *Norris* v. *Mumford*, 4 Mar. 20; cotton at N. O. sold at N. Y., and order for transfer of possession delivered to purchaser: *Olivier* v. *Townes*, 2 Mar. N. S. 93; ship at N. O., though the sale was effectual by laws of place of contract, and vendor's and vendee's domicile.

(*o*) Case put in *Thuret* v. *Jenkins*, 7 Mar. 353.

(*p*) *Lamb* v. *Durant*, 12 Mass. 57; *Lanfear* v. *Sumner*, 17 Mass. 110: commented on by Story, s. 392, and note to s. 389.

in question should be only transitory and brief, for in every case the transfer of the property rests on an instantaneous transaction, and so occupies no long space of time. It will be otherwise only in the exceptional cases in which the momentary place of the thing is so undetermined, that the parties cannot have dealt under any certain consciousness of that place. In such cases we shall have to consider that as the place of the thing supposed at which it is next destined to remain, which will often be the domicile of the present owner, the alienor" (*q*) (as when ships are on a voyage, even perhaps an outward one, but of which the home port is to be not merely the ultimate conclusion, but the first at which they are destined to make any stay).

268. In the leading case on this point, that of *Olivier* v. *Townes* (*r*), the Louisiana tribunal expressed itself thus. "We readily yield an assent to the general doctrine for which the appellee contends." This was the efficacy of the law of the vendor's domicile, coinciding in the particular case with that of the place of sale. "He has supported it by a variety of authorities drawn from different systems of jurisprudence. But some of these very books furnish also the exception on which we think this case must be decided, namely, that 'when those laws clash and interfere with the rights of the citizens of the countries where the parties to the contract seek to enforce it, as one or other of them must give way, those prevailing where the relief is sought must have the preference.' Such is the language of the English books to which we have been referred; and Huberus, whose authority is more frequently resorted to on this subject than that of any other writer, because he has treated it more extensively (*s*) and with

(*q*) V. 8, p. 184.
(*r*) 2 Mar. N. S. 93.
(*s*) Yet Huber's treatise is one of the shortest of the many on this subject.

greater ability, in his treatise *De Conflictu Legum* (n. 11), tells us, *effecta contractuum certo loco initorum pro jure loci illius alibi quoque observantur, si nullum inde civibus alienis creetur præjudicium in jure sibi quæsito.* The effects of a contract entered into at any place will be allowed according to the law of that place in other countries, if no inconvenience will result therefrom to the citizens of that other country with respect to the right which they demand." Observe that *in jure sibi quæsito* does not mean "with respect to the right which they *demand*," but "which they *have acquired*," which is very different: for if the purchaser gained the property in the ship by the law of the place of sale, then the attaching creditor acquired no right, because when he instituted his process there was nothing left in the vendor on which the attachment could operate. Yet, as we saw in Art. 144, Huber came to the same conclusion with the Louisiana judges. If the foreigner, continued Justice Porter, "sends his property within a jurisdiction different from that where he resides, he impliedly submits it to the rules and regulations in force in the country where he places it. What the law protects it has a right to regulate." The court finally examined the point of injury to its own citizens in these words:—"This city is becoming a vast storehouse for merchandise sent from abroad, owned by non-residents, and deposited here for sale; and our most important commercial transactions are in relation to property so situated. If the purchasers of it should be affected by all the previous contracts made at the owners' domicile, although unaccompanied by delivery, it is easy to see to what imposition such a doctrine would lead, to what inconvenience it would expose us, and how severely it would check and embarrass our dealings. . . . It would be giving to the foreign purchaser an advantage which the resident has not, and that frequently at the expense of the latter. This, in the language of the law, we think would be a great inconvenience to the citizens of this state, and therefore we cannot sanction it."

269. It must be regarded as unfortunate that the doctrine has been rested in Louisiana on these grounds. The appearance of a departure from general rules of law, for the express purpose of favouring the citizens of the forum, has produced an antagonism which is quite apparent in all Story's remarks, though he finally sums up by declining to express an opinion (*t*): and the preference of the *lex situs* might, as we have seen, have been grounded on the strictest principles. On the whole, I am disposed to regard the language of the judges as the somewhat loosely expressed efforts of a strong common sense, freeing itself from the trammels of the older jurists, whose dicta in favour of the *lex domicilii* formed almost the only technical material it had to work upon. The adoption of the *lex situs* would, no doubt, occasion some inconvenience in the case of ships or merchandise, of which the exact situation at the moment might be unknown to the owner, and to those with whom he dealt. We have seen that Savigny meets this by a reference, not simply to the duration, but to the nature of the chattel's continuance in its temporary situation, namely, whether it is such that its owner must be considered to have submitted himself to the *lex situs* by carrying or sending it thither: and in the ambiguous cases lying on the limits, he considers that a longer or shorter continuance will found the application of the *lex situs*, according to the rule of that law which is in question, the form of voluntary alienation being applicable, for instance, on a shorter stay than the term of prescription for clothing a *bona fide* possessor with the property (*u*). But this method leaves far too much to the court to suit the genius

(*t*) Sects. 390, 394.

(*u*) See the citation in Art. 267, and Savigny, pp. 178—181.

of English jurisprudence: and the submarine telegraph will soon remove the difficulty which it is intended to obviate.

270. It remains to observe that if the ship or goods were at sea at the date of the earlier sale, it has been decided even in Louisiana that the creditor or second purchaser cannot take or obtain possession on their arrival at New Orleans, because there was no *lex situs* to oppose the final effectuation of the earlier sale at the instant when it was made (*x*).

271. It may happen however that a British ship, or a share in a British ship, is transferred abroad to one qualified to be owner under the 18th clause of the Merchant Shipping Act, 1854; and that such transfer is good by the *lex situs*, but that a memorandum of it is not indorsed on the certificate of registry under the 45th clause of the same act, or the transferee registered as owner under the 57th. It is clear that in such a case a British court would be bound by our statute, inasmuch as the public motives of its provisions would take the case out of the class in which the maxims of international law can be applied, and assimilate it to those in which an obligation, good by its *lex loci*, is defeated in the forum by the plea of turpitude. But as this is a consideration for that forum only in which the stringent law exists, it is probable that the courts of the nation in whose harbours the ship was found would give full effect to the transfer. If the transferee be not qualified to be owner of a British ship, no difficulty arises, for the ship will, by the transfer, merely cease to be British within the meaning of the statute.

272. Next, let us suppose that by the law of the sale, whether that of the vendor's domicile or, if the transaction took place elsewhere, that of the place of sale, the vendor

---

(*x*) *Thuret* v. *Jenkins*, 7 Mar. 318.

had, in accordance with the Roman law, a lien on the goods for the price, or, in accordance with the English, a right to stop them *in transitu* in case of the consignee's insolvency. How far will either of such rights prevail against the vendee, or his assignees as representing his general creditors, or against innocent purchasers from him, the goods being found, or the sub-purchase made, where the vendor has no such security for the price (*y*)? or how far will the former of such rights prevail, in conflict with a law giving only the English or more limited security? Mr. Burge has answered these questions in favour of the vendor, as against the vendee, on the ground of the *lex loci contractus*; but against him when he competes with third parties, as the vendee's other creditors (*z*). It may be argued that the vendor, by empowering the purchaser to carry the thing into the empire of another law, has enabled him to deal, on the strength and credit of its property, with those who cannot be held to know the rights retained by the late owner under a foreign jurisprudence. But Story says that "upon the general principles as to the operation of contracts, and the rule that movables have no locality,

(*y*) The conflict here imagined did not arise in *Inglis* v. *Usherwood*, 1 East, 515, for there the vendors repossessed the goods while still in Russia, under the right given by the law of that country, which was also the place of sale. Notwithstanding therefore that the goods were afterwards found in England, by the law of which country the right to stop *in transitu* would have been lost by the delivery to the agent of the vendee, which was made previous to the vendors' repossession, yet the vendee had no colourable foundation for seeking to apply our rule to a delivery made in Russia. In *Whiston* v. *Stodder*, 8 Mar. 95, it was decided that a vendor, who has no lien by the law of the place where the sale was completed, through his final assent being given and the goods being shipped on account of the purchaser, acquires none by the law of the country where they are received by the purchaser: see Mr. Livermore's very learned argument in this case.

(*z*) V. 3, p. 770. In the case of *concursus*, Burge makes the lien to depend on the law of the owner's domicile, where he says the movable estate is by a fiction.

it would seem that these privileges, hypothecations and liens ought to prevail over the rights of subsequent purchasers and creditors in every other country: that having once attached rightfully *in rem*, they ought not to be displaced by the mere change of local situation of the property" (*a*). In this opinion that learned writer includes "hypothecations and liens recognised to exist for seamen's wages, and for repairs of foreign ships, and for salvage" (*b*): and indeed both these, and every sort of pledge or mortgage given either expressly or tacitly without possession, appear to be indistinguishable in principle. In a recent case it has been held that a mortgage without possession, but valid as between the parties to it at New York, where it was made, and where the chattels were at the time it was contracted, was yet defeated by an attachment in Vermont, into which state the mortgagor brought the chattels (*c*). But the decision has been very much questioned in a still later case, where a mortgage made by partners in Massachusetts having been there foreclosed, the chattels also then being there, though in the possession of the mortgagors, whereby the mortgagee obtained a title to the property which was assumed to be valid by the laws of that state against even *bona fide* purchasers, one of the partners afterwards took the chattels into Vermont, and sold them there to innocent persons, whose title under Vermont law was consequently preferable (*d*). The Massachusetts law was applied, as it clearly ought: and it was said, with great hesitation, that *Skiff* v. *Solace* might per-

(*a*) Sect. 402.

(*b*) Sect. 401.

(c) *Skiff* v. *Solace*, 23 Vermont, 279. It does not appear from the report whether the mortgage was valid against third persons at New York.

(*d*) *Taylor* v. *Boardman*, 25 Vermont, 581. "Has the property once been transferred," says Savigny, "then every subsequent change of the locality of the thing is indifferent to the fate of the property, which cannot be affected by it:" p. 185.

haps be distinguished, on the difference between a lien and the entire property.

273. The assignment of a debt may be either equitable or legal, the difference between the two relating to the name in which the assignee must sue, but either, when complete, enabling him to recover the debt. Now by some laws, as by ours and that of Massachusetts (*e*), the assignment is itself a complete transfer, though the debtor will be discharged if he pay the debt without notice of it: consequently notice *pendente lite* will prevent the debt being recovered by an attaching creditor or posterior assignee. By others, as the Scotch, the transfer is only completed by intimation, as the Scotch call it, to the debtor, so that such intimation *pendente lite* comes too late. Evidently then there is room for a conflict of laws analogous to that which occurs on the sale of a corporeal chattel, intimation taking the place of delivery, and the forum in which the debtor is sued that of the *situs*. And accordingly we find analogous opinions and decisions. That the assignment of a debt, complete by the law of the creditor's domicile, must be held complete and valid everywhere, is asserted by Kames, Story, and a Pennsylvanian case (*f*). That its completeness must be decided by the law of the forum where the debt is sued for, has been held in Louisiana, on the attachment of a promissory note previously assigned without delivery (*g*).

274. Nor does the conflict arise on intimation, or delivery of the instrument, alone. If a debtor make a voluntary assignment in favour of his creditors, either preferring some, or laying down rules for their payment different from those which would be followed in his bankruptcy or

---

(*e*) Story, s. 396.

(*f*) Kames on Equity, b. 3, c. 8, s. 4; Story, s. 397; *Milne* v. *Moreton*, 6 Binney, 361, 369.

(*g*) *Fisk* v. *Chandler*, 7 Mar. 24.

insolvency; and this is good in the assignor's domicile, but such preferences or rules are not allowed in the forum where the assignees seek to establish their claim to the property, against a plaintiff attaching subsequently to the date of the assignment; the attaching plaintiff is preferred in Massachusetts (*h*) and Louisiana, unless he is a citizen or inhabitant of the state of the assignment, when he has been treated as estopped by his own law from denying its validity (*i*). The same estoppel has even been applied to real estate in Louisiana, all the parties being resident in another state (*k*).

275. As a detached point on movables, this seems the place to mention that funds impressed with a trust for the establishment of a charity abroad are paid over by the court of chancery to the trustees, who must administer them under the superintendence of the local authorities (*l*); so that, even if an English testator give indefinite directions for founding a school in Scotland, the Scotch courts will have to supply whatever precise regulations may be needed (*m*). The objection to the administration of foreign charities, even through trustees subject to the jurisdiction,

(*h*) *Zipcey* v. *Thompson*, 1 Gray, 243.

(*i*) *Richardson* v. *Leavitt*, 1 Louis. Ann. 430. But the estoppel was not recognised in *Ramsey* v. *Stevenson*, 5 Mar. 23, an older case.

(*k*) *Merchants' Bank* v. *Bank of United States*, 2 Louis. Ann. 659.

(*l*) *Provost, &c. of Edinburgh* v. *Aubery*, Ambl. 236; *Emery* v. *Hill*, 1 Russ. 112; *Minet* v. *Vulliamy*, 1 Russ. 113, note.

(*m*) *Att.-Gen.* v. *Lepine*, 2 Swans. 181, 1 Wils. 465: the report in 19 Ves. 309 is incorrect, the rehearing mentioned being evidently what is reported by Swanston and Wilson. But this, together with an unreported case of *Cadell* v. *Grant*, mentioned in 19 Ves. 309 as one where a charity in Scotland was established by decree, and *Oliphant* v. *Hendrie*, 1 Bro. C. C. 571, where such a charity was also so established, is cited by Lord Brougham as though in all three schemes were directed (1 Mo. I. A. C. 293, 1 Mo. P. C. 296). It may have been so in the two last-named cases, though the reports do not show it; but the later authority of *Emery* v. *Hill*, cited in the last note, would rather lead to the conclusion that the court had always been consistent, in establishing such charities, but without schemes.

is independent of any peculiarity in the constitution of the court of chancery, and has been recognised by the Privy Council. It is that " those who are engaged in the actual execution are beyond the court's control, and those who are within the jurisdiction are answerable to the court for the acts of persons as to whom they can derive no aid from the court. Such an office will not easily be undertaken by any one, and its duties cannot be satisfactorily performed (*n*)." But before any forum will deliver funds to trustees for a foreign charity, it must be assured that the purpose can be legally accomplished in the country where it was intended (*o*). Another detached point on the jurisdiction as to movables is that a suit depending elsewhere *in personam* is no bar to a suit *in rem* (*p*).

276. A subject sometimes treated of under the head of movables is that of the law of torts, which has in this work already been considered, as to marine and other extraterritorial torts in Art. 158, and, as to those committed within territorial jurisdictions, in the chapter on obligations. I take this opportunity however of observing that, since Art. 158 was printed, the report of *Cope* v. *Doherty* (*q*) has appeared, the main point in which decides that a tortfeaser on the high seas cannot plead British law in answer to a British subject whom he has damaged, and thus, with the cases quoted before, completes the chain of English authorities for asserting that a municipal law can never be applied in marine torts where one party only is bound by it. Plaintiff's (damaged party's) law, appealed to by plaintiff—*The Zollverein*, by defendant—*Cope* v. *Doherty:* defendant's (tortfeaser's) law, appealed to by plaintiff—*The Dumfries*, by defendant

(*n*) 1 Mo. I. A. C. 295, 1 Mo. P. C. 297.
(*o*) *Mayor of Lyons* v. *E. I. C.*, 1 Mo. I. A. C. 175, 1 Mo. P. C. 175.
(*p*) *Harmer* v. *Bell*, *The Bold Buccleugh*, 7 Moore, P. C. 267.
(*q*) 4 K. & J. 367.

—*Nostra Signora de los Dolores.* But it is worthy of inquiry whether, if the English and American laws had been proved to agree, that would not have formed a case for applying their common provisions between a plaintiff of one country and a defendant of the other, no less than between parties of the same state (*r*). It is evident that the force of the general maritime law between members of different nations, as one common to the parties, does not depend on the existence of a common authority imposing it on them both, for no such authority exists: it depends on the fact that the provisions of that law are received by the community to which each belongs, as the rule to the justice of which in certain descriptions of cases it gives a free assent. Now this consideration arises with equal strength, when the municipal laws of two nations agree. How in fact did the law maritime first come into being? Simply by this very process. The laws of Wisby and Oléron, the Consolato del Mare, and all the various other sources of that code, even the Roman law in this application of it, were originally the laws of particular populations, the justice of which ensured their reception in widening circles, and which, as they spread, were applied between the merchants of the different ports which adopted them, as well as between those of the same port. Why then should this process cease now? Must all nations adopt successively a limitation of the owner's liability to the value of the ship and freight, and yet treat each other on the footing of a ruinous liability, which they all abandon individually for themselves?

(*r*) See 4 K. & J. 391.

CHAPTER IX.

Bankruptcy and Insolvency.

277. We now come to those universal assignments of movable property, for which, as they had no small part in suggesting the law of the owner's domicile as the rule for personalty, we should expect to find that rule maintained with less question than besets its application to particular assignments. Nor shall we be disappointed: for even the law of Scotland, which, as we have seen, does not admit the assignment of a particular debt, though complete by the law of the creditor's domicile, to prevail over a subsequent arrestment without intimation, yet gives effect to the general assignment which by the same law of domicile is made on the creditor's bankruptcy or marriage, without regard to the giving of intimation to any particular debtor whose liability may be therein comprised (*a*). Also even those jurists who maintain most strictly the rule of the *lex situs* for the subjects treated of in the last chapter, and who write with reference to the Roman and other thence derived laws, in which the only proceeding analogous to our bankruptcy is the appointment of a curator in the debtor's domicile, with power to sell his property for the benefit of the creditors, and with or without the debtor's discharge from the residue of his debts as a resulting consequence, mostly maintain the necessity that that officer should be authorized and assisted by foreign

(*a*) See particularly in *Selkrig* v. *Davis*, 2 Rose, 316.

judges, in selling also those parts of the estate which may be situate in their jurisdictions. They treat the process as one of the creditors' remedy, and compare the assistance thus claimed for the curator to the execution which is allowed to be had on judgments in foreign countries. There are indeed those who hold that each judge should establish a separate *concursus*, for the distribution of the property lying within his limits: but this is answered by the argument that, since a *concursus* is founded on nothing but the existence of numerous rights of action which cannot all be fully satisfied, it cannot arise in any jurisdiction on the mere ground that the debtor has property there, no forum for personal actions being, on Roman principles, founded on that circumstance. Thus, where those strict maxims of jurisdiction are upheld, the refusal of assistance to the curator of the domicile would amount to a denial of justice: and even elsewhere it is granted, though on a comity demanded by a less imperious necessity. The difference between plural and singular *concursus* is important on the priorities between unsecured creditors: for on that point, belonging as it does to the remedy on merely personal obligations, each forum would follow its own law, a rule which is well established in bankruptcies (*b*). As an English bankruptcy passes all the estate within the British

(*b*) Story, s. 323, coincides with the general opinion that priority is no part of a contract, and therefore independent of the *lex loci contractus*. Huber holds the existence of property in a given jurisdiction to vest a right in the creditors to be paid out of it in the order of priority there established, an opinion which would lead to the necessity of plural *concursus*, or at least that the *forum domicilii* should regard the *leges situs* of the different parts of the estate in the matter of priority, which was probably never done in practice: l. 3, J. P. Univer., c. 10, s. 44. Hertius, Rodenburg, the two Voets, Matthæus, Boullenois, &c., determine priorities by the law of the debtor's domicile, except as against immovables, which however Savigny would bring into the *concursus* of the same place. See Art. 280, for France.

dominions, there cannot be a second British *concursus* to compete with a prior English adjudication (*c*).

278. The English and Scotch cases may be divided into two classes: those in which the effect of an English bankruptcy in Scotland, or of a foreign bankruptcy in England, is considered, and those in which the effect of an English bankruptcy abroad is considered. As to the former class, the doctrine "that an assignment under the bankrupt-law of a foreign country passes all the personal property of the bankrupt locally situaté, and debts owing, in England" (*d*) or Scotland, was finally established for Scotland though not previously unknown there (*e*), by the leading cases of the *Royal Bank of Scotland* v. *Cuthbert* (commonly called *Stein's case*) (*f*), and *Selkrig* v. *Davis* (*g*): which also fully show, as before alluded to, that the English bankrupt's assignees prevail against an arrestment made by a Scotch creditor subsequently to the assignment, but before its intimation to the Scotch debtor. In England the same doctrine rests on still earlier authorities (*h*).

279. As to the latter class, the effect which an English bankruptcy may have abroad calls for the decision of our courts only in contests between the assignees and those

---

(*c*) As to the relative priority of adjudications and sequestrations, see *Exp. Geddes, re Mowat*, 1 Gl. & J. 414, whence it appears that the relation of the adjudication to the act of bankruptcy does not supersede a sequestration actually prior.

(*d*) These are the words of Story, s. 409.

(*e*) *Struther* v. *Reid*, cited by Lord Meadowbank, 1 Rose, 481.

(*f*) 1 Rose, 462.

(*g*) 2 Rose, 291, 2 Dow, 230.

(*h*) *Solomons* v. *Ross*, 1 H. Bl. 131, note; *Jollet* v. *Deponthieu*, 1 H. Bl. 132, note. *Neale* v. *Cottingham*, 1 H. Bl. 132, note, established the same doctrine in Ireland. And if some of the syndics appointed abroad may, by the law of their appointment, sue without joining the others, they will be permitted to do so here, their title as procurators (see Art. 280), where such is really their character rather than assignees, being recognised in England: *Alivon* v. *Furnival*, 1 Cr. M. & R. 277, 4 Tyrwhitt, 751.

who having, after the bankruptcy, obtained property belonging to the bankrupt, or received payment of debts due to him, in foreign countries, afterwards bring such property to England, or are sued here in respect of such receipt. Now in the three leading cases of *Hunter* v. *Potts* (*i*), *Sill* v. *Worswick* (*k*), and *Philips* v. *Hunter* (*l*), the assignees indeed recovered, but in all of them the defendant, who as creditor of the bankrupt had attached abroad, was a domiciled Englishman, and the debt due to him had been contracted in England, while the proceeding in attachment had been commenced by him with knowledge of the bankruptcy, and in the first two cases by swearing an affidavit in England. Some surprise may be felt that some of these circumstances should have weighed with the judges (*m*), and perhaps they might have been safely omitted from a summary statement of the facts. But the English domicile is important, for it introduces the question how far our law may not have been enforced as a rule common to all the parties, and not simply as that of the bankrupt's domicile. Now in none of the cases had there been an intimation of the bankruptcy pending the attachment, but Lord Rosslyn held that if there had, and the foreign court had notwithstanding rejected the title of the assignees, a foreign creditor would not, though he appears

(*i*) 4 T. R. 182.

(*k*) 1 H. Bl. 665.

(*l*) 2 H. Bl. 402. The attaching creditor resided in America for a temporary purpose, and his firm had no house there, so that his domicile was English: p. 404.

(*m*) It is difficult to introduce the *locus contractus* of the attaching creditor's debt into this discussion, for both the attachment, and the assignment under the bankruptcy to trustees for the creditors, concern that debt only as remedies for its recovery, and remedies are of the *lex fori*. It is not therefore true, except formally and only in the forum of the bankruptcy, that the creditor's "interest is transferred to the assignees." We have here in fact a conflict between two processes in different forums, each of which claims to be the proper remedy. But for the weight which the *locus contractus* had with the judges, see 2 H. Bl. 405.

to have thought that an English creditor would, be liable to refund (*n*). Upon the whole then the English doctrine may be said to stand thus :—

(1) The foreign court, in case of intimation *pendente lite*, ought to hold the title of the assignees superior to that of the creditor whose proceedings in attachment were commenced after the act of bankruptcy, even though it might use a different rule in the case of an assignment of a particular chattel by the owner (*o*).

(2) If it does not, but in the face of such an intimation adjudges the property or the payment to the creditor, our conceptions of private international justice have been violated, but the respect due to the *res judicata* of a competent tribunal—for in regard to the situation of the corporeal chattel, or the personal obligation of the trustee, the forum of the attachment is *ex hypothesi* competent—generally protects in the creditor's hands what he has so received. Add to this, that the attaching creditor has gained his advantage in the course of procedure, the validity of which must therefore depend on the law of the forum in which it was gained. *Utique ex lege domicilii* [*debitoris*] *discutienda causa creditorum est. Nisi forsan executio directa sit in ejus debitoris mobilia qui adhuc in possessione suorum bonorum sit: feret enim tum creditor diligentiæ ac vigilantiæ suæ præmium, si quid eo nomine loci mores, ubi in causam judicati ceperit mobilia, præ aliis creditoribus ipsi indulserint, quod privilegium illud non tam proficiscatur ex credito, quam ex actu ipso executionis qua alios creditor prævertit, adeoque hæc res, tanquam concernens*

(*n*) 1 H. Bl. 693. And see the creditor's subjection to our bankrupt laws urged in 2 H. Bl. 405, 406, 408. No light is thrown on the question by *Exp. Dobree*, 8 Ves. 82, for if the law of Jersey only vested the property "upon the completion of the judicial act" of attachment, it was not in conflict with that of England as to the effect of the bankruptcy on the debts attached.

(*o*) This is distinctly laid down in *Sill* v. *Worswick*, 1 H. Bl. pp. 691—693.

exequendi ordinem, legem accipiat a loco ubi illa peragitur" (*p*). The reasoning is the same, though in our case the advantage is not given through a priority allowed in the *situs* to a certain description of creditor (though that case also might arise, and would have to be decided in the same way), but on a systematic preference of individual creditors to the assignees or curators acting for the body.

(3) But if the creditor be an Englishman, this farther circumstance strips him of the protection he would otherwise derive from the *res judicata*, an effect which will be accomplished in legal form by raising an irrebuttable presumption that what he recovered he recovered to the use of the assignees.

(4) And lastly, we may probably add that if no intimation was given previous to the completion of the recovery by attachment, the same presumption will be raised, and the creditor, whether foreign or English, compelled to refund, although the law of the place of attachment might refuse efficacy to such intimation even if given *pendente lite* (*q*).

280. With regard to France, in which the Roman system of the *cessio bonorum* has been developed into a modern bankruptcy capable of discharging the debtor, Merlin states that, first, the syndics named by a foreign tribunal in the bankruptcy of a foreign trader may recover in France his credits and other effects, without previously causing either the adjudication of bankruptcy, or their own appointment, to be declared executory by a French tribunal. For, although the alleged bankrupt might dispute the adjudication in France, yet the syndics are but the attorneys of his

(*p*) Rodenburg, de Jure quod oritur e Stat. Div., tit. 2, c. 5, s. 16.

(*q*) At least no inquiry seems to have been made about the law of the place of attachment in *Hunter* v. *Potts*, *Sill* v. *Worswick*, or *Philips* v. *Hunter;* and the distinctions there suggested on the creditor's nationality refer only to the case of an intimation actually given.

creditors to sue for his effects; and the validity of their title, as against a debtor to his estate who does not dispute the existence of a just ground for the adjudication, must be decided, on the maxim *locus regit actum*, by the law under which they derive their appointment as such attorneys. Secondly, that he who purchases any of his French effects from a foreign trader, bankrupted in his domicile, in ignorance both of the adjudication, not yet declared executory in France, and of the actual disorder of his affairs, has a good title against the syndics, even though they afterwards cause the adjudication to be declared executory. Thirdly, that if the purchaser knew of the adjudication, he would be admitted to sustain his purchase by showing that it was not well founded. Fourthly, that if the purchaser did not know of the adjudication, but knew that his vendor had stopped payment and was selling in fraud of his creditors, his purchase would be invalid on account of his complicity in the fraud. And fifthly, that the creditor, to whom a foreign trader has mortgaged any of his French effects, cannot complete his title by obtaining a valid inscription in the *bureau des hypothèques* if the mortgage was made later than ten days before the act of bankruptcy (*ouverture de la faillite*), this being the *lex situs*, to which it makes no difference whether the act of bankruptcy and consequent adjudication be French or foreign (*r*). It is evident that these conclusions proceed, like the English doctrine, on a liberal application of international comity to bankruptcy laws; but that they are modified by the French system of declaring foreign judgments executory. This system has also, as may be seen in Merlin's reasonings, altered the basis on which the conclusions rest, even where they agree with ours. The title of the foreign assignees is not now received in France on the

(*r*) Répertoire, Faillite et Banqueroute, Sect. II., § II., Art. X.

ground of the international validity of universal assignments made by the law of the domicile; or on the ground that a trader's subjection to bankruptcy laws is in the nature of status, dependent therefore on the law of the domicile; for the validity of the adjudication may be disputed, on the demand for declaring it executory. It depends on the validity of the assignees' procuration to act for the creditors, so that in fact their authority, as that of the curator in a Roman *cessio*, is not made to turn on the conceptions of conveyance or property, but on those of procedure. Also no distinction appears to exist between movable and immovable property, with regard to any of the doctrines here abstracted from Merlin.

281. In the United States, where the policy of our bankruptcy laws is not admitted, an opposite opinion is correspondingly maintained on the first of the four points enumerated in Art. 279. Not only do they object to the discharge of the debtor, as impairing the faith of contracts—a ground which here would not be decisive, since they might assist the distribution without recognising the discharge, as an English distribution would in fact be assisted by a judge under the Roman law, in which the *cessio bonorum* does not operate a discharge—but they refuse to allow property within their limits to be distributed according to any priority not obtained under their own laws. Other reasoning will be found in the reports of the American judgments, in which it is attempted to base the same conclusion on the principles of international law, but it will be seen on examination to revert in the end to this refusal to apply those principles to the case: a refusal in which the courts and legislatures of an independent nation are fully justified, if they do not possess that community of ideas with us, on which alone comity can be founded. Thus it is said that foreign laws must not be admitted when they would prejudice the citizens of the forum, a po-

sition the value of which here depends on the degree in which priorities between creditors are thought of vital importance: that laws only operate territorially, so that the involuntary assignment made by the law of the domicile has not the same claim to extraterritorial validity which it is admitted might justly be advanced for a voluntary assignment made by an owner, a position which even in theory would only be true if the latter assignment as well as the former did not depend for its validity on its recognition by the *lex situs*, and which is disregarded in America itself in the case of transmission on intestacy (*s*), where the convenience of subjecting the whole personalty to one rule is obvious, and is only taken up in bankruptcy because the corresponding convenience is not recognised in America: and that bankruptcy laws work a kind of forfeiture, which brings them within the rule that penal statutes do not operate extraterritorially, a position not very consistent with the rejection of the discharges granted under them as being too favourable to the bankrupt. In fact, the reasons thus given go beyond the doctrines actually maintained in the United States. "In most of the cases," says Story, "in which assignments under foreign bankrupt-laws have been denied to give a title against attaching creditors, it has been distinctly admitted that the assignees might maintain suits in our courts under such assignments for the property of the bankrupt. This is avowed in the most unequivocal manner in the leading cases in Pennsylvania and New York already cited, and it is silently admitted in those of Massachusetts. The point has hitherto been a struggle for priority and preference between parties

(*s*) It may be said that the intestate assents, by his intestacy, to the statutes of distribution of his domicile: not more however than the bankrupt, by his residence and trade, and his creditors, by their dealings with him, do to the bankruptcy laws of his domicile.

claiming against the bankrupt under opposing titles; the assignees claiming for the general creditors, and the attaching creditors for their separate rights" (*t*). Story's own opinion, as well as that of Kent, was in favour of the European doctrine against that of the United States.

282. The English bankrupt cannot be compelled to execute an assignment of the movable property owned by him, or debts due to him abroad, in aid of the assignment by law which may not be respected in any foreign country (*u*): nor indeed will a confirmatory conveyance, even voluntarily made by the bankrupt, be allowed any force in New York, for the title of the assignees under the adjudication is, as we have just seen, held good there against him, so that nothing remains in him which he can convey (*x*).

283. We have already seen that his British immovables are not suffered to pass to the assignees or syndics of a foreign bankrupt, but are left as a prize for the diligence of those creditors who may proceed by our laws. The assignees in an English bankruptcy now take, by statute, the debtor's immovables throughout the British dominions (*y*): but the creditor of an English bankrupt is not bound to impart to his fellow-creditors the benefit of proceedings he has taken against the bankrupt's immovable estate situate out of those dominions, subject of course to the condition that by those foreign proceedings, and his proof in the domicile, he must not together receive more than twenty shillings in the pound (*z*). If however a creditor have attached abroad personal property of the

---

(*t*) Sect. 420.

(*u*) *Exp. Blakes*, 1 Cox, 398.

(*x*) *Holmes* v. *Remsen*, 20 Johnson, 267; reversing Chancellor Kent's decision (with which Story agrees, s. 418) in 4 Johnson, Ch. 489.

(*y*) 12 & 13 Vict. c. 106, s. 142.

(*z*) *Cockerell* v. *Dickens*, 3 Mo. P. C. 98.

bankrupt, he will not be suffered to receive dividends here without communicating what he has so received, and suspending the farther progress of his foreign proceedings. "The principle is," said Lord Wensleydale, "that one creditor shall not take a part of the fund which otherwise would have been available for the payment of all the creditors, and at the same time be allowed to come in *pari passu* with the other creditors for satisfaction out of the remainder of the fund: and this principle does not apply where that creditor obtains by his diligence something which did not and could not form a part of that fund (*a*)," as the foreign land, in the case supposed. But the principle applies to personalty, to which the assignment in bankruptcy makes even abroad an effectual title in the absence of a competing claim by attachment. Hence it may be concluded that the same doctrine would operate against even a foreign creditor, who might by foreign law obtain possession of the bankrupt's personalty in spite of an intimation of the assignment. The *res judicata* would, as we have seen, protect his retention of the property from the suit of the assignees in England, a country to the bankrupt-laws of which he is not personally subject; but our law would have a right to impose its conditions on him if he sought to avail himself of it by proving his debt.

284. It will readily be understood that in England, no less than in America, the *bona fide* payment, which the bankrupt's debtor makes under process of foreign law to his creditor, protects him from a second payment at the suit of the assignees in the bankrupt's domicile (*b*). It is only from the creditor that we ever allow the assignees to recover.

(*a*) *Cockerell* v. *Dickens*, 3 Mo. P. C. 132.
(*b*) *Le Chevalier* v. *Lynch*, Doug. 170.

285. The bankruptcy of partners gives rise to difficult questions. In *Stein's case*, before alluded to, an English commission of bankrupt issued against five copartners, of whom three resided in London, was held a bar to a sequestration against the property of the other two, who resided at Edinburgh and carried on in Scotland trades distinct from that of the firm (*c*): but it has been held in England that the assignees of a partner residing here, and separately bankrupt, cannot recover from a joint creditor of the firm any portion of the joint property which he may have attached abroad in the place where the firm has its establishment (*d*). "The difficulty," said Sir W. Grant, "seems to me to be insuperable, where a partnership originating in another country has at least a divided establishment, and some of the partners continue to reside and carry on the trade in that other country. How are the West Indian partners to be controlled in the management of their trade, or restrained, by any proceeding here, from paying and applying the partnership assets as they think fit? Equality of distribution cannot possibly be attained. Are we then to tell a creditor, that, because he happens to reside in England, and his debt has been contracted there, he shall not be allowed to take such remedies against his foreign debtors as the laws of their country may permit? In the cases before the Lord Chancellor, in which the domicile of the partnership was completely English, the court, taking from the creditor his separate remedy, professed to give him his distributive share of the whole partnership property. But it cannot in this case reach the West Indian property, or bind the West Indian partners; then you would take from the partnership creditor one remedy, without substituting any other

(*c*) 1 Rose, 462.
(*d*) *Brickwood* v. *Miller*, 3 Mer. 279.

in the place of it. This would be to say that the West India property must be left for any creditors but English creditors. Then, if English creditors are not to be restrained from suing, it would be incongruous to force them to refund what they have recovered. I think, consequently, the defendant is entitled to retain what he has recovered or received from the West Indies, to the extent of satisfying the joint debts due to him" (*e*).

286. In *Exp. Goldsmid*, A. and B. were partners at Liverpool, and A., B. and C. at Pernambuco, each firm trading under the name of A., B. & Co. The Pernambuco house, being in advance to that of Liverpool, drew bills upon it, which were accepted, and purchased by the Brazilian government. The Liverpool house then became bankrupts, and afterwards the Pernambuco house became *fallidos* by Brazilian law, and entered into a *concordata* with their creditors: and the question was whether the Brazilian government, having received a dividend under the *concordata*, was entitled to prove under the adjudication. Lord Justice Knight Bruce avowed his opinion to be that abstract justice, and the principles of commercial law and of general jurisprudence, were with the petitioners, and that the law of England was not opposed to them. Lord Justice Turner, adverting to the question whether the case ought to be dealt with according to the Brazilian or English law, considered "that, the bills being accepted here, the case must be dealt with upon the footing of the English law," of which he took a different view from his learned brother (*f*). The case however is reported as under appeal. One element in it was how far the firms should be recognised as having a personality, which might

(*e*) P. 283.

(*f*) 1 De G. & J., 257, 282, 285. See *Exp. Cotesworth, re Vanzeller*, 1 D. & Ch. 281, and *Exp. Chevalier, re Vanzeller*, 1 M. & A. 345. But could the place of acceptance of the bills affect this question of procedure?

dispense with the consideration of the identity of two Pernambuco partners with those at Liverpool. Where the same persons traded under different firms at Antwerp and in London, the superior court of Brussels in 1816 refused to admit the title of the assignees, in the bankruptcy of the London house, to interfere in any manner with the affairs of the Antwerp house, which had not been bankrupted in the Netherlands, and to which they attributed an entirely distinct personality (*g*). A joint English commission of bankrupt was not superseded on the ground of a previous separate Irish commission (*h*).

287. In all cases of *concursus* or bankruptcy, the priorities between unsecured creditors must be distinguished from any rights of mortgage or lien. These must always be enjoyed according to the laws in force in the situation of the effects to which they apply, being in fact real and not personal rights. It will be only the surplus which the assignees or curator, appointed in the domicile, can be allowed to appropriate for the benefit of the general creditors. Thus the title of the assignees will be held, even in England, inferior to that of an attaching creditor who obtained his judicial lien by commencing proceedings before the act of bankruptcy.

288. With regard to such assignments of property for the benefit of creditors as are not allowed by the law of the assignor's domicile, so far as they relate only to foreign property, they will necessarily be held valid even in the domicile, provided that, as contended for in the last chapter, the rule for the transfer of property in particular movables by the owner be there drawn from the *lex situs*. Still more will this be the case, if the assignment was made

(*g*) Merlin, Rép., Faill. et Banqu., Sect. II., § II., Art. X.; Jurisprudence de la Cour Supérieure de Justice de Bruxelles, 1816, t. 2, p. 181.

(*h*) *Exp. Cridland*, 3 V. & B. 94.

while the debtor was domiciled in another jurisdiction, where the preference of certain creditors is lawful, and he only afterwards came within the limits of the forum which has to pronounce on the assignment in case of his insolvency. But the debtor who makes a conveyance of this kind will in either case be exposed to the penalties with which, in his present domicile, an unlawful preference of certain creditors may be visited. "Although our courts might not be authorized to annul such contracts, as to their effects between the parties, yet they might well inquire whether it was not the intention of the legislature to afford the protection of the insolvent laws to such only as shall have abstained from giving an undue preference to certain creditors, in derogation of that vital principle of our system, that the property of the debtor forms the common pledge of his creditors, and although such preferences may be tolerated by the *lex loci.* If the legislature has thought proper to declare such a condition, as one upon which shall depend the right to claim the benefit of the insolvent laws, which it is not denied they had an unquestionable right to do, then there is an end to the argument, unless it can be shown that the mere residence of the party in another state, [or the existence of his effects there], dispenses him from a compliance with the condition" (*i*).

289. It will be observed that, to found bankruptcies and insolvencies, a trading establishment is a sufficient substitute for a domicile strictly interpreted. Such an establishment is in truth a domicile of the firm, the personality of which is universally recognised in commerce, and calls imperatively for a recognition in English law, such as it has already obtained on the continent (*k*). The possibility has

(*i*) *Andrews* v. *His Creditors*, 11 Louis. 464, 477.

(*k*) See Art. 286, and Mr. Ludlow's able paper in the Transactions of the Juridical Society, v. 2, p. 40.

been suggested that, with reference to the question of domicile, an English adjudication, actually prior, may be a fraud on a Scotch sequestration, which would therefore stand in spite of it (*l*). When the same merchant has a trading establishment in two places, Rodenburg agrees with Burgundus in holding that the priorities between all his creditors, as to all his effects, must be decided by the law of that place which is his true domicile: only if he has a true domicile in each, do these jurists admit a double *concursus* (*m*).

(*l*) *Exp. Geddes, re Mowat*, 1 G. & J. 414, 423.

(*m*) Rodenburg, de Stat. Div., tit. 2, c. 5, s. 16. See Lord Eldon's remarks on the difficulties attending a double *concursus*, in *Selkrig* v. *Davis*, 2 Rose, 314, 315.

CHAPTER X.

Movable Successions.

1. *Jurisdiction as to the Movable Property of a Deceased Person.*

290. Throughout Christendom, the property of a deceased person—or at least the movable part of it—is vested by law in a representative or representatives continuing the person of the defunct, who must satisfy the claims outstanding against him, either fully or to the value of his succession, and who hold the surplus either for his or their own enjoyment, or for distribution among those interested. The proximate source of this is in the Roman jurisprudence, which not only made the heir, nominated either by the law or by testament, represent his ancestor, but was so intolerant of any breach in the continuous line of representation that, until the heir took to the inheritance, it invested the estate itself with quasi-personal qualities as standing in its late owner's place. Its remoter source is in the general character of western civilization, which rests upon the family as the integrant element of the state, and thus involves the perpetuity of the family, and ex-

cludes the confiscation or dispersion of the inheritance on the death of the ancestor. But the original idea of the continuity of the person, which in the Roman heir was simply and rigidly expressed by a continuity both of interest and burdens, often throwing on him a *damnosa hæreditas*, has been so far and variously modified that in England, for instance, the continuity of burdens has been entirely separated from that of interest: the former, with the technical property necessary for supporting them, being thrown on the executor or administrator, the latter being vested in the legatees or next of kin, for whom the executor or administrator holds the surplus in trust.

291. Now suppose a movable succession comprising articles situate in different jurisdictions. First, a transferee of what I have called the technical property must be created by each jurisdiction for the portions of the succession within it, since the territorial principle allows no other sovereign to exercise authority there. It is in fact the question of creating a legal owner for certain special articles the bare property in which is considered as vacant by death, and not that of transmitting the beneficial interest of the defunct in his entire estate after discharge of burdens. Hence no one claiming to be a representative, whether *a testato* or *ab intestato*, can meddle with any portion of the succession before proving the will, or receiving a grant of administration, or some other formal induction into the property, in the forum where such portion is found (*a*).

292. But, in order to preserve as far as possible the singleness of the representation, it has been decided, first, that if there be a will, the jurisdiction of the testator's

---

(*a*) Our courts so uniformly refuse to act on foreign probates or administrations, that it is sufficient to refer for the principle to the dicta in *Pipon* v. *Pipon*, Ambl. 25, and to *Price* v. *Dewhurst*, 4 My. & Cr. 76. See also *Tourton* v. *Flower*, 3 P. W. 369.

domicile can alone decide upon its validity, and, secondly, that the person who obtains administration as next of kin in the jurisdiction of the intestate's domicile, or his attorney, is entitled to a similar grant in any other jurisdiction where the deceased had personal estate (*b*). Thus, when the will of one domiciled abroad is offered here for probate, if its validity has already been established in the forum of the domicile, it will be admitted here on the strength of the foreign judgment (*c*). If not established abroad, and not contested here, the probate will pass in England on affidavit of the law of the foreign domicile, when the will is found conformable thereto (*d*): but, if contested here, proceedings will be suspended till the foreign jurisdiction has pronounced for or against the validity (*e*). And, with regard to the second of the above rules, it does not apply to one who in the *forum domicilii* has obtained administration as a creditor: it is then discretionary in the *forum situs* to grant the local administration to the same or another person (*f*). The universal successor is appointed by the personal jurisdiction, though his title must be confirmed in the *situs* of the chattels: but the limited beneficial interest of a creditor prevents his being regarded in that light. Nor even where there is a universal successor, is the court so far bound by the mere form of the foreign proceedings but that, if it sees fit, it may only grant administration with the will annexed to one who in the testator's domicile has obtained probate as constructive executor (*g*). In all these cases, the probate or administration granted in the domicile is called the prin-

(*b*) Per Lord Mansfield, in *Burn* v. *Cole*, Ambl. 416.

(*c*) *Larpent* v. *Sindry*, 1 Hagg. Eccl. 382.

(*d*) *Maraver's goods*, 1 Hagg. Eccl. 498.

(*e*) *Hare* v. *Nasmyth*, 2 Add. 25; *De Bonneval* v. *De Bonneval*, 1 Curt. 856.

(*f*) Lord Mansfield, in *Burn* v. *Cole*, *ubi supra*.

(*g*) *Read's goods*, 1 Hagg. Eccl. 474; *Mackenzie's goods*, Deane, 17.

cipal, that in the *situs* of any other part of the succession the ancillary, administration, the latter term being used in a general sense, as including probate or any other mode of representation by judicial appointment or confirmation: and either the principal or ancillary, as limited to the chattels having a particular *situs*, may be termed a local administration.

293. And now, by st. 21 & 22 Vict. c. 56, it is "competent to include, in the inventory of the personal estate and effects of any person who shall have died domiciled in Scotland, any personal estate or effects of the deceased situated in England or in Ireland, provided that the value of such personal estate and effects situated in England or Ireland respectively shall be separately stated in such inventory" (*h*). And "when any confirmation of the executor of a person, who shall" by the interlocutor of the commissary "be found to have died domiciled in Scotland, which includes personal estate situated in England or Ireland, shall be produced in the principal court of probate in England, or in the court of probate in Dublin, such confirmation shall be sealed with the seal of the said respective court, and shall thereafter have the like force and effect in England or Ireland respectively as if a probate or letters of administration, as the case may be, had been granted by the said respective court of probate" (*i*).

294. Correspondingly, by the same statute, "when any probate or letters of administration to be granted by the court of probate in England or Ireland respectively to the executor or administrator of any person who shall therein, by any note or memorandum written thereon signed by the proper officer, be stated to have died domiciled in England or Ireland respectively, shall be produced in the commis-

---

(*h*) Sect. 9.
(*i*) Sects. 12, 13.

sary court of the county of Edinburgh, the commissary clerk shall indorse or write a certificate thereon; and such probate or letters of administration, being duly stamped, shall be of the like force and effect, and have the same operation in Scotland, as if a confirmation had been granted by the said court" (*k*).

295. In considering generally the rule that property of a deceased person cannot be possessed except under an administration granted in the *situs*, I assumed, as was necessary for the establishment of the principle, that its *situs* is not changed between the time of the death and that when the attempt is made to reduce it into possession. Let us now examine what effect such a change will have. The principle appears to be that every administration, principal or ancillary, operates on such goods of the deceased as either are when it is granted, or at any subsequent time shall be, within the jurisdiction of the court from which it issues. The property in all such goods is vacant, and the jurisdiction where they are found, and it alone, can confer it. If indeed, before the goods come into jurisdiction A., they have already been possessed under an administration granted by jurisdiction B., then the administration granted in A. cannot affect them, whatever the order of the grants as to priority, because the property in the goods was not vacant when they arrived in A.: they were in fact no longer the goods of the deceased, but of the B. administrator. But, for convenience, and also as a result of the maxim that *en fait de meubles possession vaut titre*, the same effect is not attributed to an administration in B. under which possession might have, but has not, been taken before the arrival of the goods in A. Thus in an American case, where there were stage-coaches and stage-horses belonging to a daily line

(*k*) Sect. 14.

running from one state to another, it was said that, if the administrators in the two states had been different, "the property must have been considered as belonging to that administrator who first reduced it into possession within the limits of his own state" (*l*). And, "according to the common course of commercial business, ships and cargoes and the proceeds thereof, locally situate in a foreign country at the time of the death of the owner, always proceed on their voyages and return to the home port," where "they are taken possession of and administered by the administrator of the *forum domicilii*" (*m*).

296. Let us apply these principles, established for corporeal chattels, to debts due to the deceased, which may at the time of the death be recoverable in different forums, as that of the debtor's domicile and that of the contract, and which may, by a change of the debtor's domicile, or by his coming casually within a jurisdiction where such casual presence is admitted to found the process, become after the death recoverable in still other forums. By the analogy, such a debt will be recoverable in any forum where the action will otherwise lie, by an administrator who has obtained his grant from that forum, without the necessity of a grant from the forum where the debt must have been recovered at the time of the death. The English decisions bearing on this point are curiously involved with the notion of certain kinds of debts as having a *situs* identical with that of the instrument by which they are evidenced, a notion which, as we know, was influential in our municipal law in determining the jurisdiction of local courts of probate. It has however been determined that a grant in the forum of this artificial *situs*, when that is foreign, is not necessary to sustain a suit in England (*n*):

(*l*) *Orcutt* v. *Orms*, 3 Paige, 459, 465.
(*m*) Story, s. 520.
(*n*) *Whyte* v. *Rose*, 3 Q. B. 493.

and so far this agrees with the principle that an administration in the forum of the suit is alone necessary.

297. The conclusions of the last article are subject to the remark that if by any means, such as exist in the case of negotiable paper, the debt can under an administration be reduced into what is equivalent to possession without actually receiving it from the debtor, the debtor may then be sued in any other forum without the necessity of administration being granted therein. Thus if the representative under an administration in A. becomes possessed there of notes payable to bearer, he may sue thereon in B. as the legal owner and bearer without taking out administration in B.: or if the notes were payable to the deceased's order, and they are indorsed by the representative who gets them under the administration in A., the indorsee may sue in B. without taking out any farther administration (*o*). But such a reduction into possession is not operated by getting hold of a deed of covenant, under an administration granted in the artificial *situs* attributed to it by the English rules above alluded to. To sue on such a deed in England, there must be an English administration, notwithstanding a foreign grant where the deed was *bona notabilia* at the death (*p*).

298. It is obvious that since the question, what debts are properly recoverable under any local administration, depends on rules of jurisdiction which are subject to differences of opinion, the farther question arises, whether a recovery by one local administrator will protect the debtor in a suit by another, brought in a forum by the rules of which the former recovery would not have been allowed. Thus, an English administrator recovers in England, on a contract not made in England, and from a debtor not do-

(*o*) Story, s. 517, and see above, Art. 244.

(*p*) *Per curiam*, in *Whyte* v. *Rose*, 3 Q. B. 507, notwithstanding *Huthwaite* v. *Phaire*, 1 Man. & Gr. 159.

miciled in England, the jurisdiction being founded on the defendant's casual presence here. Will that recovery protect the debtor from a suit by the local administrator of his, the debtor's, domicile, by the law of which, we will suppose, the defendant's casual presence is not sufficient to found the jurisdiction? Supposing the recovery to have been by the testator or intestate, the affirmative would admit of no doubt, because payment to the creditor is satisfaction in fact, wherever made. But we shall see that according to the preponderance of authority in England and the United States, each local administrator must administer the values received by him, for the benefit of the deceased's creditors, according to the priorities given by the law of the forum which appointed him: so that it may not be indifferent to the parties concerned by which local administrator the debt is received. But the payment made under judicial—and therefore, to a private person, irresistible—authority ought, in justice, to protect the debtor from all farther claim: and similar protection ought, I think, on the same principle, to be furnished by a payment made without suit, but to a local administrator who had at the time the power of enforcing it by suit. And these points appear to be well established in England. It is true that, in an old case of the year 1571 (*q*), a release by an Irish administrator to a merchant of Waterford was held no answer to an action by the English administrator on a bond which at the death was *bona notabilia* in England, but the reason probably was that the Irish administrator could not have recovered for want of being able to make *profert* of the bond; so that, in spite of the *prima facie* aspect given to the case by the defendant's domicile, it is rather an authority for the principles here maintained,

(*q*) *Daniel* v. *Lucre*, Dyer, 305, Dalison, 76.

which are farther supported by *Shaw* v. *Staughton* (*r*), and the argumentative remarks in *Huthwaite* v. *Phaire* (*s*) and *Whyte* v. *Rose* (*t*).

299. But what if a debtor to the estate pays a local administrator who could not have recovered from him? In that case it may be said that there is no reason why he should not suffer the loss caused by his own facility, and the old case just quoted is a direct authority for his having to pay again (*u*). But the American dicta are for the sufficiency of the discharge (*x*). "Is not," asked Chancellor Kent, "the policy of the law sufficiently answered, when our courts refuse to lend their assistance to any authority not derived from our own laws, touching the administration and distribution of assets?"

300. Lastly, if a local administrator obtain a judgment against a debtor, but payment is not made under it, he may sue in his own name upon the judgment in any other local jurisdiction, without taking out administration there, "for he makes himself accountable for it" in his own forum "by bringing his action" (*y*). And, on the other hand, it is said in the same case that after such judgment no other local administrator can sue, either on the judgment, "not being privy to it," or "on the original contract, for the defendants might plead in bar the judgment recovered abroad" (*y*). But the conclusiveness of a judgment by a foreign administrator as a bar, and the right of maintaining an action upon it, must of course be both taken subject to

---

(*r*) 3 Keble, 163.

(*s*) 1 Man. & Gr. 159, 162.

(*t*) 3 Q. B. 493, 510.

(*u*) *Daniel* v. *Lucre*, *ubi supra*.

(*x*) Chancellor Kent, in *Doolittle* v. *Lewis*, 7 Johnson, Ch. 49: Justice M'Lean, in *Mackey* v. *Coxe*, 18 Howard, 104.

(*y*) *Talmage* v. *Chapel*, 16 Mass. 71.

the limitations which apply to the international effect of foreign judgments generally.

301. When any property of the deceased has, under the rules we have been considering, been properly reduced into possession by an administrator, it is thenceforward treated as his in every jurisdiction. If he remits it to a foreign country, it cannot be taken from his agent by the administrator appointed in that country (*z*). Nor is there any difference in respect to this, or any of the preceding rules, between a principal and an ancillary administrator. We shall find a distinction in their duties as administrators, but their full legal title to the property fairly possessed by them is equally protected, and the principal cannot recover from the ancillary that which the latter has so obtained, because the latter must himself administer it in the ancillary jurisdiction (*a*).

302. Indeed, the duty of an administrator, taking, as before, that term to include any judicial representative, is to discharge the debts of the deceased out of the assets which come to his hands, and either to distribute the surplus among those beneficially entitled, or to remit it to the principal administrator to be so distributed by him. This must be done under the superintendence of the judge from whom he derives his authority (*b*), to whom, and not primarily to any private person, he is accountable. Hence he cannot be sued as administrator, whether by creditors, heirs, or legatees of the deceased, in any other jurisdiction than that of the sovereign who appointed him. If he transmit the assets into another jurisdiction, then he who would there obtain redress must constitute himself administrator there, in which character he may claim the assistance of the local courts in obtaining an administra-

---

(*z*) *Currie* v. *Bircham*, 1 Dow. & Ry. 35.

(*a*) *Preston* v. *Melville*, 8 Cl. & F. 1.

(*b*) *Jauncy* v. *Sealey*, 1 Vern. 397.

tion of the assets which have been brought by the foreign administrator within its jurisdiction (*b*). Nor again, if the relief is not sought out of assets of the deceased, still distinguishable as such, brought by the foreign administrator within the jurisdiction, but from such administrator as having so dealt with the assets as to make himself personally liable, and as domiciled or present, or having effects of his own, within the jurisdiction, still the suit will not be entertained without administration taken out here (*c*); for any value recovered in it will be unadministered assets of the deceased, which cannot, as we have already seen, be recovered in any forum without a grant of administration therein. Unless indeed the foreign "executor or administrator has so dealt with" the fund transmitted to this country, or for which he has made himself personally liable, "that it has ceased to bear the character of a legacy or share of a residue, and has assumed the character of a trust-fund in a sense different from that in which the executor or administrator held it: if it has been taken out of the estate of the testator, and appropriated to or made the property of the cestui que trust, it may not be necessary that the cestui que trust should bring before the court the personal representative of the testator in a suit to recover that part of the estate" (*d*).

303. Hence also one who has accepted abroad a grant of administration without benefit of inventory, and has consequently made himself liable for payment of the debts

---

(*b*) *Lowe* v. *Fairlie*, 2 Madd. 101; *Logan* v. *Fairlie*, 2 Sim. & Stu. 284; *Bond* v. *Graham*, 1 Hare, 482. See also *Sandilands* v. *Innes*, 3 Sim. 263.

(*c*) *Tyler* v. *Bell*, 2 My. & Cr. 89; overruling *Anderson* v. *Caunter*, 2 My. & Ke. 763. In connexion with this, it is useful to know that an executor of an executor is not executor of the original testator unless both probates were granted in the same court: *Jernegan* v. *Baxter*, 5 Sim. 568; *Twyford* v. *Trail*, 7 Sim. 92; overruling *Fowler* v. *Richards*, 5 Russ. 39.

(*d*) Sir James Wigram, in *Bond* v. *Graham*, 1 Hare, 484: and see this doctrine acted on in *Arthur* v. *Hughes*, 4 Beav. 506.

irrespective of the value of the assets, cannot, even by a creditor who has taken out administration here, be sued in the English chancery upon that liability, or, unless he has received English assets, as executor *de son tort* (*e*). It is another question whether he might not be sued at common law, on the personal obligation to the creditors contracted by him through acceptance of the unlimited administration, and, if so, the plaintiff would not need an English administration. But the defendant's liability as representing the deceased, on which alone the suit in chancery could be framed, simple personal obligations not being there enforceable, exists only in the jurisdiction from which he derives his representation. And, from the entire absence of privity between the several local administrators, in respect of the liabilities incurred by them, a judgment recovered against one will not be accepted in another jurisdiction, as even *prima facie* proof of a debt due from the estate, in an action against the different local administrator there (*f*); though it might be otherwise, if the same person were administrator in both countries at the time of the judgment (*g*).

304. But will the administrator be accountable in the jurisdiction from which he derives his title for assets of which he has succeeded in possessing himself, but for which another local administration ought to have been taken out? This may happen by a debt being paid him, or chattels being delivered to him, in a foreign country without suit, or by a recovery in a foreign country, if any such there be, which permits a suit without requiring a local administration. Now on the principle that an administration extends to the property of the deceased which

(*e*) *Beavan* v. *Hastings*, 2 K. & J. 724.

(*f*) *Brodie* v. *Bickley*, 2 Rawle, 431; *Stacy* v. *Thrasher*, 6 Howard, 44; *M'Lean* v. *Meek*, 18 Howard, 16.

(*g*) *Per curiam*, in *Brodie* v. *Bickley*, 2 Rawle, 437.

is or shall be within the jurisdiction, subject only to the condition that it shall not have ceased to be the property of the deceased, and become that of an administrator, by reduction into possession under a lawful administration, the administrator should be accountable in his own jurisdiction for these values when he brings them within it. And this was held in *Dowdale's case* (*h*), where it was said that "if the executors have goods of the testator in any part of the world, they shall be charged in respect of them; for many merchants and other men, who have stocks and goods to a great value beyond sea, are indebted here in England, and God forbid that those goods should not be liable to their debts, for otherwise there would be a great defect in the law." The same doctrine appears to be laid down by Lord Hardwicke in a case of *Atkins* v. *Smith* (*i*), of which there is only a very short and obscure note, but is objected to by Story (*k*), who however assumes that in *Dowdale's case* the foreign assets had been collected under an Irish probate. This, which neither appears in the report nor is implied in the general observations above cited, would entirely alter the case. For the Irish executor being, as we have already seen, liable only in Ireland to account for the assets received under his Irish probate, could not, as such executor, be sued in an English court of law, though a complete administration of them in chancery, as assets brought into England, might be obtained through an English grant by a plaintiff administrator under it. Story's suggestion that an administrator receiving assets in a foreign country, without a due local grant, should be accountable there as executor *de son tort* (*l*), may also be received, as it appears to have been in America; but that is no answer to the reason given in *Dowdale's case* for making him liable in his own jurisdiction as well.

(*h*) 6 Coke, 46 b, Cro. Ja. 55.
(*i*) 2 Atk. 63.
(*k*) S. 514 a.
(*l*) S. 514.

305. The administration of the assets, to which each local representative is bound in the manner we have now considered, refers to the payment of the debts of the deceased; for the principle is that until these are satisfied the property will be retained within the jurisdiction, but that the surplus then remaining is transmissible to the deceased's domicile, to be distributed by that forum among his heirs and legatees (*m*). Hence also if a testator make separate wills of his effects in different countries, the administrator *cum testamento annexo* appointed in his domicile must also have the foreign will annexed to his grant (*n*). To clear the estate, in short, is the duty of an ancillary, and of the principal considered merely as a local, administrator: to distribute it is the duty of the principal administrator as such. For it is only by regarding the estate of the deceased as a unit, that it can be claimed by his personal jurisdiction from the jurisdictions in which the several articles composing it exist: but again it is only his beneficial interest in it, or the balance of value after deducting the sum of its negative from that of its positive items, which can be regarded as a unit. The first care of the jurisdiction in which property vacant by death is found, must be to vest it in some one who shall discharge the burdens on it: not till then is it free to follow the international courtesy which refers to his personal law the beneficial continuation of his person.

306. Upon the conduct of each local administration in discharging these burdens many important questions arise.

(*m*) *Preston* v. *Melville*, 8 Cl. & F. 1; *Meiklan* v. *Campbell*, 24 Beav. 100. The latter case shows that its discretionary power of ordering service abroad will be used by the court of chancery in aid of an ancillary administration, that is, to enforce administration here of the English assets of a foreign testator. In *Weatherley* v. *St. Giorgio*, 2 Hd. 624, the difference between principal and ancillary administrations does not appear to have been considered.

(*n*) *Spratt* v. *Harris*, 4 Hagg. Eccl. 405.

First, the remuneration, if any, which the administrator receives out of the estate, depends on the practice of the court whose officer he is. Thus, if a testator domiciled in India names different executors for India and England, the Indian executors, if no legacy is accepted by them for their trouble (*o*), will be entitled to a commission of 5 per cent. on the assets received by them, though, by transmitting those assets here, they may ultimately have to receive their commission under the authority of an English court (*p*): but the English executors will not be allowed any remuneration (*q*).

307. Next, each local administrator, being only accountable to his own jurisdiction, must discharge the debts in such order, as to preference or priority between creditors, as the practice of that jurisdiction demands. The debts here spoken of are not merely those owing to creditors within the jurisdiction, or upon obligations contracted within it, but all which the deceased may owe anywhere, for it is not until all are discharged that the principal administrator can justly claim any thing on account of the succession: only a debt owing on a foreign judgment, or any other kind of foreign security which does not fulfil the technical requisites for placing it in a given rank according to the rules of the forum, will be classed among obligations of the lowest order (*r*). And if assets, by transmission after the death, come to be administered where they would not have been recoverable, the rights of the creditors against them are considered to be vested, so as not to be affected by such transmission, and the priority as to each part of the assets will depend on the law of that

(*o*) *Freeman* v. *Fairlie*, 3 Mer. 24: which shows also that the legacy, if refused, must be refused within a moderate time.

(*p*) *Chetham* v. *Audley*, 4 Ves. 72; *Cockerell* v. *Barber*, 1 Sim. 23.

(*q*) *Hovey* v. *Blakeman*, 4 Ves. 596.

(*r*) *Cook* v. *Gregson*, 2 Drew. 286.

forum by the authority of which they were originally possessed (*s*). Hence the priority as to the produce of the sale of land can never depend on any other law than that of the *situs* (*t*).

308. The doctrines of the last paragraph are firmly established in the United States (*u*). But upon the continent of Europe it has been more usual to hold that the priorities of creditors against the assets depend on the law of the deceased's domicile. This arises from what has already been alluded to, the original Roman conception of an absolute continuation of the deceased's person, throwing therefore on the heir all the burdens as well as all the benefits of the succession. For, in consequence of this uninterrupted transmission, no change is made in the several special forums of the ancestor's obligations (*x*), while, for his domicile as the general one, is substituted that of the heir upon whom they pass over personally. Hence, instead of the conception of the administration of an insolvent estate, we have that of a *concursus* of creditors against the heir; and, when the heir is allowed to limit by an inventory the extent of his liability, it follows naturally that this *concursus*, so far as concerns his ancestral debts, shall be separated from any claims of his other creditors, and held in that forum where he enters on the succession. A similar result is arrived at, though perhaps less correctly, by asserting a special forum, in the place where he enters on the succession, for the obligations, confessedly of a contractual nature, which by that entrance the heir incurs towards the ancestral creditors (*y*). It is

(*s*) *Cook* v. *Gregson*, 2 Drew. 286.

(*t*) *Hanson* v. *Walker*, 7 L. J. Ch. 135.

(*u*) Story, s. 524.

(*x*) Dig. 5, 1, 45.

(*y*) There is still another view, perhaps the least tenable of all on Roman grounds, that the heir founds for the ancestral creditors a special forum against himself in every place where he possesses himself of a part of the impossible, either way, to apply a result so reached to the jurisprudence of nations which have not restrained, but abandoned in principle, the personal liability of the universal successor; who do not in fact employ the conception of a succession, except in reference to the surplus remaining after the payment of debts; and among whom therefore any identity of the beneficial heir with the administrator, who must pay those debts out of the assets, is altogether casual. There can, under such a jurisprudence, be no *concursus* except against the assets, without relation to any forum of personal obligations. No doubt a comity might have been established in England and America to this effect, that the assets collected under every ancillary administration should be remitted to the domicile, in order that the principal administrator might there apply them in payment of creditors as well as of beneficiaries. Such a comity would have been analogous to the international recognition of the title of assignees in bankruptcy, and would have led to a similar result, in determining priorities by the laws of the single *concursus*. But no such rule has been established by the courts of this country, or of the United States; on the contrary, as we have seen, their doctrine is that only the surplus is transmissible to the domicile. Wherefore the same principles which, under the continental jurisprudence, lead to determining priorities by the law of the domicile of the defunct, in their application to our jurisprudence refer the same question to the *situs* of the assets, as determining the administration under which they are recoverable.

---

estate. This, in its application to the *concursus* of the creditors against him, would lead directly to determining their priorities as to each portion of the assets by its own *lex situs:* but for an English lawyer that doctrine requires no such questionable support. For the rest, these points are chiefly mooted abroad with regard to the query whether the co-heirs are bound *in solidum* or *pro virili parte*. See particularly Boullenois, t. 1, p. 277, *et seq.*; Merlin, Rép., Dette, § IV.; Savigny, v. 8, p. 238.

309. Nevertheless, in *Wilson* v. *Dunsany*, the view here opposed was made to prevail (*y*). The judgment is short, and does not clearly state the reasons. The argument of counsel enlarges on the topic that personal property follows the law of the owner's domicile, but without noticing that property is primarily only in a corporeal thing, that its conception is enlarged scientifically in order to include obligations so far as increasing or diminishing the means of the party, and that with obligations in this relation the questions which arise between the several creditors of the same debtor have nothing to do. It is by no means from any consideration of property, but from the maxims applicable to a *concursus*, that the continental jurists reached a similar, and in their case it seems a right, conclusion. For England, the principle of *Cook* v. *Gregson* appears more correct.

310. As to the future application however of that principle, when both the jurisdictions concerned are British, a question may arise on the recent statute. The administration granted in any one part of the United Kingdom being now capable of being made available in any other part, it may be said that a single British administration has been established, and that, with one *concursus*, we must also have one rule of priority, from whichever part of Great Britain and Ireland the assets come. Since however the Scotch confirmation, for instance, is to have the same effect, when made available here, as an English probate or administration would have had, while such a probate or administration would have produced a liability to account here for the assets received under it—and similarly for the other cases—it appears that the only relief is from the burden of proving the same facts, as to the death, domicile, &c., to several courts, and that separate local administra-

(*y*) 18 Beav. 293.

tions, with separate accountabilities, and therefore rules of priority, are still intended.

311. Thus far there is no difference between ancillary and principal administrations, but if the ancillary administration take place here, there is nothing to prevent our chancery from adopting any proceedings of the *forum domicilii*, or any accounts taken there, and it often does so for convenience when the bulk of the property lies in that jurisdiction (*z*). Also, when the ancillary administration has been completed here, although, as we have seen, the surplus is transmissible for distribution to the *forum domicilii*, yet this is only permissive, each representative being accountable to the tribunal which appoints him for all that he receives by its authority: and the same end is sometimes more easily accomplished by a distribution under the authority of our court, the decision of the strictly competent forum as to the persons beneficially entitled being for that purpose adopted (*z*). The same principle furnishes an answer to the question—suppose the estate cleared of debt without an administration suit, and the executors in both jurisdictions the same: in what forum must a claimant of the beneficial succession sue them for the surplus? It has been decided in *Innes* v. *Mitchell* (*a*) that such a plaintiff is not confined to the principal forum, that he may sue in the ancillary forum for so much of the property as was there received under the ancillary probate, and is therefore there to be accounted for: and that this will be so even though the executors, or those adverse claimants to whom they may have paid over the surplus, have removed the property into the jurisdiction of the principal forum.

(*z*) *Meiklan* v. *Campbell*, 24 Beav. 100, 104.

(*a*) 4 Drew. 141, 1 De G. & J. 423, 432; which case shows also that the court will support its jurisdiction under the circumstances by ordering service abroad.

312. In the above investigation, reference has frequently been made to the surplus which remains of the assets in any jurisdiction after a complete administration there. Now it is often a difficult question what is a complete local administration, and how it shall be made; and these points appear to have received more attention in the United States than in England. It has been there said that in the case of an estate solvent on the whole, but of which the portion recoverable in any one of their jurisdictions might be insufficient to pay all the debts in full, the citizens of each jurisdiction ought to be paid out of the assets there. "For it would be but an idle show of courtesy to order the proceeds of an estate to be sent to a foreign country, and oblige our citizens to go or send there for their debts, when no possible prejudice could arise to the estate or those interested in it by causing them to be paid here, and possibly the same remark may be applicable to legatees living here, unless the circumstances of the estate should require the funds to be sent abroad" (*b*). The difficulty is greater in the case of an insolvent estate, and on this the same learned and able judge, Chief Justice Parker, offered the following observations.

313. "What shall be done, to avoid, on the one hand, the injustice of taking the whole funds for the use of our citizens to the prejudice of foreigners, and, on the other, the equal injustice and greater inconvenience of compelling our own citizens to seek satisfaction of their debts in distant countries? The proper course would undoubtedly be to retain the funds here, for a *pro rata* distribution according to the laws of our state among the citizens thereof, having regard to all the assets, either in the hands of the principal administrator or of the administrator here,

(*b*) From the judgment in *Dawes* v. *Head*, 3 Pick. 145.

and having regard also to the whole of the debts which by the law of either country are payable out of those assets; disregarding any fanciful preference which may be given to one species of debt over another, and considering the funds here as applicable for the payment of the just proportion due to our own citizens; and if there be any residue, it should be remitted to the principal administrator to be dealt with according to the laws of his own country, the subjects of that country, if there be any injustice or inequality in the payment or distribution, being bound to submit to its laws. The only objection which can be made to this mode of adjusting an ancillary administration upon an insolvent estate, is the difficulty and delay of executing it. The difficulty would not be greater than in settling many other complicated affairs, where many persons have interests of different kinds in the same funds. The powers of a court of chancery are competent to embrace and settle all cases of that nature, even if the powers of the court of probate are not sufficiently extensive; which however is not certain. The administrator here should be held to show the condition of the estate abroad, the amount of property subject to debts, and the amount of debts; and a distribution could be made upon perfectly fair and equitable principles. The delay would undoubtedly be considerable, but this would not be so great an evil as either sending our citizens abroad upon a forlorn hope to see the fragments of an insolvent estate, or paying the whole of their debts out of the property without regard to the claims of foreign creditors. And if the probate court has not sufficient power to make such an equitable adjustment, a bill in equity, in which the administrator here should be the principal respondent, would probably produce the desired result, and then time and opportunity could be given to make known the whole condition of the estate, and all persons interested might be heard before any final decree: in the meantime the administrator could be restrained from remitting the funds until such decree should be passed" (*c*).

2. *Succession to Movables by Destination of Law.*

314. The law of an intestate's domicile as the rule for his succession has sometimes been rested on an assent which he is supposed to imply, and to this there is no objection in the case of his having enjoyed the power to vary the destination which the law would have given to his property. But no such reason can apply to the case in which the law of his domicile absolutely prescribes that destination, in whole or in part, by a provision not subject to the wills of testators: and yet it is certain that that law is then also the rule. In truth, the testamentary power, where it exists most unfettered, has attained that point by progressive enlargement, and in some countries the tide has recently set towards its restriction; so that it is more in accordance with legal history to regard destination by law as normal, and not to seek in implied assent a justification for the preference which the *lex domicilii* is allowed to have over the *lex situs*, whether in case of voluntary intestacy, or of a statute precluding the free bequest of the whole or of some fixed proportion of the individual's fortune. It is firmly based in the intimate connexion of the subject with the person of the deceased.

315. This preference appears to have been always recognised in England, though in some cases before Lord Hardwicke ineffectual attempts were made to shake it (*d*). But in Scotland the *lex situs* is upheld by the older au-

(*c*) *Dawes* v. *Head*, 3 Pick. 147.

(*d*) *Pipon* v. *Pipon*, Ambl. 25; *Thorne* v. *Watkins*, 2 Ves. 35.

thorities, nor can the true rule be considered as having been fully established for that country till the decision of *Balfour* v. *Scott* (*e*). That was a case of distribution on intestacy, and in *Hog* v. *Lashley* (*f*) it was ruled that the *lex domicilii* empowered a testator to exclude a child from the legitim given by the *lex situs*. *Balfour* v. *Scott* also settled another important point, namely, that the heir of Scotch heritable estate, though compellable to collate it if he claim a distributive share in the personalty of his intestate ancestor domiciled in Scotland, is not so compellable if the ancestor were an Englishman: for no such condition of collation is imposed by the English law, which gives him his interest in the personalty.

316. Farther, however nicely the evidence may be balanced between competing domiciles, one of them must, at least for the object of distribution, be pronounced for. "The next rule is," said Lord Alvanley, "that though a man may have two domiciles for some purposes, he can have only one for the purpose of succession. That is laid down expressly in Denisart under the title Domicile; that only one domicile can be acknowledged for the purpose of regulating the succession to the personal estate. I have taken this as a maxim, and am warranted by the necessity of such a maxim, for the absurdity would be monstrous, if it were possible that there should be a competition between two domiciles as to the distribution of the personal estate. It could never be possibly determined by the

---

(*e*) 6 Bro. P. C. 550. As the house of lords held the intestate's domicile to have been English, the point must have arisen on the cross-appeal, on which it was decided in effect that the personal estate in Scotland was distributable by English law. The true doctrine had been laid down by Lord Thurlow in the Scotch case of *Bruce* v. *Bruce*, 2 Bos. & Pul. 229, n. (see dictum in page 230), 6 Bro. P. C. 566; but the point did not arise there, as the domicile was ultimately held to be English, and there were no effects in Scotland.

(*f*) 3 Hagg. Eccl. 415, n., 6 Bro. P. C. 577.

casual death of the party at either. That would be most whimsical and capricious. It might depend upon the accident whether he died in winter or summer, and many circumstances not in his choice, and that never could regulate so important a subject as the succession to his personal estate" (*g*). Supposing however that there is an absolute impossibility of fixing the domicile, even that of origin being uncertain, his lordship, as we saw in Art. 34, considered a recourse to the *lex situs* necessary: but Savigny solves the same difficulty by the casual place of death (*h*).

317. One application of the general rule is, or may be, to the legitimacy of the successors. "The law of the domicile," says Story, "is to decide whether a person is legitimate or not, to take the succession" (*i*). "It holds," says Savigny of the same law, "also for the conditions of kinship generally, and thus for the existence of kinship traceable through wedlock, as for legitimation" (*k*). On the other hand, it is plain that all the reasons which have been given for determining the legitimacy of a claimant once for all, by the appropriate law, as against the *lex situs* when he seeks to inherit land, apply with equal force against the *lex domicilii* of the deceased when he would succeed to personalty (*l*). And accordingly it was not on the ground of the *lex domicilii testatoris* that the word "children," when the question of legitimacy arose on it, was interpreted in a will (*m*): a precedent which is fairly in point here.

318. In *Potinger* v. *Wightman* (*n*) it was held that a

(*g*) *Somerville* v. *Somerville*, 5 Ves. 786.

(*h*) V. 8, p. 296, note (*b*).

(*i*) Sect. 481 a.

(*k*) V. 8, p. 314.

(*l*) See above, Arts. 90—94.

(*m*) *Re Wright's trust*, 2 K. & J. 595.

(*n*) 3 Mer. 67.

mother may through a change of residence acquire a benefit in the succession of her child whose domicile is hers, provided the change was made without improper motive: and it seems as though Sir William Grant considered that any direct view to the law of the new abode, as being more favourable to the mother, would be an improper motive.

319. Distributive shares do not give rise to all the questions properly belonging to succession. When the claims of creditors against the estate have been satisfied, the question by what portion of the estate the burden of those claims is primarily to be borne, being as I may say one internal to the inheritance, must be decided by the law of the deceased's domicile. Thus the Scotch heir of an English intestate, who has paid in Scotland movable debts of his ancestor, has been allowed to exercise here the right of relief given by our law against the personalty (*o*). This principle however must give way when it conflicts with the authority of the *lex situs* to decide both what is realty, and to whom it is transmitted; so that, if in the case just put the debts paid had been by Scotch law immovable, the heir could not, as we have already seen, have availed himself of our right of relief (*p*). In effect the ancestor's heritable bond would have been equivalent to an alienation by him of so much of his immovable property, which therefore might be justly regarded as having never, to that extent, been included in his succession.

320. Again, two descriptions of imposts are commonly set by governments on successions: those on their collection, and those on their transmission. Each in fact bears on the amount ultimately transmitted, but the former class,

---

(*o*) *Winchelsea* v. *Garetty*, 2 Keen, 293. See also *Anon.*, 9 Mod. 66, and *Bowaman* v. *Reeve*, Pre. Ch. 577.

(*p*) *Elliott* v. *Minto*, 6 Mad. 16; *Drummond* v. *Drummond*, in *Brodie* v. *Barry*, 2 Ves. & Be. 132. See above, Art. 76.

duties on probates and administrations, being regarded as a remuneration to the state which protects the property and aids the representative to get it in, are charged in respect of the *situs* of the assets at the death. We exact them on property left by foreigners in our funds, or otherwise in the United Kingdom (*q*), but not on the foreign property of any one, though dying and even domiciled here, or though his executor may bring the property to this country and administer it here (*r*). The other class, duties on legacies and distributive shares, being directly imposed on the right of succession, are payable to the government and according to the law of the deceased's domicile, wherever the legatees or successors may reside, and wherever the property may be situate at the death, or may be afterwards remitted (*s*).

321. Distributive shares and legacies will carry the interest of the country in which the assets have been placed by the administrators since they became payable, on the presumption that that interest has been made (*t*). And when a testator left assets in two jurisdictions, in each of which his will was proved by certain of his executors, the legatees who sued in one of the forums, where there was an ample fund for their satisfaction, were held bound by their election, and could receive only the interest current there (*u*).

(*q*) See the dictum in *Thomson* v. *Advocate-General*, 13 Sim. 164, 12 Cl. & F. 29. These duties are in fact coextensive with the necessity for probate or administration.

(*r*) *Att.-Gen.* v. *Dimond*, 1 Cr. & J. 356; *Att.-Gen.* v. *Hope*, 1 Cr. M. & R. 530, 8 Bl. N. R. 44, 2 Cl. & F. 84; *Att.-Gen.* v. *Bouwens*, 4 M. & W. 171.

(*s*) *Thomson* v. *Advocate-General*, 13 Sim. 153, 12 Cl. & F. 1; overruling *Att.-Gen.* v. *Cockerell*, 1 Price, 165, *Att.-Gen.* v. *Beatson*, 7 Price, 560, and *Logan* v. *Fairlie*, 2 Sim. & Stu. 284; and superseding, by a more general statement or decision, *Att.-Gen.* v. *Jackson*, or *Forbes*, 8 Bl. N. R. 15 and 2 Cl. & F. 48, *Re Ewin*, 1 Cr. & J. 151 and 1 Tyr. 91, *Re Bruce*, 2 Cr. & J. 436, and *Arnold* v. *Arnold*, 2 My. & Cr. 256.

(*t*) *Malcolm* v. *Martin*, 3 Bro. Ch. 50; *Raymond* v. *Brodbelt*, 5 Ves. 199.

(*u*) *Bourke* v. *Ricketts*, 10 Ves. 330.

322. It remains to notice the opinion which subjects immovable successions to the same law as movable ones, and which for a century past has gained ground in Germany, though in other parts of Europe the *lex situs* is maintained for land with less uncertainty than once attached to it. I can however scarcely suppose that even in countries living under the Roman law the immovable property, there situate, of an intestate domiciled in England, would be subjected to the mode of succession pointed out by our statutes of distribution; for they are so absolutely confined to personal estate, that they do not seem to constitute such a *lex domicilii* as would admit of extra-territorial application to land. The case is different, when in two countries there exist laws of distribution, unlike, but neither distinguishing land from chattels. A case which deserves to be here mentioned is *Iha* v. *Rae*, showing that by the native law, as administered between Gentoos in India, the Mitheela rule of inheritance is applied, even as to land situate where the general rule is that of another sect, on the death of one who performs his domestic ceremonies of mourning and rejoicing according to the Mitheela Shaster (*x*).

3. *Validity of Wills of Movables.*

323. On the continent, the formal requisites of a will as to attestation, holograph redaction, &c., &c., are of course submitted primarily to the maxim *locus regit actum*: and the first question is whether this maxim is facultative or imperative. Supposing it to be facultative, which has been in all ages the opinion of most jurists, then there is the farther question whether the proper seat of the trans-

(*x*) 2 Moore, I. A. C., 132, 160.

action, the forms used in which the testator has the option of employing, is his domicile, or the situation of the property; and again, whether any difference is made in the last question by the property being movable or immovable. There are, besides, the extreme opinions, on the one side, that the forms of the situation are imperative; and on the other that those of the domicile are imperative, at least on those who die there, for I am not aware that the latter forms have been held on the continent to be imperative on wills made abroad by those who die from home: and farther variations may be introduced by asking, for instance, whether the judges of the *locus actus*, if their own jurisprudence regards the maxim *locus regit actum* as imperative, will be bound to apply the *lex domicilii testatoris* to a foreigner's will made within their jurisdiction in the forms of his domicile, supposing that law to regard the same maxim as only facultative. The English lawyer will probably thank me for sparing him a dry list of the jurists who have passed their opinions on these endless combinations, since the total absence of any maxim in English law at all analogous to the *locus regit actum* prevents the subject from having here even an historical importance. He will be more interested to know that the French court of cassation has declared for the imperative obligation on wills of the forms of the place of redaction, even in reference to the will of a foreigner made in France in the forms of his domicile (*y*): and that in Germany, though the better opinion inclines to a free option between the forms of the domicile and place of redaction, yet Savigny recommends a German who makes his will abroad by the *lex loci actus* to make another for safety, on his return home, by his *lex domicilii* (*z*).

(*y*) Decree of March 9th, 1853; Dev.—Car., 53, 1, 274; Fœlix, 3me édit. p. 166, n. (*a*).

(*z*) V. 8, p. 356. See above, Arts. 174, 175, on the analogous questions in contracts.

324. In England it is well settled that we refer the formal validity of a will of movables to the law of the testator's domicile. Thus, if that domicile be English, we require the English Wills Act to be followed even though the will be made abroad, not having, as before remarked, any such maxim in our jurisprudence as *locus regit actum* (*a*). If the domicile be foreign, the only inquiry we make is whether the will would be admitted to operate there, without regarding whether its validity in the domicile results from its pursuing the forms ordinarily there required, or from the adoption in that forum of a will made in foreign form (*b*). This appears to be the just application of the principle that movable successions are governed by the personal law of the decedent. The same doctrine is firmly established in the United States (*c*).

325. Admitting then the *lex domicilii testatoris* as a basis, we next come to certain questions which were raised in *Curling* v. *Thornton* (*d*), where Sir John Nicholl admitted to probate a will which was said to be wholly null by the French law, on the grounds that, first, a British subject could not divest himself of a British domicile, and secondly, that if the testator had so acquired a French domicile that it would have governed in case of intestacy, yet he retained a secondary one here sufficient to give effect to a will made in England in conformity with our

(*a*) *De Zichy Ferraris* v. *Hertford*, 3 Curt. 468, 4 Moore, P. C. 339; *Page* v. *Donovan*, Deane, 278.

(*b*) In *The Duchess of Kingston's case*, probate was granted here, as late as 1791, of the will of a lady domiciled in France both at the time of making her will and at her death, such will being conformable to the English and not to the French form: in *Curling* v. *Thornton*, 2 Add. 21. Also the form of the *lex situs* was anciently demanded in Scotland for Scotch movables: but that the forms of that law are not to be considered was decided in *Hare* v. *Nasmyth* (2 Add. 25), both for Scotland and England.

(*c*) Story, s. 468.

(*d*) 2 Add. 6.

law. But the principle laid down by Lord Alvanley in intestacy, that for purposes of succession there can be but one domicile, has since been established for testacy also by the case *De Zichy Ferraris* v. *Hertford* (*e*), in which a codicil to the will of an English peer, domiciled here, was rejected, though made by him at Milan, where he had a second residence, in Austrian form, and disposing of Austrian property. And the first ground was overruled by the decision of the court of delegates in *Stanley* v. *Bernes* (*f*), reversing the judgment of Sir John Nicholl, who adhered to the opinion he had expressed in *Curling* v. *Thornton*, and establishing that a testator, though he may continue entitled to the privileges of a British subject, may yet so acquire a foreign domicile that his will made in English form, and disposing of English property, will be held invalid for non-compliance with the foreign requirements as to attestation.

326. In interpreting the above rules on the formal validity of testaments, the question may arise whether by the domicile is meant that at the date of the will, or that at the death, supposing the testator to have changed his residence during the interval. In the general continental view, it is the former alone which is intended: no other meaning can be given to the permission accorded to the testator to choose between the forms of his domicile and those of the *locus actus*, and as a will made in the latter manner would remain valid notwithstanding the change of a domicile which was no element in its validity (*g*), so also would one which the testator, in obedience to no rule of law, but for his own convenience, had preferred to make in the former. In the English view the thing assumes a

(*e*) 3 Curt. 468, 4 Mo. P. C. 339.

(*f*) 3 Hagg. Eccl. 373, 447. The decision of the delegates was followed in *Moore* v. *Darell*, 4 Hagg. Eccl. 346.

(*g*) Fœlix, No. 117.

different aspect. By referring ourselves to the law of the domicile, as that of the succession, we of course mean the domicile at the death. If therefore the change be from an English domicile to a foreign one, as this will be no longer the forum of principal administration, the continuing validity of the English will, when offered for probate here, will have to be referred to the law of the country where the testator resided at his death, and thus will ultimately come to be determined on the answer given there to this international question. But if the change be from a foreign domicile to an English one, we shall have to decide for ourselves on the continuing validity of the foreign will, and then I submit that it should be maintained whenever conformable either to the *lex loci conditi testamenti*, or to the law of the then domicile: for it never can be imagined that by the transference of his domicile to England the testator intended tacitly to revoke his will, more especially since by the continental law, with which alone from his previous life he can be supposed to be acquainted, such transference would not have that effect. "It has been held however that unless the will was executed according to the law of the person's last domicile, and the place of his death, it would not be valid although made according to the laws of the testator's domicile at the time it was made" (*h*).

327. A question sometimes arises how far the foregoing rules are applicable to instruments which partake in certain limited respects only of the testamentary character. And with this may be taken the analogous question, how far a power given by contract to executors or administrators is to be taken as tied by the same rules which apply to the powers given them by law. Thus, where an English

---

(*h*) *Nat* v. *Coon*, 10 Missouri, 543; cited in the late editions of Story, s. 479 g.

will gave a power to appoint personal property by a will, or by any writing purporting to be, or being in the nature of, a will, and attested by two witnesses, and the donee was domiciled at Naples, it was necessary to ascertain whether a will made by him conformably to English law and to the terms of the power, but not to Neapolitan law, was a good execution (*i*). It was held that since, by the construction put by English law on the terms of the power, no instrument could be a good execution of it which had not been declared testamentary by being admitted to probate, it was incumbent on the English court of probate to pronounce on the testamentary character of the instrument in question: but it was not said by what law that court should guide itself in so doing, though perhaps it was assumed that it would follow the English law, and so the decision was understood by Story (*k*). I should say that whether its want of conformity to Neapolitan law prevented or did not prevent the writing from being a proper testament, it was in the nature of a will within the true meaning of the power, being revocable during life, and that therefore, being attested as the power demanded, it was a good execution: the law to which, as a testament, the writing would have been amenable, seems irrelevant to its operation in declaring the trust of property held in trust under a former will. But if English law, which alone could be heard on the construction of that former will, would entertain no execution except by a writing declared by probate to be a proper testament, it would appear that the same law was bound to solve the difficulty it had created, by admitting the writing to probate. Chancellor Kent held that a power of sale, given to the executors and administrators of a mortgagee, might be exercised by the

(*i*) *Tatnall* v. *Hankey*, 2 Mo. P. C. 342.
(*k*) Sect. 473 a.

administrators appointed in the domicile of the deceased, without the necessity of an appointment in the *situs* of the land (*l*).

328. There is a universal agreement in referring to the law of the domicile at death, as opposed to that of the domicile when the will was made, all questions of its intrinsic validity: as of the proportion of his estate of which the testator may dispose, legitim, disherison of natural heirs by simple preterition, and so forth (*m*). These points belong essentially to the law of the succession, which is not opened till the death: and they slide into those which belong to the next section.

4. *Construction and Operation of Wills of Movables.*

329. Two classes of cases fall under this head, which it is perhaps impossible in practice to distinguish by a very accurate line: those where the question is of interpreting the testator's meaning, and those where it is of the operation of law upon that meaning. If his meaning be plain, but opposed by the law of his domicile at death, there is no doubt but that that law must prevail, whether it declare his intention illegal, or indirectly frustrate it by a positive rule of construction obliging the courts to take his words in a certain sense. Thus we have already seen that a testator's power to exclude a child from legitim depends on the law of his domicile (*n*), and so also a condition in restraint of marriage will be valid or not according to the same law, irrespective of the situation of the property to the bequest of which it is attached (*o*). And if the testa-

(*l*) *Doolittle* v. *Lewis*, 7 Johnson, Ch. 45.

(*m*) Fœlix, no. 117; Savigny, v. 8, p. 312. And see the next paragraph.

(*n*) *Hog* v. *Lashley*, 3 Hagg. Eccl. 415, n., 6 Bro. P. C. 577. See Art. 328, and *Price* v. *Dewhurst*, 8 Sim. 279, 4 My. & Cr. 76.

(*o*) *Ommaney* v. *Bingham*, 3 Hagg. Eccl. 414, n.

tor have used words which by the law of his domicile are not suffered to carry a legacy to the representatives of the legatee, no attention will be paid to the most irrefragable proofs of his intention that the legacy should not lapse (*p*). All this proceeds upon the plain principle that, when the claims of creditors have been satisfied, the testator's domicile is the forum for the administration of the surplus as between the heirs or legatees; and to what wills does the law of that forum apply if not to those which come before it in the course of its regular jurisdiction? Whence foreign courts also must admit that law, if a will which would regularly be subject to it happens from any circumstances to come before them. Thus the grant of an English probate decided even for the English court of chancery merely who was executor, and no farther question as to the operation of the will of one domiciled in France (*q*). And the court of session must interpret the will of a domiciled Englishman as it would be interpreted in England (*r*); so that even if the personalty is to be invested in Scotch land, the English law must decide whether the first taker under the settlement to be made will be entitled to the interest of the fund during the year after the testator's death (*s*).

330. But this principle is not taxable with the conclusion which has sometimes been drawn from it, that all words of technicality, quantity, or other, used by the testator must be understood according to the law, measures, or language of his domicile. If indeed any absolute rule in force there requires that, it must be done; but all that

(*p*) *Anstruther* v. *Chalmer*, 2 Sim. 1.

(*q*) *Thornton* v. *Curling*, 8 Sim. 310. As to the grant of probate in this case, see above, Art. 325.

(*r*) *Trotter* v. *Trotter*, 3 Wils. & Sh. 407, 4 Bl. N. R. 502.

(*s*) *Macpherson* v. *Macpherson*, 1 Macq. 243. See, as to the interpretation of foreign wills, *Bernal* v. *Bernal*, 3 My. & Cr. 559, C. P. C. 55.

is generally necessary is that the system of interpretation prevailing in the courts of the domicile be applied, and if that be a rational system, and so far as it is unfettered by absolute rules fixing certain interpretations regardless of circumstances, it will itself look to the circumstances of the testator or of the property for the explanation of many things, and may so be led to understand words with reference to foreign technicalities, measures, and languages. Thus an annuity charged on Irish land, by an English will, for a wife living in England, was held, upon the manifest intention, to be payable here in our currency without charge for remittance (*t*). And if a testator, having funds in his domicile and also abroad, bequeaths a legacy generally without separating the funds, it will be payable in the money of his domicile (*u*); but if he separates the property, and charges the legacy on the foreign assets, that will be a very strong argument that he intends its value to be taken in the foreign currency (*x*). Thus also where a testator domiciled in Jamaica devised an estate there, on the question whether the stock on it passed also, the probable sense in which the particular words employed would have been used by a Jamaican was appealed to in the judgment, but no arbitrary rule of construction laid down (*y*). And when it is contended that a will puts the heir of foreign immovables to his election by an ineffectual attempt to devise them, the

(*t*) *Wallis* v. *Brightwell*, 2 P. W. 88.

(*u*) *Saunders* v. *Drake*, 2 Atk. 465; *Pierson* v. *Garnet*, 2 Bro. Ch. 38; *Malcolm* v. *Martin*, 3 Bro. Ch. 50.

(*x*) Dicta in *Saunders* v. *Drake*, 2 Atk. 466, and *Pierson* v. *Garnet*, 2 Bro. Ch. 47. Whatever currency be held to have been intended, if the legacy be paid out of a fund in court in England, the course of chancery is to pay it at the sterling value, without reference to the exchange: *Cockerell* v. *Barber*, 16 Ves. 461; *Campbell* v. *Graham*, 1 Ru. & My. 453, 461. This is as much as to say that, as against the residuary legatee, no particular place of payment was intended by the testator.

(*y*) *Stewart* v. *Garnett*, 3 Sim. 398.

question whether those immovables were meant to be devised by it must be answered as the courts of the testator's domicile would answer it (*z*). The case in which this was decided supplies also another lesson, that however clear, in appearance, may be the meaning of a foreign will, no tribunal can with safety or propriety act on it without obtaining the opinion of lawyers of the domicile (*a*). To act otherwise would be to assume a knowledge of foreign law, which might prove treacherous where little suspected, as with regard to the precise degree of clearness with which in any country an ineffectual intention to devise must be manifested in order to put an heir to his election.

331. But although, when the data are before the foreign judges, they must attribute to the testator the same meaning which, upon them, he would be held to express in his domicile, yet, as they are bound only by their own rules of evidence, this may influence the data which come before them, and so, indirectly, their conclusion. Thus a revoked will cannot be proved, and therefore no English court can look at it, but a Scotch court may, though the testator was English, to get the benefit of the light it may throw on a later will (*b*). "Had Mr. Yates died intestate," said Lord Brougham, "the English statute of distributions, and not the Scotch law of succession in movables, would have regulated the whole course of the administration. His written declarations must, therefore, be taken with respect to the English law. I think it follows from hence, that those declarations of intention touching that property must be construed as we should construe them here by our principles of legal interpretation . . . . . . The Scotch court must inquire of the foreign law as a

(*z*) *Trotter* v. *Trotter*, 3 Wils. & Sh. 407, 4 Bl. N. R. 502.

(*a*) But see *Bernal* v. *Bernal*, 3 My. & Cr. 559, C. P. C. 55.

(*b*) *Yates* v. *Thomson*, 3 Cl. & F. 544. The following extracts are from pages 585—591.

matter of fact, and examine such evidence as will show how in England such instruments would be dealt with as to construction. I give this as my opinion upon principle, for I am not aware of the question ever having received judicial determination in either country. But here I think the importing the foreign code (sometimes incorrectly called the *comitas*) must stop: what evidence the courts of another country would receive and what reject, is a question into which I cannot at all see the necessity of the courts of any one country entering . . . . . It by no means follows that where a sentence of a foreign court is offered in evidence, the probate, for example, of an English will, it should not be admitted, nor do I think it should be denied its natural and legitimate force. But that it must, like all other instruments, be received upon such proof as is required by the rules of evidence followed by the court before which it is tendered, I hold it to be quite clear: it will follow, that though a probate striking out part of a will would be received, and the court of session would have no right to notice the part struck out—for this would be reversing or at least disregarding the very sentence of the court of probate—yet the non-probate of a person's will would not prevent the court from receiving and regarding that will, if its own rules of evidence did not shut it out."

332. It remains to observe that a stringent prohibitive law, existing in their situation, will exclude the operation of the law of the domicile even on the chattels comprised in a succession. This is the case with a direction to emancipate slaves, invalid by the former though good by the latter jurisprudence (*c*).

(*c*) *Mahorner* v. *Hooe*, 9 Smedes & Marshall, 247.

CHAPTER XI.

Marriage.

1. *Constitution of the Marriage.*

333. In pursuance of my plan of considering first all the dealings of men as transacted between persons confessedly capable with regard to them, and afterwards introducing those limitations to the general doctrines which arise from incapacity, it becomes the time, after having discussed the subjects of obligation and property, to enter on that of marriage. But it is necessary on the threshold of this topic to point out its relation to the question of incapacity, as that is understood in private international law: for there are three objections to the constitution of a marriage which turn on incapacity in some sense or other, and clear ideas in respect to them are indispensable from the beginning. These are, that the parties have not attained the age of consent: that they have attained it, but not that farther age at which the authorisation of parents or guardians is necessary to the validity of the consent: and that the parties are within the prohibited degrees of affinity, or are affected by religious vows.

334. The first of these is a question of capacity in the

strictest sense. Marriage is a status, but it is constituted by a consensual contract, and to the force of the consent, nay, to its existence, a certain ripeness of judgment is necessary, not by any positive law, but by the nature of consent itself, which universal jurisprudence merely recognises. All that law can do is to lay down the rules for determining when such ripeness of judgment shall be presumed; and if, on this, the code of one nation accepts the provisions of another as to its members, it does so merely by way of adopting the best evidence it can procure as to the existence, in the particular case, of an incapacity the general assertion of which it does not borrow from that foreign code.

335. The necessity of an authorisation by parents or guardians is a protection which positive law throws round a will presumed to be weak, and is therefore in principle a matter of policy and institution, like the relief granted to expectant heirs against catching bargains. It can therefore, from its own nature, claim no recognition at the hands of a foreign law. But since the age of consent is in most, or all, civilized nations placed so early that such a protection is held to be necessary for some period after it, a weakness of judgment remaining after the age of consent may, in the mutual dealings of members of those nations, be accepted for a fact as general and primary as those of nature: and in mutually receiving the evidence of positive law with regard to its existence, and the remedies supplied by positive law for it, they will be acting in a manner analogous to the former case.

336. The third point arises from vows, and the prohibited degrees of affinity. It is at once apparent that there is here no natural incapacity, such as we have been considering hitherto. The parties are both physically and mentally capable of a marriage in fact. Yet if an act or contract is illegal, so that the external semblance of it is,

for any juristic consequences, a mere nullity, except in so far as it may possibly subject the parties to penalties for the attempt, then, in one sense of the words, a personal incapacity is created as to such act or contract. It is precisely this personal incapacity which is created by a law prohibiting a time-bargain as gambling. No legal obligation arises by such a bargain, and therefore the parties, in spite of the concurrence of their wills, are incapable to contract a legal obligation that way. The words in which such laws are couched are of course very various. It may be that no action shall lie on such a bargain; or "that all marriages which shall hereafter be celebrated between persons within the prohibited degrees of consanguinity shall be absolutely null and void" (*a*); or "that no descendant of the body of his late Majesty King George II. (other than, &c.) shall be capable of contracting matrimony without the previous consent of" (*b*) the reigning sovereign. Or again, there may be no words at all, as when by the common law no obligation arises on a *turpis causa*. But to suppose that any difference is made, to the nature of the incapacity produced, by the presence or absence of any particular words, or of any words, would be to return to the point from which Bartolus set out: *bona decedentis veniant in primogenitum* is a real statute, *primogenitus succedat* a personal one (*c*). Hence the third objection, being of the same kind with the illegality of pecuniary contracts, is properly within the scope of the present chapter, and cannot be deferred: the first is not so, but from the early age which in most countries, and certainly in England, is regarded as sufficient for consent, it is of small practical importance: while the second is of a mixed character, ranking with the third in principle,

(*a*) 5 & 6 Wm. 4, c. 54, s. 2.
(*b*) 12 Geo. 3, c. 11, s. 1.
(c) See Art. 142.

though with the first in its practical aspect. On the whole then, there is no sufficient reason for not taking here the whole subject of the constitution of marriage together.

337. But before entering on the international questions, one more remark must be made on marriage, considered simply from the municipal point of view. It is established by a contract, in which not only is no place of execution stipulated, but none even enters into the expectations of the parties in any such manner as to become an element of their consent. On the contrary, it is, by its very nature, a contract the parties to which intend that the status produced by it shall arise immediately, as in fact it does, without reference to their possibly being from home at the time: and they farther intend that the continuance of that status, as resulting from the contract, shall be independent of any subsequent change in their domicile, and of all place whatever, so that if they at any time seek to dissolve it, and have récourse to some territorial law for that purpose, the operation of that law shall in no way flow from their contract: and moreover, that no disappointment which either side may experience, in those pecuniary consequences of the marriage which must depend on place, shall in any degree affect the existence of the status itself.

338. Now the most obvious international view of marriage, considering the ubiquity and immediate inception of the status produced by it, is to assimilate it to those contracts causing obligations of which an immediate performance can be demanded anywhere: and for these there was no doubt, wherever the *forum contractus*, with the principle of the *lex loci contractus*, was received, that both the form and the legality, the extrinsic and intrinsic validity, depended on the *lex loci celebrationis*. This is very clearly asserted by the jesuit Sanchez, who is among the most ancient authorities on the subject, and one to whose opinions a very high respect is paid in the Roman church.

He lays down, in passages often quoted, the general rule that the solemnities of contracts are to be regulated by the *lex loci contractus* (*d*): he applies it not only to marriage generally, but also expressly to those who visit a foreign country *in fraudem decreti Tridentini, ut ibi possent libere absque parocho et testibus matrimonio copulari*, using the two reasons that *est enim fraus licita cum contrahentes utantur jure suo*, and that *bona vel mala intentio conferre potest ad committendum vel non committendum peccatum, non tamen ad annullandum actum, cum intentio maneat in mente, nec effectum influat in opus externum* (*e*): and he farther expressly extends the doctrine to the diriment impediments, in a passage which I will cite at large, as it has not been noticed in many of the subsequent controversies on the point. *Tandem deducitur, si fidelis contrahat matrimonium apud infideles apud quos domicilium habet, cum impedimento aliquo dirimenti ab ecclesia inducto, matrimonium fore nullum, quia leges ecclesiasticæ ubique terrarum fideles adstringunt. At secus erit dicendum si infidelis contrahat extra patriam in loco principi Christiano subdito aut alii principi infideli, cum impedimento dirimenti statuto a suo solo principe, quia non adstringitur legibus suæ patriæ extra illam* (*ut late probavi lib.* 3, *disp.* 18, *n.* 18). *Dixi a suo solo principe, quia si etiam esset impedimentum dirimens sancitum a principe loci in quo contrahit, non valeret, quia peregrini adstringuntur legibus communibus suæ patriæ et loci in quo reperiuntur* (*ut probavi ea disp.* 18, *n.* 3). *Si autem esset ab ecclesia inductum illud impedimentum in loco fidelium ubi infidelis contrahit, et in suo oppido a principe infideli, valeret matrimonium, quia lex illa ecclesiastica non est generalis in illo oppido, sed solos fideles adstringit* (*f*).

(*d*) De Matrimonio, lib. 3, disp. 18, passim.
(*e*) Ib., lib. 3, disp. 18, n. 29.
(*f*) Ib., lib. 7, disp. 3, n. 11.

As there is now no ecclesiastical law on marriage which is recognised as having any force, except as far as the civil power may have adopted it, it is only what Sanchez says of the marriage of *infideles* that can be still applied by us.

339. From the Voets and Hertius I do not find any statement of opinion on these points farther than as to the mere solemnities, but on those they all follow lines different from each other and from Sanchez. Paul Voet takes the *lex loci contractus* for the general rule, but makes an exception (in which, as to the solemnities, he is perhaps singular)—*nisi quis, quo in loco domicilii evitaret molestam aliquam vel sumptuosam solemnitatem, adeoque in fraudem statuti sui, nulla necessitate cogente alio proficiscitur, et mox ad domicilium, gesto alibi negotio, revertatur* (*g*). John Voet decides a particular case on principles which would always require the solemnities of the domicile, and which leave it uncertain whether he would not have also demanded any farther ones imposed by the *lex loci contractus* (*h*). And Hertius declares for the latter, as the *locus actus*, on his general rule with regard to the *lex quæ actui formam dat*, but admits that between foreigners who are compatriots the solemnities of their domicile will be sufficient (*i*).

340. Huber on the other hand says nothing expressly about the solemnities: but he subjects the prohibited degrees to the condition *si licitum est eo loco ubi contractum et celebratum est*, with the two only exceptions of *si incestum juris gentium in secundo gradu contingeret alicubi esse permissum*, and of two persons who betake themselves (*se conferunt*) to a foreign country and return after marrying there, *quia sic jus nostrum pessimis exemplis eluderetur* (*k*).

(*g*) De Statutis, § 9, c. 2.
(*h*) Comm. ad Pand., lib. 23, tit. 2, n. 4.
(*i*) De Coll. Leg., s. 4, § 10, non valet (6).
(*k*) De Confl. Leg., s. 8.

341. The ancient jurisprudence of France on this subject, as stated by Bouhier, is just so far modified from the doctrines of Sanchez, as might be expected in a country where, in consequence of the deviation from the common ground of the *forum* and *lex contractus* in reference to obligations, the analogy did not exist on which the common international theory of marriage was founded. It referred the solemnities always to the *lex loci actus,* but, in the case of two French persons marrying abroad, whether they went abroad for that purpose or not, subjected them to the necessity of all those consents which they would have required in France. If however a marriage was celebrated abroad between a French subject and a foreigner, Boubier cites a uniform current of decisions to the effect that even the necessary consents were then limited to those required by the *lex loci contractus:* and some of these decisions are particularly strong, being in cases where the husband was the party of minor age, and French by origin and domicile (*l*). But these doctrines have not been maintained in the modern law of France. The 170th article of the Code Napoleon runs thus:—*le mariage contracté en pags étranger entre Français, et entre Français et étrangers, sera valable, s'il a été célébré dans les formes usitées dans le pays, pourvu qu'il ait été précédé des publications prescrites par l'art.* 63, *au titre des actes de l'état civil, et que le Français n'ait point contrevenu aux dispositions contenues au chapitre précédent.* The chapter referred to is that which regulates the validity as to age, consent, and degrees of affinity: and as to these points, the French law, permitting to those of other nations the same extent which it claims for itself, will regulate the marriages of foreigners in France by the laws of their nationality or domicile (*m*).

(*l*) Observations sur la Coutume du Duché de Bourgogne, ch. 28, n. 59—66.

(*m*) Merlin, Répertoire, Loi, § 6, Art. 6.

And as the omission of the publications ordered by Art. 63 is not an absolute cause of nullity when the marriage is contracted in France, so it has been decided that it will only nullify the marriage of a Frenchman contracted abroad, when it took place *dans un but de clandestinité et afin de se soustraire aux exigences de la loi Française* (*n*).

342. The opinion of Savigny is so far similar to that which now rules in France, as that he refers every impediment to marriage to the law of the domicile, in consequence of the purely personal character of the whole subject. But he takes this exclusively of the husband's domicile, the law of which, as the true seat of the marriage, must prevail over that of the previous domicile of the wife. He admits the sufficiency of a religious ceremony, which the inhabitants of a country where that is required perform in a country where a civil one is generally needed: and he considers that if in such case the parties should have used the civil rite of the *locus actus*, the stringent character of a law demanding a religious ceremony would, without any reference to the question of their intention to evade it, oblige them to undergo such a form on their return home, which however, when completed, would operate by relation to the previous civil ceremony (*o*).

343. It is impossible not to see in this historical sketch that the international theory of marriage, having been originally framed at the time when personal and mixed statutes were not well distinguished, has been since modified through the influence of that clearer demarcation which towards the end of the sixteenth century was made between those two classes (*p*): also that in the passage from the earlier to the later theory, the *lex domicilii* was first timidly introduced through the *in fraudem legis* doc-

(*n*) *Giovanetti* v. *Orsini*, Dalloz, 1856, première partie, p. 9.

(*o*) V. 8, pp. 326, 357, 359.

(*p*) See above, Art. 149.

trine, before it ventured to assert itself in its own right. In that intermediate form the doctrine appears to be entirely reprehensible. Not to mention that a law which cannot speak in its own name can have no claim which the parties can defraud (*q*), to make the validity of a marriage depend on so uncertain an element as the opinion which a court may form as to the motive of a journey appears to be, in its practical bearings, one of the most extravagant proceedings which it ever entered into the mind of a jurist to recommend. Indeed it is not without grave hesitation that the certainty, which was the great advantage of the old rule of the *lex loci contractus*, can, on a matter where uncertainty is more immoral and of more dangerous example than marriage with a deceased wife's sister, be exchanged for even that degree of doubt which always attends the determination of domicile where there is the suggestion of a removal. There is, besides, the regret which must be felt that the judgments in *Brook* v. *Brook* have left it uncertain whether it is on domicile or allegiance that the binding force of the British marriage laws is in future to rest: but for domicile there speak so many considerations—the purpose of such laws in protecting the morals of the inhabitants, the general concurrence of foreign opinion, and the uncertainty which would otherwise exist whether the law of England, Ireland or Scotland should be applied to a subject domiciled abroad—that perhaps no great practical difficulty will hence arise. The other difficulty might be removed or lessened by appropriate enact-

(*q*) The argument can derive no benefit from the illegality asserted in Art. 199 of contracts, otherwise legal where made, but subsidiary to the breach of a foreign law. The analogy does not hold, because of the total *non constat* that the parties will ever return to the domicile, and the total independence of their contract on the question whether they do return there. It is more like the knowledge of an illegal purpose, which in *Pellecat* v. *Angell* and *M'Intyre* v. *Parks* did not vitiate the contract.

ment with reference to the conditions of domicile for this particular application.

344. The status of marriage is created on the contract of the parties, immediately, and therefore by the *lex loci contractus*, which then alone has power over them. Into whatever jurisdiction they afterwards come, the status being recognised as identical throughout Christendom, it will be accepted, unless some strong motive be shown for looking behind it to the contract on which it was created. Hence the form is justly referable to the *lex loci contractus*, and so the English cases have decided (*r*): while, if the marriage be void by that law, whether for form or any other reason, there is an end of the question (*s*). To this however an exception must be made, when from any cause it is impossible to comply with the local solemnities. Thus a marriage between Protestants celebrated at Rome by a Protestant clergyman was admitted by Lord Eldon, on its being sworn that two Protestants could not there be married by the *lex loci*, as no Roman priest would be allowed to marry them (*t*). Marriages in ambassadors' chapels are scarcely exceptions,

(*r*) Foreign marriage in local form good here: *Herbert* v. *Herbert*, 3 Phil. Eccl. 58, 2 Hagg. Cons. 269; *Smith* v. *Maxwell*, 1 Ry. & Mo. N. P. 180. Foreign marriage not in local form bad here: *Lacon* v. *Higgins*, 3 Star. 178, 1 Dow. & Ry. N. P. C. 38: even though the parties were British subjects, and followed the rites of the church of England: *Butler* v. *Freeman*, Ambl. 303; *Kent* v. *Burgess*, 11 Sim. 361. Protestants having abjured, for the purpose of being married at Rome by Roman Catholic rites, the question whether, and in what sense, their abjuration was required to be sincere, in order to the validity of the marriage, was decided by the law of Rome: *Swift* v. *Kelly*, 3 Knapp, 257.

(*s*) *Scrimshire* v. *Scrimshire*, 2 Hagg. Cons. 395; *Middleton* v. *Janverin*, Ib. p. 437.

(*t*) Cruise on Dignities, 276. The Roman law was however incorrectly deposed, for the marriage at Rome of persons not of the Romish religion is governed by the old common law of Europe, as it stood before the Council of Trent: *Sussex Peerage*, 11 Cl. & F. 152.

partly from the fiction of extraterritoriality, and partly because they are allowed by all laws, and therefore by that of the country in which the chapel is really situate: and as factories in heathen countries are beyond the pale in which laws are allowed to operate territorially, marriages there are properly regulated on the footing of personal laws. Both classes have received a statutory recognition here, and a statutory sanction, binding on British tribunals, has been given to marriages, at least one of the parties to which is a British subject, in British consulates and factories in civilized countries, and in the lines of a British army abroad, solemnized in such manner as the acts direct (*u*).

345. I have already intimated my opinion that the *lex loci contractus* may reasonably adopt any consent of parents or guardians, required for the marriage of either party in his or her domicile, as the condition without which it will not give binding force to the forms of their contract. In doing so, it would simply follow a comity so widely spread that the language of laws, when not positively excluding it, may be fairly taken to presuppose it. And although in the domicile it may be possible to evade the necessity of any consent, through a marriage by banns which may not come to the knowledge of the parent or guardian, yet the distinction between this and an absolute necessity seems too thin to be taken account of. It is certain however that the British courts have not hitherto adopted this view, but have persevered in maintaining that no other consents than those which the *lex loci contractus* demands for the marriage of its own subjects are necessary for the marriage

---

(*u*) See 4 Geo. 4, c. 91; 12 & 13 Vict. c. 68; and above, Art. 157. If a marriage under these acts should be invalid by the *lex loci contractus*, its validity here will carry with it, for our courts, and for such property as may be within their reach, the validity of a collateral marriage contract: *Este* v. *Smyth*, 18 Beav. 112.

of foreigners celebrated within its jurisdiction. The point arose on the English Marriage Act, 26 Geo. 2, c. 33, when English minors married in Scotland, and was by no means decided in advance, as has been sometimes imagined, by the proviso "that nothing in that act should extend to Scotland," for the question affects the interpretation of this proviso. On the old view, as represented by Sanchez, such a proviso would except marriages celebrated in Scotland: on the modern view, it would except the marriages, wherever celebrated, of domiciled Scotchmen. The former was held to be its meaning, which is nothing else than a direct decision that, first, the Scotch *lex loci contractus* does not adopt the necessary consents of the domicile, and, secondly, that the English *lex domicilii* submits to such non-adoption of them (x). Considering however the intimate connexion between these points and that on illegality by consanguinity, it may well be doubted whether such a decision will be made, since *Brook* v. *Brook*, in a new case: Lord Brougham's act settles that of Scotland.

346. Next, a statute which, like 5 & 6 Will. 4, c. 54, declares marriages between persons within certain degrees invalid, without specifying between whom or where contracted, appears *prima facie* to do two things. First, to express the refusal of the legislature to create the status of marriage, upon a contract entered into here between any two persons whatever who are within those degrees. Secondly, to direct the judges who are subject to it not to recognise the status of husband and wife, which any two persons whatever who are within the same degrees may import with them from abroad. If the generality of either

(x) *Compton* v. *Bearcroft*, 2 Hagg. Cons. 444, note; *Dalrymple* v. *Dalrymple*, 2 Hagg. Cons. 54; &c. In *Roach* v. *Garvan*, 1 Ves. sen. 157, it does not appear that there was any conflict of laws. *Harford* v. *Morris*, 2 Hagg. Cons. 423, was ultimately decided on the ground of force and custody: see p. 436. As to *Ruding* v. *Smith*, 2 Hagg. Cons. 371, see above, Art. 157.

of these interpretations is to be restrained, it cannot be on any consideration of the limits of the legislature's authority, for authority to do all this it unquestionably has, but must be on the presumption that the legislature intended to conform to some widely acknowledged rule of international jurisprudence. Now I know of no such rule which would restrain the former interpretation, and on the contrary it seems to be demanded by the ethics on which the act proceeds. If such marriages be wrong in the sight of English law, it cannot be right that English law should make them, however it may tolerate them: and I therefore submit that persons whose affinity is no bar in their domicile cannot, nevertheless, marry here. But the latter interpretation would lead to the consequence of the same persons being married by one law and unmarried by another: nay, of our law enforcing, as a good marriage contracted here, that which would be bigamy by the law of the parties' home. This can never have been intended, and while it can only be obviated by an international agreement as to the cases in which such invalidating statutes shall not apply, so also the only terms in which such an agreement is possible are that marriages contracted in the husband's domicile, and good by the law of that place, shall be thenceforward held good everywhere. Such an understanding would meet every purpose of the enactment, for the marriage of the woman is indifferent to the morals of the people whom she quits: nor can any inconvenience be apprehended from recognising the status which two new inhabitants bring with them from their old domicile, at all equal to what would result from divorcing a married couple against their will. I should therefore submit that from those bars which depend on what is called incapacity, whether absolute, as from Romish orders, or relative, as from degrees of affinity, the parties must be free both by the law of the place where the marriage is celebrated, and by that of the husband's domicile: that if they are so free, their marriage will be good, always and everwhere. In *Brook* v. *Brook* it has been decided that "English subjects" within the degrees prohibited here cannot validly marry abroad (*y*).

347. "We regard Christian marriage," said Lord Brougham, "as wholly a different thing, a different *status*, from Turkish or other marriages among infidel nations, because we clearly never should recognise the plurality of wives, and consequent validity of second marriages standing the first, which second marriages the laws of those countries authorize and validate. This cannot be put upon any rational ground, except our holding the infidel marriage to be something different from the Christian, and our also holding the Christian marriage to be the same everywhere" (*z*). The principle, fairly carried out, ought to prevent our enforcing here any conjugal rights resulting even from a first Turkish marriage. "If," said Lord Brougham, in a passage immediately preceding that last quoted, "there go two things under one and the same name in different countries, if that which is called marriage is of a different nature in each, there may be some room for holding that we are to consider the thing to which the parties have bound themselves according to its legal acceptation in the country where the obligation was contracted." Certainly we must not, from a mere coincidence of name between different things, enforce an obliga-

---

(*y*) 3 Sm. & G. 481, 523, 531. Story and Kent supported the *lex loci contractus* in the most absolute manner short of incest *juris gentium*, which they place with Huber at the second degree. Whether they also held with Huber the *in fraudem legis domicilii* exception, it does not appear. See Story, ss. 114, 116 a.

(*z*) *Warrender* v. *Warrender*, 9 Bl. N. R. 112, 2 Cl. & F. 532. A curious attempt was made, and repelled, in *Herbert* v. *Herbert* (3 Phill. Eccl. 58, 65, 2 Hagg. Cons. 269) to make the conjugal rights depend on the *lex loci contractus* of a valid marriage.

tion never really accepted: and therefore, since we cannot carry out a Turkish first marriage on Turkish principles, we ought not to fix the parties with an English marriage in its stead.

348. It remains to notice the case of *privilegia*. Although a law which professes to make any persons or class of persons incapable as to any act or contract is in fact a mere declaration that such act or contract, when attempted by them, is illegal and null, and is not therefore, on general international principles, necessarily to be respected by foreign sovereigns when the act or contract is attempted in their dominions, yet if such an artificial incapacity is contained in the jurisprudence of the both of any two countries, they may reciprocally recognise it as though it were a natural one. Of this kind is the incapacity of nobles to engage in trade, and consequently to bind themselves by mercantile contracts, which existed in many European states, and may possibly exist still in some. Such an inability of each other's subjects would be reciprocally recognised in those countries, but would be disregarded elsewhere (*a*), as we disregard the native inability of a foreign slave to exercise any of the rights of freedom in these dominions. Another example is the inability which by many foreign laws attaches to persons in general to become parties to a bill of exchange, the peculiar obligations implied by such an instrument being regarded as so perilous that they are only allowed to be incurred by those classes, variously defined in different countries, for whose trading pursuits they are held to be necessary. Between such countries, the capacity to become a party to a bill of exchange is decided by the domicile (*b*); but I know of no authority for supposing that the domicile

(*a*) Story, s. 104.

(*b*) Savigny, v. 8, p. 263.

would be referred to by our courts for such a purpose, if a foreigner drew, accepted or indorsed a bill of exchange within their jurisdiction. These are not *privilegia*, but they pave the way for considering them, since the English Royal Marriage Act is but an extreme case dependent on the same principles. It professes to make certain persons incapable of contracting matrimony without the consent of the sovereign, but what it really does is what it can do, namely, to prevent such persons from contracting matrimony within the British dominions without such consent, and to prevent British judges from acknowledging any matrimony which the same persons may similarly contract out of the British dominions. This however is amply sufficient for its purpose, which will be equally effected whether foreign judges should or should not, as to marriages contracted abroad, recognise the incapacity which the statute creates (*c*).

2. *Divorce.*

349. The dissolution of the marriage tie gives rise to several great international questions, into which the consideration of the laws applicable to the different cases enters abundantly, but which take the form rather of disputes on jurisdiction, because in no civilized country is

(c) The *Sussex Peerage case* is reported in 11 Cl. & F. 85. Some curious cases may be put. Suppose an escaped slave should marry here, but without having acquired an English domicile, and, after returning to his own country, where we will suppose slaves are incapable of marriage, should there be liberated, and marry another woman, living his first wife. I apprehend we should hold the first wife to be the real one here. If before the first marriage he had acquired an English domicile, I suppose the case would admit of no doubt on this side of the Atlantic, although the country from which he had escaped might deny his power of changing his domicile for an English one, or might set up nationality against domicile.

divorce permitted to be made by the independent act of the parties, without the interposition of judicial authority. The first of these questions in their natural order is whether any country should ever recognise a divorce granted for a cause insufficient by its own laws; a point which has been mooted on the continent of Europe, but not, so far as I am aware, in the British Isles or in America. The negative answer would not entirely preclude an international system of jurisdiction in divorce, but reduce its applicability to the cases arising between those countries of which the laws on divorce agreed: thus it would remain an inquiry of interest on what circumstances the jurisdiction should be grounded, that the divorce pronounced might be of authority in countries where its cause was recognised, though no circumstances could give it authority in any other. The next question, which has been chiefly mooted in England, is whether the causes of dissolution are not necessarily prescribed by the law of the marriage, whether that be taken to be the law of the place of celebration or that of the matrimonial domicile (the husband's at the time of the marriage), so that no forum can have jurisdiction to divorce for a cause insufficient by that law, however competent its authority over the parties may be on other grounds. This point arises within whatever limits are left to the subject by the previous question, from which it differs in that the former supposes an objection to the divorce from the public policy and ethics of the nation called on to recognise it, while this supposes a private right to indissolubility acquired by the parties through their contract. I am not aware that the converse proposal, to extend the causes of divorce beyond the *lex fori* to all those permitted by the law of the marriage, has ever been made. Thirdly, we shall have to consider the jurisdiction by and the causes for which divorce may be decreed, with reference to the place of commission of the offence on which the application is based, or to the nationality or domicile of the parties at the time of the suit: and in this discussion again the argument for the law of the existing domicile or nationality will proceed on public grounds alone. But these public grounds may be differently conceived. They may be based on the assumption that a divorce judicially granted ought to be universally recognised, as is generally done by the continental jurists, and then the aim will be to establish such rules as may be equitable between nation and nation: or the principle may be, as it seems to be in the Scotch and American courts, that divorce, being instituted for the sake of public morals, ought to be decreed with a view to the interests of the forum in that respect; and then the same considerations on which the rules themselves would otherwise be established, will apply to the inquiry what validity can be allowed abroad to divorces granted under such rules. The whole of the third question is subject to the first, on the extent to which an international recognition of divorce is possible.

350. *First question of Art.* 349.—An Englishwoman was divorced by act of parliament in 1822: in 1824 the mayor of the third arrondissement of Paris refused to marry her to a Frenchman; and in the same year the royal court of appeal at Paris, confirming the judgment of the court below, held that the mayor was justified in his refusal, because divorce had been abolished in France by the law of the 8th of May, 1816. The pith of the decision is contained in the following passage of the judgment of the inferior court;—"*attendu que la loi civile en France dispose qu'on ne peut contracter un nouveau mariage avant la dissolution du premier, et que la loi française ne reconnaît plus le divorce comme un moyen de dissolution de mariage:*" and its principle admits of a natural extension to the case of a foreign divorce granted for a cause insufficient by the law

of the country called on to recognise it, but which law does not altogether prohibit divorce. Merlin has carefully discussed this decision, which he concludes would be correct if the law of France regarded the marriage of a divorced person as adulterous. But that such is not the mind of the French law he proves from the fact that the law of 1816 permitted the marriage of persons who had been divorced before its date, though their former consorts might still live: and hence he infers that a jurisprudence which merely refuses the means of divorce, without condemning the marriage of a divorced person, ought to have been taken to accept the status of a foreigner who has been lawfully divorced in his own country (*d*). This leaves it uncertain what Merlin would have held if divorce had never been established in France, in which case he could not have deduced the mind of the French law from the circumstances attending its abolition. That divorce is morally lawful, but that it is inexpedient to provide regular means for obtaining it, is an opinion shared by respectable authority, but which there seems no more reason, *a priori*, for attributing to the law than the opinion that divorce is morally unlawful: and the best way to escape from such slippery arguments is to accept all men with that condition of married or unmarried with which courts of competent jurisdiction have impressed them. The French courts, on the occasion referred to, said that marriage is *juris gentium*, but that divorce is not. But it is not the mere contract of marriage which is *juris gentium:* it is the status to which the contract leads, and in which it is immediately merged, that preeminently merits that title. And the consequence is that, being *juris gentium*, we must take the status of married or unmarried as we find it, as foreign competent authority has left it: nor can any thing

(*d*) Questions de Droit, Divorce, § XIII.

be more inconsistent with allowing that universal character to marriage than to insist on taking a certain past fact, as the solemnisation, and deducing all its effects by our own law without reference to circumstances. These principles have been recognised in England, except in the case, hereafter to be noticed, of marriages contracted here (*e*).

351. *Second question of Art.* 349.—Next, where, as in contract or the transfer of property, the rights of parties originate in their own dealings, only interpreted and effectuated by the law, the part of the law is prior to that of justice, which has merely to declare and enforce the right already existing by the operation of law on the facts. Hence, as we have often seen, though the law which was applicable to the facts when they occurred was a different one from that of the forum, yet the right it then created was already in existence before the cause reached the forum, and must be declared and enforced accordingly. But where, as in divorce, it is the justice itself which first creates the right, there can be no question of any claim arising out of a law which was only applicable before the parties stood in justice: and this at once shows why it has never been contended that either the *lex loci contractus* of the marriage, or any other foreign law, can give a claim to divorce for causes which do not sustain it by the *lex fori;* why, in such cases, there is in the forum a total defect of jurisdiction to divorce. In fact, a jurisdiction which does not *consider* that the parties *are* divorced, but *decree* that they *shall be* divorced, gives not a private but a public remedy, and can never therefore be put in motion but on the grounds which the public law of the forum contemplates: nor, if those grounds are present in the case, ought

(*e*) *Ryan* v. *Ryan*, 2 Phil. Eccl. 332; *Connelly* v. *Connelly*, 7 Moore, P. C. 438. In the latter case, the separation was by vows of chastity, which must be considered on precisely the same ground as divorce, being in fact divorce by consent.

the circumstance that the parties were married under another law to prevent the *lex fori* from pronouncing a divorce which it desires from public motives. In this spirit it has been well said by the supreme court of Massachusetts, that "regulations on the subject of marriage and divorce are rather parts of the criminal than of the civil code, and apply not so much to the contract between the individuals as to the personal relation resulting from it, and to the relative duties of the parties, to their standing and conduct in the society of which they are members; and these are regulated with a principal view to the public order and economy, the promotion of good morals, and the happiness of the community. A divorce for example in a case of public scandal and reproach is not a vindication of the contract of marriage, or a remedy to enforce it, but a species of punishment which the public have placed in the hands of the injured party, to inflict under the sanction and with the aid of the competent tribunal; operating as a redress of the injury when, the contract having been violated, the relation of the parties and their continuance in the marriage state have become intolerable or vexatious to them, and of evil example to others. The *lex loci* therefore by which the conduct of married persons is to be regulated, and their relative duties are to be determined, and by which the relation itself is to be in certain cases annulled, must be always referred, not to the place where the contract was entered into, but where it subsists for the time, where the parties have had their domicile and have been protected in the rights resulting from the marriage contract, and especially where the parties are or have been amenable for any violation of the duties incumbent upon them in that relation" (*f*).

352. I cannot refrain from adding here the clear state-

(*f*) Justice Sewall, in *Barber* v. *Root*, 10 Mass. 265.

ment of the same reasoning which was given by Merlin on a question precisely analogous, that in which the conflict is not between the laws of two countries, but between those of the same country at different periods. It brings out pointedly the distinction to which I have already alluded between a proceeding in justice which declares rights already existing through a contract, and one which creates in the public interest rights which have no existence prior to the proceeding itself. "Peut-on," says he, "en vertu d'une loi nouvelle qui introduit le divorce, dissoudre par cette voie un mariage contracté sous une loi qui le prohibait? Et réciproquement, un mariage contracté sous une loi qui autorisait le divorce, peut-il être dissous par cette voie sous une loi qui le prohibe? L'affirmative ne serait pas douteuse si le divorce était, comme l'état d'époux, l'effet immédiat et la simple conséquence du mariage. Dans cette hypothèse, le divorce ne pourrait, comme l'état d'époux, dépendre que de la loi du temps où le mariage a été célébré, parceque, dans le premier cas, l'époux qui s'opposerait au divorce serait fondé à dire qu'en se mariant il a entendu contracter une union indissoluble; que, dans le second cas, l'époux, qui demanderait le divorce, serait fondé à dire qu'en se mariant il n'a entendu contracter qu'une union qu'il lui serait un jour ou l'autre libre de rompre; et que, dans l'un comme dans l'autre, ce serait à la loi du temps du contrat qu'il faudrait s'en rapporter sur la force du lien que les parties contractantes auraient formé. Mais ce n'est ni par conséquence ni par interprétation de l'intention dans laquelle a été contracté le mariage, que le divorce est permis ou prohibé. En le permettant comme en le prohibant, le législateur ni s'arrête ni ne doit s'arrêter à ce que les époux ont ou sont censés avoir voulu au moment où ils se sont unis; il ne s'arrête et il ne doit s'arrêter qu'aux considérations d'ordre public qui lui paraissent en commander impérieusement la faculté ou la prohibition d'après la conduite respective des époux. Et cela est si vrai que vainement deux époux qui se marieraient sous l'empire d'une loi prohibitive du divorce se réserveraient-ils la faculté de divorcer, comme ce serait en vain que, se mariant sous une loi qui permettrait le divorce, ils renonceraient d'avance à cette faculté, parce-qu'à l'une et à l'autre hypothèse s'appliquerait nécessairement la grande maxime consacrée par l'art. 6 du Code civil, *qu'on ne peut déroger par des conventions particulières aux lois qui intéressent l'ordre public et les bonnes mœurs.* Aussi personne n'oserait-il prétendre aujourd'hui en France que des époux mariés sous l'empire du titre *du divorce* du Code civil peuvent encore divorcer, depuis que le divorce a été aboli par la loi du 8 Mai 1816 . . . . . . Et par la raison inverse, il n'y a nul doute que la faculté de divorcer introduite pour la première fois en France par la loi du 20 Septembre 1792 n'ait été, tout le temps qu'elle a subsisté, commune aux époux qui s'étaient mariés avant cette loi, comme aux époux qui s'étaient mariés sous son empire (*g*)."

353. These principles have been thoroughly maintained in every country but England where divorce exists. In Scotland it was firmly settled that judicial divorce was not precluded by the mere circumstance of the marriage having been solemnised in England, or of the spouses having at the time of marriage been domiciled in England, even when divorce was here obtainable only by act of parliament. I may refer to the leading case of *Warrender* v. *Warrender* (*h*), which will be noticed again on the other

(*g*) Rép., Effet Rétroactif, Sect. III., § II., Art. VI. Merlin himself applies the passage above cited to conflicts of territorial laws, in his Questions de Droit, Divorce, § XI., Art. I.

(*h*) 2 Cl. & F. 488, 9 Bl. N. R. 89. This decision was made necessary by the doubt raised in consequence of *Lolley's case*, in *Tovey* v. *Lindsay*, 1 Dow, 117, in which the pursuer died before there was any decision under the judgment of remit: Fergusson on Marriage and Divorce, 50.

points which arose in it, and in which, so far as it turned on the marriage having been contracted in England, Lord Brougham not only suggested as a possible ground that which, with the French and American authorities, I have already put forward, that divorce is not a remedy on the contract (*i*), but also observed that, even taking it as such, remedies depend on the *lex fori* and not on the *lex loci contractus* (*k*). Another part however of his lordship's reasoning requires more particular notice: that in which, putting, for argument's sake, even the *lex fori* out of the question, he considers that, as the matrimonial domicile was Scotch, the parties must be considered as having contracted with reference to it as the place of execution (*l*). I have already urged the objections which lie to regarding the matrimonial contract as having any definite place of performance: and I only revert to the subject here in order to caution the student against supposing, from the passage in *Warrender* v. *Warrender* referred to, that the Scotch courts would be at all influenced by such a consideration. On the contrary they regularly dissolve marriages contracted, whether in England or in Scotland, by persons whose domicile at the time of the contract was English (*m*). The courts of those American states where judicial divorce is established proceed with the same disregard of the matrimonial domicile and place of contract (*n*).

(*i*) 2 Cl. & F. 537, 9 Bl. N. R. 117.

(*k*) 2 Cl. & F. 533, 9 Bl. N. R. 114.

(*l*) 2 Cl. & F. 535, 9 Bl. N. R. 116.

(*m*) In *Trevelyan's case*, in 1789 (Fergusson on the Consistorial Law in Scotland, p. 33), in *Tewsh's case*, in 1811 (ib., p. 42), in *Levett's* and *Rowland's cases*, finally disposed of in 1816 (ib., pp. 70—84), and in many others, the contract and matrimonial domicile were both English. It is superfluous to quote those in which the contract was Scotch and the matrimonial domicile English, as they are included *a fortiori* in the former kind.

(*n*) Bishop on Marriage and Divorce, s. 745.

354. As the English ecclesiastical courts separated only *a mensa et toro*, and there is no country of which the laws do not permit a separation to that extent, and for the same causes for which it was decreed in England—since that separation and its causes are derived from the canon law, which was of general authority throughout Christendom—it follows that those courts were never called on to decide whether they would divorce for causes insufficient by the *lex loci contractus* of the marriage, or by the law of the matrimonial domicile. But that question must arise before the new divorce-court, inasmuch as it can divorce *a vinculo*, and may be called on to do so in the case of a marriage celebrated under a law by which divorce is prohibited. The cases will then be in point in which the dissolution of such marriages by foreign divorce-courts has been canvassed in England, and these are also of great interest on their own account. The first of them is *Lolley's case*, where a Scotch divorce from a marriage contracted in England did not save the prisoner from a conviction for bigamy in consequence of a second marriage in the latter country (*o*). Both Lolley and his first wife retained their English domicile throughout the proceedings which were had for the Scotch divorce, and which were founded on the Scotch doctrine of transient residence as sufficient to ground the jurisdiction, which will have to be examined under the next head. Now as that doctrine is not generally received, the conviction might have been sustained without asserting the absolute indissolubility of an English marriage. But when the points reserved were argued before all the judges, they "held the conviction right, being unanimously of opinion that no sentence or act of any foreign country or state could dissolve an English marriage

(*o*) Russ. & Ry. 237.

a vinculo matrimonii, for ground on which it was not liable to be dissolved *a vinculo matrimonii* in England" (*p*).

355. Next, in *M'Carthy* v. *Decaix* (*q*), in became necessary to consider whether a Danish divorce had dissolved the marriage of a Dane with an Englishwoman celebrated in England; for, under the supposition that it had, he had renounced some pecuniary rights, which renunciation was invalid if made upon an error as to so important a fact. Lord Eldon hesitated, apparently considering that the dictum in *Lolley's case* went beyond the facts there; but Lord Brougham, who had been counsel for Lolley, and took the seals while *M'Carthy* v. *Decaix* remained undecided, pronounced that the marriage had not been dissolved. "If," said he, "it has not validly, and by the highest authorities in Westminster Hall, been holden that a foreign divorce cannot dissolve an English marriage, then nothing whatever has been established. For what was *Lolley's case?* It was a case the strongest possible in favour of the doctrine contended for. It was not a question of civil right, but of felony. Lolley had *bona fide*, and in a confident belief, founded on the authority of the Scotch lawyers, that the Scotch divorce had effectually dissolved his prior English marriage, intermarried in England, living his first wife" (*r*). It will be observed that the facts in *M'Carthy* v. *Decaix* not only go beyond those in *Lolley's case*, from the Danish domicile and nationality of the husband, Mr. Tuite, at the time of the divorce, but also, since the same circumstances existed at his marriage, show that in Lord Brougham's apprehension the English character of the contract depended only on its having been solemnized here, contrary to what might have been expected

(*p*) Russ. & Ry. 239.
(*q*) 2 Ru. & My. 614.
(*r*) Ibid., p. 619.

from his remarks in *Warrender* v. *Warrender*, above referred to, as to the matrimonial domicile being the place of execution. And this is important, because it shows that the indissolubility attributed in *Lolley's case* to an English marriage can by no means be treated, as Chief Justice Gibson of Pennsylvania attempted to treat it, as "an unavoidable consequence of the British tenet of perpetual allegiance" (*s*). The consequences of that tenet could not at any rate have been extended to a Dane, who never owed allegiance to the sovereign of the British Isles, even if it were easy to see how Lolley's allegiance could bind him to the law of England more than to that of Scotland; and thus it appears that the doctrine has no other foundation than a supposed private right to indissolubility acquired through the contract.

356. In the same year with the decision of *M'Carthy* v. *Decaix*, 1831, Dr. Lushington, in the consistory court of London, pronounced a second marriage null under circumstances which differed from those in *Lolley's case* only in that the second marriage was solemnized in Scotland (*t*): and he did so expressly on the ground that the continuing English domicile was a vital defect in the jurisdiction of the Scotch court which assumed to dissolve the first or English marriage. Finally, there is *Warrender* v. *Warrender*, in which it was held that the Scotch commissary court had jurisdiction to dissolve an English marriage, and in which Lord Brougham rejected *Lolley's case*, not as not involving a point of Scotch law, but as decided by judges who had no authority to declare the law for Scotland. For, said he, "I do not see how, consistently with any principle, the judges who decided the case could limit its application to England, and think that it did not decide

(*s*) In *Dorsey* v. *Dorsey*, 7 Watts, 349.

(*t*) *Conway* v. *Beazley*, 3 Hagg. Cons. 639.

also on the validity of the divorce in Scotland. They certainly could not hold the second English marriage invalid and felonious in England, without assuming that the Scotch divorce was void even in Scotland" (*u*). But if this be so, then the dictum in *Lolley's case* will be in point when a divorce from a French marriage, for example, shall be sought under our new law: and if the able argument by which Lord Brougham in *Warrender* v. *Warrender* disputed that dictum, and of which I have given a considerable extract in Art. 248, be combined with my previous citations from Merlin and Justice Sewall, the reader may appreciate the amount and character of the authority arrayed against the opinion of the judges.

357. It is impossible not to perceive that the opinions of jurists are sometimes influenced by considerations more proper for the politician, and as the dictum in *Lolley's case* may thus be probably traced to a national feeling which must have been very much changed when judicial divorce was established in England, it may be expected to be restrained in future to the facts which were then before the judges. And thus we may conclude that whether in deciding on the validity of divorces granted abroad from English marriages, or in decreeing divorces from foreign marriages, the *lex loci contractus* will not in future prevent our courts from lending their aid towards establishing such rules of jurisdiction in this matter, as that divorces may neither be granted when they will not be internationally respected, nor refused when they are demanded by the policy and morals of the forum.

358. *Third question of Art.* 349.—The first principle on which it is possible to raise such rules of jurisdiction as here contemplated is, that every thing must depend on the circumstances existing at the time the suit is brought.

(*u*) 2 Cl. & F. 550.

This principle is common as well to the Scotch theory, which grounds divorce on the necessity of upholding morality within the territory, and therefore rejects the condition of a permanent domicile therein, as to that more generally received abroad, which grounds it on the authority of a government to determine the status of its domiciled subjects. The possible quarters from which the principle may be impugned are, besides the place of celebration of the marriage and the then domicile of the parties, which have been already considered and rejected, the place where the adultery or other offence for which the divorce is sought was committed, and the domicile of the parties at the time of its commission: and the notion on which these have been put forward appears to be that divorce is a private remedy for a breach of contract, which however, if it were better founded than it is, would only be in point when there should be a conflict of laws between the forum and the *locus delicti*, without reference to the domicile at the time of the delict. But, as Mr. Bishop says, "the place where the offence was committed, whether in the country in which the suit is brought or in a foreign country, is quite immaterial. This is the universal doctrine; it is the same in the English, Scotch and American courts, and there is no conflict upon the point." Farther also, "the domicile of the parties at the time the offence was committed is of no consequence:" and although "a contrary doctrine has been maintained in New Hampshire and Pennsylvania, in which states it is held that the tribunals of the country in which the parties were domiciled when the *delictum* occurred have alone the jurisdiction," yet "there is probably not a single analogy in the law to sustain this New Hampshire and Pennsylvania rule . . . . . . Who ever heard of a court refusing to sustain an action, either of tort or contract, on the bare ground that the parties, at the time of the injury or breach, were domiciled in another jurisdiction? Then, is the right of every government to determine the status of its own subjects limited or controlled by any such exception" (x)?

359. On precisely the same principles depends the question which arose in Belgium and Piedmont, when those countries were incorporated into the French empire, whether divorce could be granted there, under the French Code Civil, for causes which had occurred previous to its introduction. The affirmative was decided, for reasons which will be understood from the following expression of them by the court of appeal of Turin, given in one such case where the cause of divorce was judicial infamy incurred under the independent government of the country, but from which during that independence divorce could not follow:—"*il suffit que lors de la publication de la loi l'état et la condition des personnes soient tels que la loi l'exige pour donner lieu au divorce, pour qu'on puisse y avoir recours sans blesser d'aucune manière que ce soit le principe de la non rétroactivité*" (y). The argument holds, if for the status of infamy we substitute the actual condition of the persons in regard to the having been guilty of adultery or other misconduct, and is strengthened when, as in many of the cases to which the contrary doctrine is applied in New Hampshire and Pennsylvania, there is no conflict of laws, but only a question of jurisdiction. But even where there is a conflict of laws between the forum and the place where the offence was committed, Merlin, who here also points out the analogy to a change of law in the same

---

(x) Law of Marriage and Divorce, ss. 740, 741, 744. In *Tovey* v. *Lindsay*, 1 Dow, 131, it had however been thought that the place where the offence was committed might be of importance; but the case came to nothing, and the doubt, like so many others thrown out in the course of that unlucky cause, has since been repudiated by the highest authority: see particularly 2 Cl. & F. 562, 9 Bl. N. R. 146.

(y) Journal des Audiences de la Cour de Cassation, an 1809, Supplément, p. 15: and Merlin, Répertoire, Effet Rétroactif, sect. III., § II., Art. VI.

country, decides absolutely for the forum, even though the offence may have been committed in a country where not merely is divorce prohibited, but of which the parties were then citizens (*z*).

360. Next, the Scotch doctrine with regard to the defender is that his mere presence in the country renders him amenable to the jurisdiction, so that he is well cited personally the moment he sets foot in Scotland, or by a citation left at his dwelling-place after a sojourn of forty days (*a*). This was established in *Utterton* v. *Tewsh* (*b*), on appeal to the court of session, where the defect of Lord Meadowbank's reasoning appears to be in an over estimate of the necessity of a speedy procedure in cases of divorce: Scotch morals could not suffer much from the irregularities of persons transiently there, even if, which the argument begs, no other means could be found of correcting them than a divorce *a vinculo*. And, as the government of their domicile has the strongest interest in the morals of men, it is not probable that any country will recognize these foreign divorces of its resident subjects. They are certainly not recognized in England (*c*).

361. Admitting then the necessity that the jurisdiction shall be founded in domicile, it follows that if the husband

---

(*z*) Questions de Droit, Divorce, § XI., Art. II.

(*a*) Upon this forty days' residence has been raised the question whether it will still ground the jurisdiction, if in fraud of a foreign law: *Allison* v. *Catley*, 1 Sec. Ser. 1025. But as the very theory of the short residence is that no foreign law has a right to be heard in the matter, the question of *mala fides* has been repudiated as inapplicable by Lord Truro, in *Geils* v. *Geils*, 1 Macq. 275. Lord St. Leonard's, in the latter case, held *Allison* v. *Catley* sustainable on another ground: 1 Macq. 265. When the jurisdiction is admitted to be founded on domicile, the *mala fides* comes in fairly, as a flaw in the reality of the domicile, which is excluded by the intention to return on obtaining the divorce.

(*b*) Ferguss. Rep. 23.

(*c*) *Conway* v. *Beazley*, 3 Hagg. Cons. 639; *Robins* v. *Dolphin*, Sw. & Tr. 37. The Scotch practice is equally repudiated in the United States: Bishop, s. 721.

be plaintiff, his domicile being in law that of his wife also, the domicile of both is the same, and is the proper forum for divorce. She is bound to follow him, and, if in fact she has a separate residence, she cannot take advantage against him of her own wrong. This has been the constant practice as well of the American (*d*) as of the English ecclesiastical courts, as it doubtless will also be of our new divorce-court: and it was finally decided for Scotland by *Warrender* v. *Warrender* (*e*), which proved also by its very point that an actual separation by consent will not preclude the husband from suing in his own forum, provided there has been no attempt to secure by contract the continuance of that separation, and which also opposed the powerful reasoning of Lords Brougham and Lyndhurst to Lord Eldon's assertion in *Tovey* v. *Lindsay*, that, when the husband has agreed that the wife shall live separate, he can only sue her in the new forum which she may have acquired (*f*).

362. But Merlin, speaking with reference to the prohibition of divorce in France, asks whether a husband, once French, but who has naturalized himself abroad without his wife having done so too, can sue her for a divorce in his new country, whether by consent, as divorce was originally allowed by the Code Civil to be had by consent with the sanction of a court of justice, or contentiously. And he answers both questions in the negative. For, says he, " de même en effet que pour contracter un mariage il ne suffit pas que l'une des deux parties soit capable de se marier, qu'il faut qu'elles le soient toutes deux, que l'incapacité de l'une ne peut pas être couverte par la capacité de l'autre; de même aussi

(*d*) Bishop on Marriage and Divorce, s. 729.
(*e*) 2 Cl. & F. 488, 9 Bl. N. R. 89.
(*f*) 1 Dow, 119, 138.

pour que l'on puisse valablement dissoudre par le divorce un mariage contracté légalement, il ne suffit pas que l'une des deux époux soit capable de divorcer, il faut qu'ils les soient l'un et l'autre ; et la capacité qu'en acquiert l'un par un fait qui lui est absolument personnel ne peut pas y habiliter l'autre à qui ce fait reste étranger. Or le mari Français qui sans le concours de sa femme abdique sa patrie et se fait naturaliser, par exemple, dans le royaume des Pays-Bas où le titre *du Divorce* du Code civil est encore en pleine vigueur, acquiert sans doute la capacité de divorcer, mais la communique-t-il à sa femme? Non, évidemment non. Pour que sa femme pût l'acquérir en même temps que lui, il faudrait que la naturalisation du mari en pays étranger fùt de plein droit commune à la femme, il faudrait que la femme perdit la qualité de Française par cela seul que le mari perdrait la qualité de Français, et cela est impossible. Sans doute c'est un principe général que la femme suit la condition de son mari, et c'est pourquoi l'art. 12 du Code civil déclare Française l'étrangère qui épouse un Français. Mais conclure de là que la femme qui est devenue Française par son mariage avec un Français, ou qui l'était par droit de naissance au moment où elle s'est mariée, puisse en perdre la qualité par la naturalisation que son mari acquiert en pays étranger, ce serait une grande erreur . . . . . . Vainement objecterait-on qu'aux termes de l'art. 108 du Code civil, *la femme mariée n'a point d'autre domicile que celui de son mari* . . . . . . Il est clair que quand même la femme Française devrait être réputée de plein droit domiciliée dans le pays étranger où son mari s'est fait naturaliser ; je dis plus, quand même elle y serait domiciliée de fait ; elle ne serait pas pour cela régie, quant à son état, par la loi de ce pays ; elle ne pourrait pas pour cela, en vertu de la loi de ce pays, consentir à la dissolution de son mariage par le divorce ; elle ne pourrait pas pour cela, en vertu de la loi de ce pays, être actionnée par son mari à l'effet de voir prononcer cette dissolution malgré elle" (*g*).

363. It is plain that this reasoning rests on two grounds, neither of which is admitted in Great Britain or America. One, which however Merlin probably intended to apply only to the case of a divorce by mutual consent, makes it a question of capacity, and as such to depend on the law of the nationality: the other makes a divorce claimed even *in foro contentioso* to depend on the law of France, on the pretension which the Code Civil puts forward to regulate the status of French persons even abroad. We know nothing of a divorce by consent, but if persons of British national character should obtain one in any foreign country where they might be domiciled, we should probably recognize it: and, regarding divorce as a public measure, our own interests would prevent our holding French subjects to be exempt from it here, if amenable to the jurisdiction by a permanent domicile, however the French courts might in such case refuse to recognize the acts of ours.

364. But now let us suppose the wife to be plaintiff, and to be living *de facto* separate from her huband. That she may sue him for divorce in his domicile is apparent on every ground, whether we consider the remedy as a private one between the parties, or as partaking also of a public character. In the former case, that is the jurisdiction to which he, the defendant, is *prima facie* amenable: in the latter, it is that which is most interested in the question, as being the place where the matrimonial duties should rightfully be performed. And the same also is the determination of the canon law, in the contemplation of which divorce *a mensa et toro* bore neither altogether a public character, nor merely that of a remedy appertaining of

(*g*) Questions de Droit, Divorce, § XI., Art. IV.

right to the plaintiff, but of a proceeding intended for the health of the defendant's soul: his soul could only be corrected by the ordinary of his domicile, who alone had jurisdiction over him in respect of his person. But in several of the American states it is necessary by the local law that plaintiffs in divorce controversies should be domiciled in the country: and here consequently a doubt arose. Yet inasmuch as the wife can only obtain her divorce upon grounds which would prove her to have been justified in living apart from her husband, it has been justly held there that she may sue him in his domicile upon the legal fiction of being herself domiciled there also, and that he cannot set up in answer the foreign residence into which he has driven her by his own wrong (*h*). In Scotland the pursuer's domicile is of so little account that the oath of calumny may be taken by commission.

365. But can the wife sue her husband for a divorce in the state in which she resides apart from him? The notion that she can do so when the separation, whether provoked or not, has been made by her, has probably never been entertained out of America: but there it is well established. For, says an American authority, "it is practically impossible for a party to proceed in another state than that in which he lives; because in probably all, unless possibly we may except Louisiana, there are either statutory provisions requiring that the plaintiff shall have resided within the state a certain number of years before he brings his suit, or there are other technical statutory impediments which are tantamount in their effect to this. But nearly or quite all the statutes provide for notice, by publication" in newspapers, "to absent defendants; and unless the judicial tribunals give effect to each other's decrees rendered under these statutes in favour of *bona fide*

(*h*) Bishop, s. 729.

subjects, we shall be in a most distressing condition of conflict and confusion" (*i*). The same American authority justifies this as follows. "The general doctrine is familiar, that the domicile of the wife is in law that of the husband. But it will probably be found on examination that the doctrine rests upon the legal duty of the wife to follow and dwell with the husband wherever he goes. If he commits an offence which entitles her to have the marriage dissolved, she is not only discharged thereby immediately, and without a judicial determination of the question, from her duty to follow and dwell with him, but she must abandon him, or the cohabitation will amount to a condonation and bar her claim to the remedy. In other words, she must establish a domicile of her own separate from the husband, *though it may be or not in the same judicial locality as his*. . . . . It is the burden of her allegation that she is entitled, through the misconduct of her husband, to a separate domicile. If she fails to prove this, she fails in her cause. . . . . Having therefore arrived at the conclusion that the husband and wife may have, for purposes of divorce, separate domiciles, we shall find no difficulty in settling upon principle that the courts of the actual *bona fide* domicile of either may entertain the jurisdiction. If it were not so, then both states would be deprived of the right to determine the status of their own subjects, each must yield to foreign power in the management of its domestic concerns. A state would thus be compelled to refuse redress to the wrongs of a citizen" (*k*). It is apparent that the force of this argument lies in the words which I have printed in italics, for it does not follow that the duty of breaking off the cohabitation drives the wife to change her forum: nor has she, on general legal prin-

(*i*) Bishop, s. 732.

(*k*) Bishop, ss. 728, 731.

ciples, the power to do so, till freed from the marriage by sentence, with which the right to a sentence must not be confounded. And therefore the reasonable rule would seem to be that for which the same learned writer assures us that there is some American authority, though greatly overweighed; namely, "that the wife cannot, by a removal of her habitation after the commission of the offence, acquire a new jurisdiction in which to prosecute her claim for divorce" (*l*). It would be often impossible for the wife to obtain redress, could the husband by a removal after the offence, prevent her suing him in his former domicile, for in many cases she would not even know his new abode: and her condition interests the state in which she continues to reside, and from the citizenship of which she has never been rightfully withdrawn (*m*). And even if the wife should, after the husband's offence, remove into another jurisdiction, and he should sue her there for the restitution of conjugal rights, she may then fairly, in answer, ask for a divorce, because the husband has by his suit submitted himself to the forum, and the mere dismissal of his demand would afford the wife no substantial protection from him (*n*).

(*l*) Bishop, s. 730.

(*m*) That the English judge ordinary would order substituted service in such cases may be inferred from *Chandler* v. *Chandler*, 27 L. J., N. S., Ma. & Pr. 35. See also *Robotham* v. *Robotham*, Ibid., p. 33. His power to do so rests on stat. 20 & 21 Vict. c. 85, s. 42, and the 10th rule made thereunder.

(*n*) *Geils* v. *Geils* (in England), 6 Notes of Cases, 97; *Geils* v. *Geils* (in Scotland), 1 Macq. 255, 269. The latter case shows that the having obtained a divorce *a mensa et toro* in this manner does not preclude the wife from obtaining one *a vinculo* in the husband's domicile: and from the reasoning it may be concluded, as might be expected, that the having exhausted the remedies given in this direction in the then domicile does not preclude either party from obtaining the larger ones given in a new *bona fide* domicile.

3. *Pecuniary Effects of the Marriage.*

366. It is universally allowed that, when a marriage takes place without settlement, the mutual rights of the husband and wife in each other's movable property, whether owned at the time of the marriage or afterwards acquired, are to be regulated by the law of the matrimonial domicile, so long as that remains unchanged. The reasons given are four. First, that though the matrimonial domicile has nothing analogous to the place of performance in contracts, when considered with reference to the status itself, yet that it must be held to have entered into the expectations of the parties with reference to the pecuniary effects of that status, since there is no other law by which they could have supposed that they would be regulated, and, if they had not acquiesced in their regulation by that law, they could have provided against it by express agreement, or by declining the marriage. This theory, known as that of a tacit contract, extends the law of the original matrimonial domicile to acquests also made after its change, since that change depends on the single will of the husband, which cannot affect rights founded on a concurrence of wills in a common expectation. It is identified with the name of Dumoulin, from the ability with which he maintained it, but has been adopted by most of the greatest jurists, both before and since his time (*o*). Secondly, that though an expectation as to the pecuniary effects of the marriage cannot be attributed to the parties,

(*o*) With Dumoulin (t. 2, p. 963; t. 3, p. 555, ed. 1581), for the indifference of a change of domicile, are, besides Savigny, P. Voet, de Stat. s. 9, c. 2, n. 7; J. Voet, ad Pand. l. 23, t. 2, n. 87; Hertius, de Coll. Leg., s. 4, § 48, 49; Merlin, Rép., Communauté de Biens, § I., Art. III.; Fœlix, n. 91. In the same sense are four judgments of the parliament of Paris, of the dates of 1640, 1700, 1718, and 1746, adduced by Merlin, *ubi supra*.

since it is certain they do not always think of those effects at all when concluding the contract, yet the same result follows, and with the same extension to the case of a change of domicile, from the consideration that they both did in fact submit themselves to the law of the matrimonial domicile, by the concurrence of their wills in the matrimonial contract itself. This is Savigny's modification of Dumoulin's theory (*p*).

367. Thirdly, that movables are governed by the law of the owner's domicile. This reason is limited to the case in which the matrimonial domicile remains unchanged, and, after a change, would refer the rights of the spouses to the law of the new domicile. But from its extreme vagueness, it is impossible to say whether it would refer to the law of the new domicile merely the rights of the spouses in such property as either may acquire after the change, regarding those in the property which they bring with them into the jurisdiction as finally vested, or whether it would displace and remodel even the latter rights (*q*). Against the latter interpretation speaks strongly the injustice of permitting the wife's vested rights to be devested by the husband's act, nor does even the more restricted

(*p*) V. 8, pp. 329—334.

(*q*) Huber (de Confl. Leg., s. 9) determines the rights, in property acquired after the change, by the law of the new domicile, *sicut res antea communes factæ maneant in eo statu juris quem induerunt.* And this is the opinion of Story (s. 187), and has been consecrated in the Louisiana code (Art. 2370), after having been established there by the leading cases of *Gale* v. *Davis's Heirs*, 4 Mar. 645, and *Saul* v. *his Creditors*, 5 Mar. N. S. 569. But the code happens to mention the case of *persons* who come to live within the state; wherefore, when the husband removed his domicile to Louisiana without being *de facto* accompanied by the wife, the court, thinking itself remitted to the general principles, held the subsequent acquests not to follow the law of the new domicile, which was less favourable to the husband, unless his assent to it could be proved: *Dixon* v. *Dixon's Executors*, 4 Louis. 188. Eichhorn (Deutsches Recht, s. 359, 307 d, 310 e, f) determines the rights by the law of the new domicile, for property acquired as well before as after the change.

one escape the accusation of subjecting the wife's interests to a needless uncertainty, which cannot have been in her intention. The maxim on which either proposition is based seems to slip through our fingers when we try to grasp it. We saw in the chapter on movables how questionable was the doctrine that particular assignments of chattels depended for their validity on the law of the assignor's domicile: but the present doctrine has nothing to do even with that. If the husband or wife acquires in the new domicile, and *ex hypothesi* does nothing to assign this acquest, or any interest in it, to the other consort, can the law step in, and make an assignment *inter vivos* upon no human act intervened? It would be difficult to parallel this in jurisprudence, if it is so. *Cadit quæstio*, however, if the marriage has already assigned this acquest by another law.

368. Fourthly, that universal assignments of movables, made by or in accordance with the law of the owner's or assignor's domicile, are effectual everywhere, irrespective of the situation of the chattels which enter into the mass (*r*). This reason agrees with the first and second in referring to the law of the matrimonial domicile the rights of the spouses even in acquests made after a change, since the prospective assignment made by and at the moment of the marriage may include these, as well as the future acquests to be made in the matrimonial domicile, and there is certainly no universal assignment wrought by the change of domicile which can include any description of property.

369. The two last reasons differ from the two first in

(*r*) "The legal assignment of a marriage operates, without regard to territory, all the world over:" Lord Meadowbank, in *Stein's case*, 1 Rose, 481. I do not know whether his lordship would have accepted my conclusion, that it must also operate without regard to a subsequent change of domicile.

excluding immovables, which must, on principle, be included either in a tacit contract or a tacit submission: or at least, if any one will say that the contract or submission refers to the law of the situation for each individual article of the mass, he must, on principle, say so for the movable articles as well as for the immovable ones (*s*), whence those who side with Dumoulin and Savigny have generally refused in this matter the distinction between the two classes of property (*t*). The position of those two great jurists appears to me unassailable, but its consequence as to land cannot be admitted in England, partly from the strict forms of conveyance to which we tie the acquisition, not only of the full property in land, but even of any interest in it; and partly from the discrepancy between the nature of those limited estates which our system of real property recognizes, and those interests which would be created under most continental marriage laws. Indeed, even in movables, we find it best not to inquire too particularly into the extent of the difference between the English and other legal systems, lest all international communion of law should be impossible. The favourite basis for the theory with English lawyers would probably be the universal efficacy of the assignment by marriage, suggested to them by the sweeping assignment operated by an English union: but, very much as in the case of a foreign bank-

(*s*) That is, on the ground taken by Dumoulin and Savigny, who regard the absence of express contract as a reference or submission to the particular provisions of some law, and therefore to that of the domicile. Vandermeulen, whose tract may be seen at length in Merlin (*ubi supra*), does not seem to perceive this meaning of Dumoulin, whom he supposes to regard the parties as referring to some law as law; whence he is of course able to deduce that, if so, they must refer to the *lex situs* for land, without being driven to the same conclusion for chattels.

(*t*) The Voets indeed accept this distinction here, as they usually pushed far the reality of statutes: Paul, de Stat., s. 4, c. 3, n. 9; Johann., ad Pand., l. 23, t. 2, n. 60. But the other jurists mentioned in note (*o*), p. 352, refuse it, as does also Huber. See Fœlix, n. 90.

rupt's syndics, if we found that the husband could receive or sue for the wife's property by the law of the matrimonial domicile, we should not be over nice in considering whether his title was an assignment or a procuration (*u*).

370. Whatever arguments there are for deciding by the law of the matrimonial domicile the interest of the spouses in the foreign immovables owned by them at the time of the marriage, the same apply equally to those afterwards purchased out of the movable property of either consort, or of the community if the couple are in community, and with an important addition: for if the *lex situs* were allowed to prevail as to the latter, movable property might be withdrawn from the dominion of its own law, to the damage of interests already vested in one or the other party. Hence even Vandermeulen, whose opposition as to the former point we have seen, held as to the latter that, notwithstanding a conveyance must necessarily operate according to the *lex situs*, yet the interest given by the *lex domicilii* may be realized by an action either on the implied matrimonial contract, or on the right to compensation for the purchase-money. Of course if in any country the legal ownership of land does not depend on strict forms of conveyance, but follows that of the purchase-money, there, upon these principles, the land itself would be immediately affected by the law of the matrimonial domicile: and this appears to have been the case in the old jurisprudence of the parliament of Paris. That tribunal, by judgments of 1549, 1745, and 1746, decided that acquests of land *en pays coutumier* were not common,

(*u*) *Campbell* v. *French*, 3 Ves. 321, 323; *Sawer* v. *Shute*, 1 Anstr. 63; *Dues* v. *Smith*, Jacob, 544; *M'Cormick* v. *Garnett*, 5 D. M. G. 278. I know of no English authority for the case of a change of domicile, unless a dictum of Lord Eldon in *Lashley* v. *Hog* (1 Roberts., Sc. Ap. Ca. 4; 1 Burge, 625) be, as it sometimes is, considered in point. But, as to the real nature of the case of *Foubert* v. *Turst*, to which that dictum applied, see below, Art. 373.

when made by one whose matrimonial domicile was *en pays de droit écrit;* and in 1539, and again in 1718, that acquests of land *hors pays coutumier* were common, when made by one whose matrimonial domicile was *en pays coutumier* (*x*).

371. If there be a settlement, or collateral marriage contract, executed by the parties, its validity, and their rights under it, will be determined by the same rules which would apply to any other contract made in the place where the marriage is celebrated, and to be performed in that where the matrimonial domicile is first established. Thus the formal or external requisites will depend generally on the place of celebration; the interpretation generally, and the legality and operation always, on the domicile. Only if it relate to land, it cannot operate as a conveyance unless it pursue the forms of the *situs*, though even then it will be allowed in the *situs* such operation as it may claim in the character of a contract. Also, on these express agreements, there can be no substantial question as to the consequence of a change of domicile before making any acquest which may come under them, for they will affect according to their terms all property wherever and whenever acquired (*y*). It has been held in Louisiana that a matrimonial contract which

---

(*x*) Merlin, *ubi supra.*

(*y*) English cases where effect has been given to foreign marriage contracts according to these principles are *Foubert* v. *Turst*, Pre. Ch. 207; 1 Bro. P. C. 38 fol., 129 oct. (change of domicile): *Anstruther* v. *Adair*, 2 My. & Ke. 513: *Williams* v. *Williams*, 3 Beav. 547: *Este* v. *Smyth*, 18 Beav. 112, where the domicile was really French, and the contract interpreted in effect by French law: *Duncan* v. *Cannan*, 18 Beav. 128, 7 D. M. G. 78 (change of domicile). See also *Forbes* v. *Adams*, 9 Sim. 462, where a wife effectually conveyed her interest under her settlement, in money charged on land, in the form of the *situs*, which was also the matrimonial domicile: and *Duncan* v. *Campbell*, 12 Sim. 616, where the rights of the consorts under a post-nuptial settlement were decided by the law of the domicile. The doctrines of this article are asserted also by Story, s. 184.

would adopt a law foreign to the domicile must set out its provisions, and not merely refer to the law *eo nomine* (*z*): but a contrary opinion has been expressed by the present Master of the Rolls (*a*).

372. If a settlement, or other express contract, be made on the marriage not comprising all the movable property of either party, the question whether it excludes any rights which would otherwise arise in the part not settled or contracted on will be decided by the law of the matrimonial domicile, as appropriate both to the operation of the settlement or contract, and to the destination of the remaining property. And the residue on which the settlement or contract is held not to operate, either expressly or through effect of law, will of course go by the same rule (*b*).

373. It is universally admitted in principle that the succession to either consort on death must be separated from the subjects treated of in this section, and be regulated by the law of the last domicile of the deceased (*c*). In practice however there is often a great difficulty, on the question what matters belong to the department of succession, and what to the pecuniary effects of the marriage. In *Foubert* v. *Turst* (*d*), the admitted effect of the contracts, of which there were both an ante—and a post-nuptial one, was that the consorts were in community as to all the property in the cause, except a sum of 800 *livres*, which

(*z*) *Boucier* v. *Lanusse*, 3 Mar. 581. A similar rule is provided by Art. 1390 of the Code Napoleon, for contracts adopting any of the old local laws or customs of France.

(*a*) In *Este* v. *Smyth*, 18 Beav. 122. See *Byam* v. *Byam*, 19 Beav. 58, where some reference was made in the Italian articles to the law of England, but at any rate the domicile was English, the husband being in the English army.

(*b*) These were the points in *Watts* v. *Shrimpton*, 21 Beav. 97, which however was decided on the national character at the time of the marriage, against the domicile.

(c) Savigny, v. 8, p. 336.

(*d*) Pre. Cha. 207; 1 Bro. P. C. 38 fol., 129 oct.

was to go to "the wife and her heirs of her part." The wife predeceasing the husband, and without issue, after a removal of the domicile from the custom of Paris to England, "her heirs of her part" according to the custom were of course entitled, by contract, to the 800 *livres:* but the husband, as his wife's heir by the law of England, claimed her share in the community as to the rest; while her relations claimed this also, evidently on the ground that the ante-nuptial contract had been made with the intervention of the wife's mother, who should therefore be considered as having stipulated for them by implication, when she stipulated for the community in return for the portion which she gave with her daughter. Lord Keeper Wright repelled this implication, holding that a contract, which, so far as it went, coincided with the custom of Paris, must be taken as an adoption of the custom. But his decree was reversed in the House of Lords, and the wife's share in the community given to the heirs of her part, on their counsel pointing out that in certain particulars, collateral to the general stipulation of community, the contract deviated from the custom of Paris, whence it was argued that it could not in any part be considered as an adoption of it. The contract was probably most correctly interpreted by the higher court (*e*), but in both courts the true nature of the contention appears to have been understood. If there had been an ante-nuptial contract between the husband and wife alone, with no particular reason for implying a stipulation in favour of her relations, or if the parties had married under the custom of Paris without express agreement, there is no reason to suppose that the House of Lords would not have held the

(*e*) The post-nuptial agreement went to the very point, and was in favour of the husband: which showed pretty clearly that when it was made the ante-nuptial agreement was not understood in his favour.

husband entitled, as successor by the law of her last domicile, to the share in the community which the contract, or the law of her matrimonial domicile, would have given the wife on her death. In *Lashley* v. *Hog*, Lord Eldon distinctly said that, had there been no contract, the decision in *Foubert* v. *Turst* must have been for the husband (*f*).

(*f*) This is the dictum the unlucky wording of which, in the very brief note of it, has caused it to be sometimes cited for the new domicile, in the case of a contention *between the husband and wife:* see above, p. 356, note (*u*). It is not likely that Lord Eldon meant any thing of the kind, or confounded a question of succession with one between the consorts.

CHAPTER XII.

Foreign Judgments against the Person.

374. Having now gone through the international questions of jurisdiction and law which arise in the trial of original causes of action, so far as these are independent of the status of the parties, we have to consider the effect which will be allowed to the personal judgment of a foreign tribunal pronounced *in foro contentioso*. Now since a judgment is merely an act of sovereign power, it can of itself have no extraterritorial effect. The officers of the state in which it is pronounced must carry it into execution, whether with or without the intervention of any farther formalities, but it can convey no authority to the officers of another state. Hence it is universally admitted, even as between those countries in which, as in France, a judgment contains a direction to the officers of justice and is therefore, if domestic, immediately executable on being delivered to such an officer by the party (*a*), that a foreign judgment, though possessing the same character at home, can only obtain effect through the sanction accorded to it by the territorial courts (*b*). This sanction however may be given either directly or indirectly; that is, either by the declaration of the local judge that the foreign judgment is *exécutoire*, or admitted to execution within his jurisdiction, or by a new judgment pronounced

---

(*a*) Such a judgment *emporte la voie de l'exécution parée.*

(*b*) On this ground it has been held, that, in a suit in chancery to have the benefit of a foreign judgment, a receiver cannot be appointed before decree: *Houlditch* v. *Donegall*, Beat. 390.

by the local judge in favour of the same party in an action brought on the former one. The first method is used in most parts of the continent of Europe, the second in the British Isles and the countries colonized from them (*c*). Many of the questions which arise are common to both the systems, though with a slightly different appearance, for the objections to declaring a foreign judgment executory are analogous to the defences to an action on such a judgment: but the question of the effect to be given to a foreign judgment, when declared executory, in charging by a tacit lien the goods of the party, has no analogue in the English system, for the judgment in the new suit will of course operate precisely as any other rendered by the same court. We will now suppose an action brought in England or the United States on a foreign judgment, and examine in order the questions to which it gives rise.

375. First, the judgment sued on must, in England, be proved in the manner pointed out by the st. 14 & 15 Vict. c. 99, s. 7. "All proclamations, treaties, and other acts of state of any foreign state or of any British colony, and all judgments, decrees, orders, and other judicial proceedings of any court of justice in any foreign state or in any British colony, and all affidavits, pleadings, and other legal documents filed or deposited in any such court, may be proved in any court of justice, or before any person having by law or by consent of parties authority to hear, receive, and examine evidence, either by examined copies or by copies authenticated as hereinafter mentioned; that is to say, if the document sought to be proved be a proclamation, treaty, or other act of state, the authenticated copy to be admissible in evidence must purport to be sealed

---

(c) In Spain, Sweden and Norway foreign judgments are neither declared executory, nor is an action brought on them, but the successful plaintiff must bring a new action on the original cause: Fœlix, n. 398, 400, 401.

with the seal of the foreign state or British colony to which the original document belongs; and if the document sought to be proved be a judgment, decree, order, or other judicial proceeding of any foreign or colonial court, or an affidavit, pleading, or other legal document filed or deposited in any such court, the authenticated copy to be admissible in evidence must purport either to be sealed with the seal of the foreign or colonial court to which the original document belongs, or, in the event of such court having no seal, to be signed by the judge, or, if there be more than one judge, by any one of the judges of the said court, and such judge shall attach to his signature a statement in writing on the said copy that the court whereof he is a judge has no seal; but if any of the aforesaid authenticated copies shall purport to be sealed or signed as hereinbefore respectively directed, the same shall respectively be admitted in evidence in every case in which the original document could have been received in evidence, without any proof of the seal where a seal is necessary, or of the signature, or of the truth of the statement attached thereto, where such signature and statement are necessary, or of the judicial character of the person appearing to have made such signature and statement" (*d*). And, to sustain the action, the examined or authenticated copy must be that of the judgment itself: a monition, which "is either the equivalent of a writ of execution, or a prelude to it by way of attachment, is not sufficient evidence of a judgment of the same amount" (*e*).

376. Next, the judgment thus proved must be one *in personam* for an ascertained sum. Thus an action would not lie, where a definite sum had been adjudged, but liable to reduction by the amount of costs which the plaintiff

---

(*d*) By the interpretation clause, British colonies here include all British possessions.

(*e*) *Obicini* v. *Bligh*, 8 Bing. 335, 354.

might have had taxed (*f*). If however the judgment have been rendered with a stay of execution for the purpose of determining the amount of a cross demand, that will not prevent an action on it here in the mean time, though our court will, on application, stay proceedings for such a time as "to give the defendant the fair benefit of the reservation" made by the foreign court (*g*). But, the sum being certain, it may have been adjudged merely for costs in a suit of which the primary object was not pecuniary, as for divorce (*h*), provided a general personal liability to pay those costs was created by the sentence: for an action will not lie on an order of a foreign court to pay costs, enforceable only by attachment in the court where the order was made, inasmuch as no action at law can be maintained on such an order even of the English chancery (*i*). While on the other hand, if the foreign judgment created a general personal liability to pay money, the action will lie on it in a court of law here, notwithstanding that it may have been rendered by a court of equity in a country where the English distinction between law and equity is adopted (*k*).

377. But need the foreign judgment be final? The question does not often arise on the continent, as it is there a peculiarity of France, and of the other states which have taken this particular from the French codes, that even a domestic judgment can be executed before the time for appeal has expired; and no one can think of giving an earlier validity to a foreign than to a home sentence. In England, a colonial decree may be sued on while an appeal to the Privy Council is still open and intended (*l*):

(*f*) *Sadler* v. *Robins*, 1 Camp. 253.

(*g*) *Hall* v. *Odber*, 11 East, 118, 126.

(*h*) *Russell* v. *Smyth*, 9 M. & W. 810; and see Justice Gaselee's judgment in *Obicini* v. *Bligh*, 8 Bing. 354.

(*i*) *Sheehy* v. *Professional Life Assurance Company*, 2 C. B., N. S. 211, 256.

(*k*) *Henderson* v. *Henderson*, 6 Q. B. 288.

(*l*) *Henderson* v. *Henderson*, 3 Ha. 100.

and after judgment for the plaintiff in an action on a French sentence, stay of execution pending an appeal already instituted from the latter was refused (*m*). And this seems quite fair, but when the judgment is of no force in its own country pending the appeal, it would seem that it ought on principle to receive no force here. And where the foreign order is interlocutory, so that it "may be varied by the subsequent proceedings in the cause," the English court will entertain no proceedings in relation to it (*n*).

378. Such foreign judgment thus proved is considered in England and America as *prima facie* evidence of a promise, by the party against whom it is rendered, to pay its amount. It therefore constitutes a debt by simple contract, to be sued for, says an old case, in " an *indebitatus assumpsit*, or an *insimul computasset*, &c., so that the statute of limitations is pleadable" (*o*). And the same principles will be applied if, as may be done in suitable circumstances, the plaintiff files a bill in chancery to have the benefit of the foreign proceedings (*p*). But this fiction of a promise was only resorted to in order to bring the liability within the English forms of action: it may not be rebutted by proof of its unreality, if the judgment stand the other tests to which we shall presently see it subjected, and the promise will therefore be equally presumed whether the judgment was given *in invitum*, or confirmed an award made under submission to a reference. " We cannot think," said Lord Denman, "that the parties' previous consent to be bound makes a stronger obligation, than that

(*m*) *Alivon* v. *Furnival*, 1 Cr. M. & R. 297.

(*n*) *Paul* v. *Roy*, 15 Beav. 433, 440; *Patrick* v. *Shedden*, 2 E. & B. 14.

(*o*) *Dupleix* v. *De Roven*, 2 Vern. 540, 541. See also *Walker* v. *Witter*, Doug. 1.

(*p*) *Houlditch* v. *Donegall*, 2 Cl. & F. 470, 8 Bl. N. R. 301. As to whether a simple decree for an ascertained amount can be sued on in chancery, see *Paul* v. *Roy*, 15 Beav. 433, 443.

of every subject of the state to perform the duties imposed on him by a court of justice exercising lawful jurisdiction over him" (*q*). These words indeed contain the pith of the reason for which, in any case, a foreign judgment is either declared executory on the continent, or is upheld as a cause of action under the English law. It is that on the person against whom the decree was made a duty was imposed by lawful authority to obey it, so that another court, in lending its aid to the right correlative to that duty, does but follow out the principle of recognising internationally rights which have once well accrued. The competence then of the court, that is, the lawfulness of the authority which imposed the duty, is the foundation of all faith given to the *res judicata* of a foreign tribunal: and the want of such competence is the first objection we must consider as urged against the judgment.

379. Now we have seen in the preceding chapters, under the several divisions in which the causes of action arise, that civilized nations differ widely as to the rules of jurisdiction. Naturally, therefore, when called on to enforce foreign judgments, each tries by its own maxims the competence of the courts which pronounced them (*r*). To do otherwise, would be to license every foreign state to draw to itself all causes which it pleased; nor can any judge be required to enforce a duty not imposed on the defendant by an authority held lawful in his own tribunal. These principles are said to be well settled in continental practice, and at least any deviation from them is not made on the side of admitting more widely the competence of foreign tribunals. Thus, we have seen in Art. 113 that the Code Napoleon establishes a personal forum of the

(*q*) In *Henderson* v. *Henderson*, 6 Q. B. 298. The objection thus answered arose out of the fact that in *Henley* v. *Soper*, 8 B. & Cr. 16, the decree sued on had been made on the result of an arbitration.

(*r*) Fœlix, n. 321, 327.

plaintiff, and this has been followed in the Sardinian code; but no authority is allowed in France to a Piedmontese judgment resting on the Piedmontese character of the plaintiff (*s*). It would seem as if the competence of a foreign court was tested primarily by the Roman principles of the *forum rei* and the *forum speciale obligationis*, besides being subjected to the farther condition that the particular rule on which it is based must also be received in the country where the execution of the judgment is sought.

380. The farther condition just mentioned has not been exacted in England from judgments satisfying the general maxims on jurisdiction, because the authority of the superior courts at Westminster was anciently limited by service of the writ within the realm, so that to have insisted on a similar circumstance for the support of a foreign judgment would have led to the too inconvenient result of ignoring the *forum rei* in every case of the defendant's absence. It may, I believe, be said that the *forum rei* is always allowed in England to be a valid foundation for a foreign judgment (*t*): and in one case that maxim has been pushed to an extreme length, a Scotch judgment being enforced here *in personam* against a native Scotchman who was in India, and appears to have been even domiciled there, when it was rendered (*u*). The professed ground was allegiance, but, after the transference of his domicile, it is difficult to see how that, even if otherwise a proper basis for jurisdiction, subjected the defendant more to the Scotch courts than to the British courts in India.

(*s*) Judgment of the royal court of Grenoble, of 3rd January, 1829; Sirey, 1829, II, 176; Fœlix, n. 321.

(*t*) *Cowan* v. *Braidwood*, 1 M. & Gr. 882, 1 Sc. N. R. 138. But not the French forum of the plaintiff: *General Steam Navigation Company* v. *Guillou*, 11 M. & W. 877, 894.

(*u*) *Douglas* v. *Forrest*, 4 Bing. 686. See the reference to allegiance in p. 703.

381. It is much less clear in what cases we admit a foreign *forum speciale obligationis*, for, in accordance with the tendency of our own courts to assert jurisdiction on the mere ground of the defendant's casual presence, or actual notice of our process (*x*), the main effort in the cases has generally been to ascertain whether the defendant had, or but for his own fault might have had, such notice of the foreign proceedings as to enable him to be heard in them (*y*). Hence, when the defendant was actually present, there is no hesitation in admitting the competence: but difficult discussions have arisen when he was absent. In the latter case, on general principles, the jurisdiction is only founded, as we saw in Art. 109, on the defendant's possession of property within the territory; and the simple rule would be, when that condition is satisfied, to respect the title gained to any property by the plaintiff in the attachment suit, at the same time admitting the payment as a discharge of and protection to the garnishee, but not even then to enforce the judgment *in personam* for the balance not liquidated by the attachment, because the *locus contractus*, without either domicile or presence, does not found a purely personal jurisdiction (*z*). The cases however do not answer to this rule, as might be expected from the fact that they often arise on the judgments of colonial and other courts, which, their law being modelled on the English, themselves base their competence in these attachment suits on the legal presumption that notice is conveyed by the artificial citations used, to which it makes no difference whether the property seized be substantial or

(*x*) See above, Arts. 116, 120, 123, 125.

(*y*) See *Reynolds* v. *Fenton*, 3 C. B. 187; *Cowan* v. *Braidwood*, 1 M. & Gr. 882, 1 Sc. N. R. 138; *Sheehy* v. *Professional Life Assurance Company*, 13 C. B. 787, 2 C. B. N. S. 211. If the defendant appeared by attorney, it will be presumed that the foreign court saw that the attorney was properly constituted: *Molony* v. *Gibbons*, 2 Camp. 502.

(*z*) That an attachment can never bind the defendant beyond the property seized is recognised by Story, s. 549.

nominal (as a chip or a hat), or whether the forum was or not the *locus contractus*. The actual result of the cases is that where the constructive notice has been thought insufficient, payment under the foreign or colonial judgment in attachment has, without any inquiry as to whether it emanated from the *forum contractus*, been held not even to protect the garnishee from a suit by the principal defendant (*a*): while, where it has been thought sufficient, the foreign judgment against an absent defendant, unsatisfied by any property possessed by him in the forum, has been enforced against him *in personam* in England (*b*).

382. As to what constructive notice is sufficient,—where the actual notice was served on a public officer appointed to represent absentees, it was presumed that he would do his duty, and the judgment was enforced (*c*): and it appears that a judgment will be good, if rendered against one who, having been within the jurisdiction, has left an attorney there to act for him (*d*). In *Obicini* v. *Bligh*, it seems to have been thought that the decree of a foreign court of admiralty was good, which condemned in damages a captor who would have been present if, as he ought, he had brought in his prize for adjudication (*e*).

383. There is however one case of the *forum speciale obligationis* which must be distinguished. It is that in which an instrument does not leave the *forum contractus* to be deduced from its general circumstances, but contains on either side the clause that the party in question elects,

(*a*) *Cavan* v. *Stewart*, 1 Star. 525.

(*b*) *Becquet* v. *M'Carthy*, 11 A. & E. 179, 3 P. & D. 143. This ground was also taken in *Douglas* v. *Forrest*, 4 Bing. 686.

(*c*) *Becquet* v. *M'Carthy*, *ubi supra:* but see Lord Brougham's remarks on this case in 5 Cl. & F. 21.

(*d*) *Cavan* v. *Stewart*, 1 Star. 530. Foreign judgments were held bad in *Buchanan* v. *Rucker*, 3 Camp. 63, 9 East, 192; and in *Ferguson* v. *Mahon*, 2 B. & Ad. 951.

(*e*) 8 Bing. 335, 352, 354.

for the purpose of the instrument, a certain spot as his domicile. Not only is such a clause binding, but so also, even without an express stipulation to that effect, is a provision of the law of the place of contract declaring a certain transaction to be of its own force an election of domicile there (*f*). The contractor having by his own act given to the *forum contractus* the efficacy of a *forum rei*, a judgment there pronounced against him will be enforced *in personam* here without reference to the question of notice.

384. Supposing the competence of the foreign court established, or that actual or constructive notice to the defendant of its process which we in many cases accept instead of a competence strictly interpreted, there arises the great question whether the foreign judgment has the force of *res judicata*. In the continental system of declaring judgments executory, the form of this question is whether such declaration must be preceded by an examination of the substance of the judgment, as to accuracy in fact and law. In the Anglo-American system of suing on a foreign judgment, the form is whether such judgment is a conclusive proof of the claim decreed for by it, or merely a presumptive one, which the defendant may rebut by showing it to be erroneous in fact or law. The judgments of the several states which composed the German empire had mutually the force of *res judicata*, but those of states foreign to the empire had not that force within it: and a similar system is still pursued in the Germanic states and portions of states east of the Rhine, as well in those which have adopted codes, as in those which adhere to the Roman law, the condition of reciprocity being substituted for that of membership of the Germanic body. The same condition is exacted in Denmark, Switzerland, and the Sardinian and Papal States: so that in any of these the

(*f*) *Vallée* v. *Dumergue*, 4 Exch. 290; *Meeus* v. *Thellusson*, 8 Exch. 638.

judgment of any other of them, or of a state which allows the force of *res judicata* to foreign judgments without demanding reciprocity, is admitted to execution without examinantion (*g*). In France the practice of the courts has at last fully settled that every foreign judgment must be examined, though this opinion, depending as it does on the interpretation of the codes, and of the 121st article of the ordinance of 1629, allowed to be still in force, was long disputed by many jurists, and is so yet by some (*h*). In Belgium and Rheinish Prussia, as the question rests on the French codes received there without the ordinance of 1629, foreign judgments have the force of *res judicata*; except, in Belgium, French judgments, by the special law of September 9th, 1814, and in Rheinish Prussia, by the decisions of the courts, judgments given against inhabitants of Prussia in countries where Prussian judgments are submitted to examination (*i*).

385. In England, there is a classical dictum of Chief Justice Eyre, against allowing the force of *res judicata* to a foreign judgment. "We examine it," said he, "as we do all other considerations of promises"—he had just before alluded to the fiction with which in England the true liability is encrusted—"and for that purpose we receive evidence of what the law of the foreign state is, and whether the judgment is warranted by that law (*k*). To the same effect were the opinions of Lord Mansfield (*l*) and Justices Buller (*m*) and Bayley (*n*), and such also is

(*g*) Fœlix, n. 331—345.
(*h*) Fœlix, n. 347 *et seq.*
(*i*) Fœlix, n. 377 *et seq.*
(*k*) In *Philips* v. *Hunter*, 2 H. Bl. 410.
(*l*) *Walker* v. *Witter*, Doug. 1, 6.
(*m*) *Galbraith* v. *Neville*, Doug. 6, note.
(*n*) *Tarleton* v. *Tarleton*, 4 M. & S. 20.

that of the present Master of the Rolls (*o*). Against these high authorities must be set those, equally high, of Lords Nottingham (*p*) and Kenyon (*q*), Sir L. Shadwell (*r*), and Lords Denman (*s*) and Campbell (*t*). The opinion of Lord Brougham is perhaps doubtful. In *Don* v. *Lippmann* he used language which would rank him with Lord Nottingham: "A foreign judgment is good here as a ground of suit, provided that it has not been obtained by fraud or collusion, or by a practice contrary to the principles of all law" (*u*). In *Houlditch* v. *Donegall* he expressed himself more at large to a very similar purpose, referring to the defect of jurisdiction which would invalidate a foreign judgment, and to the possibility that it might emanate from a country of which the laws were so different from ours that it could not be admitted within the pale of juridical intercommunity: and none of his lordship's remarks in that case would have led to the conclusion that he regarded the judgment of an ordinary Christian state examinable for error in fact or in law, had he not made them in express opposition to those learned judges who have maintained that it is not so examinable (*x*).

386. But the recent decisions in the Queen's Bench are probably the safest to follow. "Several pleas," said Lord Denman in *Henderson* v. *Henderson*, "were pleaded to show that the defendant had not had justice done him in the court of chancery at Newfoundland. This is never

---

(*o*) *Reimers* v. *Druce*, 23 Beav. 150. In Spain. Sweden, and Norway, the foreign judgment is treated, in the new action brought on the original cause, as at the utmost a presumption favourable to the plaintiff: Fœlix, n. 398, 400, 401.

(*p*) *Gold* v. *Canham*, 2 Sw. 325; *Cottington's case*, *ib.*, p. 326.

(*q*) *Galbraith* v. *Neville*, Doug. 6, note.

(*r*) *Martin* v. *Nicolls*, 3 Sim. 458.

(*s*) *Henderson* v. *Henderson*, 6 Q. B. 288.

(*t*) *Bank of Australasia* v. *Nias*, 16 Q. B. 717.

(*u*) 5 Cl. & F. 20.

(*x*) 8 Bl. N. R. 337, 2 Cl. & F. 476.

to be presumed, but the contrary principle holds, unless we see in the clearest light that the foreign law, or at least some part of the proceedings of the foreign court, are repugnant to natural justice: and this has been often made the subject of inquiry in our courts. But it steers clear of an inquiry into the merits of the case upon the facts found: for whatever constituted a defence in that court ought to have been pleaded there" (*y*). The value of this language is enhanced by the clearness with which it puts a strictly foreign on a level with a colonial court (*z*). It is well known that even the courts of Scotland and Ireland have always been treated here as foreign, but some expressions have been used in a modern case which may be read as if a colonial decision, being subject to an appeal to the Privy Council, was more entitled to the force of *res judicata* than one of another nation. It was not however of re-examining the substantial accuracy of a foreign or colonial decision that the expressions alluded to were used, but of the notice of process to the defendant, with reference to the point of competence, of which the learned vice-chancellor felt confident that a British court of appeal would test the sufficiency on English principles (*a*).

387. There is however one case in which it is generally admitted that a foreign judgment is examinable for error in law. It is when the original suit fell within the province of private international jurisprudence, the force *rei judicatæ* not being then acquired unless the right municipal law was selected as the groundwork of the decision. For of its own code the foreign court will be allowed to be the best interpreter, but international maxims belong equally to all courts, and if they have not been followed, as under-

(*y*) 6 Q. B. 298.

(*z*) This is also the effect of Lord Campbell's language in *Bank of Australasia* v. *Nias*, 16 Q. B. 735, 737.

(*a*) *Henderson* v. *Henderson*, 3 Ha. 117, 118.

stood by the tribunal where the judgment is to be enforced, the defendant will not be held to have been bound by a lawful authority acting lawfully (*b*). So too if the foreign judgment avowedly repose on the view taken by the foreign court of English law, whether as that considered applicable to the case, or as constituting a fact in the relations of the parties, it will not be enforced here, if the English law was erroneously interpreted in it (*c*).

388. The citations made above from Lords Denman and Brougham establish the principle that, whatever respect we should otherwise pay to a foreign judgment, we cannot enforce one which we consider contrary to natural justice. Indeed the laws which, on the doctrine of Arts. 196—198, we could not directly apply ourselves, we can no more apply indirectly, by enforcing their results when embodied in a judgment of the country where they exist. An example is furnished by the sentence of a court composed of interested parties (*d*), and others have been suggested (*e*). Also it cannot be imagined that we should enforce here a foreign judgment sustaining a claim founded in a breach of the English revenue-laws.

389. Another objection to enforcing a foreign judgment is that it was obtained by fraud, which of course does not impeach its intrinsic authority, unless the circumstances charged as fraudulent were before the foreign court, so that the plea was in effect disposed of there (*f*).

390. If a judgment obtained against a company in its domicile, or in the country under the laws of which it was

(*b*) Fœlix, note to n. 327: *Reimers* v. *Druce*, 23 Beav. 145, 156. See also this doctrine acted on in *Arnott* v. *Redfern*, 2 C. & P. 88, and above, Art. 231.

(*c*) *Novelli* v. *Rossi*, 2 B. & Ad. 757.

(*d*) *Price* v. *Dewhurst*, 8 Sim. 279.

(*e*) See *Paul* v. *Roy*, 15 Beav. 440.

(*f*) See *Bowles* v. *Orr*, 1 Y. & C., Exch., 464; and the reporter's note to *Innes* v. *Mitchell*, 4 Drew. 102.

established, in an action brought against it either in its corporate character or in the name of one of its officers, be by those laws capable of execution against the members of such company as though they had been severally the defendants, such judgment will also found an action in England against an individual shareholder. He is bound by the law of the company to which he has chosen to belong, and the notice to its officer who represents him must be held sufficient to protect his interests (*g*).

391. A foreign judgment by confession is of course essentially different from one pronounced *in foro contentioso*, being merely a peculiar title by contract; and, when it is sued on, the court will examine whether it was really and duly authorized by the party against whom it is recorded (*h*). The same principles apply to the awards of foreign arbitrators, when made a rule or order of court by the consent of the parties: those defences only will be admitted which attack them as contracts, or tend to their rescission as such, but, when established as contracts, the force of *res judicata* will be allowed then *ex contractu*, without regard to their substance, or the competence of the court which sanctioned them. But the award in an arbitration forced on the parties by the law, though with the permission to name their own arbitrators, as in the proceedings of the French tribunals of commerce, or in a private one in which the law has intervened to name the arbitrators, or which has been judicially confirmed not by consent but by law, is not to be distinguished from an ordinary judgment *in foro contentioso* (*i*). On the other

(*g*) *Bank of Australasia* v. *Harding*, 19 L. J., N. S., C. P. 345; *Bank of Australasia* v. *Nias*, 16 Q. B. 717.

(*h*) *Frankland* v. *M'Gusty*, 1 Knapp, 274. See also *Guinness* v. *Carroll*, 1 B. & Ad. 459.

(*i*) *Alivon* v. *Furnival*, 1 Cr. M. & R. 277, 4 Tyrwh. 751, as well as others in our reports, was a case of this kind. The rules laid down in the text as to awards are fully recognised by Fœlix. l. 2, t. 7, c. 2.

hand, if a private foreign award be sued on before receiving judicial confirmation even by consent, it constitutes a mere title by contract.

392. The maxim *transit in rem judicatam* does not in England apply to foreign judgments, so that the plaintiff has here the option of suing on the original cause (*k*).

393. A foreign judgment for the defendant, in a court competent as to the matter, is a conclusive bar to any attempt by the plaintiff to reopen his claim here (*l*). But it must be a final judgment in its own country (*m*), it must have been given upon the merits (*n*), and it is besides liable to all the objections which may be urged against a foreign judgment sought to be enforced by the plaintiff (*o*). If these tests are satisfied, "the plea of *res judicata* applies, except in special cases, not only to points upon which the court was actually required by the parties to form an opinion and pronounce a judgment, but to every point which properly belonged to the subject of litigation, and which the parties, exercising reasonable diligence, might have brought forward at the time" (*p*). But the foreign proceedings must not terminate in a sentence

---

(*k*) *Maule* v. *Murray*, 7 T. R. 470; *Hall* v. *Odber*, 11 East, 118; *Smith* v. *Nicolls*, 5 Bing. N. C. 208; *Bank of Australasia* v. *Harding*, 19 L. J., N. S., C. P. 345; *Bank of Australasia* v. *Nias*, 16 Q. B. 717; contrary to the opinion of Lord Nottingham in *Newland* v. *Horseman*, 1 Vern. 21. See *Bayley* v. *Edwards*, 3 Sw. 703.

(*l*) *Ricardo* v. *Garcias*, 12 C. & F. 368; and Lord Cranworth's judgment in *Ostell* v. *Le Page*, 2 D. M. G. 895. And the English chancery, after decreeing against the plaintiff, has granted an injunction to restrain him from prosecuting elsewhere a suit for the same claim: *Booth* v. *Leycester*, 1 Keen, 579.

(*m*) *Plummer* v. *Woodburne*, 4 B. & Cr. 625.

(*n*) *Garcias* v. *Ricardo*, 14 Sim. 265.

(*o*) As the mistake of English law, *Novelli* v. *Rossi*, 2 B. & Ad. 757. "If the decree is conclusive upon one party, it must be conclusive upon both; and, if not conclusive upon both, it ought to be conclusive upon neither." Sir J. Wigram, in *Henderson* v. *Henderson*, 3 Ha. 117.

(*p*) Sir J. Wigram, in *Henderson* v. *Henderson*, 3 Ha. 115.

against the particular demand framed in them, leaving it possible that some other demand might be sustained on the same facts (*q*); which is sometimes expressed by saying that the proceedings relied on as a bar must have been taken for the same purpose as those in which they are pleaded (*r*).

394. Nor does the efficacy of the bar considered in the last paragraph depend upon the same person being plaintiff both here and abroad. If the party defendant here obtained judgment there in a suit instituted by him in order to be discharged from a possible claim, he will be equally protected (*s*). Or if there was damage incurred by both parties, through an accident which each charges to have happened by the negligence of the other, then a judgment of a competent forum will be conclusive, so as to prevent the person on whom it threw the blame, though the defendant there, from suing here on the same facts (*t*).

395. The plea of a suit depending abroad, in which character a decree for account must be considered until the accounts are taken, is closely connected with that of a foreign judgment, and it is now held to be good (*u*), though a different opinion was formerly entertained (*x*). Also if the rights of the parties have been fully determined by the foreign court, but have not yet been satisfied, the English chancery will not interfere to enforce them while

---

(*q*) *Callandar* v. *Dittrich*, 4 M. & Gr. 68, 4 Sc. N. R. 682.

(*r*) *Behrens* v. *Sieveking*, 2 M. & Cr. 602.

(*s*) *Burrows* v. *Jamereau*, 2 Str. 733, Dick. 48. The bar pleaded in *Novelli* v. *Rossi*, *ubi supra*, was of this kind, and only failed for the reason mentioned above in Arts. 387, 393.

(*t*) See *General Steam Navigation Company* v. *Guillou*, 11 M. & W. 877, 894; where however this doctrine, not being directly in point, is not positively advanced.

(*u*) *Ostell* v. *Le Page*, 5 De G. & S. 95, reversed in 2 D. M. G. 892.

(*x*) *Bayley* v. *Edwards*, 3 Sw. 703. See *Imlay* v. *Ellefsen*, 2 East, 453; and *Naylor* v. *Eagar*, 2 Y. & J. 90.

the parties are still before the foreign court, and there is no defect of power in that forum to secure the property out of which the satisfaction must be made; though otherwise a bill will be entertained for the purpose of securing the property pending the litigation abroad (*y*).

396. Every state must admit that a forum competent on the title to property renders the property what it pronounces it to be: and to this is analogous a foreign judgment on status, which however we shall see in the next chapter is not generally recognised here. The exception is furnished by the judgments in matrimonial causes, and results from the ancient connexion of that subject in England with the law of contract, whence these judgments were assimilated to those on the existence of an obligation. The effect of foreign divorces has already been considered: that of sentences on the validity of marriages is highly uncertain, the place of contract and the domicile being confused in our views of the jurisdiction no less than of the law (*z*). It is only certain that on marriages contracted in the domicile the sentence of that jurisdiction would be received as final.

(*y*) *Cruikshank* v. *Robarts*, 6 Mad. 104.

(*z*) See *Cottington's case*, 2 Sw. 326, note; *Roach* v. *Garvan*, 1 Ves. Sen. 157; *Scrimshire* v. *Scrimshire*, 2 Hagg. Cons. 395, 408, 419; *Sinclair* v. *Sinclair*, 1 Hagg. Cons. 294, 297.

CHAPTER XIII.

STATUS.

397. IN the present chapter I propose to bring together a number of questions which have this in common, that some state of facts is pronounced upon, and dispositions are made concerning it, by some law or jurisdiction. Such facts are sometimes of natural importance, as infancy or lunacy, so that they cannot be overlooked in any country, but there is some degree of conventionality in their juristic treatment. Thus, in infancy, the period of natural incapacity terminates at a limit conventionally fixed: and the fact of lunacy, established or disproved in proceedings taken for that purpose, is, to a greater or less extent, accepted accordingly in other proceedings where it is incidentally in question. Now so far as any country possesses in its own jurisprudence a conventional determination of a natural status, it is convenient for it to recognise any foreign determination of the same status: as, when a law fixes twenty-one years as the full age of its own subjects, it may give credit to another law, which, considering the climate and social life of its territory, pronounces its subjects to attain their full age at twenty or twenty-five. Besides this, with every conventional determination of a naturally important fact, there are connected institutions by which the exigencies arising out of it are provided for, as, with minority, the power of the father, and, after his death, the guardianship both of person and property: and there is an obvious convenience in admitting such foreign institutions whenever the domestic jurisprudence does not condemn their principle. There are besides in most countries more or fewer kinds of artificial status, as for in-

stance nobility, the mercantile character, or coverture by marriage, are made the grounds of peculiar privileges or disabilities: and not only may these, and the institutions connected with them, be mutually recognised for convenience as between those countries in which any the same status exists, but they may even be recognised where they do not exist, as applying to foreigners, on the ground that, where no particular property or transaction is primarily in question, it belongs to every sovereign to regulate the general condition of those domiciled within his territory. This however is again subject to the principle that the foreign status must not be opposed to the spirit of the domestic legislation, as slavery is to that of free states.

398. It may at first sight appear to make a difference, whether in any case a foreign disposition concerning status depends on law or on jurisdiction. Thus if any law makes the nearest relation guardian to a fatherless child, or permits the father to appoint a guardian by will, such a guardianship may be thought, as to its international recognition, a very different thing from an act of jurisdiction by which the sovereign power in any country names a guardian. But the distinction, closely examined, is unimportant. The provisions of a law on personal status are made for its domiciled subjects, and the exercise of jurisdiction on such status is also limited to domiciled subjects: or at least, if the latter be extended beyond that, as when a court names a guardian for a foreign child found within its territory and needing protection, such an act of jurisdiction, however humane, does not even pretend to recognition in the domicile of the person affected. This is the universal sentiment of the jurists of all countries, who refer personal status to the law and the jurisdiction of the domicile (*a*). It is

(*a*) "*Méme dans les états,*" says Fœlix, "*qui, comme la France, refusent de reconnaître l'autorité de la chose jugée en pays étranger, on admet généralement l'autorité des actes de juridiction volontaire passés à l'étranger:*" n. 454.

only then, to revert to our example, for regular subjects that either law or jurisdiction ever appoints guardians, and the recognition of such guardians in a foreign territory must, in each case, rest on the same ground, namely, their constitution by the sovereign power of their own state. In the case which seems strongest to the contrary, that of a foreign guardian constituted by a law coinciding with that of the state where his character is recognised, it is not from the provisions of the latter law that he is held to derive his character, for they form a personal statute, and were only intended by the legislator to apply to his own subjects.

399. There exist on the continent two principal modifications of the general theory just laid down, which apply equally to all the kinds of status. One is that of the French code, which claims to regulate the status of Frenchmen wherever domiciled: *les lois concernant l'état et la capacité des personnes régissent les Français, même residant en pays étranger* (b). There is no corresponding provision as to the status of foreigners, and French writers are in consequence often inexact in their language on this subject, as Fœlix, who speaks loosely of the personal statute being that of "the nationality or domicile (c):" his posthumous editor, Demangeat, contends for the common rule of domicile, which is expressly adopted by Savigny, and by the Prussian and Austrian codes for subjects as well as for aliens. Nationality is indeed a purely political fact, and is moreover not subject to a free change at the choice of the person. It is to domicile that we must look for a clue to the intentions, and actual personal and social condition, which are the determining considerations in private law.

(b) Code Civil, Art. 3.
(c) Nos. 27, 28.

400. The other modification is that already noticed in Art. 146, namely, that the fact of any particular status as affecting the person is to be determined by the personal law, but the question what the person, as affected thereby, may or may not do, by the *lex situs*, or the *lex loci actus aut contractus*. Thus the limited capacity which a French minor acquires at eighteen would be ignored in a country where such grades of capacity are unknown, and he would there enter on all his powers at once on attaining his French majority at twenty-one. But this doctrine, as usual with half measures, seems to have no tenable foundation. If the personal statute is to receive faith at all, as furnishing the best measure of the actual personal condition of its subject, or deference, as having rightful authority to dispose artificially of such condition, it is just for his capacity that it can claim that faith or deference. Nor can there be any greater difficulty in ascertaining the foreign law as to the acts permitted to any one, than as to the name of the status or class under which it ranges him: besides that every degree of capacity is in truth a separate status, though it may not be separately named. Accordingly the French, Prussian and Austrian codes distinctly reject this doctrine, declaring the "personal qualities and capacities" to depend, the two latter on domicile, the first, for Frenchmen, on its own provisions (*d*).

401. The rule of accepting either capacity in detail, or even status generally, as determined by the personal law or jurisdiction, has never been adopted in England, because, as I have had occasion to observe before, the maxims of international jurisprudence were filtered into our private law from the practice of the ecclesiastical and admiralty courts, which became fixed at a very early period (*e*). Be-

(*d*) Preus. All. L. R., Einl., ss. 23, 34; Oester. Gesetzbuch, ss. 4, 34; Code Nap., *ut supra*.

(*e*) See above, Arts. 149 and 345.

sides the old authorities for determining by the *lex loci contractus* the absolute capacity to marry without consent of parents or guardians, now very much shaken by the decision, that in legislating on the relative incapacity to marry arising from affinity parliament had all domiciled Englishmen in view, there is a case at *nisi prius* where it was assumed that a minor's capacity to contract for unnecessary articles depended on the *lex loci contractus* (*f*): and that there is not more authority on the subject may be referred to its not having been questioned. Considering however the weakness of this array, as well as the recent decision alluded to, it might not be too late to establish judicially the presumption that the common and statute laws of England on capacity are intended to apply to those domiciled here, and to them only, were it desirable to do so. But from the late age at which majority is fixed in some countries, as in Prussia at twenty-five, it would be undesirable to expose Englishmen to the risk of finding their contracts made here, say with Prussians of twenty-four, invalid. A foreigner's contract made in Prussia on a movable subject is good there by enactment, if either his personal law or the Prussian sustains his capacity (*g*); and with a similar provision here the recognition of foreign status would be advantageous, not more for its own sake, as validating the contracts of those who may be of age at home, though under twenty-one, than as a step towards the establishment, by treaty and legislation, of uniform maxims throughout the world on private international jurisprudence. But inasmuch as the general rule, when so modified, could

---

(*f*) *Male* v *Roberts*, 3 Esp. 163. In *Huet* v. *Le Mesurier*, 1 Cox, 275, one baptized in Guernsey, but it is not said whether domiciled or even born there, was held to attain his age at 21. Majority in the island is at 20, and the possibility of a question was not noticed.

(*g*) All. L. R., Einl., s. 35. A similar interpretation has sometimes been put on the 35th section of the Austrian code, but erroneously: Savigny, v. 8, p. 145.

not be brought under any presumption as to the intention of the English law, it cannot, in that form, be adopted here without the intervention of parliament. As to America, Story, speaking for all the states where the basis of the law is English, rejects entirely the personal law as to capacity, and refers it always to the special law of the transaction (*h*).

402. While the English law remains as it is, it must, on principle, be taken as excluding, in the case of transactions having their seat here, not only a foreign age of majority, but also all foreign determination of status or capacity, whether made by law or by judicial act, since no difference can be established between the cases, nor does any exist on the continent. Thus an act facilitating the transfer of property vested in lunatics cannot be applied on the strength of a judgment, by a foreign competent court, declaring the person a lunatic (*i*): nor will the committee appointed by such court have any authority over the lunatic's person here (*k*). These doctrines may be of serious consequence to the personal safety of foreign lunatics and infants in England, for though a foreign father is indeed held to have authority over the person of his child here by English law (*l*), yet that a foreign testator should provide for the contingency of his child's being

---

(*h*) Sect. 103.

(*i*) *Sylva* v. *Da Costa*, 8 Ves. 316. Lord Hardwicke had ruled otherwise, thinking the case might be brought within the wide latitude allowed in England to foreign sentences as evidence in collateral proceedings: *Exp. Otto Lewis*, 1 Ves. Sen. 298.

(*k*) *Re Houstoun*, 1 Russ. 312.

(*l*) Lord Cottenham, in *Johnstone* v. *Beattie*, 10 Cl. & F. 114. This is equivalent to recognising the foreign status, for the foreign *patria potestas* would not on the continent be recognised beyond the extent allowed by domestic law. The question whether the constitution of the *patria potestas* demands conception, or only birth, in wedlock, is to be judged by the law of the place where the father was domiciled at the time of the child's birth: Savigny, v. 8, p. 338.

casually in England by appointing guardians for it pursuant to English law is a very improbable contingency (*m*): and hence, in the leading case of *Johnstone* v. *Beattie* (*n*), an attempt was unsuccessfully made to establish that the foreign guardian, as such, has authority over his ward's person here. The facts were that the court of chancery, in the entire absence of special circumstances, ordered a reference to the master for the purpose of appointing guardians to a Scotch minor (*o*), having Scotch guardians, and no property in England: and this Lords Lyndhurst, Cottenham and Langdale sustained, as a proceeding of course, on the ground that the infant had no guardians possessing lawful authority in England (*p*), where she happened to be when the bill was filed. They also admitted, or rather claimed, that the effect of appointing guardians by the court would be to impound the child in England, transferring from Scotch to English authority, namely to that of the chancellor, the decision on her residence, secular and religious education, and marriage, during all the remainder of her minority: and it would necessarily follow that the duration of such minority would be measured by English law, or at least that any earlier emancipation would depend on the pleasure of an English judge. But Lords Brougham and Campbell, while reserving the jurisdiction, which obviously might call for exercise if the guardians of the domicile were neglecting their duty, reprobated its exercise in the case, on the ground that the infant had guardians possessing lawful authority in England, namely her Scotch ones (*q*): and it

(*m*) If indeed it can be understood what appointment by the will of one domiciled abroad could be interpreted as being pursuant to English law.

(*n*) 1 Phil. 17, 10 Cl. & F. 42.

(*o*) After the father's death, *there being guardians*, the mother could not change the child's domicile, at least against their consent.

(*p*) 10 Cl. & F. 87, 112—119, 148.

(*q*) 10 Cl. & F. 94—97, 130—132.

is difficult to believe that their opinion will not prevail, if ever a writ of *habeas corpus* should be sued out to set free a foreign child, being in England under the care of its guardian or his agent.

403. There are kinds of status which we could not recognise here, even were it certain that we recognised foreign status generally, because they are either, as slavery and disability for heresy, condemned in principle by our legislation, or, as judicial infamy and excommunication, their recognition would militate against the rule, well fixed in England, that no effect is ever given to foreign penal laws, otherwise than in pursuance of a treaty (*r*). There are also others, as interdiction for prodigality, and the incapacities relating to trade and exchange mentioned in Art. 348, which, in the case of a transaction having its seat here, we should ignore, as we do foreign determinations of those kinds of status which are known to our law. It becomes however, as to some of these, a question what would be the effect of ignoring a status which is, in form, attributive, and not privative, of capacity; as in the case of the limited class of persons who in some countries may become parties to bills of exchange. In such a case the real status, or exceptional condition, is that of the majority who do not enjoy the so-called special capacity, for the presumption is always in favour of the largest capacity of the adult: and the effect of ignoring the foreign status would be to enable any inhabitant of the foreign country, of full age by English law, to become a party to a bill of exchange here.

404. The validity of a contract made out of England, with regard to the personal capacity of the contractor, will

---

(*r*) Lord Loughborough, in *Folliott* v. *Ogden*, 1 H. Bl. 135; Justice Buller, in *Ogden* v. *Folliott*, 3 T. R. 733, 734. The same doctrine is established in the United States; Story, ss. 104, 621: and Martens denies the extraterritorial operation of judicial infamy. But Hertius says, *in uno loco infamis ubique infamis habetur.*

be referred in our courts to the *lex loci contractus;* that is, not to its particular provisions on the capacity of its domiciled subjects, but in this sense, that, if good where made, the contract will be held good here, and conversely. Hence if an Englishman of twenty-three should contract in Prussia, where the age of majority is twenty-five, his contract will be good here, because the Prussian courts would apply our law on a question of status. Thus too, if a foreign wife may trade at her residence, she may sue here on her contracts made there (*s*).

405. In the same manner, where a title to property has accrued abroad as a consequence of foreign status, it will be admitted here on the ground of the *lex domicilii* as governing universal assignments of movables, without looking back to the status in which it originated. Thus a Scotch *curator bonis* can sue in England for the personal estate of a Scotch lunatic (*t*), and the assignees of an Australian minor, capable of trading and being bankrupted in the colony, have maintained a suit in Ireland for his personalty (*u*): also it has been laid down that the father's usufruct in the English movables of his unemancipated child will depend on the law of his domicile (*x*). Hence it will follow that a Prussian of twenty-three cannot obtain payment of personal property belonging to him here, because his guardian alone could make title to it during his minority.

406. In Arts. 90—94 I considered the conflict between the *lex situs* and the personal law of the claimant, on legi-

(*s*) *Cosio* v. *De Bernales*, 1 C. & P. 266, Ry. & Mo. 102; whence also it appears that the English law determines the name in which the action must be brought.

(*t*) *Scott* v. *Bentley*, 1 K. & J. 281.

(*u*) *Stephens* v. *M'Farland*, 8 Ir. Eq. 444.

(*x*) *Gambier* v. *Gambier*, 7 Sim. 263. The father's domicile for the time being governs the pecuniary relations between him and his child, in case of a change of domicile after its birth: Savigny, v. 8, p. 338.

timation *per subsequens matrimonium*, in the succession to land. We must now consider what that personal law is. The mere places of the birth of the child, and of the marriage of its parents, can have no claim to furnish a personal law, the basis of which must always be domicile (*y*). The real conflict is between the father's domiciles at the times of the birth and of the marriage, when they differ. The pretension of the former is refuted by the considerations that, first, if it could legitimate upon the marriage, it would, by doing so, declare the child to belong to its father's new domicile, and therefore not to be subject to its law; and, secondly, that the child's domicile while still illegitimate, that is, up to the marriage, is not that of its father but of its mother. Hence the status of bastardy is generally referred to the matrimonial domicile (*z*). But this has been opposed by Schäffner, on the theory that the father's domicile at the birth gives the child an inchoate right to legitimation, which the former must not be allowed to defeat by choosing a new domicile disadvantageous to his child: a theory remarkably weak, since, as Savigny observes in reply to it, the father need not marry at all, and need not acknowledge the child if he does, either of which events would be fatal to the supposed inchoate right. A decision has however been made in England for the father's domicile at the birth, though not for Schäffner's reasons (*a*).

(*y*) *Dalhousie* v. *M'Douall*, 7 Cl. & F. 817, 1 Rob., Sc. Ap., 475; *Munro* v. *Munro*, 7 Cl. & F. 842, 1 Rob., Sc. Ap., 492. See *The Strathmore Peerage*, 6 Paton, 645; *Rose* v. *Ross* (al. *Munro* v. *Saunders*), 6 Bl. N. R. 468, 4 Wils. & S. 289; *Shedden* v. *Patrick*, 1 Macq. 535.

(*z*) Savigny, v. 8, p. 339: opinions of the Scotch judges in *Munro* v. *Munro*, 1 Rob., Sc. Ap., 504, 517.

(*a*) *Re Wright's trust*, 2 K. & J. 595. From Art. 317, above, it will be seen that Savigny would have made the same decision as to the persons intended by the bequest in this case, though not as to the general bastardy of the claimant.

407. The personal status of bastardy will give way in England to the *lex situs*, as to the inheritance of land from as well as by one legitimated by subsequent marriage (*b*): and neither this decision nor that of *Birtwhistle* v. *Vardill* is affected by the st. 21 & 22 Vict. c. 93, which establishes an English declaration of legitimacy, and of the validity of marriages. That declaration is to bind all persons, for all purposes—to the extent, of course, of the legitimacy, or validity of marriage, declared by it: but the act stops short of pronouncing what was denied in *Birtwhistle* v. *Vardill*, that legitimacy is sufficient for an English heir, without the farther condition of birth after marriage (*c*).

(*b*) *Re Don's estate*, 4 Drew. 194.

(*c*) See above, Arts. 90-93.

CHAPTER XIV.

Procedure.

408. *Aut quæris*, says Bartolus, *de his quæ pertinent ad litis ordinationem, et inspicitur locus judicii* (*a*): nor has this been ever questioned in theory, though doubts occur on some of the practical applications. It would be impossible to import into any court a new system of procedure for every case in which foreign things or acts might be involved: there would exist neither the machinery nor the minute and curious learning necessary for it. Nor is there any reason why it should be desired to do so. The principle, be it comity or justice, of enforcing rights which have accrued abroad, can be carried no higher than to place them on a level with domestic rights, entitling to the same remedies and subject to the same rules of procedure: and if we examine the matter fundamentally, the laws of civil process are not like those which originated the rights, commands addressed to the parties by their then permanent or temporary sovereign, but they are commands addressed to the judge at the time of the suit and by his own sovereign, as the conditions under which his justice is to be administered. It merely remains to mention the chief applications of this rule on which dispute has arisen.

409. The question of the name in which a suit must be brought, so far as it can be separated from that of the title sued on, must be decided by the *lex fori* (*b*). There is

(*a*) See above, Art. 166.

(*b*) Story, ss. 565, 566; *Wolff* v. *Oxholm*, 6 M. & S. 92, 99; *Jeffery* v. *M'Taggart*, 6 M. & S. 126.

often much difficulty in effecting this separation, on which I may refer to the places where the several titles have been treated of (*c*).

410. The rank or privilege of any title, as whether it be a specialty, depends on the *lex fori.* This we have seen exemplified in the case of foreign judgments, which form here titles by simple contract only: and a bill of exchange, drawn where a peculiar process exists for those contracts, must be subject to the ordinary process where no such peculiarity exists, and conversely will be entitled to the peculiar remedy of the *lex fori,* though such do not exist in the place of drawing (*d*).

411. Arrest of the body, and the writ *ne exeat regno,* depend on the *lex fori,* though, from a confusion between arrest of the body and personal liability, they were formerly held in England to depend on the *lex loci contractus* (*e*). The admissibility of set-off or compensation belongs to the remedy, and depends on the *lex fori* (*f*); but not the answers to the contract itself, for they concern its validity (*g*). Priorities between creditors depend on the *lex fori,* but liens on the law of property; so that no property can be distributed in any bankruptcy or administration, according to the priorities allowed in the forum, till it has been first cleared of all charges affecting it (*h*). Statutes of limitation, as to obligations, I have discussed in Arts. 250—252. In property, prescription concerns the ownership, which depends on the *lex situs,* unless for movables

---

(*c*) See particularly Arts. 241, 242, 278, 297, 369.

(*d*) Savigny, v. 8, p. 151.

(*e*) *Imlay* v. *Ellefsen,* 2 East, 453, 455; *De la Vega* v. *Vianna,* 1 B. & Ad. 284; *Brettilot* v. *Sandos,* 4 Sc. 201: overruling *Melan* v. *Fitzjames,* 1 Bos. & Pul. 138; *Talleyrand* v. *Boulanger,* 3 Ves. Jun. 447; *Flack* v. *Holm,* 1 J. & W. 405, 417.

(*f*) Story, s. 575.

(*g*) Above, Art. 229.

(*h*) Above, Arts. 272, 277, 307.

the law of the owner's domicile may claim to be heard (*i*); but the *situs* is the forum. The time for appealing depends clearly on the *lex fori* (*k*).

412. The admission and force of any particular kind of evidence depends on the *lex fori* (*l*), a rule however which there is the utmost difficulty in applying, from the uncertainty of the true limits between questions of evidence and the substantial questions in the cause. The doubts which arise on contracts I have considered in Arts. 172 and 177. In the title to property, the effort must be to distinguish between the foreign conveyance, the efficacy of which must depend on its proper law, whether *lex situs, lex domicilii testatoris,* or any other, and the proof of that conveyance tendered in the suit. Thus, if an enrolled and recorded copy has by the *lex situs* the same force as the original, such copy is itself a conveyance, and an examined copy of it is receivable here without evidence of search for the original, because it is not regarded as a copy of a copy, but as being made from a duplicate original (*m*). Yet it has been said that where the title to personalty depends on a foreign will, although the court must, upon the facts and documents before it, interpret the testator's intention as, upon the same facts and documents, it would be interpreted in his domicile, yet that it must follow its own rules of evidence as to what facts and documents it shall admit: whence it would result that it may come to a different conclusion as to the destination of the property from that which the *forum domicilii* would arrive at (*n*). A witness is not

---

(*i*) See Savigny's opinion, cited in Art. 269.

(*k*) *Lopez* v. *Burslem,* 4 Mo. P. C. 300.

(*l*) *Bain* v. *Whitehaven and Furness Junction Railway Company,* 3 H. of L. 1.

(*m*) *Tulloch* v. *Hartley,* 1 Y. & C., C. C., 114.

(*n*) Lord Brougham, in *Yates* v. *Thomson,* 3 Cl. & F. 544, 585—92. See above, Art. 331.

protected from disclosing what may expose him to criminal prosecution in a foreign country, because the judge cannot know what may be penal there (*o*).

413. The proof of foreign laws gives rise to important questions, and the *lex fori* governs as to the method of it, as for instance whether a written code, or the certificate of a public officer, shall be received. The matter stands in England thus. Foreign laws, not being within the cognizance of the court, must be proved as facts, and if they are not alleged and proved, judgment will pass according to the law of England (*p*). This will be so, even if the plaintiff's right is founded on a foreign law, though then it might be argued that, if he does not prove it, the law of England cannot help out his claim (*q*); so that, in effect, there is a presumption that the foreign law agrees with the English till its difference is proved. If there be a jury, they must judge of the proof of such difference, because the foreign law is merely a fact in the cause: the judge confines himself to instructing them how far the law in question is the right one to be applied. Being a fact, the foreign law must be proved afresh in every cause in which it is alleged (*r*): indeed it would be highly unsafe to refer to its proof in some preceding English case, for it may have been changed in the interval. And all the above is true even of the Scotch law when in point here, except in the House of Lords: that court, in an appeal from either country, will take notice of the law of the other, and not be bound by the evidence given of such law in the court beneath (*s*).

(*o*) *King of Two Sicilies* v. *Willcox*, 1 Sim. N. S. 301, 329.

(*p*) *Smith* v. *Gould*, 4 Mo. P. C. 21. As to the mode of pleading a foreign law, see *M'Leod* v. *Schultze*, 1 Dow. & L. 614; *Benham* v. *Mornington*, 4 Dow. & L. 213, 3 C. B. 133.

(*q*) *Brown* v. *Gracey*, Dow. & Ry., N. P., 41, note.

(*r*) *M'Cormick* v. *Garnett*, 5 D. M. G. 278.

(*s*) *Douglas* v. *Craig*, 2 Dow. & Cl. 171.

414. The nature of the evidence which must be given of the foreign law has been the subject of much doubt, nor is it certain that the same views are now entertained on it in England and the United States. In the latter country, " a written foreign law may be proved by a copy properly authenticated, which may be verified by an oath, or by an exemplification of a copy under the great seal of a state, or by a copy proved to be a true copy by a witness who has examined and compared it with the original, or by a certificate of an officer properly authorized by law to give the copy, which certificate must be duly proved" (*t*). And these methods of proof were formerly admitted in England (*u*), though much doubt has now been thrown on them by the dicta in the *Baron de Bode's case* (*x*), in which it was pointed out that if the words of the foreign law are before the English court, still the latter may err in interpreting them, from the want of a general acquaintance with the jurisprudence of the country in question; and I may add that the point to be proved is always what the foreign law was at a certain moment of time, so that if the written law be of an earlier date, it may have been altered during the interval, and if of a later, no similar provision may have existed at the critical instant. Still, the cases in which such proof has been received have not been directly overruled (*y*), though it has in the *Baron de Bode's*

(*t*) Justice Wayne, in *Ennis* v. *Smith*, 14 Howard, 426; adopting the language of Story, s. 641.

(*u*) *Lacon* v. *Higgins*, 3 Stark. 178. And see Lord Ellenborough's dictum in *Picton's case*, 30 Howell's State Trials, 491.

(*x*) 8 Q. B. 208, 246.

(*y*) *The Sussex Peerage*, 11 Cl. & F. 85, 134, has been thought to overrule them (2 Phillips on Evidence, 10th edition, p. 220): but in that case the law proved was unwritten. See Lord Campbell's remark on the proof of a written law at p. 114. Lord Denman's account of the decision in the *Baron de Bode's case*, at p. 116, goes beyond the report in 8 Q. B., from which it appears that the non-admissibility of the foreign text did not arise. It was well remarked by Lord Langdale, in *Nelson* v. *Bridport*, that " if the utmost *case* been established that the most proper mode of proving a written law is by the parol testimony of experts (*z*), and that they will not be called on to produce its text, even when they mention it as the ground of their opinion. Unwritten laws are also proved by the parol testimony of experts, and both in this and the other case, when such persons are examined, it is on their statements alone that the court or jury must rely; and though they may read extracts from books, to refresh their memory, or as containing the authentic letter of the law, the force of such extracts will be only that which they derive from being incorporated with the parol statement (*a*). The expert, if not a practising lawyer of the country whose law is in question, must be "*peritus virtute officii*, engaged in the performance of public duties, connected with which, and in order to discharge them properly, he is bound to make himself acquainted with that law. That being so, his evidence is of the nature of that of a judge (*b*)."

415. As to the proof of foreign judgments and acts of state, see the statutory provision cited at length in Art. 375. A commission was granted by Lord Hardwicke to examine at Paris into the extent of the jurisdiction of a court there (*c*). Besides the effect of the judgment *in rem*

---

strictness were required in every case" of proving foreign laws, "justice might often have to stand still; and he was not disposed to say that there might not be cases in which the judge might without impropriety take upon himself to construe the words of a foreign law, and determine their application to the case in question, especially if there should be a variance or want of clearness in the testimony." 8 Beav. 527, 537.

(*z*) If however a written contract incorporate a written foreign law by reference, the text of that law must be produced: *Millar* v. *Heinrick*, 4 Camp. 155, as explained in 8 Q. B. 252.

(*a*) *The Sussex Peerage*, 11 Cl. & F. 85, 114. See *Cocks* v. *Purday*, 2 C. & K. 269.

(*b*) *Ibid.*, p. 134, overruling *Regina* v. *Dent*, 1 C. & K. 97. See *Böhtlink* v. *Schneider*, 3 Esp. 58; *Clegg* v. *Levy*, 3 Camp. 166.

(*c*) *Gage* v. *Stafford*, 2 Ves. Sen. 556.

of a competent court, in vesting the property in the party whose it is pronounced to be, in England and some of the American states it is held also conclusive, against persons not parties to it, as to the facts on the proof of which it was founded ; a doctrine chiefly in point when the sentence of a prize court is invoked by marine insurers in order to falsify the warrantry of neutrality. The refinements raised as to the cases in which such a sentence will have that effect turn on questions of public international law.

INDEX

(*The* NUMBERS *are those of the* ARTICLES.)

London: printed by C. Roworth and Sons, Bell Yard, Temple Bar.

Spotted something that isn't quite right?

Let us know and we'll fix it for future reprints. And as a thank you for your diligence, we'll send you a free Sothis book of your choice.

publisher@sothis.press

This page intentionally left blank

Made in United States
Orlando, FL
04 November 2026

90201505R00254